The research makes clear that  we
are going to support the menta   low
should we work with them? A   ...ently
when working with the parents of a toddler compared with, say, a teenager?
This brilliant book draws on a mentalizing model to show how we can all learn
to do this work better. It is the kind of book that I wish I could have read when
I first started working in this field; but it also offers important insights and
practical advice for the experienced psychotherapist.

—**Nick Midgley, PhD,** Professor of Psychological Therapies With Children
and Young People, University College London and the Anna Freud Centre,
London, United Kingdom

Adults who become parents are developing alongside their infants and children.
They are especially learning how their mental life shapes and is shaped by their
children. In this very accessible and clinically rich volume, the authors describe
this developmental journey that is the privilege and responsibility of parenting.
Their insights are invaluable to clinicians and parents alike.

—**Linda Mayes, MD,** Arnold Gesell Professor, Yale Child Study Center, Yale
School of Medicine, New Haven, CT, United States

WORKING WITH PARENTS IN THERAPY

WORKING WITH WITH PARENTS IN THERAPY

A Mentalization-Based Approach

Norka Malberg,
Elliot Jurist,
Jordan Bate, &
Mark Dangerfield

 AMERICAN PSYCHOLOGICAL ASSOCIATION

Published by
American Psychological Association
750 First Street, NE
Washington, DC 20002
https://www.apa.org

Order Department
https://www.apa.org/pubs/books
order@apa.org

In the U.K., Europe, Africa, and the Middle East, copies may be ordered from Eurospan
https://www.eurospanbookstore.com/apa
info@eurospangroup.com

Typeset in Charter and Interstate by Lumina Datamatics, India

Printer: Gasch Printing, Odenton, MD
Cover Designer: Gwen J. Grafft, Minneapolis, MN

Library of Congress Cataloging-in-Publication Data

Names: Malberg, Norka T., author. | Jurist, Elliot L., 1953- author. |
   Bate, Jordan, author.
Title: Working with parents in therapy : a mentalization-based approach /
   by Norka Malberg, Elliot Jurist, Jordan Bate, and Mark Dangerfield.
Description: Washington, DC : American Psychological Association, [2023] |
   Includes bibliographical references and index.
Identifiers: LCCN 2022043976 (print) | LCCN 2022043977 (ebook) | ISBN
   9781433836114 (paperback) | ISBN 9781433836121 (ebook)
Subjects: LCSH: Parenting—Psychological aspects. | Parent and
   child—Psychological aspects. | Psychotherapy. | Mentalization Based
   Therapy. | BISAC: PSYCHOLOGY / Psychotherapy / Couples & Family |
   PSYCHOLOGY / Clinical Psychology
Classification: LCC BF723.P25 M253 2023 (print) | LCC BF723.P25 (ebook) |
   DDC 155.9/24—dc23/eng/20221017
LC record available at https://lccn.loc.gov/2022043976
LC ebook record available at https://lccn.loc.gov/2022043977

https://doi.org/10.1037/0000341-000

Printed in the United States of America

10 9 8 7 6 5 4 3 2 1

Contents

Foreword

We often refer to the group of professionals, clinicians and researchers, all of whom follow a mentalization-based approach to psychotherapy, as "the mentalizing family." The authors of this book, Norka Malberg, Elliot Jurist, Jordan Bate, and Mark Dangerfield, are all core family members; some like Malberg and Jurist were present at the birth of the baby and are in a position to claim parenting rights.

It has been a pleasure and a privilege to watch over the past 3 decades not just the growth of this family but also its collective achievements. Mentalization-based therapy (MBT) is now a recognized orientation for supporting infants, children, young people, adults, and families with mental health difficulties using a coherent transdiagnostic and largely, transtheoretical approach. Put "mentalizing" into Google Scholar and you get 34,000 hits. Neuroscientists, particularly Uta and Chris Frith, popularized the term in the 1990s, although psychoanalysts can claim to have used it first (Fonagy, 1989). Its use in the mental health community has become genuinely transtheoretical, which reflects its proximity to the core of what it means to be a person. In 2006 we wrote,

> In advocating mentalization-based treatment we claim no innovation. On the contrary, mentalization-based treatment is the least novel therapeutic approach imaginable: it addresses the bedrock human capacity to apprehend mind as such. Holding mind in mind is as ancient as human relatedness and self-awareness. (Allen & Fonagy, 2006, p. xix)

The authors of *Working With Parents in Therapy* are to be congratulated for producing a wonderful volume that perfectly exemplifies the claim to "relatability" or "ordinariness" which the MBT tradition upholds. Anyone who picks up this book will be able to access the rich ideas and explore the practical advice and suggestions because of the sense of transparency, unpretentiousness, and (yes) humor that permeate its pages.

The origin of MBT dates back 3.5 decades, but it is closely linked to the subject matter of the present volume. In work with Miriam and Howard Steele we, for the first time, demonstrated that the quality of attachment between parent and child at 1 year (with mother) and at 18 months (with father) could be predicted from an interview that concerned the parents' own attachment histories, their childhood experiences of care, neglect, or abuse. This work, based on Mary Main's ingenious coding system, revealed that it was not so much the content of the narrative but its manner of delivery that enabled transgenerational prediction. The work with the Steeles and other colleagues helped us understand this relationship. The interviews revealed that it was the parents' capacity to make sense of their early experiences and relationships in terms of their current thoughts and feelings, reflections and ambitions, and mental states, that undergirded the transgenerational relationship (Fonagy et al., 1991).

The key implication of such research, which runs through every chapter of this fascinating book, is that insecure relationships will be perpetuated from one generation to the next unless these experiences are reflected on (Fonagy et al., 1994), and that these reflections find their way into the caregiving that parents offer their children (Slade et al., 2005). The transmission of attachment security may have heritable components (Austerberry et al., 2022), but multiple experimental studies have by now clearly demonstrated that enhancing parental mentalizing increases the child's chances of thriving in a range of domains (Slade et al., 2019). This thinking has become central to our understanding of how vulnerability to mental disorder is generated and directs us to how it may be prevented, breaking the intergenerational cycle of disadvantage. This book makes a major contribution to refining these initiatives further based on a thorough exposition of the relevant research literature and building on the authors' unparalleled cumulative experience of working with caregivers and parents. It could be titled as a genuine guide to breaking the cycles of disadvantage.

This volume does far more than support work with early intervention. It takes a lifespan perspective. It takes on as its challenge that generating of support for mentalizing to enhance outcomes for an infant, a young child, an adolescent, or a mature adult. The golden thread that runs through the pages is the hypothesis that attachment-related trauma impairs the development of mentalizing, which subsequently leads to the pattern of emotion dysregulation and self disturbance that is characteristic of individuals with severe and persistent emotional and relational problems. Of course, Elliot Jurist was there contributing to the laying down of these ideas (Fonagy et al., 2002). His original and creative thinking on mentalized affectivity shines through. At the heart of this book is the idea that the mind, when not alone, is more likely to withstand adversity. The presence of a mentalizing influence, the support that the caregiver or parent can give, or the support the therapist can offer to the parent or caregiver, is the vital element to protect the child's mind from being traumatized through adverse experience.

What we were unaware of at the time was just how important the presence of a concerned mentalizing other was for the protection of the child, or indeed adolescent, in the presence of adversity. For example, a retrospective study of the effects of adverse childhood experiences (ACEs) on adult health behaviors and levels of well-being found the impact of adversity to be powerfully moderated by both social deprivation and the reliable availability of adult support (Bellis et al., 2017). Risks of low well-being and poor health behaviors were exacerbated (as is usually the case) by deprivation (Propper et al., 2005; Stimpson et al., 2007) even after ACE count had been taken into account. Higher ACE counts and deprivation increased risk of negative outcomes, but their impacts were substantially mitigated by support from an always available adult during childhood. Thus, for self-destructive health behaviors, the least deprived to most deprived difference was 12% for those without support but only 4% for those with support—a threefold reduction of risk. The risk from the combination of ACEs and deprivation was similarly almost halved by the availability of reliable support in childhood. These findings are in line with the expectation that social and economic differences in the prevalence of mental health problems may be at least partially mitigated if we can create a situation in which an adult is there to mentally absorb the stress that the child faces. In terms of the message of this book, we know how an understanding social environment can be created for a child so they have an adult whose understanding of them mitigates the toxic level of stress they face. The message from this book is about what is possible to achieve with sensitive support offered to a child coping with the highest levels of stress. It is now a matter for us to take this message forward and enhance the capacity of carers to make available the psychological support that can enhance the social capital of their community.

The thinking around parental mentalizing of course takes us to the concern that we all have to go beyond the dyadic and support for mentalizing within the family system, to encompass the ecological systems that the child and the family occupy (e.g., school, neighborhood, community). We face significant cultural changes as we observe some components of our society to have gone into reverse in relation to considering actions in terms of the thoughts and feelings that might be genuinely driving them, and treating actions in the most concrete way possible, without seeking the intentions or meanings that drive them. This book was written with the challenges faced by 21st-century parents in mind. It does not idealize the nuclear family, and its clinical cases have a deep sense of reality about them. I would argue that the mentalizing approach they recommend is needed now, in the digital age, more than ever before. The authors make the strongest case possible for engaging with transgenerational trauma and undertaking a mentalizing-informed approach to addressing the struggles which parents might experience with children and adolescents turning away from personal contact, making it all the more important for parents to emphasize the basic elements of social understanding. This book takes a courageous and broad approach, engaging with social trends and holding parents' hands as they navigate these contemporary challenges, to improve children's chances across many contexts and settings.

The demands on parents are undoubtedly increasing. Among other things, there is far more advice given to them about parenting than they could possibly take on board. The limitation of most parenting books is the lack of a conceptual framework; therefore, the suggestions, however practical, turn out to be of little value beyond the immediate situation for which they are offered. What the reader will see in this book is the palpable advantage of having a coherent and powerful theoretical framework that can address itself to age-specific problems within the normative and the clinical range that parenting in the 21st century has to encompass. The advice that is given has the hallmarks of mentalizing and the prerequisites for generating trust. It is honest and transparent, and, in many instances, it's accompanied by a touch of humor. It is unusual in offering suggestions in a nuanced and subtle manner which, surprisingly, appears not to place the person giving the advice in any sense above the person receiving it. In this way it loosens the unidirectional nature of knowledge transfer that can characterize clinical books that tell you how to do therapy or engage in other interventions. This book succeeds in enabling the parent/carer to be recognized as the person who knows the child and their story better than the person giving the advice. What also runs through the gripping case histories is how developing understanding may be fostered together through a joint exploration—not just by delivering truths but by also offering opportunities for active shaping of a narrative and giving tools to solve problems rather than solutions that appear to make them far less challenging than they are in reality.

What gives the reader confidence in reading *Working With Parents in Therapy* is the obvious trust that all the authors have in the model that's being used. They confidently build, not just cite, evidence and use it to create a structure that does not just tell the reader how to deliver support but actually gives them a great deal of flexibility to discover for themselves the sense of agency that mentalizing gives. Mentalizing is a key element of modern parenting. To stop, rewind, and reflect is, in most contexts, a "big ask." The authors of this volume are fully aware of this, and their major focus is on finding a way to practical delivery. This is an outstanding contribution the authors make. This book does not stop at describing the ideal but offers practical steps for getting closer to it. It will be treasured in training programs but also, I believe, by parents. To create such a multipurpose book requires insight, dedication, and deep clinical experience. This book represents the most comprehensive volume on mentalization-focused parenting that I have read. And that is no exaggeration.

Parenting is about social development, and social development is about learning. Learning is best when delivered by a good teacher—a teacher who the reader can walk along with and who validates rather than aims to fix problems too quickly and too easily. In reading this book I experienced the kind of positive feedback loop that I think the authors are aiming to generate. There seems to be a cycle of exchanges between the reader and the authors, generating increased trust with the turn of each page and an increased interest and curiosity about how common problems can be understood, disentangled, and once laid bare, solved in the context of a mentalizing exploration that holds onto but does not take over the process of learning, and takes advantage of the clinicians' and—through them—the parents' drive to understand and achieve.

—*Peter Fonagy*

REFERENCES

Allen, J. G., & Fonagy, P. (Eds.). (2006). *Handbook of mentalization-based treatment.* Wiley. https://doi.org/10.1002/9780470712986

Austerberry, C., Mateen, M., Fearon, P., & Ronald, A. (2022). Heritability of psychological traits and developmental milestones in infancy: A systematic review and meta-analysis. *JAMA Network Open, 5*(8), e2227887. https://doi.org/10.1001/jamanetworkopen.2022.27887

Bellis, M. A., Hardcastle, K., Ford, K., Hughes, K., Ashton, K., Quigg, Z., & Butler, N. (2017). Does continuous trusted adult support in childhood impart life-course resilience against adverse childhood experiences—A retrospective study on adult health-harming behaviours and mental well-being. *BMC Psychiatry, 7*(1), 110. https://doi.org/10.1186/s12888-017-1260-z

Fonagy, P. (1989). On tolerating mental states: Theory of mind in borderline patients. *Bulletin of the Anna Freud Centre, 12*, 91–115.

Fonagy, P., Gergely, G., Jurist, E., & Target, M. (2002). *Affect regulation, mentalization, and the development of the self.* Other Press.

Fonagy, P., Steele, M., Steele, H., Higgitt, A., & Target, M. (1994). The Emanuel Miller Memorial Lecture 1992: The theory and practice of resilience. *Journal of Child Psychology and Psychiatry, and Allied Disciplines, 35*(2), 231–257. https://doi.org/10.1111/j.1469-7610.1994.tb01160.x

Fonagy, P., Steele, M., Steele, H., Moran, G. S., & Higgitt, A. C. (1991). The capacity for understanding mental states: The reflective self in parent and child and its significance for security of attachment. *Infant Mental Health Journal, 2*(3), 201–218. https://doi.org/10.1002/1097-0355(199123)12:3<201::AID-IMHJ2280120307>3.0.CO;2-7

Propper, C., Jones, K., Bolster, A., Burgess, S., Johnston, R., & Sarker, R. (2005). Local neighbourhood and mental health: Evidence from the UK. *Social Science & Medicine, 61*(10), 2065–2083. https://doi.org/10.1016/j.socscimed.2005.04.013

Slade, A., Grienenberger, J., Bernbach, E., Levy, D., & Locker, A. (2005). Maternal reflective functioning, attachment, and the transmission gap: A preliminary study. *Attachment & Human Development, 7*(3), 283–298. https://doi.org/10.1080/14616730500245880

Slade, A., Holland, M. L., Ordway, M. R., Carlson, E. A., Jeon, S., Close, N., Mayes, L. C., & Sadler, L. S. (2019). Minding the Baby: Enhancing parental reflective functioning and infant attachment in an attachment-based, interdisciplinary home visiting program. *Development and Psychopathology.* Advance online publication. https://doi.org/10.1017/S0954579418001463

Stimpson, J. P., Ju, H., Raji, M. A., & Eschbach, K. (2007). Neighborhood deprivation and health risk behaviors in NHANES III. *American Journal of Health Behavior, 31*(2), 215–222. https://doi.org/10.5993/AJHB.31.2.10

Acknowledgments

We dedicate this book to our parents and stepparents, especially our fathers, three of whom passed away during the writing of this book. We also thank those in our lives who keep us honest, humble, and self-observing.

The world of mentalization-based research, theory, and clinical practice has grown exponentially in the last 2 decades. We recognize the multitude of colleagues who have followed the initiative of a small group of pioneers under the leadership of Peter Fonagy at the Anna Freud National Centre for Children and Families in London. The concept of mentalization has come as a way of translating and applying some of the knowledge developmental psychoanalysis holds dear in a way that has awakened clinical and research creativity. The proliferating wealth of scientific publications one finds under the keyword "mentalization" is evidence of its impact. Those of us who are psychodynamically informed and trained can hear the whispers of psychoanalytic voices as they are integrated with systemic thinking and cognitive behavioral, neuropsychological, and developmental science, under the rubric of mentalization-based practices. We feel grateful for being beneficiaries of this way of thinking and working and being able to share our clinical and research experiences and knowledge in this way.

We begin by collectively thanking Susan Reynolds, from the American Psychological Association, for her encouragement and vision during the process of conceiving and writing this book. Also, a big thank-you to Anna Lalaouna for her support and contributions in the laborious process of editing.

Norka Malberg thanks her dad, Tomas Malberg, for his feedback during the initial stages of this book before his passing in late 2020—nothing like the analytic mind of an engineer to ground one's thinking, and proof that two very different minds can mentalize each other. Thank you to her mentalization-based treatment for children (MBT-C) core team colleagues—Nick Midgley, Karin Ensink, Nicole Muller, and Karin Lindqvist—who continually inspire her with their creativity, commitment, and hard work. A special thanks to Peter Fonagy for introducing to her, at a pivotal time in her career, the concept and practice of mentalization-based treatment and for continuing to support her in a kind and generous manner. Thanks to Linda Mayes and her colleagues at the Yale Child Study Center for offering a wonderful community in which to grow as a person and a professional. To her friend and colleague Abigail Tishler for reading the earlier versions of this book. To all the parents who entrust her with the emotional well-being of their children: a big, big thank-you. Finally, a heartfelt "I love you" to her two sons, Luis Tomas and Sebastian—although far, always close—and to her partner in life and in work, Mark, and their two pugs, Bowie and Ziggie: Thanks for all you do.

Elliot Jurist mourns his father, Sumner Jurist, who loved good conversation and dry martinis and who was a subtle mentalizer of emotions. His death in September 2021 is too recent to try to say more. Elliot also mourns his father-in-law, Lennard Wharton, who passed away in November 2021. Lennard was a scientist, a chemist, and an engineer who loved literature and music and was devoted to—and beloved by—everyone in the family. Elliot thanks the students in his research lab at the doctoral program in clinical psychology at The City College of New York, City University of New York: Will Holland, I Wang, Dan-Bi-Lee, Brian Neff, Leecey Cameron, Elliot Raymon, Ellie Sherwin, Rachel Ende, Nandita Sharma, Molly Tow, Alana Docherty, Nishanthi Anthonipillai, Rhyan Toledo, Nicole Slater, Shaun Halper, Amarelis Raudales, and Simge Huyal. Special thanks to collaborators: Sasha Rudenstine, David Greenberg, Rozita Alaluf, Michael Perez Sosa, and Gulsen Kaynar. More thanks to Elliot's stalwart colleagues: Deidre Anglin, Diana Diamond, Eric Fertuck, Ben Harris, Bob Melara, Sara O'Neill, Diana Punales, Margie Rosario, Steve Tuber, Paul Wachtel, and Lissa Weinstein. And here's to his friendship with György Gergely for decades of undaunted, skeptical, and serpentine lucubration. Elliot is deeply grateful to his family for their constant support and love: his wife, Rebecca Wharton, and his children, Julia and Joshua. Thanks, too, to their two dachshunds, Pretzel and Maggie, for reminding him that—pandemic be damned—there remains an outside world.

Jordan Bate acknowledges—first and foremost—the presence and support of her parents and stepparents, as well as the mentorship and friendship of Miriam and Howard Steele, her academic parents. The Center for Attachment Research at The New School and the Group Attachment-Based Intervention (GABI) program at Montefiore Medical Center, led by Anne Murphy, gave her tremendous opportunities that have been the foundation of what she works to continue alongside colleagues and her students at Ferkauf. Her classmates from The New School help her maintain her mentalizing stance; translate research and theories into writing; and think in more sensitive and critical ways about trauma, culture, and systems of power and oppression—most especially Hannah Knafo, Shana Grover, William Jock, Jessica Joseph, and the rest of Jordan's doctoral cohort. Alessandro Talia has been a valued source of intellectual stimulation for many years. The list of supervisors whose voices shape Jordan's approach is long and includes Jeremy Safran, Jerome Kogan, Verna MacCornack, Wooster Welton, Herb Schlesinger, Francine Godet, Karin Ensink, Chris Bonovitz, and Inga Blom. On a personal level, watching her younger sister, Kendall, become a parent to Khajit and Dojin has been a profound experience. Jordan has deep appreciation for all of her friends who are parents. Her husband, Seb, is her No. 1 partner, attachment figure, and coparent to their rescue dogs, Nucky and Dax, and has tolerated her many hours absorbed in this work. Finally, Jordan acknowledges that while parents are not well-enough supported in our society, being a parent remains a valued position in it. She acknowledges all of those who find themselves on the margins of this social norm and assures them that they should also feel loved, valued, and nurtured.

Mark Dangerfield thanks his parents for helping him believe in epistemic trust much before he knew what mentalization was—with a special memory of his father, who passed away in early 2020, as an intuitive and curious Englishman who facilitated Mark's interest in mental health without knowing it. Mark acknowledges the first colleagues who introduced him to the fascinating mentalizing world through Adaptive Mentalization-Based Integrative Treatment (AMBIT): Dickon Bevington and Peter Fuggle. He is very grateful for their valuable help and collaboration in the development of the El Equipo Clínic de Intervención a Domicilio (ECID) project in Barcelona, Spain. He also thanks his colleagues at the ECID project of the Fundación Vidal y Barraquer in Barcelona: Anna Oriol, Jordi Artigue, Marta Montaner, Valentina Bruno, David López, Eli Rodríguez, Elsa Coll, Gemma Segura, Laia Ferrer, Lina Gutiérrez, and Oriol Canalías, with whom they continue working together to recover their mentalizing capabilities and keep on learning to work with parents who have histories of great suffering. His gratitude and respect go to all the adolescents and parents with whom he has worked throughout his years of clinical practice. Finally, with love to his son, Nico, who is still making him learn through experience what being a father is, and to his partner, Norka, the best companion in this profession—and in life.

WORKING WITH PARENTS IN THERAPY

INTRODUCTION

Our Framework to Mentalization-Based Therapy With Parents

Over the last half-century, the world has changed fundamentally, shifting the expectations and experiences of how parents raise their children (Faircloth, 2014). As family composition and living arrangements have diversified—with an increase of unmarried or divorced families, single and same-sex parents—so has the face of parenting. This shift requires a systemic and integrative clinical approach more than ever.

HOW WE DEFINE THE TERM *PARENT*

Throughout this book and the therapeutic framework it proposes, we take the term *parent* to be broad and encompass all who are in a parenting role, whether they are the parent of an unborn child or have lost a child, or parent children or young adults whom they did not give birth to. We recognize parenting as an identity, a role, and an experience that is not tied to one definition.

https://doi.org/10.1037/0000341-001
Working With Parents in Therapy: A Mentalization-Based Approach, by N. Malberg, E. Jurist, J. Bate, and M. Dangerfield

As pointed out by Sisk (2020), in the past 20 years, many psychoanalytically informed authors (Altman, 1994; Chazan, 1995; Lieberman & Van Horn, 2005, 2008; Novick & Novick, 2005, 2013; Siskind, 1996, 1997; Slade, 2008a, 2008b; Stern, 1995; Tsiantis, 2000) have advocated for increased work with and consideration for the parents of children in treatment. Our approach considers the impact of generational transmission of relational patterns, in the same way that many psychoanalytic authors (Badoni, 2002; Blos, 1985; Fraiberg et al., 1975; Hoffman, 1984) identified the intergenerational transmission of psychological disturbance as a critical factor in influencing the development of pathology in childhood.

Current evidence shows that maltreatment-related childhood adversity is the leading preventable risk factor for mental disorders and substance abuse (Teicher et al., 2016). This highlights the need for organizing frameworks and substantial treatments for parents to ameliorate present distress; alter historical patterns of dysfunction; and support a more permeating sense of recovery, revitalization, and strengthened capacity to engage meaningfully in life and relationships in the context of parenting. One must search books and articles on child treatment to find mention of parent work, often described as brief, cursory, and confined to what are viewed as practical considerations: how often to see the parents, how much to tell them, or how to gain their cooperation. Furthermore, too often one finds a cautionary tone when discussing parent work regarding parents as threatening or "attacking" the treatment by undermining the therapist's work. As Siskind (1999) pointed out, there frequently seems to be an attitude of resignation—one that suggests that parents are the special burden that the child therapist must bear.

Approaches to parenting are rooted in parents' value and belief systems (Bornstein et al., 2012). Parents, for example, orient their efforts toward important developmental goals they have for their children, which are rooted in sociocultural norms but are also personally motivated and inform their parenting style. For example, independent of culture, parents who aim for obedience, interdependence, and school achievement as primary goals in child-rearing tend to be more authoritarian and controlling (Meng, 2012). Moreover, migration and globalization have led to unprecedented ethnic, cultural, and religious diversity within many societies. Immigration to a country that differs in parenting norms, along with the subsequent changes in family structures, dynamics, and roles, presents significant challenges for families. For instance, parents may feel that their native sociocultural context prior to migration conflicts with the new one. This might be reflected, for example, in experiences with the legal and educational systems, in which the parents feel an undermining of their family dynamics and values (Nauck & Lotter, 2015).

Although there are good reasons to question a binary perspective on gender, parenting tends to remain gendered, in terms of (a) the parents' experience and identity as a parent and (b) how parents approach their children. The experiences of parents and parenting are in a state of constant change, as they follow children's age and developmental stage. As a result, we need working frameworks that go beyond prescriptive and obscure ways of describing parent work. A developmental and relational framework informed by contemporary psychodynamic research and theory potentiates the emergence of a lens through which the therapist can organize, understand, and reflect on their work with parents and truly meet them where they are.

OUR APPROACH

In this book, we present a mentalizing framework for working with parents that aims to take into consideration the current sociocultural environment and how it impacts the developmental process of parenting. We do this by using a model that is based on developmental principles, thinking about the process of parenting as a developmental line (Freud, 1965)—one that fluctuates and transforms throughout the lifespan. This developmental approach structures the therapeutic process in our work with adults who are parents (Malberg, 2015). This means that the process of assessment, formulation, and tailoring of the intervention is informed not only by the specific challenges motivating the parent to seek help regarding their child but also by the individual characteristics of the parent, such as personality organization, attachment style, and temperament. In a nutshell, we propose a *transactional and developmental framework* of working with parents, one that considers what the parent brings, what the child brings, and what the therapist brings.

The approach presented in this book is the result of integration of psychodynamic clinical research, theory, and practice. Each of the authors brings the experience of such integration in their daily professional functions. Norka Malberg, coauthor of the 2017 book on mentalization-based treatment (MBT) with school-age children (Midgley et al., 2017), has further elaborated—in the last 15 years of her career as a child and adolescent psychotherapist and MBT child and adolescent supervisor and trainer—models, to work with parents and teachers, that substantially support the work with children and adolescents (Malberg, 2015, 2019, 2020) in the context of mental health settings as well as the larger community. Her work emphasizes the intersection of child and adult work in the context of working both as a child and adult psychoanalytic psychotherapist.

Elliot Jurist is a coauthor of the 2002 book (Fonagy et al., 2002) that first laid out the theoretical foundations for what is now known as MBT, currently a widely used, evidence-based clinical practice that has come to radically shift views about the role of the psychotherapist in the context of psychotherapy (Bateman & Fonagy, 2016). He has developed the construct of mentalized affectivity (Greenberg et al., 2017, 2021; Jurist, 2005, 2008, 2010, 2018) in the effort to focus on working with emotion in a more targeted and specific fashion supported by his extensive research and clinical practice.

Jordan Bate brings her clinical and research experiences in the context of contemporary attachment theory in the tradition of illustrious mentors and colleagues such as Miriam and Howard Steele, with particular emphasis on (a) parental and child reflective functioning in the context of adverse childhood experiences and (b) how to train therapists in these approaches (Bate et al., 2016, 2018; Bate & Malberg, 2020; Murphy et al., 2014, 2015; Steele et al., 2014, 2015; Talia et al., 2019). She is also a coauthor of *Deliberate Practice in Child and Adolescent Psychotherapy* (Bate et al., 2022), part of the American Psychological Association's Essentials of Deliberate Practice series.

Mark Dangerfield (2020, 2021), a clinical psychologist; psychoanalyst; MBT for Adolescents (MBT-A) psychotherapist, trainer, and supervisor; and lead Adaptive Mentalization-Based Integrative Treatment (AMBIT) trainer, contributes both (a) his extensive clinical experience in working with families and adolescents with severe psychopathological problems and (b) his research and clinical explorations into the impact of adverse childhood experiences and their profound consequences on the lives of children and families—and, specifically, the process of parenting as well as adult psychological functioning. All four authors are psychodynamically informed in their clinical approach and strongly influenced by a tradition of clinical research that guides the process of formulation and treatment planning and implementation.

This book is a model of intervention based on a scaffolding process shaped by the core theoretical elements of contemporary mentalization theory and its clinical applications—not an intervention manual. We believe that working with parents, whether in parallel to our work with their children or in individual or couple's psychotherapy, is a process that is best served when the therapist can hold in mind the benefits of effective mentalizing as a protective factor in the lifelong journey that parenting represents. The framework presented in this book approaches the diversity in contemporary parenting configurations and practices by focusing on strengthening and revitalizing a single capacity: that of parental reflective functioning (Slade, 2005), otherwise known as *mentalization*.

HOW WE DEFINE *PARENTAL REFLECTIVE FUNCTIONING*

We define *parental reflective functioning* as a caregiver's capacity to flexibly use different facets for mental reflection, by (a) focusing on self or other, (b) shifting between and integrating affective or cognitive ways of understanding, and (c) using external or internal sources of information as well as relying on quick implicit forms and more controlled explicit forms of reflection, specifically in the context of the parent-child relationship. In the next pages, we invite the reader to explore the elements that guide our intervention with parents and consider a specific way of relating, while keeping in mind the uniqueness of each parent's experience.

Our goal in this book is to provide the reader with parameters—guiding principles, if you will—to inform the process of evaluation, formulation, and treatment in the work with parents. Our emphasis on *parenting as a developmental process* allows for the necessary flexibility to *meet the parent where they are in the developmental line of parenting* and employ a scaffolding process to navigate the task of supporting and growing with parents as they define and revisit who they are, how they are, and who they feel they ought to be in the context of the parenting experience. Anna Freud (1965), one of the founders of child psychoanalysis, advocated for the use of the concept of developmental lines to articulate both the fluidity of the developmental process and its transactional nature. She felt that speaking of developmental lines to parents and teachers communicated clearly and effectively the importance of a flexible scaffolding to meet children where they are developmentally and as people. The framework presented here, as well as MBT, emerged from Anna Freud's legacy of clinical and theoretical integration.

THE STRUCTURE OF THIS BOOK

We begin by presenting the key concepts of mentalization and parental reflective functioning in the context of development and their clinical applications. Through clinical vignettes,[1] Chapter 1 illustrates the clinical applications

---

[1] The cases in this book have been disguised to maintain client confidentiality.

of the concept of parental reflective functioning as a guiding lens in the process of assessment and treatment planning. Specifically, we explore the value of a therapist's mentalizing stance in eliciting and modeling the relational ingredients of reflective functioning. We underline the value of providing parents a safe environment where they can feel mentalized. Furthermore, as working with parents can often be experienced by the therapist as a treacherous and frustrating process, we illustrate, in this first chapter, the emergence of prementalizing modes of functioning and the value of both identifying them and working to return to mentalizing with parents in a coregulating, bidirectional fashion. We highlight how working with emotion from a mentalizing stance proves helpful in this context. The chapter ends with a clinical illustration of the case of the O family and their daughter, Cristina. This clinical example, which has been modified to preserve anonymity, will accompany us throughout Part I of this book, in which we explore the different pieces of the puzzle that form our framework.

In Chapter 2, we explore our mentalizing framework, based on a foundation of epistemic trust and mentalized affectivity. The concept of epistemic trust has been advanced in recent years by Fonagy and Allison (2014), in a search to expand the scope of attachment theory and for research to be more systemic and culturally sensitive by drawing from communication theory. The concept of natural pedagogy, derived from Gergely and Csibra's (2005) work and a developmental perspective, affords more freedom to the therapist working with parents—but also more responsibility in the context of the therapeutic relationship. As we reflected at the beginning of this Introduction, the expansion of diversity that we are encountering in contemporary society demands the exploration of valuable concepts such as epistemic mistrust, as well as a focus on rupture and repair within the therapeutic relationship with parents. We cannot any longer afford to work from a place of certainty and from the safety of our established wisdom. More than ever, in order to open the door to mutual social learning, we must work on our capacity for genuine interest, nonjudgmental attitude, and, most of all, sincerely a curious and not-knowing stance. We hope to illustrate these principles once more through clinical vignettes with Cristina's parents.

The other central component of our framework, that of mentalized affectivity, refers to a capacity that is central for the promotion of safety and social learning required to activate or rehabilitate a parent's reflective functioning. Often, when working with parents, it is easier to stay connected at a cognitive level; somehow, it seems to create the semblance of progress and of "fixing something." In this chapter, we attempt to illustrate the value of integrating both emotion and cognition in our therapeutic work—one of the four dimensions that influence our capacity to mentalize. We take account of identifying, processing, and expressing emotions and strive to help patients integrate cognition and emotion by recognizing how emotions in the present are influenced by the past.

Chapter 3 addresses the "ghosts in the nursery," a concept—coined by psychoanalyst Selma Fraiberg (Fraiberg et al., 1975) and present throughout this book—that has been widely used, in the attachment literature, to speak of the impact of a parent's relational past and its influence in the capacity and quality of parenting. Furthermore, the term addresses the strength of generational transmission of relational patterns in the context of potentially traumatic experiences and how it presents itself as a strong inhibiting force while working with and supporting parents. The concept of adverse relational experiences is explored in this context and illustrated via clinical vignettes.

In Chapter 4, we address what we understand to be an essential part of the therapeutic process—and one that will determine its outcome. We are referring to the assessment phase with parents from our mentalizing approach, in which assessing the complexities and conflicts around parenting is described in detail.

Finally for Part I, in Chapter 5, we bring it all together and present an integrative framework for assessment, formulation, and intervention, from a developmental and relational perspective, when working with adults who are parents, in the various clinical contexts. We offer an illustration of the application of this integrative framework to the fictional case of the O family.

Moving forward in this book, Part II illustrates the application of our mentalizing framework across the developmental continuum to diverse parenting situations in the context of today's society, keeping in mind the role of a transactional model of parenting where the parent—with their relational history, personality, and temperament—impacts the child, and vice versa. We understand that parenthood is an ongoing developmental process throughout one's life trajectory. However, in this book, as seen in Chapters 8 through 11, we focus our exploration in the period from infancy to young adulthood. Each of these chapters outlines key considerations for specific developmental stages of the child and the parent: the transition to parenthood and to parenting during infancy, toddlerhood, school age, adolescence, and young adulthood. Chapter 12 specifically addresses working with couples, and the overlap between couples therapy and parent work. In the concluding chapter, we highlight the impact, on the clinician, of parent work from a mentalization-informed perspective. From this perspective, a relational framework informed by mentalization principles includes the emotional impact of the work on the professional and the importance of supervision and peer support to encourage and sustain a mentalizing stance.

PART I

A MENTALIZATION-BASED FRAMEWORK FOR WORKING WITH PARENTS

1 MENTALIZATION AND PARENTAL REFLECTIVE FUNCTIONING IN THE CONTEXT OF DEVELOPMENT

The goal of a mentalization-informed clinical model for working with parents is to promote a self-sustaining parental capacity to manage a child's difficulties and the accompanying emotional challenges, while opening the potential for connection and satisfaction in the experience of parenting. Quite often, clinical formulations that guide work with parents become focused on what the parents are not doing or how they are affecting the child in a less than optimal way. There is a tendency to ignore the importance of developing safety and trust in the relationship with parents and seeing them as whole persons, beginning with an exploration of their own experience, their thoughts and feelings, and their hopes and fears, in the context of parenting. Our mentalization-informed model to parent work promotes a benign, nonpathologizing attitude, which seeks to facilitate the activation of a "mentalizing system" in the working relationship between parent and therapist that is parallel to the caregiver–child system. Our goal is to offer a relationship to parents where they can feel seen and understood in their strengths and difficulties as parents. By doing so, we assess and adapt to their own developmental competency, as well as their emotional and relational patterns that are predominant in the relational

https://doi.org/10.1037/0000341-002
Working With Parents in Therapy: A Mentalization-Based Approach, by N. Malberg, E. Jurist, J. Bate, and M. Dangerfield

dynamics with their child. We intend to offer them a relational experience that, if generalized with their child, can help them offer a different way of being with their child and managing the inevitable challenges and difficulties that parenting implies. This is a relationship where their curiosity and availability prevails, which facilitates the child's experience of being seen and considered by their parents.

Let's begin with a clinical moment: Imagine a mother who comes to therapy and, in explaining her 10-year-old daughter's separation anxiety, describes her daughter's "fear." The therapist asks the mother, "How do you know your daughter feels fear?" To which the mother replies, "I spend so much time with her, we're very connected. I just worry about her future . . ."

The way that we understand this mother's reply is shaped by the lens of our therapeutic approach. At first, the therapist might be impressed with the mother's investment in her child's well-being and reinforce it by praising it. Validation and empathy could begin to emerge between the mom and the therapist. After all, coming to see a mental health professional for support has multiple meanings to a parent, but before exploring those, trust and basic safety need to be established.

On the other hand, a therapist could also feel concerned by the level of closeness and certainty with which this mother speaks of her daughter, who is struggling to develop a sense of agency and independent functioning. The therapist might choose a psychoeducational approach and speak about the child's developmental needs, perhaps out of her concern for what she might perceive as an intrusive mom. This approach may result in the establishment of an expert–patient relationship, one that parents usually enjoy initially but that sends both clinician and parents into a blind search for solutions that bypasses the internal reality of the child and the family dynamic surrounding it.

Alternatively, the therapist could focus on the mother's fear about her daughter's well-being and try to bring into the room a balance between validating her current fears and inviting a new way of thinking of her child's strengths, thus opening the door to thinking about her child's developmental and emotional functioning, activating her reflective functioning and encouraging a mentalizing stance.

Mentalization refers to the uniquely human ability to interpret the meaning of one's own and others' behavior by considering underlying mental states and intentions, as well as the capacity to understand the impact of one's own affects and behaviors on others—and vice versa (Fonagy & Target, 1996). Although the capacity to mentalize is partly an innate one in humans, with its own biological underpinnings (Kovács et al., 2010), there is little doubt that the development of our ability to mentalize also depends on the quality of the social environment in which we are raised.

As we hope to illustrate throughout this book, the goal of a mentalization-informed clinical model working with parents is to promote a self-sustaining parental capacity to manage a child's difficulties and the emotional challenges, while opening the potential for connection and satisfaction in the experience of parenting.

ATTACHMENT AND MENTALIZATION

Secure attachment facilitates the development of mentalization but does not guarantee it. John Bowlby (1969), the founder of attachment theory, studied children who exhibited antisocial behavior; he became curious about the connection between (a) the absence of consistent and predictable parenting figures and (b) children's behavior. Furthermore, he began to observe the impact of loss and separation in children's development of self-esteem and overall functioning in relationships. His work impacted the way we think about schools and hospitals and understand separations between parents and children from the child's perspective. Later, Mary Ainsworth (Ainsworth et al., 1978) developed more systematic scientific ways of exploring these issues across cultures. Her studies were very important, as they showed that attachment is universal—that we find it in all humans across cultures.

These two pioneers developed the basic language of attachment theory. The field of attachment has been influenced by other disciplines—such as developmental and cognitive psychology, neuroscience, and anthropology. Contemporary theorists and researchers have expanded the language of attachment, because of this cross-fertilization.

Research on mentalization blossomed within the field of attachment and psychodynamic research and theory. The term *mentalization* has its roots in 1960s French psychoanalytic terminology (Marty, 1991), but the modern use of the term owes much to the work of Peter Fonagy and his colleagues at the Anna Freud Centre. It can be thought of as an umbrella concept (Luyten & Fonagy, 2015) that overlaps and encompasses a number of other important constructs such as theory of mind (Premack & Woodruff, 1978) and mindfulness (Masterpasqua, 2016). The focus on mentalization as a clinical construct has contributed to the emergence of a new contemporary psychodynamic clinical modality that integrates the findings of neuropsychology, developmental psychology, genetics, and anthropology under the umbrella of developmental psychoanalysis. Working from this perspective approaches the work with parents from a truly curious and flexible stance that makes no assumptions about the developmental and relational journey of a parent, while being supported by a sturdy theoretical and clinical framework.

Mentalization is a developmental capacity inherent in all human beings, very much dependent on the quality of a child's relationships (Fonagy et al., 2002). The development of mentalization critically depends upon interpersonal experiences and, specifically, upon interactions with more mature minds—assuming these interactions are benign, reflective, and sufficiently attuned (Fonagy, 2006). Early in our development, when we are, in the words of Fonagy and Target (1997), "playing with reality," we manifest different ways of approaching the relational world that precede the development of mentalization. These ways of functioning manifest early in life and reflect the existing emotional and cognitive capacities of the child.

Starting from infancy, children recognize contingencies in behavior; if I cry, someone—probably my parent—will come help me. This understanding of mental states is referred to as *teleological,* and these contingencies cohere into implicit relational patterns, ways of being with other people. But children in infancy do not yet have a concept of their own mind or other people's minds or the language to articulate internal experiences. This develops over time from implicit mentalizing abilities. When mentalizing emerges remains controversial and depends upon the experimental paradigm that is used to assess it.

In the toddler years, children begin to comprehend mental states, but they do not yet understand that what is in their mind may differ from what is in the minds of others—a state referred to as *psychic equivalence.* By the time children are 5 years old, if they have been exposed enough to the experience of adults trying to understand who they are (what they need, want, fear, etc.), they develop what developmental psychologists call *theory of mind* (Bartsch & Wellman, 1995). An established way, which has been replicated hundreds of times, to explain how theory of mind manifests itself is the *false-belief task.* In it, a researcher shows a 3-year-old a box of crayons and asks, "What is in here?" The child says, "Crayons" and then opens the box to see candles inside. The researcher closes the box and asks, "If your friend came in and I asked him what is inside this box, what would he say?" Most 3-year-olds will respond, "Candles!" Three-year-old children believe that what they think and know is what others think and know. If we ask the same of 6-year-olds, they will answer, "Crayons, of course!" indicating their capacity for perspective taking. It is during this time that children begin to understand that just because they know something, it does not mean that other people know it, too. Translated to the emotional world, they may have an emotion, but that does not mean that others have it, too; their being angry does not mean that others are angry. This capacity lays the foundation for a change in the child's mentalizing abilities (Ensink & Mayes, 2010; Gergely & Jacob, 2012). However, as noted, by the 2nd year of life, infants can discern that others have views that differ from their own, as they monitor, infer, and attribute beliefs to them (Onishi & Baillargeon, 2005). Another issue about theory of mind concerns culture as a factor, as research has suggested that East Asian infants acquire theory of mind later than do Western infants (Liu et al., 2008; Wellman et al., 2006).

Between the ages of 5 and 8 years, children display a growing ability to play, including the ability to use play symbolically (Fonagy & Target, 1996; Muller & Midgley, 2020). In this stage, they develop a more complex understanding of mental states in their play but are not necessarily able to apply this more nuanced and complex understanding to their own mental states or the mental states of others in the real world (Fonagy & Target, 1996; Muller & Midgley, 2020). Thus, this form of prementalizing is called *pretend mode.*

Ideally, around the age of 6 or 7 years, if we have been exposed to curious, holding, and predictable adult minds, we naturally begin to integrate the three modes of prementalizing—teleological, psychic equivalence, and pretend mode—into our behavioral and emotional functioning. As a result, although these ways of responding continue to appear when we are confronted with higher levels of emotional arousal in the context of relationships, hopefully none of them will become the primary way of managing interpersonal life.

However, when the child does not have enough of a secure base in their primary relationships or when the child experiences relational trauma, prementalizing functioning may become prevalent at older ages. Most of us resort to prementalizing modes at times but have developed ways of recovering our mentalizing capacities (i.e., our resilience capacity). However, under extreme levels of stress, these modes manifest themselves more prevalently, and it is more difficult to recover our reflective function.

Parenting is one of the most stressful challenges that a person can choose. Regardless of all of the gains that this task might bring a person, parenting challenges one's capacity to cope with uncertainty, lack of control, and at times high levels of helplessness, as well as one's capacity for containing strong and overwhelming feelings more generally. Seeing one's child suffer without being able to "take the pain away" is a difficult task that at times awakens one's "ghosts in the nursery" (a concept we explore in depth in Chapter 3). Thus, we often see parents in prementalizing modes when they are in our treatment rooms. They often present initially with strong teleological needs: "Show me that I am not a terrible parent! Please give me strategies so I can feel I know what I am doing! Help my child learn how to control their emotions!" At other times, they may seem locked into their current perspectives in a psychic equivalence position: for example, "She just hates me! Like everyone else in my life, I guess." For other parents, a pretend mode is a safer place, psychologically speaking, and they may approach the therapy from an intellectual perspective or with an idealistic hope that the child "will grow up and this will all go away." As mental health providers, we feel the pressure to educate and validate parents—both of which, if done in a timely fashion, can help to establish a spirit of collaboration with parents.

PREMENTALIZING MODES

1. **Teleological mode:** Infants are described as being *teleological* because they rely heavily on behaviors: for example, they feel safe and secure because the parent does physical things such as hold them, stroke them, cuddle them, and feed them. In the context of parenting, these teleological needs might be manifested in requests such as "Could you give me some strategies to manage my child?" hence demanding objective guidance and proof of the therapist's expertise, effort, and efficacy.

2. **Psychic equivalence mode:** After the 1st year, around age 2 to 3 years, children develop an awareness of mental states; however, developmentally, they are egocentric. They do not realize that other people might have a different perspective. At this time in development, this is referred to as *psychic equivalence*—where internal thoughts and feelings are treated as real, and there is only black-and-white, good-and-bad thinking. We encounter this prementalizing way of functioning in parenting in situations where parents accuse the therapist of being judgmental because of a comment or nonverbal expression. The parent asserts their own impressions as truths and with no margin for uncertainty, often leaving the therapist feeling paralyzed and attacked.

3. **Pretend mode:** This reflects even more sophistication in the ability to consider and explore mental states, but this is done only when the child can completely separate the pretend world from the real world: for example, in a fantasy world. This mode is exemplified by the parent who comes for support but seems to fill the therapy hour with random facts, theoretical explanations they have read and how they relate to their difficulties with their child, but is disconnected from their child's underlying emotional states. Although this parent seems motivated to receive support, the therapist tends to feel disconnected from the parent and with no clear sense of how to explore their emotional experience.

The terms *mentalization* and *reflective functioning* are often used interchangeably, although *reflective functioning* was initially considered to refer to the measurement of mentalization as manifested within narratives regarding attachment relationships (Fonagy, Steele, Steele, Moran, & Higgitt, 1991; Midgley et al., 2017). The early research showed that a parent's capacity for reflective functioning when talking about their own childhood experiences was predictive of their children's attachment security with them (Fonagy, Steele, Steele, Moran, & Higgitt, 1991). When parents had themselves experienced deprivation in childhood, the ability to reflect in this way was particularly important in their children developing a secure relationship with them. This early research led to the defining of reflective functioning as an understanding of how minds work, which goes beyond the ability to label mental states and includes recognition that (a) one cannot truly know or be sure of mental states (they are opaque), (b) mental states can be disguised, (c) mental states underlie behavior, (d) relationships have an impact on mental states, (e) people's mental states affect and are affected by each other, (f) mental states can change over time, (g) people can have different perspectives from each other, and (h) people can have different perspectives over time.

Research conducted since the 1990s has looked at reflective functioning when adults are speaking about a range of material, including their children (Slade, 2005), trauma (Berthelot et al., 2015), and topics they discuss in therapy (Kivity et al., 2021). In this book, *reflective functioning* is used primarily to refer to the capacity to mentalize, especially *explicit mentalizing*—that is, the conscious ability to stop and reflect on the states of mind of self and other.

Mentalization is a complex concept. In their attempt to define it, Bateman and Fonagy (2016) have described mentalization as having four dimensions:

1. Self and Other: People can mentalize with regard to themselves (self) and others.

2. Internal and External: Mentalizing includes reflection on what is happening internally in someone's mind and externally in terms of their behavior.

3. Cognition and Affect: Mentalizing includes reflection on both thoughts (cognition) and emotions (affect).

4. Implicit and Explicit: Mentalizing often occurs automatically but can also be slowed down for more conscious processing.

This conceptualization is central to mentalization-based treatment (Bateman & Fonagy, 2016), a manualized, structured therapy approach centered on mentalization as a core capacity implicated in personality disorders and other forms of psychopathology. While Fonagy and Bateman emphasized balance between the two components for each dimension, we find it more helpful to think about integration as the goal, insofar as this is possible—so, for example, the capacity to integrate mentalizing oneself with mentalizing others, or integrating mentalization of cognitions with mentalization of affect.

REFLECTIVE FUNCTIONING AND QUALITY OF PARENTING

One of the questions that has intrigued both developmental researchers and clinicians is how parents communicate an interest in infants' minds and feelings and thereby help them to develop their own capacity to recognize and know their feelings and regulate emotions (Midgley et al., 2017).

In their seminal work on attachment assessment, Ainsworth and colleagues (1978) proposed that the mother's awareness of the infant's communication, coupled with her capacity to empathically identify and put herself "in the infant's shoes," is central to her understanding of the infant and to her responding in a well-timed, appropriate manner. Most importantly, Ainsworth et al. (1978) introduced the Strange Situation, an observational method to assess parents' internal representations of relationships in young children and how those manifest in different attachment patterns of behavior. Ainsworth's work gave way to a robust body of empirical research, which has supported the notion that the parent's capacity to make sense of their own and the child's mental states plays a crucial role in parental sensitivity, thereby helping the child develop flexible and adaptive means of self-regulating and establishing productive and sustaining relationships.

While Ainsworth focused on sensitive and responsive caregiving, the notion of "attunement" introduced by Daniel Stern (1985) involves the demonstration of parental behaviors that capture and reflect the emotions of the child. Some parents display difficulties with attunement and have trouble recognizing signals associated with negative emotions displayed by their infant. Furthermore, Stern spoke of the importance of the "mutual looking" between parent and baby as a key element in the development of the internal world (how we see ourselves in the world of relationships) in which attachment can be represented and regulated. Simply put, the quality of the relationship infants—and, later on, small children—have with grown-ups who take care of them lays the foundations for learning how to think about feelings and how to manage feelings, especially anxiety. As children become older, their emotional reactions become more their own and increasingly complex. By the time children reach preschool, they begin to understand implicit rules (there is no need to use words) about displaying emotions and seem to have deliberate control of facial expressions. The way in which parents respond and react to this new capacity is very important in terms of letting the child know that expression of feelings, positive and negative, is allowed and, most importantly, that adults make an effort to understand what is behind them. What is the motivation? Is the child showing us that they are feeling afraid, alone, confused?

Reflective functioning is a dynamic, developmental, and bidirectional capacity, which arguably is, to a large extent, context and relationship specific. This might explain why parents can show very different levels of mentalizing with regard to their different children and why—much as in genetic research, at least within the confines of an average expectable environment—it could be primarily child features, such as temperament, and contextual features, such as early trauma, that drive these interactions among the child, environmental factors, and parental reflective functioning (Luyten et al., 2017).

From its inception, reflective functioning has provided both clinicians and researchers a starting point to explore the quality of the relationship between the caregiver and the child and development longitudinally. The awareness of the importance of the role of the caregiver's mind-mindedness (Meins et al., 2002, 2003) in the emergence of the infant's sense of self has been acknowledged and emphasized in psychoanalytic theory (Fenichel, 1946; Mahler et al., 1975; Stern, 1985; Winnicott, 1965) and explored both clinically and theoretically. Reflective functioning itself is considered highly present in a parent's functioning when the parent

- demonstrates an awareness of the nature of mental states;

- makes explicit efforts to tease out mental states underlying behavior;

- recognizes the developmental aspects of mental states (that they can change over time, and how a person feels and thinks now may be different than what that person felt and thought in the past);

- recognizes mental states in relation to the person the parent is speaking to (Fonagy et al., 1998; Katznelson, 2014);

- displays awareness that emotions can vary in intensity and over time; and

- is aware that feelings can be disguised or unobservable, that feelings can trigger other feelings and that internal states can conflict, and that mental states are key to understanding behavior (Fonagy et al., 1998; Katznelson, 2014).

CONSTRUCTS RELATED TO MENTALIZATION

Theory of mind: the psychological capacity to explain and predict people's actions and interactions based on an understanding of their thoughts, feelings, beliefs, and intentions (Wellman, 1992).

Mind-mindedness: seeing others (and yourself) as having a mind capable of intentionality and agency (Meins et al., 2002).

Metacognition: the ability to think about, monitor, and reason about mental states and in the context of interactions between people.

Slade (2005) expanded the concept, applying it to parents' reflections on their own children and their relationships with them, referring to this skill specifically as *parental reflective functioning*. Parental reflective functioning allows children to develop their own reflective functioning capacity. Though reflective functioning is most often assessed by looking at the way people speak, much of the transmission likely occurs through nonverbal aspects of these processes, beginning with the caregiver's ability to regulate the child's affective state, especially in moments of increased arousal. Parents who respond to their children's manifestation of emotions with contingent marked affective displays (and this includes tone of voice, facial expression, bodily distance, and motion) allow their babies to modulate their own emotional states. This practice, also referred to as *marked mirroring,* is thought to be particularly important when it comes to the management of negative emotions (Fonagy et al., 2002) because it is central in the early development of recognition of self and affective states and self-regulation. Furthermore, it represents a powerful protective factor against hyperactivation of the attachment system and the associated proximity-seeking behaviors automatically in response to perceived threat (in some cases, based on previous relational experiences, and in other cases, due to the child's temperamental vulnerabilities, and so on; Fonagy et al., 2008). Central to the framework explored in this book is the belief that in the context of this first relational dance between parent and child, the parent's mentalized affectivity capacities will be pivotal in the development of moments of contingent and congruent marked mirroring.

Parental reflective functioning allows the child to adapt to emotional states without being destabilized and to experience and recognize the affects that they feel. This experience permits the development of the child's ability to know the subjective meaning of their feelings beyond a mere intellectual understanding and to begin to exercise control over those feelings. It also promotes the ability to acquire mentalized affectivity (a concept we explore in depth in Chapter 2), which would allow the child to feel thoughts and think about feelings (Jurist, 2005, 2018).

Regarding a parent's attachment patterns, H. Steele et al. (2008) and M. Steele et al. (2002) have shown that both mothers' and fathers' security with respect to their own childhood experiences is predictive of their child's ability to recognize painful feelings, acknowledge difficult situations, and understand emotions—especially negative ones. More recently, Rosso et al. (2015) found that although no significant differences were observed between the average mentalization abilities of children of secure versus insecure mothers, all children with high levels of mentalization were the children of secure mothers. Furthermore, the authors found that mothers' use of dismissive strategies, based on idealization of experiences with their own parents and insistence on a lack of recall for early childhood experiences, was significantly and negatively correlated with a marker of children's mentalization ability.

A DEVELOPMENTAL APPROACH TO MENTALIZING WITH PARENTS

An innovation of mentalization-based treatment for children (MBT-C) was the elaboration of the developmental lines of mentalization—specifically, the addition of a developmental line of interpersonal and intrapersonal capacities that are integral to mentalization, consisting of (a) attention regulation, (b) affect regulation, and (c) explicit mentalizing. This line does not replace the unfolding of the prementalizing modes but occurs alongside it. While prementalizing modes are markers that mentalization has not developed or has broken down, often, when mentalizing breaks down, these related capacities of attention regulation and affect regulation have been disrupted as well.

The term *attention regulation* was used by Fonagy et al. (2002), who argued that the development of self-regulation in infancy depends on the development of mechanisms to react to stress (*affect regulation*), maintain focused attention (*attention regulation*), and interpret mental states in the self and others (*explicit mentalizing*). The development of these three areas is "arguably the most important evolutionary function of attachment to a caregiver" (Fonagy et al., 2002, p. 313). These three mechanisms are interdependent and each feed back to the others, constituting the developmental line of mentalizing.

FOUNDATIONS OF ATTENTION REGULATION AND AFFECT REGULATION

Beatrice Beebe's (2006) research with parent–infant dyads has shown that subtleties of nonverbal interactions between parents and children, at just 4 months of age, are predictive of children's later attachment patterns and illuminated the roles of attentional control and affect regulation as foundational to secure attachment. Beebe and her team observed parents and infants interacting face-to-face for 10 minutes. One of their most influential observations was that while parents spent most of the task gazing at their child, babies at times turned their gaze or orientation away from the parent. Beebe explained that while gaze and facial interactions are fun and pleasurable, they are also stimulating, so when the baby starts to feel overaroused or something becomes uncomfortable, the baby will withdraw—often by looking away—to self-regulate. Beebe reassured parents that if they can recognize these moments and just wait, with openness, for the baby to self-regulate, then in time, the baby will come back. However, this withdrawal from the interaction to self-regulate can make parents anxious, if they are not aware of how normal and important this is for the child's development.

Parents, particularly those whose own early attachment relationships contributed to the development of internal working models of themselves as unlovable and unworthy, can feel as though their baby is rejecting them or does not love them or that they are failing as a parent. But Beebe (2005, 2006) cautioned that if parents respond to these concerns by trying to follow the baby and get them to come back sooner, or what she calls "chase," then the baby will likely "dodge"—that is, need to move away again in order to get the space needed to self-regulate. Similarly, if the parent misinterprets this move away as a rejection from the baby, the parent might be inclined to give up—or even reject the baby in return. Both of these reactions are understandable if we put ourselves in the shoes of a parent who is wanting and trying to do their best and does not realize the meaning of the baby's communications here. In later chapters, we discuss how we work with parents of infants both to understand their children and to understand their own internal reactions and responses, including their strengths and the moments where they connect with each other; however, we describe this research here because of what it has taught us about the importance of attention regulation and affect regulation as the foundational building blocks of mentalizing. While the baby does not yet have the capacity to mentalize in the way that adults are capable of, both parent and baby are in an ongoing process of attending to the other, or an object of joint attention, and regulating their arousal. It is perhaps most obvious in the case of the parent: that in order to mentalize their experience or their baby's, they need to have the capacity to focus their attention either on their baby's communications or on themselves internally and then regulate the emotions that are aroused, whether they are negative (e.g., anxiety, fear, disappointment, shame, anger) or positive (e.g., excitement, joy, curiosity).

Parents often seek help while in a state of dysregulation themselves, informed by fear, helplessness, or feelings of guilt and rage, which are difficult to speak about for fear of being judged or feeling further shame. As a result, to accomplish the goal of helping parents mentalize their children, we may need to remain as much as possible in a therapeutic stance that provides the parent with an environment that fosters epistemic trust—an environment characterized by joint attention and coregulation, that facilitates an experience of the parent feeling adequately seen and emotionally validated by the therapist.

The parent's own attachment styles influence their affect regulation and reflective functioning capacities. Identifying, processing, and expressing a range of emotional experiences in the context of a safe and mentalizing therapeutic relationship can represent a protective factor for parents. In fact, current research literature shows that more frequent maternal mental state talk about positive feelings was found to be associated with less maternal reflective functioning and less sensitivity to child needs (Borelli et al., 2012). Another study by Dunn and Brown (2001) demonstrated that family dialogue involving negative emotions was predictive of better performance on tests of understanding emotions. Among school-age children, it appears that parents' child-focused reflective functioning is associated with their children's attachment and, more specifically, children's emotional openness (Borelli et al., 2016, 2021). And Sharp et al. (2006) demonstrated that a child's tendency to avoid recognizing and facing negative emotions was negatively correlated with the maternal ability to understand the child's mind. Further down the developmental road, Benbassat and Priel (2012) investigated the role of parental reflective functioning correlated with adolescent reflective functioning and social competence in a sample of adolescents aged 14 to 18 years. These findings have important relevance for clinicians technically, as they suggest the importance of creating a therapeutic environment in which parents feel safe to explore difficult and often-avoided emotions regarding their children.

This link between emotion recognition, mental state talk, and children's emotional tolerance highlights the value of creating a baseline of both the child's/adolescent's and the parents'/family's mentalizing profile. This approach helps us in our attempt to meet the parents and child "where they are." It is very important to assess the parents' relational developmental path and how it is contributing to, or inhibiting, their capacity to mentalize in the current relationship with their child.

Parental reflective functioning promotes the quality of interactions, which sets the foundations for the development of the child's own mentalizing capacities. Working with parents, keeping in mind attention regulation and affect regulation, alongside mentalization, to guide our clinical interventions is a central aspect of a mentalization-informed approach.

For instance, during the early stages of working with parents, a focus on epistemic trust (a concept we explore in Chapter 2) can be built through moments of attention regulation (e.g., "Tell me the story of the fight with your daughter, and let's try to understand it together"). Working at an attention-regulation level promotes the process of identification, modulation, and expression of emotion in an increasingly safe and trusting relational environment for the parent. The main aim is to encourage and strengthen the parent's mentalized affectivity while providing the parent the experience of feeling thought about and accompanied in the expression of painful emotions. Parental reflective functioning is about not only what is verbally communicated but also the way in which it is conveyed. Mentalized affectivity in a parent facilitates their capacity to maintain an environment of safety and trust for themselves and their children, in the context of stressful situations.

A NEW RELATIONAL EXPERIENCE: FEELING MENTALIZED

Psychoanalyst and pediatrician Donald Winnicott (1960) famously said, "There is no such thing as a baby"—meaning that we find ourselves in the eyes of our caregivers, in the way they hold us and the way they respond to our nonverbal expressions. These expressions at first all come from bodily experiences: feeling hungry, feeling cold, feeling sick, feeling excited. The way in which a caregiver receives them, tries to decipher their meaning, and reacts to them is vital in the process of learning how to experience and manage our emotions—and with it, the sense of who we are in the world of relationships.

Central to our mentalizing-informed model to working with parents is the task of helping them to retell their story and their child's story in a way that their self-observation increases and with it, their capacity to "play with ideas" of what might be going on for their child and themselves.

Many times, this capacity to play relationally needs to be modeled and practiced in our work with parents before we can begin the process of focusing on what is going on for the child. In other words, we need to give parents the experience of being mentalized before they can do the same for their child. In this way, we first work on the parent's capacity for self-reflective functioning in order to facilitate child-centered reflective functioning.

Teaching an able child to ride a bike typically requires that you have done it, too. Through experience, (a) you can teach the child what to pay attention to, (b) you are able to ride your own bike as the child mirrors you, and (c)—most important—you experience the satisfaction of sharing an experience filled with connection and mutual enjoyment. Parental reflective functioning and the child's own development of the capacity for mentalization similarly requires that parents have some experience being mentalized and have had the chance to practice and hone their own mentalizing skills, in the context of a safe and predictable relationship.

The main purpose of this mentalization-informed approach to working with parents is to offer them a new and different model of a relational experience from what they likely received earlier in their lives. In this new relational experience, the therapist makes efforts to be available to receive the emotional impact of the parents' unpleasant emotional states, without responding in a problem-solving mode and without focusing solely on the child's difficulties as the only problem that needs to be addressed. Our main goal is to mentalize the parents, with the idea that this different relational approach can be generalized by the parent and will invite them to take a more genuine interest in what lies behind their child's behavior—which will better serve their child's social and emotional needs and improve their relationship. This new attitude is characterized by higher levels of (a) flexibility, (b) curiosity, and (c) genuine openness.

As previously explained, reflective functioning supports parents' sensitive responsiveness by helping caregivers to mentally put themselves in the place of the infant and imagine the infant's experience (Fonagy & Target, 1997). By the same token, reflective functioning can be expected to play a role in inhibiting negative parenting by helping parents mentally step back and be cognizant of their own emotions and their impact on the child (Ensink et al., 2016). For example, Arietta Slade (2005) proposed that parental reflective functioning is a factor in the intergenerational transmission of attachment, and expanded the research showing that parents' own states of mind about attachment predicted their children's attachment, by demonstrating a link between the quality of caregiver–child attachment relationship and the infant's attachment style. Furthermore, parental reflective functioning is thought to play an important role in the development of the child's own capacity for reflective functioning, which in turn is thought to foster affect regulation, effortful control, and—ultimately—the development of a sense of autonomy and agency, as well as the capacity to develop secure attachment relationships.

A parental reflective stance is implicit in interactions (Ensink et al., 2016), and it is characterized by some of the following:

- a benign interest in the mind of the child and emotional availability to help the child make sense of their own reactions and those of others

- a capacity to look past the child's behavior to determine what it communicates about their experience, feelings, and difficulties

- a capacity to play, joke, and imagine with the child

- a motivation to consider the meaning and sense of a child's thoughts and feelings, even if one cannot be exactly sure what is in the child's mind

- an availability to help the child put feelings into words and elaborate autobiographically meaningful narratives

- a motivation to see the child's perspective and an awareness that the child's experience may be very different from one's own

- an ability to have a sense of one's own thoughts and feelings when interacting with the child and to modulate one's own aggression

- an appreciation that one's own feelings and moods, and their history, will affect and have an impact on one's children

We have described mentalization and reflective functioning as a construct, a developmental process, and a capacity, and we now shift to mentalization as a therapeutic stance and the basis for an intervention approach. When we model these characteristics in our interactions with parents, we are offering them a different relational experience. We offer them the most valuable skill of all: that of imagining in a curious way what is motivating their behaviors and those of their children, especially during moments of stress.

WORKING WITH PARENTS FROM A MENTALIZING STANCE: AWAKENING, REVISITING, AND MODELING REFLECTIVE FUNCTIONING

Good mentalizing is characterized by the following: a kind of comfort with exploring the mental world, a curiosity about oneself and others, the capacity to imagine the point of view and emotional states of others, the ability to reflect upon oneself, the ability to tolerate uncertainty and that minds change, the capacity to be playful and flexible, and the understanding that mental states are opaque by nature (Luyten et al., 2012). *Concrete mentalizing* is characterized by

(a) a lack of reflection, (b) rigid adherence to one's own perspective and interpretations, (c) a kind of certainty about oneself or someone else, (d) automatic and distorted interpretations, (e) defensiveness, and (f) an inability to regulate one's emotional distress in relation to others (Luyten et al., 2012).

Much of the mentalization-based literature (Bateman & Fonagy, 2012; Fearon et al., 2006; Fonagy, 2006) highlights the importance of the mentalizing clinician's awareness and self-observation of their own fluctuations in mentalizing, in response to interactions with parents. The following are central aspects of the stance in the process of establishing a safe environment where to activate and model reflective functioning for parents and families.

KEY PRINCIPLES OF A MENTALIZING STANCE

- active "wondering" and "not knowing"
- monitoring of one's own mistakes
- genuine curiosity
- staying in the here and now
- identifying mentalizing impasses and lowering arousal levels
- paying attention to nonverbal ways of communicating
- keeping a developmental focus as the main exploratory lens

One of the key components of any mentalization-informed clinical intervention is the mentalizing posture of the therapist. It is important to highlight that a mentalizing stance is impossible to sustain at all times, as the therapist's mentalization capacities are also affected by the emotional impact of the client's responses. However, a conscious focus on mentalization helps the therapist to exercise their own mentalized affectivity capacities in the context of clinical stressful situations.

Active "Wondering" and "Not Knowing"

The therapist does not presume to know what is going on until the other person explains it. Parallel to this, one insists on inviting alternative perspectives to the discussion. In this way, the therapist models an inquisitive stance, based on understanding mental states of others as "opaque" and assuming an attitude of curiosity. A therapist in an inquisitive stance attempts to "imagine" what the other thinks and feels, followed by recruiting the other to figure it out—something that often results in improvement of affect regulation and overall quality of interpersonal relationships.

Monitoring One's Own Mistakes

The therapist acknowledges their inability to really know what is in the other person's mind and speaks of the therapist's own mistakes (use of self)—for example, "I am sorry, I think I misunderstood you." In certain moments, it is helpful for therapist to articulate what you were thinking and why the misunderstanding might have occurred.

Genuine Curiosity

Genuine curiosity about other's experience (inquisitive stance) reflects a mentalizing stance, for example, "I wonder how you feel when you have to hold your child down so she stops kicking you—what goes through your mind at that moment?" Similarly, though a more advanced position to take, the therapist models genuine curiosity about their own experience at the time, for example, "I've been talking a lot today; I wonder what that's about?"

Staying in the Here and Now

A mentalizing stance stays in the present moment, "in the room," as much as possible, instead of moving to the past. For example,

> I can imagine your childhood experiences make dealing with these issues with your child challenging; however, I would like to stay for a minute with what you just said, regarding your fight with your child yesterday, and what you experienced just now when you were telling me about it.

At times, this is difficult, such as when the strength of the past trauma is keeping the parent away from thinking psychologically, out of fear and anxiety. It is crucial in the therapeutic work during these times to really slow down and allow for exploration of these issues.

Identifying Mentalizing Impasses and Lowering Arousal Levels

Simmering down the emotional temperature in the room can be done by bringing in the therapist's experience in the here and now:

> Can we pause here a minute? I think I can see how this that you are sharing with me is quite painful—and I can imagine why, because I am quite moved by the difficulties you had to go through with your child.

Inviting the parents to "stop and rewind" to the moment before mentalizing stopped or broke down is a straightforward technique for lowering arousal levels and beginning to mentalize difficult moments, for example, "What do you think just happened here just now?" This commonly occurs during early sessions with parents, which are often characterized by defensive or sometimes openly aggressive behaviors.

Paying Attention to Nonverbal Ways of Communicating

Mentalizing is not just verbal and cognitive—it is also embodied. Therapists also work to help parents become aware of the power of nonverbal communication. The therapist identifies facial and bodily cues that communicate affective shifts in the family and thinks with parents about how these cues are experienced by the therapist and how they might be experienced by the child. At times, we are unaware of culturally mediated nonverbal expressions that have been passed on from generation to generation, carrying profound meaning in families. We also tend to overly invest in words and in explaining things to children—when, at times, all they need is a calm physical presence from their caregivers.

Keeping a Developmental Focus as the Main Explanatory Lens

Whenever possible, identify the difference between child and adult thoughts and feelings. At times, utilizing a psychoeducational approach to understanding a behavior helps parents create benign explanations of children's behaviors.

In the next chapters of Part I, we explore some of these constructs and how they are observed and intervened within the clinical realm. To bring these concepts to life, we follow the case of Cristina.

CRISTINA AND HER PARENTS: SPECIMEN CASE

Cristina is a 9-year-old biracial girl who was referred to treatment by her school's counselor because of what the counselor reported as obsessive-compulsive behavior. Cristina was described as constantly checking, before going to bed, where her mother was and constantly calling her mother up to her room for long periods of time. She was also concerned about cleanliness and order and avoided activities where she feared getting dirty or hurt. Most recently, Cristina had begun to isolate at school and asked her teacher if she could stay in the classroom to help, because she feared getting hurt by the "rough" play of the other children.

Cristina lives with her parents and her younger brother, Jack, who is 7 years old. Both parents, Mr. and Mrs. O, are college educated. Cristina's dad is the primary breadwinner, as her mom scaled back from a profitable full-time job to working as a freelancer after giving birth to Cristina. At the time of referral, Cristina's parents were discussing separating, but they believed that Cristina and Jack were not aware of their conversations and plans. When asked about sources of marital stress, Mr. O spoke of feeling that their marriage had become cold and distant, especially after the children were born. Mrs. O agreed and added that Mr. O's job required long hours away and that this had been tough for everybody, including Mr. O.

Both parents came from intact families. Mrs. O had a history of depression, which she linked to growing up in a White, middle-class home where she was physically provided for but where her emotional needs were neglected. Mrs. O had never sought support regarding her difficult childhood, as she felt that nobody would believe her. Mr. O described his family as close-knit. His parents emigrated from Latin America to the United States before his birth, and he grew up in a "typical American suburb." His parents spoke Spanish to each other, but he never learned Spanish at home. Mr. and Mrs. O met online when they were both in their early 30s.

Cristina was described by both parents as a well-behaved and caring child, who was slightly nervous all the time and quite perfectionistic. She was seen as loving and sensitive toward her brother; however, sometimes he could provoke her, and she would become rageful and aggressive toward him. Often, though, as Cristina's parents described, she would just run to her room and hit a pillow. When asked about how the family manages feelings, Mrs. O spoke of her husband's Latin American temper and her difficulties dealing with it due to her history of emotional maltreatment in her family of origin.

Mrs. O seemed anxious and apprehensive about how to help Cristina with her difficulties, whereas Mr. O seemed to think that this was a phase that she would grow out of. When they were asked about how they thought their children might be affected by the tension in their marital relationship, their responses were markedly different: Mrs. O went to great lengths to explain the reasons they were having difficulties, but she did not address the impact on the kids. Mr. O presented as defensive and somewhat dismissive of the impact on the children, responding, "They are kids! If they have a roof over their heads and a predictable schedule, they know they are OK, they know we love them." The interviewer, in turn, felt disconnected and somewhat annoyed with both parents during the interview and, in supervision, casually described them to a colleague as narcissists.

The following is an excerpt from Cristina's parents' Parent Development Interview (Slade et al., 2004), an instrument used to assess parents' states of mind and representations of the parent–child relationship and parental reflective functioning.

THERAPIST: Describe a time in the last week that you and your child really clicked.

MOM: Well, Cristina and I spend a lot of time together. I'm with them a lot more than [Mr. O] is, because of his work schedule. I think it's difficult for Cristina to feel clicked, because she's so anxious, especially lately, with adolescence knocking at her door. It's so difficult to witness your child not expressing herself because of fear.

THERAPIST: How do you know when she feels fear?

MOM: I spend so much time with her, we're very connected. I just worry about her future . . .

DAD: I think that's the whole problem, she worries too much about her. And that's why she has OCD, she learned it from you to worry all the time.

THERAPIST: There seems to be a lot of worry about your daughter, but also, it's difficult to think about where it all comes from. It's a bit confusing . . .

MOM AND DAD: [*both nod positively*]

[*a few minutes later in the interview*]

THERAPIST: Are there any experiences in your child's life that you feel were particularly difficult or challenging for her?

MOM: Well, it's not her life really, but my pregnancy with her was really difficult, and breastfeeding was hard, and I wasn't diagnosed but I think I probably had postpartum depression. And she was our first. It was really overwhelming and hard to make the decision to stop working, because my work was my whole life and I loved it, but I also felt like I couldn't do both.

DAD: But she was just a baby then, she doesn't remember that. Her life has been pretty great. She's a lucky girl, and that's why I don't understand when people think she is so miserable. Like my son, he's really happy-go-lucky and really appreciates the life he has and enjoys it!

MOM: Yea, but still, he got things from us that she didn't get. We were much more settled by the time he was born.

DAD: I think it's that school. The kids all have one issue or another, I think she's just trying to compete or something.

MOM: [*speaking directly to the therapist*] He doesn't understand what it's like to be a 9-year-old girl these days.

THERAPIST: [*prompting both parents*] You both seem to agree that things are difficult for Cristina, even though you see them from different perspectives . . . Am I right?

MOM: I suppose, in the end she is the one struggling in the playground . . . I remember being her age and being in the playground, it was terrible . . . I used to feel the other kids did not like me because of something I said or did. I always tell Cristina she is kind and nice and pretty, that she should not worry so much . . . but it does not work . . .

DAD: [*laughs*] She is not going to believe you because you tell her . . .

THERAPIST: I sense things are getting tough in here between the two of you, I am asking some difficult questions, what do you think Cristina makes of moments like this? How do you imagine she feels?

CONCLUDING SUMMARY

- We all lose our capacity to mentalize on a daily basis.

- *Good-enough reflective functioning* is the capacity to mentalize one's experiences and those of one's child simultaneously, in a consistent and predictable way, that serves as a protective factor for the parent as they embark on the lifelong task of parenting.

- Parenting, as a developmental stage, is a fluid process that requires flexibility, curiosity, imagination, and appropriate sense of humor—all characteristics of good reflective functioning.

- This book seeks to provide the therapist with a framework from which to safely explore, with the parents, the ever-changing challenges of parenting, by modeling, encouraging, and reinforcing parental reflective functioning.

- In this context, we seek to invite the parent to embark on a journey where they can experience epistemic trust while feeling held and validated by a mentalizing therapist.

- We seek to provide an environment of safety, wherein mentalized affectivity can be practiced and experienced.

In Chapter 2, we introduce two of the key concepts that are central to the clinical scaffolding of our mentalization-informed model of working with parents. These concepts facilitate the emergence of self and other mentalizing capacities, while also promoting the balance between emotion and cognition in the context of the therapeutic process. By referring to epistemic trust and mentalized affectivity, we seek to offer the reader a comprehensive understanding of two concepts that will be important to follow the clinical chapters in Part II of this book.

2 OUR MENTALIZING FRAMEWORK

Building on a Foundation of Epistemic Trust and Mentalized Affectivity

The theoretical underpinning of our model is found in the related constructs of epistemic trust and mentalized affectivity. Both constructs can be understood in terms of two coordinates: (a) the integration of affect and cognition and (b) the negotiation of self and other relationships. Epistemic trust is established within the early parental relationship; it exceeds basic trust by the incorporation of knowledge that is valuable and is transmitted though communication. Mentalized affectivity is a more advanced way to integrate the experience of emotions in relation to autobiographical memory and history. Epistemic trust concerns reliance on caregivers; epistemic vigilance marks the advance to be more circumspect about knowledge, corresponding to when children start to become influenced by others outside of the family. Mentalized affectivity occurs when processing, which is more agentive in nature, emerges. This entails more developed capacities to pursue, receive, and utilize information. In this chapter, we clearly define the respective constructs and illustrate how they can be incorporated into work with parents.

https://doi.org/10.1037/0000341-003
Working With Parents in Therapy: A Mentalization-Based Approach, by N. Malberg, E. Jurist, J. Bate, and M. Dangerfield

When asked about how he thought their children might be affected by the tension in his and Mrs. O's marital relationship, Mr. O presented as defensive and somewhat dismissive of the impact on the children: "They are kids! If they have a roof over their heads and a predictable schedule, they know they are OK, they know we love them."

Therapists of almost any orientation would identify points of intervention in this response from a father when he is asked how he thinks his children might be affected by his separation from their mother. Through the lens of reflective functioning, the response given is concrete, is certain, is all-knowing, and lacks curiosity about the other's mind. In fact, Mr. O's response suggests that he does not think of his children's minds as being shaped by the relationships in their family but instead as being determined only by whether their physical needs are met.

In their 2014 paper, Fonagy and Allison introduced a new term to the literature on mentalization and attachment theory: *epistemic trust,* a concept borrowed from Gergely et al. (2007), Csibra and Gergely (2009), and Sperber et al. (2010). The term is useful for clinicians to further understand parents' communications with regard to their openness and readiness to learn from the relationship with the therapist.

Epistemic trust is the capacity to "trust in the authenticity and personal relevance of interpersonally transmitted knowledge. Epistemic trust enables social learning in an ever-changing social and cultural context and allows individuals to benefit from their (social) environment" (Fonagy et al., 2014, Epistemic Trust and the Transmission of Culture section, para. 1). The role that it plays in social learning allows humans to generalize knowledge beyond a specific relationship—that is, as children's early experiences consolidate into longer lasting patterns of epistemic trust in adulthood, they continue to shape communication and relational skills. In this chapter, we translate the theory and research on epistemic trust into therapeutic work with parents, where epistemic trust is central to the mechanisms of action of therapy and targets for change in parents' relationships with their children. We continue to use the case of Cristina and Mr. and Mrs. O to explicate this concept, in the same way we did with reflective functioning in the previous chapter.

NATURAL PEDAGOGY AND EPISTEMIC TRUST

The question that is important for many, if not most, parents and communities is not, "Is [this individual] child 'securely attached'?" but rather, "How can I ensure that my child knows whom to trust and how to share social connections with others? How can I be sure my child is with others and situations where he or she will be safe? (Weisner, 2014, p. 263)

Learning plays an important role in psychotherapy from any orientation, although we as clinicians might (and perhaps should) be reluctant to see ourselves as "experts" or "teachers." As therapists, we hope that patients will learn, from our work together, new things about themselves, their relationships, and their emotions and that this knowledge will help them to understand themselves and others better and improve the quality of their lives. Parents especially often come to our offices wanting to learn—or, rather, to be taught:

- They ask to be taught strategies to control their child's behavior, skills to change their interactions with them, and ways to understand them.

- They often feel as though their children are not listening to and hearing them; they feel as though their children are not learning social and emotional skills, and they are not able to teach them.

- They are frequently concerned about their children's development and whether they are good parents, wanting to learn about what is wrong and what they can do about it.

As such, therapeutic work with parents necessarily involves enhancing the pathways for learning—first, so that they can learn through their relationship with us and then so that their children can learn from them and others in the world. What is being learned in therapy might differ depending on the model. In our approach, the focus is on learning to mentalize and/or restore mentalizing and to improve relational functioning.

Importantly, the model of learning that we put forward in this chapter, to foster epistemic trust in the therapeutic relationship, implies that the learning process is not a one-way street where parents take in and learn from the therapist/therapy. We posit, and describe further below, that channels for learning (and epistemic trust) are opened when the therapist is open to learning from the parent, as well, recognizing the parents' agency and intentionality. We begin with a description of how we as humans have evolved to learn.

MENTALIZING WITH PARENTS: THE MAP OF PARENTING

Ask parents about what the map of parenting is that was given to them by their own parents. What are the expectations, what are the fears, what are

(continues)

MENTALIZING WITH PARENTS: THE MAP OF PARENTING (*Continued*)

the core values? What are the areas where they feel they could easily be lost or have felt at a loss in the context of being a parent?

What aspects of their map would they like to erase and rewrite? Do they feel they have no map given, and what do they feel is the impact of that on their parental self-esteem and capacity to see their small victories as a parent? What is the legacy they hope to leave their kids?

NATURAL PEDAGOGY AND THE EVOLUTION OF SOCIAL LEARNING

Humans acquire knowledge about the world in two ways: The first is through direct observation and experience. We can explore a novel object and figure out what it might be useful for. However, it would not be efficient or adaptive for young infants to learn everything by observing and experiencing it themselves. Therefore, we have evolved a second pathway for knowledge: indirect experience, which is afforded to us by language. A great deal of information we acquire about the world is learned through communication from others who tell us and/or teach us. We learn about the physical world in this way. For example, our parents or other trusted adults teach us how to feed ourselves and use the toilet. Information about the social world is also learned or transmitted in this manner. For example, we learn about people's preferences, how to express our desires and needs, and how to obtain comfort or security from our interactions with others.

These are the basic ideas that compose Csibra and Gergely's (2009) *natural pedagogy theory,* which posits that young children come into the world prepared to learn from social relationships, with biologically wired systems to trust their caregivers. This stance, termed *epistemic trust,* is characterized by the learner's openness to taking in new information and modifying their understanding of the world, based on the perceived reliability of the informant to provide accurate and relevant information. In our social environment, learning is not always meant to be generalized—it is often considered specific to the situation we are in. For example, if your partner tells you, "I'm really in the mood for Thai food tonight," you do not take this to mean that Thai food is something that is generally desired—you merely learn that this is what they would like to order for dinner tonight. Epistemic trust is, therefore, a stance that needs to be activated when it is needed: that is, when the information is relevant and also generalizable.

Natural pedagogy theory suggests that through evolution, humans have developed ways of indicating, in our communication, that information we are sharing with others is relevant to others—not just in the here and now, as in the above example, but more generally. *Ostensive cues* are the overt, observable, or demonstrative signals of "communicative intent" (Csibra & Gergely, 2009; Fonagy & Allison, 2014) that direct the listener's attention to the communicator. Ostensive cues include eye contact and gaze, turn taking, marked mirroring, contingent responsiveness, greeting, using the person's name, gestures and pointing, and voice intonation. When presented with ostensive cues, children and adults become open and expect to see or learn something about a referent (person or object) that is relevant beyond the here and now.

For example, if a parent wants to teach a child about an object such as a hammer, they might say, in a singsong voice, to the child, "Look at this hammer, see . . ." and move their eyes back and forth between the child and the object. Then, they might smile and say, "It's cool, isn't it? It's used for banging things. Look—we can go 'tap, tap, tap.'" And they might look at the child's face and smile when the child smiles and say, "Cool, right?" These ostensive cues described would indicate to the child that the child should encode characteristics of the hammer, because this is going to be useful information to know outside of this immediate situation. If, however, the child observed their parent using a hammer, without any ostensive cues, then the child would encode the information specific to that occasion but would not encode this information as something that is relevant to them or other situations. Alternatively, the parent might not use any ostensive cues but might say, "hammer" and use hand-over-hand to show the child how to bang it. Similarly, this information would be encoded on some level, but epistemic trust would not be activated so that the knowledge is treated as relevant and generalizable. Do you notice what is missing in these interactions, due to the lack of ostensive cues? Hopefully, you could tell how the latter ways of interacting did not reflect the parents' sense of the child's intentionality and internal world—that is, they did not embody a mentalizing stance.

The same is true for social–emotional information. Imagine a young child who hits his playmate: The parents might tell the child to apologize, but they might do so without any ostensive cues. In this case, the child might do what they are told, but they would not encode any of the social information (e.g., that the parents do not like hitting, that another child might feel hurt, that an apology is a way to repair hurt feelings) as something relevant to be generalized in other situations.

Alternatively, imagine the parent gets down on the child's level, makes eye contact with the child, changes their tone of voice, and uses marked mirroring to show that they see and understand the child's frustration, while saying, "I know you're angry, but hitting hurt Johnny, and so you need to apologize for hitting him." These ostensive cues would indicate to the child that the information being communicated is not just relevant for this moment: Not only do the parents not like hitting right now, but, in fact, people in general do not like hitting most of the time—and apologies are generally encouraged to repair.

There is not yet clear evidence on how and why ostensive cues work in this manner, but one way that ostensive cues are understood is that they signal to the learner that the communicator grasps and recognizes their mind as intentional. This feeling of one's mind being seen is part of the feeling of security in attachment and the corresponding internal working model of the self as being worthy, and it engenders epistemic trust—trust needed to take in the social and emotional information being communicated.

A series of experiments with children around 18 months old, conducted by Egyed and colleagues (2013), demonstrated the role that ostensive cues play in determining the likelihood the listener will accept and utilize new information learned. In a laboratory setting, children interacted with two confederates, in two different scenarios. In the first scenario, a confederate entered the room and interacted with the child using ostensive cues and then showed a preference for a red ball over a blue ball. When the confederate asked the child to pass them a ball, the child passed the red ball the confederate had shown a preference for. After this exchange, the child then interacted with a second confederate, who used no ostensive cues and did not show a preference for either ball but then asked the child for one of the balls. In this scenario, the child (more often than not) passed the confederate the red ball that the previous confederate had been interested in. This behavior, the authors suggested, indicates that the child learned from the first confederate and generalized that learning.

In the second scenario, the first confederate did not use any ostensive cues but showed a preference for the red ball over the blue ball. When asked for one of the balls, the child provided the confederate the red ball, having learned, like the child in the first condition, that the red ball was preferred by the confederate. However, the difference in the two conditions is observed in the second interaction. When the second confederate, using no ostensive cues, requested one of the balls, the child was equally as likely to give the blue ball as they were to give the red ball. This behavior appears to indicate that in the absence of ostensive cuing, the child learned the preference at the individual/episodic level but did not generalize this learning to other interactions.

EPISTEMIC VIGILANCE

Epistemic trust is similar to attachment, in that we all need some way of trusting information from others, just as we need ways of seeking proximity to those who are bigger, stronger, older, and wiser, when we are in distress or under threat. It is not possible to get through life without acquiring knowledge about the world from other people.

Theorists (Grice, 1975; Sperber & Wilson, 1986) have pointed out, however, that while listeners are motivated to acquire true information that they did not already know, communicators have their own motivations—to make the listener think or act in a certain way. To achieve their own goals, communicators want the information they share to be understood and to be accepted or believed; in some cases, this may be their intention regardless of whether the information is true.

When a communicator presents information with ostensive cues, they are making it clear that they are seeking to be understood and believed by the person they are speaking to—that is, they are looking for epistemic trust. Communication of this nature offers great opportunities for collaboration, which is central to social life and at the heart of therapy. But when one person communicates information that they want to be understood and believed, the other person is in a vulnerable position, because they can be exploited if the communicator's intentions are at odds with their own. Sperber and colleagues (2010) argued that it is for this reason that the capacity for epistemic trust evolved alongside a stance of epistemic vigilance, which balances the system. *Epistemic vigilance* is not to be confused with being mistrustful—instead, it is considered the opposite of "blind trust" (Sperber et al., 2010); it is the system that determines whether epistemic trust should be granted or withheld. Whether epistemic trust is given depends on both

- our perception of the communicator's knowledge and intent; and

- the content of the information—whether it fits or conflicts with our background knowledge or beliefs, and how entrenched or confident we are in our previous knowledge or beliefs.

Recent thinking by cognitive evolutionary psychologists stresses the complex challenge of social life, where reputation is often a determining factor in trust, for better or worse. Being able to trust is crucial, but so is being able to withdraw trust.

PROBLEMS WITH EPISTEMIC TRUST

Over the course of our early lives, though, we have varied experiences in learning from other people. We may interact with people whose ostensive cues are not clear, and thus we must resort to other ways of determining whether the information they are communicating is relevant or generalizable. In the worst-case scenario, the people we interact with may be intentionally or unintentionally deceptive, leaving us uncertain or dubious about their motives. In cases such as these, epistemic trust remains low, which is protective, but if it remains chronic, then it interferes with social learning in the long term.

When one's epistemic stance is chronically not trusting, the process of taking in information and using it to modify one's worldview is disrupted. The term *epistemic hypervigilance* has been used to describe situations when the listener is chronically uncertain about the intent of the communicator or believes their intentions are bad, and so resists taking in or generalizing information communicated more broadly from different communicators. It is also problematic when a person does not know how to determine whom they can and should trust, a state that Knox (2016) described as *epistemic confusion*. This can be a valuable entry point in working with parents.

As therapists, we can recognize when patients either are prone to misread our cues, showing a lack of epistemic trust, or blindly accept what we say or offer, out of their need for approval. Further study is needed to determine whether these are two different terms for the same pattern or not. But for clinicians applying this concept, it is useful to remember that no matter what terms we use, it can be adaptive to have low epistemic trust (or high epistemic vigilance) when one has been repeatedly exposed to others who were abusive or deceitful.

Fonagy and colleagues (2015) referred to this shutting down of epistemic trust as *epistemic petrification* and suggested that it accounts for why patients with personality disorders are often difficult to treat and considered hard to reach. It has not been adaptive for them to adopt a stance of epistemic trust. Thus, they may be skeptical of the therapist's motivation, and it can take time before they are more open to hear the therapist. Even when they begin to acquire skills and begin to interact with the therapist in new ways, these skills might not generalize to other relationships and areas in their lives.

The model presented in this book emphasizes attending to parents' patterns of epistemic trust and conceptualizes the link between mentalization and epistemic trust as bidirectional. A mentalizing stance facilitates epistemic trust in the relationship, and epistemic trust facilitates the patient taking in and learning to mentalize in relationships more generally.

Many parents come from backgrounds where it was not clear whether they could or should trust the caregivers in their life. Consequently, they did not develop a flexible balance of epistemic trust and epistemic vigilance, instead adopting stances of epistemic trust that resulted in them either taking in information that was maladaptive or feeling consistently uncertain about whom to trust. We refer to these disruptions in epistemic trust as positions of *epistemic isolation,* where the person is cut off from the ability to flexibly rely on relationships as sources of information.

Corriveau et al. (2009) demonstrated that patterns of epistemic trust may be associated with different attachment patterns in children. Secure attachment, in this study, was associated with a pattern where in ambiguous/uncertain conditions, children preferentially turned to their caregiver rather than a stranger, but when there was information that indicated to the child that their caregiver's response was not accurate, the child was able to endorse a stranger's view over their caregiver's. These findings suggest that secure attachment is associated with the capacity to use the information in the environment to make decisions, but when the situation is too ambiguous or uncertain, you are able to reliably turn to a caregiver (or trusted other) for help. In contrast, children who were classified as avoidant did not preferentially turn to their caregivers for help in an ambiguous situation, while children who were classified as resistant tended to listen to their caregivers over a stranger—even when there was clear information that their caregiver was giving incorrect information.

We use this understanding to inform our approach to working with parents. The goal in our work is to enhance parents' abilities to access and utilize the information available to them in their environment and within themselves but to recognize when the situation is ambiguous and/or emotionally overwhelming and turning to another trusted person may be adaptive. This goal contrasts with being overly reliant on others (perhaps their own caregivers or even the therapist) and taking in maladaptive information or not being able to turn to anyone else for input and help.

MENTALIZATION AND EPISTEMIC TRUST

Epistemic trust was first linked to mentalization by Fonagy and Allison (2014). Implicit mentalizing, they argued, is a form of ostensive cueing. When the parent (or therapist) adopts a mentalizing stance, they indicate to the child (or patient) that they regard them as an intentional being with agency; this builds epistemic trust. That epistemic trust then enables the child (or patient) to generalize what they learn, through the relationship, to other parts of their life.

Furthermore, one of the skills learned within the context of relationships is mentalizing itself. So, once the pathways for learning are open, then children and adults learn to mentalize and then are able to begin mentalizing in other relationships. But this can then benefit them even further. As people become effective mentalizers, they begin to communicate using ostensive cues, which then foster other people's epistemic trust with them. The cascading impact of both epistemic trust and mentalizing thus has the potential to shift the quality of interpersonal interactions more broadly. As Fonagy and Allison (2014) wrote,

> Mentalizing is our route to garnering knowledge relevant to us and being able to use it across contexts, independent of the learning experience. Put simply, the experience of feeling thought about in therapy makes us feel safe enough to think about ourselves in relation to our world, and to learn something new about that world and how we operate in it. (p. 375)

ATTENDING TO OSTENSIVE CUES AND GENERATING EPISTEMIC TRUST

There is a slight problem, though, that needs to be worked out in the therapy, with the sequence just described. The problem is that mentalizing is needed in the first place to interpret ostensive cues. As described previously, lower epistemic trust is adaptive in contexts where people are exposed to others who cannot be trusted. Not only might people start to ignore the communicator's ostensive cues in such environments where they have been repeatedly exposed to communicators who deceived them, but eventually, the cues may not even register with the listener.

This is critical to remember when treating parents in psychotherapy. Many of the parents we work with have grown up and lived in such contexts where the information given to them was not useful or true (see Chapter 3, this volume). As a result of adapting to such adverse contexts, these parents may have stopped attending to and registering ostensive cues and thus are closed off to epistemic trust and the learning it makes possible. A crucial part of the work of therapy, then, is restoring patients' attention so that they can notice and register ostensive cues. Once this occurs, we can work on helping parents to be discerning about whom and how much to trust in relationships outside of therapy.

APPLICATIONS TO WORKING WITH PARENTS

From an attachment perspective, Bowlby thought of the therapist as a secure base from which the patient could feel safe to explore their own internal world and the social world. Through the lens of epistemic trust, the therapist and patient are communicators of information.

In much of this chapter, we have referred to the therapist as the communicator, fostering epistemic trust with the parent so that the parent can learn from them. But parents and patients in treatment are not only learners, they are also communicators. They come into treatment wanting the therapist to trust (i.e., understand and accept) them and their view of themselves and their child. It can often feel like they are making a case about the child, proving what is wrong (or not a problem), with an accompanying explanation of where the problem comes from. Sometimes parents share the same view and agree with each other on how they view and understand the child, but very often they have different perspectives—and, therefore, the therapist must find a way to build trust with both.

Like parents, who establish epistemic trust with their children by being reliable in attempting to understand and accept their communications, we begin to establish epistemic trust in therapy by showing parents that we perceive them as having agency and intention, both when we communicate and when we listen. As listeners, we accept and attempt to understand what parents communicate to us. To emphasize, we want parents to value their own sense of agency, not to regard what the therapist says as unconditionally valid.

Epistemic trust is approached in this framework from a developmental perspective. The same way in which Bowlby (1969) suggested that humans come into the world ready to form attachments, they also enter the world genetically prepared for social learning—that is, they have epistemic trust. However, like with attachment, real experiences with significant others shape the ways in which they trust and, specifically, how they balance epistemic trust and epistemic vigilance (Fonagy & Allison, 2014) in ways that are adaptive.

The parents' style of trusting may be revealed in how they relate to the therapist. Take, for example, a parent who tends to hear the therapist's responses as advice or suggestions and might frequently say, "I did what you told me to do, and . . ." This parent has adopted a style of epistemic trust that is overly trusting, privileging the perceived competence of others over this parent's own knowledge, and does not engage an adaptive measure of vigilance. At the other end of the spectrum is the parent who, regardless of their need for help, perceives the therapist or others as not capable or willing to help them and who is not able to identify trustworthy resources. Theoretically, secure attachment is associated with the ability to establish appropriate epistemic trust and epistemic vigilance. We posit that when breakdowns in mentalizing (and prementalizing modes) occur, the ability to engage epistemic trust has been disrupted. Let us return to Mr. and Mrs. O. The therapist must orient the starting point of therapy to establish a therapeutic alliance and epistemic trust. As described earlier in this chapter, the development of epistemic trust often begins with the therapist interacting with the parent in a way that communicates that the therapist trusts the information being shared by the parent.

Epistemic trust and mentalization may be difficult to cultivate with Mr. and Mrs. O, given the insecurity of their attachment styles. Mr. O tends to appear highly regulated, while Mrs. O, on the surface, is more anxious and shows a wider range and depth of emotions. We learned from Mr. O that in his own childhood, his emotional world was not really attended to or understood; at this point in his life, he does not see the point in further exploration, believing it only overcomplicates things. When his mentalizing goes offline, he is likely to go into pretend mode and is disinclined to turn to others. In contrast, Mrs. O appears more psychologically minded but is vulnerable to psychic equivalence modes of nonmentalizing where she feels closely attuned to her daughter's experiences and has difficulty with (a) distinguishing between self and other and (b) the uncertainty of the not-knowing stance. She tends to bother Mr. O and the therapist when she goes into long, emotionally charged examples that continue to make the same point, leaving the therapist to wonder why Mrs. O continues to tell these stories as if the therapist has never heard them before.

While considering their differences in attachment and communication of emotions, the therapist works to show Mr. and Mrs. O that the information they are both sharing is seen as relevant and to activate mentalization around it using four key techniques:

- a focus on slowing down, emphasizing the importance for the therapist to gain all of the information necessary to understand the situation and see the parents' perspective
  Example: "I can see that this is a difficult topic for both of you, am I right? I wonder if we could slow down a little to look at this difficult topic together. It will really help me to help you think about this."

- the use of ostensive cues and curiosity about the parents' own minds (what they think) and internal experiences (believing their feelings)
  Example: The therapist adjusts their tone of voice, facial expression, and posture to send the explicit message that they are trying to "stay with" the parents and understand them.

- empathic validation that is derived from a full understanding of interactions, allowing the therapist to (a) validate the basic emotions (e.g., anger, sadness, fear, happiness) and more complex emotions that underlie their behaviors and (b) provide the contexts in which they make sense
  Example: "If I were you, I would probably feel very tired and frustrated . . . What do you usually do when those feelings get too much?"

- capacity to name, notice, and repair "breakdown of mentalizing" in the here and now of the session
  Example: "You know . . . it might be my impression, but I noticed that I asked you about your relationship with your other child and you got silent. Was there something about my question that was difficult or annoying? I am sorry if it was . . ."

Once epistemic trust has been established, we have a two-person system—parent and therapist together—coconstructing an understanding of the relationship between parent and child in interaction with each other. The parent does not take in everything the therapist says indiscriminately, nor does the parent fail to turn to others for input and collaboration.

For some parents with relatively secure attachment histories, establishing epistemic trust can feel rather straightforward, as the parent's own style of communication is open and collaborative, and they are receptive to the therapist's perspectives, as well. For others, the development of epistemic trust will be the focus for much of the treatment. As described earlier in this chapter, epistemic trust and mentalization are considered related. The therapist's mentalizing stance—encapsulating curiosity, not-knowing, and playfulness—communicates to the parent that the therapist regards them as having a mind with agency and intentionality that is worth understanding. For some parents, this might be the first time in their developmental journey that a trustworthy person offers such an experience. It is a delicate balance between (a) aiding the parent and (b) keeping the child in mind while they learn and practice thinking about their own mind and the interaction and impact it has on others.

DEVELOPING A SHARED LANGUAGE OF MENTALIZING

Depending on the parents' capacities for attention regulation, affect regulation, and explicit mentalizing (including *perspective taking*—the capacity to make links between emotion and behavior), the therapist will begin treatment with the parent in different ways. However, common to any starting place is the creation of a shared language with which to communicate about emotions and experiences. In this context, psychoeducation plays an important role. Psychoeducation is used in the following ways:

- The therapist shares knowledge about how minds work (e.g., the brain and how it informs our behavior during moments of stress) and mentalizing, in ways that are connected to the reality of the parent in order to promote that knowledge's application and avoid it being used too concretely.

- The goal is for the parent to apply new knowledge at home with their child, eventually even after they are no longer in therapy.

- The creation of a shared language for mentalizing and emotion is therefore a starting point for the social learning needed to enhance mentalization.

Therapists may have different ways of explaining the concept of mentalizing—some may choose to use the term, and others may prefer to describe the concept without using technical language. These choices will often depend on the parent themselves. What is important in creating a shared language is a recognition of the other person's mind, thus creating a "we"—a space for coconstruction of goals and objectives. Creating a shared language is a process of first making sense of the language that the parent already uses and the connotations of the words they rely upon, while also sharing what is in your own mind as far as how working on the capacity to mentalize may help them achieve their goals as a parent.

Culture and gender in general shape both how people experience and how they communicate about emotions, and, thus, creating a common language (rather than the therapist introducing or teaching their own language) is an opportunity for the therapist to learn and incorporate salient aspects of the parent's identity into the mentalizing process and identify culturally relevant goals and ways of assessing treatment effects.

One element of the shared language that the therapist attempts to create with the parent is terms to describe their own internal feelings. For example, when a mother was speaking about her anxiety, the therapist asked about times earlier in her life when she had a similar feeling. She then recalled the shame she felt as a child when she did not finish her food, which her parents yelled at her for. The therapist and mother then referred to this feeling as the "completion shame." This opened the door for this mother to speak about her difficulties with feeling that she never did her job as a mother in a complete way, leading to a lot of guilt and lack of patience toward her children. From that moment onward, completion shame became a way in which both therapist and parent could "mark and observe" the feelings behind certain behaviors in a humorous way, while honoring the parent's early experiences.

The therapist and parent together create a shared language to describe the kinds of experiences the parent and their children have from week to week. For example, a father reported that his child's school used a system of "shines" and "rain drops" to refer to the high and low points of the day, so that language was adopted in the therapy room, as well.

Checking with parents on how they are experiencing interventions is an important way to explicitly remind them that we are paying attention and care about the impact of our work on them—for example, asking, "Does that resonate with you at all?" while gesturing to the body leads to a shared understanding that the therapist wants to know when empathic reflections or exploratory ideas do or do not resonate, prompting parents spontaneously to note when they do or do not.

While the development of a shared language takes place from the beginning of treatment, it continues throughout the therapy. As the parent and therapist achieve a better understanding of the parent themselves, the child, and each other, the language might be refined and updated. Metaphors relevant to the culture and life experience of the parent can prove to be very powerful ways of helping the parent to stay online while feeling strong and painful emotions in the context of parenting. For example, a mother who was trying to understand her adolescent's depression commented, "What you are describing, how he looks OK on the outside but he's keeping it all in makes me think of ducks. They look like they are gliding across the surface of the water, but underneath their feet they are paddling so hard." This metaphor provided an opportunity for the therapist to validate the mother's efforts to understand and put words to her child's feelings in ways that were meaningful to her. As the mother felt more confident that she could potentially understand her child, her anxiety lessened. Thus, the shared language embodies the mentalizing stance, which is creative and evolving.

ESTABLISHING EPISTEMIC TRUST WITH MR. AND MRS. O

Mr. O wants the therapist to understand and accept that nothing is wrong with his daughter, whereas Mrs. O wants the therapist to understand and accept that she knows her daughter and all of her daughter's anxieties very well and feels that she and her husband are to blame for the difficulties that Cristina is having.

From this very moment, we are having to mentalize what the parents' intentions are with these communications, and also how the parents might be perceiving our intent. Operating from our own position of epistemic trust as therapists means interpreting what the other communicates as being relevant. From this stance, we can most easily mentalize—that is, explore with curiosity alongside the parent. But the way that parents speak about their children or the parents' own difficulties can also be difficult to trust—that is, to understand and accept. For example, it is easy to understand what Mr. O thinks about his daughter, but it is difficult to accept as accurate, because he provides no evidence. On the other hand, it is clear that Mrs. O believes she knows her daughter inside and out, but it can be difficult to follow her when she speaks, because she does not answer questions directly, her emotions muddy her clarity, and she uses flowery or canned language that seems to lack real meaning when describing her daughter's experiences. As noted earlier, Mrs. O seems to be functioning in what we call "the prementalizing pretend mode of functioning." Usually, parents use prementalizing modes to avoid painful and conflicting emotions. (In this chapter, the italicized wording in brackets represents examples of the MBT-based technique used during the session.)

To establish epistemic trust, the therapist might say to these parents, "I think Cristina is very lucky with two parents that are working so hard to understand her [*recognizing parents' benevolent intentions*]. I think it must feel confusing at times when you see all the strengths your daughter has, and yet, she struggles so much, very confusing . . ." [*reflecting on parents' internal experience, not knowing, curious*]

The therapist here mentalizes the parents—that is, reflects and validates their experience, intentionality, and helplessness, accepting it and letting them know that the therapist can imagine how frustrating and daunting the whole situation might feel. To help parents move away from guilt, fear, and helplessness and toward a more effective reflective functioning stance about themselves and the child, we often need to start this way, by giving parents an experience of being empathized with and validated. In this way, we send a clear signal to the parents that we care and are genuinely interested in their experience and want to learn more. We hope that then the parents will become more interested in learning from our experience as well as their own and reflecting on and managing it using a mentalizing stance.

REPAIRING WHEN EPISTEMIC TRUST IS LOST

Mrs. O arrives to a session looking quite angry: She had words with Cristina's teacher, who is asking Cristina to rewrite her summer essay. Mrs. O rages about how teachers don't appreciate how difficult it is to get kids to do things during the summer—especially her daughter, who is very stubborn and fragile. The therapist listens for a while and then speaks of how difficult the summer was with Cristina overall. Mrs. O agrees. The therapist speaks of how difficult it must have been for everybody, without the structure of school and therapy. Mrs. O agrees reluctantly and says that the matter of the teacher remains tough. The therapist wonders whether, at these moments when solutions are needed, maybe these sessions feel frustrating. Mrs. O smiles and says, "Sometimes . . ." The therapist smiles back and adds, "I would probably find them frustrating if I was in your shoes . . . I want you to know that . . . Let's see, why don't we think together about what happened with this teacher who seemed to have ignored how tough it must feel when you work so hard on this essay with Cristina and now, she wants her to rewrite it . . . Should we try working on seeing the best way to manage this awful situation?"

While the first goal of our treatment approach is to foster epistemic trust between the parents and the therapist, epistemic trust is not something that can be ignored or taken for granted once maintained—it must continue to be monitored, fostered, and repaired when broken or shut down. As therapists working from this framework, we must feel comfortable explicitly speaking, during sessions, about what seems to be going on between us and parents. Whenever possible, if we are successful in working through a mentalizing impasse, we can try to (a) highlight how we have managed to do that together and (b) reinforce parents' attempts to look at the multiple perspectives and stay close to difficult and painful emotions and experiences, for instance.

It is tempting, when parents are in distress—as Mr. and Mrs. O are in the above vignette—to want to offer solutions and help them to problem solve. Incorporating an understanding of epistemic trust into our approach, we can recognize when parents are open and able to take in information that we might be able to offer, whether it is a solution, psychoeducation, or another perspective. As we described earlier in the chapter, depending on a parent's experiences (usually early in life), their epistemic trust may vary. Mrs. O enters this session not actually turning to the therapist for help with the problem yet but communicating how angry and distressed she is and how unseen she feels by the teacher and the school. And she is likely anxious about whether the therapist will be able to see and help her with these strong feelings.

In this example, the therapist invites Mrs. O to overcome a feeling of low epistemic trust by marking her experience and acknowledging her emotional state. In this way, epistemic trust can become reactivated. When a parent is in a position of low epistemic trust, they are likely to experience the therapist as untrustworthy—or even, at the extreme versions, as an abuser or enemy. As is recommended in various therapies for borderline personality disorder, the therapist is often wise to accept this projection instead of attempting to explicitly mentalize (Knox, 2016). But to reestablish epistemic trust, the therapist must not only choose not to react to the projection but also strive to experience the world as the parent does, including feeling helplessness and being destroyed. In being able to grasp the parent's experience, the therapist can then reflect it back and support the parent in mentalizing these experiences, so that the parent can regain a sense of their own agency that will enable the restoration of epistemic trust.

Fonagy et al. (2017a, 2017b) described this process as shifting the dyad from "vicious cycles" to "virtuous cycles." In these new virtuous cycles, the therapist's attunement and responsiveness invite the parent into a stance of epistemic trust (and out of epistemic isolation), positioning the parent to begin learning and applying skills such as mentalizing and sensitive caregiving behaviors. Change in the parent's life and their social relationships may be the result of the therapeutic interactions themselves; however, it is also possible that they are prompted or supported by interactions with other people in their life, from whom the parent can now learn because epistemic trust has been enhanced. According to Fonagy and colleagues (2017a), while mentalizing interventions may serve as ostensive cues facilitating epistemic trust in the therapeutic relationship, (a) the capacity to mentalize or, conversely, (b) impairments in mentalizing may also impact how the parent interprets the therapist's ostensive cues and whether those ostensive cues promote epistemic trust.

MENTALIZED AFFECTIVITY

THERAPIST: [*prompting both parents*] You both seem to agree that things are difficult for Cristina, even though you see them from different perspectives . . . Am I right?

MOM: I suppose, in the end, she is the one struggling in the playground . . . I remember being her age and being in the playground, it was terrible . . . I used to feel the other kids did not like me because of something I said or did. I always tell Cristina she is kind and nice and pretty, that she should not worry so much . . . but it does not work . . .

DAD: [*laughs*] She is not going to believe you because you tell her . . .

THERAPIST: I sense things are getting tough in here between the two of you. I am asking some difficult questions. What do you think

Cristina makes of moments like this? How do you imagine she feels?

MOM: She probably just wants to tell us to stop it [looks at her husband].

DAD: I agree . . . but fights are part of a family's life, you can't protect your kids from everything . . .

Affect regulation is widely regarded as a crucial challenge in child development, and it has a continuing important role throughout the lifespan. Over the last 20 years, the construct has been taken up and investigated across many subfields of psychology, as well as in related fields like neuroscience and philosophy. Yet, we do not yet have a comprehensive theory of affect regulation, which would have to include differentiation of the specific challenges that belong to each stage of life. In this chapter, we focus on mentalized affectivity, a form of affect regulation that pertains primarily to adults, as it entails the capacity to mentalize about emotions and, in particular, to utilize autobiographical memory as part of the effort (Fonagy et al., 2002; Greenberg et al., 2017; Jurist, 2005, 2008, 2010, 2018; Jurist & Meehan, 2009). Affect regulation is not merely an online process—it is influenced by past experiences, fantasies, and the values of one's family and culture. Mentalized affectivity can be conceived of as a more sophisticated kind of affect regulation that is dependent upon some knowledge of the self and that is critical in terms of helping us to move toward well-being.

Mentalized affectivity overlaps with affect regulation, insofar as it involves modulating and crafting emotions to be granular. However, it departs from models of affect regulation that place an emphasis on cognitive reappraisal, which alters the emotion to fit the situation and circumstance. Mentalized affectivity, as the term suggests, incorporates the live experience of the emotion as it is shaped and modulated by cognition, and cognition cannot be divorced from a sense of agency or self. So, mentalized affectivity blends and aims to establish a higher level of integrating cognition and affect, as part of the process of reevaluating the meaning of emotions. The mentalizing aspect of mentalized affectivity highlights that we can observe and reflect on emotions, without being propelled to act upon them. Mentalized affectivity helps us to appreciate that mentalization is not exclusively cognitive, although it is possible to mentalize about other things than emotions, such as beliefs. Mentalizing about emotions is especially germane to psychotherapy. Mentalized affectivity fosters better use of emotions. This includes some acceptance of how emotions can be confusing and difficult to identify. Patients frequently report what can be termed *aporetic emotions*—emotions that are unclear and undifferentiated. The experience of knowing that you feel something that still remains elusive is universal and ought to be distinguished from the phenomenon of *alexithymia,* in which there is a chronic inability to recognize emotions. Psychotherapy often entails the effort to render these aporetic emotions intelligible and granular.

Mentalized affectivity can foster insight into the links between past and present. For example, through mentalized affectivity, Mrs. O might come to see that anger was not acknowledged in her family of origin; thus, she tends to underestimate anger and often ends up becoming too angry, because there is no room for anger to be expressed and communicated. Improving mentalized affectivity can allow us to have a wider palette of emotions and to become more adept at shaping our emotions to exist in a way that is what we consider culturally or socially appropriate. We become more flexible in our responses, being willing to revise and rethink our feelings in light of our own reflection or feedback from others.

It is worth emphasizing that we can mentalize our own or others' emotions. Moreover, consistent with what we have said, in the previous chapter, about epistemic trust, mentalizing emotions can mean looking to the other as a way to help us understand ourselves better. In other words, it is not an either/or concerning self-mentalizing or mentalizing about others. A related point, which we discuss in connection with the clinical example, is that affect regulation often depends upon relying on others. Affect regulation is a factor in transforming infants' reliance on coregulation to more autonomous functioning; however, we are prepared to argue that affect regulation, not only in young children but also in adults, includes a role for others to help us with this work.

There is a good analogy between adult affect regulation and Kohlberg's (1981) highest stage of moral development, in which one is aware of social expectations but can autonomously choose how to recognize and benefit from them without accepting convention and without deferring to the authority of others. Mentalized affectivity provides a path toward greater agency, but the construct resists equation with socialization. People who are excluded from the dominant culture have reason to protest, rather than to defer to, social and cultural norms, and even people who are part of the dominant culture might resist accepting their privilege in an unjust social world.

Research about mentalized affectivity has differentiated three components: identifying emotions, processing emotions, and expressing emotions (Greenberg et al., 2017; Jurist, 2018; Rinaldi et al., 2021). *Identifying emotions* means labeling and distinguishing among different emotions. *Processing emotions* means adjusting or modulating emotions; it can also entail comparing how one is feeling against one's ideals. *Expressing emotions* means communicating what one feels to others, but it also encompasses inward expression, where one fully experiences emotions without necessarily revealing the emotion outwardly. Expressing emotions, we have learned, has a strongly cultural valence. Some cultures discourage expression of certain emotions, but all cultures have their own norms around which emotions are expressed and how they are expressed.

The movement from (a) identifying emotions to (b) processing emotions to (c) expressing emotions requires an increase in the exercise of agency: identifying represents the inception of agency, processing the actualization of agency, and expressing the realization of agency.

From a clinical perspective, it is helpful to determine patients' comfort level with emotion—and, specifically, whether they are able to identify, process, and express emotions. Jurist's research lab has created a 60-item report measure, the Mentalized Affectivity Scale (MAS), and also a shorter, 12-item version, the Brief-Mentalized Affectivity Scale (B-MAS), as well (Greenberg et al., 2021). So far, our findings in both nonclinical and clinical samples suggest that people with any diagnosis struggle with processing emotions, which thus ought to be a focus in psychotherapy. We are currently investigating links among different forms of psychopathology and identifying, processing, and expressing emotions. We are also currently asking therapists to fill out the B-MAS version, as well as their patients, in order to counterbalance the limits of a self-report measure. Appendix A presents the two versions of the measure and further details about our findings. Thus, mentalized affectivity is a valuable way not just to discern psychopathology but to predict well-being.

MENTALIZED AFFECTIVITY WITH MR. AND MRS. O

In considering our case example, we see that Cristina's struggle with affect regulation is a central concern and part of her obsessive–compulsive behavior. At times, she can be provoked to be too aggressive to her brother; other times, rather than lashing out, she withdraws to her room and hits a pillow. The fact that she has more than one way of responding to her brother is significant and bodes well for helping to regulate her emotions. She does not seem to have trouble identifying her emotions; rather, the problems lie in processing and expressing those emotions. The fact that Cristina can choose to retaliate on a pillow rather than a person suggests that she is aware of her emotions and is able to act in a way that is less destructive. A mentalizing-informed approach in therapy can work on building this capacity, giving her a wider realm of options. We might want to help her use words to express her anger, although our expectation must be tempered to what is realistic and appropriate for a

9-year-old and for a sibling interaction with a 7-year-old brother. It would be interesting to know, too, if Cristina has angry outbursts with others: at home with her parents or at school with her friends. Cristina's symptoms of obsessive-compulsive behavior coincide with a style in which emotions tend to be overregulated; thus, we would want to help her to acknowledge, tolerate, and modulate her emotions—not to distance herself from them.

While we conceptualize Cristina's symptoms through the lens of mentalized affectivity, it is clear that Cristina's parents have an important role to play in helping her, which is the focus of our therapeutic model. Cristina's mother sees her as emulating her father's expressive style, with her acting out to her brother, which Cristina's mother attributes to being culturally normative, as Latino. We wonder what it means that she externalizes Cristina's style as like her husband, without reflecting on what her own style is like. Is she unwittingly discouraging the expression of emotion for Cristina?

It is noteworthy that Cristina shows signs of separation anxiety from her mother and anxiety about being around children who are her own age. Here, we would like to refer to the dynamic between mother and daughter found at the head of this chapter, as Cristina's mother is inclined to see Cristina through her own experience and registers that her efforts at containment are not successful. Mentalizing would help Cristina's mother to differentiate between their experiences and to be more receptive to tune in to what Cristina is feeling. It is a positive that Cristina is open to seeking help from her mother; there is room for her mother to listen more closely, and, of course, it would help if Mrs. O felt supported by her husband. In the interaction highlighted above, Cristina's father distances himself by criticizing his wife, and conflict between them comes to the surface.

We imagine that Cristina's current difficulties are, in part, manifestations of the tenuousness of her parents' marriage and their trouble being on the same page in trying to help her. The therapist attempts to draw their attention to this very point, so that both parents might be more aware of their impact on their daughter and be open to hear her fears around their possible separation. In thinking about Cristina, we would focus more on affect regulation and helping her to process and express emotions; in thinking about her parents and how we would intervene to help them with their daughter, we would focus on improving their mentalized affectivity. Cristina's mother needs to be able to back off: In seeing Cristina through Mrs. O's own experience, Mrs. O could work on better self–other differentiation, creating more space between them. In contrast, Cristina's father could work on more engagement, creating more closeness between them.

Much depends on the fate of their marriage. If they separate, they will need to reassure both of their children that they will remain their parents, although things will change. If they stay together, we will work with the parents on recognizing differences between themselves, negotiating those differences openly rather than allowing them to be an irritant. Sometimes this will mean both parents compromising and agreeing on adhering to the middle ground, not insisting on their individual preference. Being able to tolerate and accept differences in style is also necessary. Moreover, we would want to encourage both parents, whether they stay together or not, to tune in to Cristina's feelings. For example, in hearing that she reports feeling new fears about aggressive play from friends her own age, perhaps the family could identify a potential friend and encourage a playdate, aiming to build on reinforcing a sense of safety and gratification.

We see our role of mentalizing parental emotions as an integral part of the therapy. We carefully consider which emotions are most central and then develop a more complex experience of those emotions and a narrative around them. Most importantly, with parents, we want to promote each parent to explore how their style of parenting reflects their own history and experience. We might encourage Cristina's mother to think about how her marriage seems to replay her childhood experience of being ignored. We might wonder, with Cristina's father, whether one or both of his parents had a laissez-faire attitude toward him and, if so, how this made him feel growing up. We would explore the family dynamic in which Cristina's mother is too involved as a result of feeling alone as a parent and as a wife. We would ask each parent to notice when they were, and try to refrain from, blaming and criticizing their partner, asking themselves instead to pause and dwell on what's going on with the other person and why they might be feeling that way.

Mentalized affectivity can serve to help both parents to communicate better with each other and to strive to make this effort with Cristina. Finally, we want to mentalize the positive emotions and make sure that Cristina's parents voice their appreciation of her: She might have some bad sibling moments, but, according to their report, she also manages to show love and care to her younger brother. It is an important aspect of mentalized affectivity to help patients move in a way that is consistent with their cherished ideals.

MENTALIZED AFFECTIVITY AND EPISTEMIC TRUST

In order to understand how mentalized affectivity can be utilized clinically, we would like to clarify its relation to epistemic trust, the other foundational construct in our model (Fonagy & Allison, 2014; Fonagy et al., 2015, 2017a,

2017b). On the face of it, epistemic trust refers to children, whereas mentalized affectivity refers to adults. Yet, mentalizing capacities begin in the second year of life (that is, much earlier than 3–4 years old, as false-belief experiments suggested) and become more sophisticated through childhood; mentalized affectivity, which depends upon autobiographical memory, commences during middle childhood. Moreover, epistemic trust underlies adult relationships and is germane for making sense of Cristina's parents' marriage and their respective relationships with her.

Let us recall that epistemic trust is a mechanism that developed through evolution and serves as a way for culture to reproduce itself, with parents providing natural pedagogy to infants, and infants being receptive to taking up and utilizing such knowledge. Epistemic trust represents the value of heteronomy—that is, the value of others' will—not just autonomy, one's own will, to borrow Kant's well-established terms. In our account of autonomy, however, we do not cease to turn to and depend on significant others.

Much remains to be clarified about epistemic trust, a construct that has been imported from cognitive psychology, as we have discussed in Chapter 2. For example, in cognitive psychology, epistemic trust is rooted in the child as a learner, instructed by caregivers, but this might be problematic in being applied to the clinical context, as it is inconsistent with our own mentalization-based and psychodynamic perspective that resists granting power to the therapist as an instructor. Epistemic trust, from a clinical perspective, must include recognition of the therapist's own history and, most importantly, in working with children and families, the parents' own experience of epistemic trust.

Various circumstances, such as neglect or abuse, can result in epistemic trust diminishing or being turned off—a loss that makes social functioning much more fraught. As Duschinsky and Foster (2021) emphasized, epistemic trust is a complex notion, which has multiple components in its original use in cognitive psychology and which must be able to distinguish between phenomena such as (a) the absence of epistemic trust and (b) persistent epistemic mistrust. Presumably, with the former, epistemic trust can be nurtured; with the latter, there is a longer road to go down to undo the damage that has occurred. It remains to be determined how problems with epistemic trust link to various kinds of psychopathology.

When epistemic trust thrives, it leads in the direction of autonomy, where epistemic vigilance can be exercised and cultivated. As we have argued, the term "vigilance" denotes the discerning ability to trust or not trust, depending upon the circumstance. There is ambiguity in how vigilance has been understood, as the clinical connotations of suspiciousness (connotations including even paranoia) are departures from the meaning of the term in cognitive psychology, where it is benign and even positive. Epistemic vigilance is a critical term for our model because it affirms perspective taking, wherein one is in the position of having to decide whether to rely on someone else's knowledge or not. Epistemic vigilance bears a close connection to reality testing, with the proviso that epistemic vigilance is particularly relevant to what is socially meaningful. Both epistemic trust and epistemic vigilance provide a language that help to capture our sociality; however, social life often requires complex judgments about additional factors, such as the reputation someone has. As previously noted, knowing both whom to trust and whom to hesitate to trust are necessary.

Let us keep in mind the relational quality of epistemic vigilance—that it most commonly entails an interaction between people. As with epistemic trust, the sender as well as the receiver will have histories that are being played out. So, in considering what we know about Cristina, it is hard to be certain, but it does seem that her fears about other kids are met with a response from her mother that is not helpful, because it is mainly based on the mother's own experience. To her credit, Cristina's mother is aware of this and perhaps might try another strategy besides identifying with her daughter as having had the same experience. It would be beneficial, of course, to know more about how the therapist experiences Cristina: whether the therapist finds her receptive to help, how vulnerable she is, and how comfortable warming up to the therapist she is. Although it is speculative, Cristina's father provides little help in inspiring epistemic trust for his daughter, and his epistemic vigilance functions to make him seem quite defensive.

In the cognitive psychology literature, epistemic vigilance is about discerning the trustworthiness of knowledge. Some translation is necessary to render the construct to be relevant clinically, given the relational quality of the interaction. It is not so much about possessing and imparting knowledge as it is about being able to apply knowledge in a useful way—that is, closer to the ancient Greek notion of *phronesis,* or applied wisdom. For instance, Cristina's father might recognize that when his daughter reports distress, it will invoke in him distancing, which is familiar to him from his own family of origin. In recognizing this about himself, he has the opportunity to compensate, and not just criticize his wife but offer Cristina genuine concern and understanding.

At this point, we are able to clarify how epistemic vigilance aids us to be on the way toward mentalized affectivity. While epistemic trust implies receptiveness, it seems passive in contrast to epistemic vigilance, which requires the exercise of agency, deliberating, and determining trustworthiness. Epistemic vigilance becomes relevant in engaging the world, where there is the potential for others to be deceptive. Epistemic vigilance would be impossible without mentalizing skills, helping us to discern whom to question trusting, along with whom to endorse trusting. Mentalizing provides the active search to consider multiple hypotheses and to keep an open mind before making conclusions.

Epistemic trust fits easily with attachment, where safety and felt security are paramount, but it veers beyond attachment in manifesting the goal of communication—that is, beyond the less well-formulated attachment notion of exploration. Epistemic vigilance brings us into the muddy water of negotiating potential danger, and it affirms an even stronger investment in communication. This effort is likely to be more successful in recognizing emotions, rather than being purely cognitive. We can trace the connection between epistemic vigilance and mentalized affectivity to perspective taking and the willingness to welcome evidence that might make us revise our beliefs. Mentalized affectivity allows us to integrate cognition and affect in a more developed way than epistemic trust.

Mentalized affectivity relies on autobiographical memory and must draw from past experiences of successful and unsuccessful epistemic vigilance. Few people possess mentalized affectivity naturally; most of us need to work at it and struggle to improve, and some people are resistant to considering how the past continues to influence the present. As part of mentalization theory and practice, mentalized affectivity differs from the old-fashioned pursuit of the past as containing the buried truth, and it encourages more of a focus on how the past perpetuates itself in the present. The reluctance of mentalization-based treatment to dwell on the past is most germane to the treatment of borderline personality disorder. Other kinds of patients, however, are likely to be more curious and receptive to making sense of how their past continues to influence the present, and there is good reason to accept and even to foster this interest, particularly with parents.

Without autobiographical memory and narrative, mentalized affectivity remains implicit. With children and teens, we can help them to engage their emotions—learning to identify, process, and express them. With adults, this becomes more integral to the experience of being in therapy. It is hard to imagine a successful treatment, regardless of orientation, in which mentalized affectivity does not increase. Mentalized affectivity might not be the aim of psychotherapy, but it is the means by which one makes strides in terms of narrowing the gap between one's ideals and reality.

WORKING WITH PARENTS AND MENTALIZED AFFECTIVITY

Mentalized affectivity is a key aspect of working with the parents of child patients, as we have discussed. It is a common experience of parenthood to experience one's own childhood again in various ways. There is an activation of the past that replays itself in the relation to one's children. It can feel shocking that automatic behavior can occur, as if one is somehow directly channeling one's own parent(s). Mentalized affectivity can be understood as the reverse direction: where patients can pose and explore questions about whether they want to replay their own history in the way they parent their own children. As Selma Fraiberg (Fraiberg et al., 1975) famously wrote,

> There are many parents who have themselves lived tormented childhoods who do not inflict their pain upon their children. In remembering, they are saved from the blind repetition of the morbid past. Through remembering they identify with the injured child (the childhood self), while the parent who does not remember may find himself in an unconscious alliance and identification with the fearsome figures of that past. In this way, the parental past is inflicted upon the child. (p. 195)

The links with developmental psychopathology are elaborated in the next chapter.

A STEPWISE APPROACH

Working with mentalized affectivity establishes the therapist's curiosity about the parents and should allay, rather than exacerbate, parents' common fear that psychotherapy will point an accusing finger in their direction. Indeed, parents seek out psychotherapy when they are already under the influence of negative emotions related to feelings that they have failed to overcome their children's problems.

Step 1 for the therapist is to listen well—that is, tuning in to the emotions of the parents so that they feel reassured that we are motivated to understand them and their side of things. This is more difficult, of course, when the parents are divided and perhaps hostile to each other.

Step 2 in using mentalized affectivity entails setting a boundary of inclusion: that everyone in the family affects and is affected by the dynamics. It is not unusual for parents who fear being blamed to deal with this by blaming the child. Life often becomes more challenging when couples make the choice to have children. Our emphasis on boundary inclusion helps to mitigate against blaming children and functions to lead parents to join together in the process, where everyone must be open to making changes.

Step 3 depends upon having a therapeutic alliance in place. Here, based upon the curiosity we have shown and the boundary of inclusion, we encourage parents to reflect upon how they may be contributing to the family dynamics in undesirable ways (from their own point of view). It is enormously important that such inquiry feels like an invitation and does not automatically evoke a defensive response, reigniting the fear of being blamed. With a couple like our case example, who are teetering on falling apart, we would want them to appreciate how their uncertainty might be having an impact on their daughter. Think about how Cristina wavers between expressing her emotions with too little regulation but sometimes can contain this: Her behavior might be seen as mirroring the uncertainty of her parents' relationship. In order to address the parents' relationship, couples therapy might well be recommended, adjunctive to this work with the parents, which would attempt to maintain a line of communication that is bound by love for their children, regardless of whether they remain together or not.

MENTALIZED AFFECTIVITY AND CULTURE

Mentalized affectivity is still in a stage of being developed. Research on the construct is expanding, and the MAS has now been translated into Italian, Spanish, German, Korean, Japanese, Taiwanese Mandarin, Mandarin, Turkish, Farsi, Bulgarian, Lithuanian, and Russian. The B-MAS has shown promising results with a clinical sample, predicting well-being better than other measures of affect regulation, such as the Difficulties in Emotion Regulation Scale (DERS; Gratz & Roemer, 2004). Also, see Appendix A, this volume. As we have mentioned, though, the expressing component of mentalized affectivity needs revision in light of cultural differences.

A new direction for mentalized affectivity, and for mentalization in general, is to investigate and affirm culture as a factor (Aival-Naveh et al., 2019; Jurist & Sosa, 2019). This is not a matter of ascertaining the culture from which someone comes and making generalizing inferences from there. What we mean begins with this question: How do you think of yourself? What group identities do you see yourself a part of—starting with family and culture, but also considering race, ethnicity, gender, social class, and immigration history? It is also necessary for therapists to become aware of these things about themselves and be attuned to how these things influence the therapist's countertransference to patients.

Culture comes up in our case example, when Cristina's mom suggests that her daughter's hyperbolic expression of emotions is influenced by Cristina's dad's Latino identity. We have no information about how the father sees himself, other than noting that he had a "normal American" upbringing. His affirmation of belonging to the dominant culture does not address whether or how he identifies as Latino. It is revealing that Cristina's mother implies that she sees her husband as an "Other," and it is striking that she does not acknowledge her own Whiteness or specify anything about her own cultural identity.

There is much that we would need to probe about culture in this family in order to improve their mentalized affectivity. We would want to encourage Cristina's mother to tell us about her own identities, and we would give her father the opportunity to say more about his own. For example, we would want to know more specifics about his family of origin and about their immigration history, insofar as that is relevant. We do not know his reaction to his wife's perspective or how he sees Cristina. Significantly, we do not know how Cristina is being raised—are there values and rituals from either parent's cultural heritage? Does Cristina think of herself as both/and, or either/or, or none of the above?

The only information we have to work with is the association of Cristina's anger as excessive and, from the mother's perspective, an emulation of the father. The testimony about Cristina's excessive anger states that it is a reaction to being provoked by her brother. So, we would want to acknowledge the legitimacy of her anger and not to miss that the brother is a part of the dynamic. Connecting Cristina's anger to culture is open to question, especially as it seems like a covert way for the mom to blame her husband. Given what we learn, it can be only a matter of speculation as to whether the father would verify this association or not. We might also wonder about an oedipal aspect of the mother's perspective: Does she feel left out of the relationship between her husband and daughter?

We conclude with more questions than we can answer. A mentalizing approach to therapy is comfortable with the awareness of how much we do not know. This is not a pessimistic result—just a recognition of the knowledge we lack, and a direction for how we imagine we could be helpful to Cristina and her family.

CONCLUDING SUMMARY

- Building epistemic trust is no simple matter, and it is not a process that once established is to be taken for granted. However, once a parent truly feels thought about, supported, and held by a therapist's mind and heart, the process of new social learning can take place.

- Asking for help from a mental health professional can mean many things for parents, among them failure, a sense of guilt, shame, and fear—but it can also become, with the right kind of support, a source of hope and support.

- For a therapist to engage parents, the therapist needs to be aware of their own biases and blank spots and be willing to accept accusations of failure, lack of ability, and, at times, dishonesty—all manifestations that parents bring to the work with a therapist when they feel helpless, frustrated, or afraid about the welfare of their child.

- To accomplish a truly safe environment in the context of parent work, to truly allow the parent to go through the natural process of epistemic vigilance and land in a place of epistemic trust, opens the door for the therapeutic experience to serve as a new developmental experience, which might have a domino effect in the way the parent understands and manages their child.

- We see mentalized affectivity as a useful tool that helps to locate how people understand various aspects of emotional experience and to link them to cognition.

- Mentalized affectivity has three components: identifying, processing, and expressing emotions.

- Research suggests that processing emotions is a crucial aspect of psychotherapy.

- Mentalized affectivity overlaps with affect regulation but emphasizes how past history influences how emotions are experienced in the present.

- Mentalized affectivity pushes us to define the relation between our hopes and our realities, and it holds the potential to narrow that gap, allowing our sense of agency to flourish, as much as humans are able to do so.

3 DEVELOPMENTAL PSYCHOPATHOLOGY

Ghosts in the Nursery

In every nursery there are ghosts. They are the visitors from the unremembered past of the parents; the uninvited guests at the christening. Under all favorable circumstances the unfriendly and unbidden spirits are banished from the nursery and return to their subterranean dwelling place. The baby makes his own imperative claim upon parental love and, in strict analogy with the fairy tales, the bonds of love protect the child and his parents against the intruders, the malevolent ghosts. (Fraiberg et al., 1975, p. 387)

The high prevalence of adverse childhood experiences (ACEs) and their causal relationship with mental disorders is indisputable. Maltreatment-related childhood adversities are the leading preventable risk factor for mental disorders and substance abuse (Teicher et al., 2016), and ACEs have been linked to leading causes of adult morbidity and mortality (Merrick et al., 2019). When working with parents from our mentalization-informed model, an indispensable part of the assessment phase is a comprehensive understanding of what has happened to parents we work with throughout their lives. We cannot formulate a case and start a treatment without understanding the family dynamics that have been present throughout

https://doi.org/10.1037/0000341-004
Working With Parents in Therapy: A Mentalization-Based Approach, by N. Malberg, E. Jurist, J. Bate, and M. Dangerfield

generations. The purpose of this chapter is to remind the reader of this key aspect of our understanding of the work of any professional in the mental health field: the systematic assessment of the presence of ACEs in the person that we are taking care of. When working with parents, we must assess and identify the presence of transgenerational relational trauma and its consequences on the functioning of the parents, in order to be able to offer a treatment plan that accurately addresses the core difficulties that very probably organize the dysfunctional dynamics. Furthermore, by doing so, we facilitate the emergence of epistemic trust and open the door to working on mentalized affectivity while helping parents create narratives of their relational past and linking them to the understanding of their own responses to their child's behaviors.

Mrs. O suffered emotional neglect during her childhood. She had never received psychological treatment but, in spite of that, had managed to cope with life by organizing her identity around her professional skills and achievements. This way of functioning also included dissociating frequently from her unpleasant and painful emotions, as she felt overwhelmed by them and did not trust any other way of dealing with them than keeping them away. Consequently, she had always felt very isolated with her suffering and described what sounded like a history of depression, which she linked to growing up in a house where she "was physically provided for but where her emotional needs were not understood or met."

In the early years of their relationship, Mrs. O saw Mr. O as being very different from her own parents because of his greater openness with his emotions. But, more recently, she no longer felt as though her marriage to Mr. O offered a different experience on this emotional level. Mr. O, in spite of regarding his childhood as happier, similarly had difficulties describing aspects of his developmental process apart from his academic and professional achievements. They had both found a balance in their relationship, with a common tendency to disconnect from emotional aspects that felt overwhelming, in different ways, while focusing primarily on the benefits of their coping system based on their cognitive and professional lives.

The equilibrium that kept this couple together was challenged when Cristina was born, which greatly impacted how they felt toward each other. At the time of referral, they were discussing separating. When asked about the source of marital stress, Mr. O spoke of feeling that their marriage had become cold and distant, especially after the children were born. Mrs. O agreed and added that Mr. O's job required long hours away and that this had been tough for everybody. They were not able to understand or identify other sources of tension or conflict, apart from describing how the changes in their professional lives were affecting them. Mrs. O scaled back from a profitable full-time job to working as a freelancer after giving birth to Cristina.

The birth of Cristina inevitably confronted them both with their own experiences as children—as daughter and son. Mrs. O was now also adding her role as a mother to her fragile adult identity, something that triggered worries, fears, and anxieties that interfered with her caring and loving capacities. Mr. O seemed to base his expectations about parenting and children on a family myth he had constructed, one that seemed to be making him and his family feel like they were failing. He seemed to hide his shame behind a minimizing façade, which spurred Mrs. O to feel as though she was over-reacting all the time. This was a very confusing state of affairs for all involved, especially Cristina and her sibling.

At first glance, Cristina's case seems quite straightforward: a child with pretty clear symptoms and what many could quickly identify as "overinvested, anxious parents" who presented with affect regulation issues themselves. In a nutshell, seen from the usual categorical psychopathological perspective, it would be easy to come up with a diagnosis, formulation, and treatment plan. However, this would draw the treatment away from a relational and develop-mental focus. For example, based on the most-prescribed evidence-based treatments, one might choose a cognitive behavioral approach to help Cristina with her anxiety, or a psychoeducational protocol with the parents to help management of affect regulation by using specific behavioral strategies. These ways of addressing the difficulties in the child and parents might well help to some extent, but, from our perspective, they would be leaving aside the core aspects of what research and clinical practice have taught us about what is essential in mental and relational functioning.

ASSESSING FOR ADVERSE RELATIONAL EXPERIENCES IN THE PARENT'S CHILDHOOD

During the assessment phase and case formulation of our mentalization-informed model, we conduct a comprehensive evaluation of the parents' own history. A key issue to explore in this case, and in most cases that we see, is that of the adverse relational experiences (AREs) suffered by both parents, and the barriers to acknowledging and resolving these painful experiences—which they are currently at risk of repeating in the relationship with their daughter, Cristina. It is always tricky and complex to do so, though, as it is rarely part of the initial demand that parents bring to our consulting rooms, and it leads parents' attention toward places that they dread. However, not doing so has the liability of ending up with a partial or superficial resolution of the difficulties that the child and parents present. Thus, our goal during the assessment period is to open the door by demonstrating a nonjudgmental and curious stance alongside explicit expressions of validation and empathy toward the parent's experiences.

Very often, mental health providers consciously and unconsciously avoid asking difficult questions too quickly, as they fear that parents will not return or that they themselves will be perceived as intrusive or unprofessional. In this context, we are faced with a challenge as mental health providers: How do we prevent intergenerational patterns of interaction, while staying close to the difficulties that motivated parents to seek help in the first place and not blaming the parents? In the following chapters, we describe how a mentalizing stance can accomplish this task.

In today's reality, with scarce resources dedicated to mental health in many communities, and with parents feeling frustrated and overstretched— exacerbated by social, economic, political, and public health stressors (most recently, the global pandemic)—it is difficult to entertain an approach that slows down the process and considers a different perspective: one that invites both parents and providers to put the pieces of the puzzle together, by focusing on a more dimensional and developmental approach of the presenting diffi- culties. Using our model's lens, we engage parents from a scaffolding style, one that begins with the building of epistemic trust and seeks to help them approach the difficulties they experience in the process of parenting from a developmental perspective that includes their own developmental history and how it affects their current relational and emotional life.

This approach to working with parents who have an appreciation for both past and current relational trauma is supported by the strong and growing evidence on the prevalence of ACEs (Felitti et al., 1998) and their psychopath- ological consequences (Artigue & Tizón, 2014; Dangerfield, 2012, 2020; Murphy et al., 2014; Varese et al., 2012). ACEs include physical, emotional, and sexual abuse; physical and emotional neglect; and household dysfunction, such as intimate-partner violence in the home, divorced or separated parents, an incarcerated parent, or a parent or other adult in the household who has a mental illness or substance abuse problem.

Following Dangerfield (2020), we use the concept of AREs in childhood as an expanded concept of ACEs. Adding the term "relational" emphasizes the importance and makes more explicit the level at which these adverse experi- ences occur in childhood: the relationship. Relationships make us human, and we run the risk that mental health care loses this essential quality if it ignores the relational dimension in suffering, disorder, and its etiology. We consider that using the ARE concept to refer to ACEs includes more explicitly the relational dimension of adversity (Dangerfield, 2020).

We can understand AREs suffered during childhood as traumatic experiences—understood as relational trauma, which must be differentiated from isolated traumatic events—that have caused significant damage to the organization of the emotional sphere, affecting the ability to modulate emotions, the ability to make sense of one's emotional experience, and the capacity for mentalization (Dangerfield, 2016, 2017). The damage caused increases if this abuse is intrafamilial, as the relational environment in which the child grows up will be dominated by a disturbed relational dynamic and we can understand that in this context, the child will not receive physical and emotional care and support from their parents—essential protection for good physical and mental development. In addition, the minor will incorporate highly disturbed emotional and relational life-management styles.

Being born and growing up in a relational environment where AREs predominate implies growing up with a level of extreme abandonment in the face of emotional impacts that cannot be contained or worked through. Disturbed relational dynamics stimulate confusion, denial, dissociation, and a sense of threat. Throughout the process of psychic maturation, the child's emotional experience will not be recognized or contained but, rather, despised. This scenario lays the foundations for damaged and disorganized thought processes in the child's fragile developing psyche, seriously affecting the ability to modulate emotions and mentalization abilities. All of this contributes to a lack of integration of the mental structure, increasing the psychopathological risk.

Attachment theory describes and demonstrates the crucial value of the relationship with carers, the same context in which most adversities occur in childhood. In turn, studies carried out for years by the team from the Center on the Developing Child at Harvard University, led by Professor Shonkoff, showed that

> the absence of responsive relationships poses a serious threat to a child's development and well-being. Sensing threat activates biological stress response systems, and excessive activation of those systems can have a toxic effect on developing brain circuitry. When the lack of responsiveness persists, the adverse effects of toxic stress can compound the lost opportunities for development associated with limited or ineffective interaction. This complex impact of neglect on the developing brain underscores why it is so harmful in the earliest years of life. It also demonstrates why effective early interventions are likely to pay significant dividends in better long-term outcomes in educational achievement, lifelong health, and successful parenting of the next generation. (Center on the Developing Child, n.d., para. 1)

The operationalization of the concept of AREs would be the following: experiences that have an impact of proven toxic stress suffered by the minor, which threatens their sense of security and well-being on an emotional and physical level as well as their psychoevolutionary development. These experiences can be exposure to sexual abuse, physical abuse, psychological abuse, and parental neglect, or the death or loss of a parent, something that implies the loss of one of the attachment figures. These factors increase the level of toxic stress, a fact that has repercussions at the neuroendocrine-immune level and affects the overall development and psychosocial functioning (National Scientific Council on the Developing Child, 2014).

Relational trauma plays a central role in the organization of the way people relate to themselves and others throughout their lives, including, of course, when they become parents. There is alarming evidence that adverse events in childhood are insufficiently assessed by mental health professionals, which interferes with the ability to establish a trusting relationship that can have real therapeutic effects (Cavanagh et al., 2004; Dangerfield, 2020; Read et al., 2018). Parents and children who have suffered from these experiences but are then assessed on only a symptomatic level will not feel adequately understood, and their real needs will not be adequately addressed.

Many of us have heard the joke "It would be good if they gave you a manual when you become a parent." Unfortunately, there is not such a manual. However, parents' own relational pasts do have an influence on the way they approach the task of parenting: We tend to repeat what we know or what we experienced in our own relationships with our parents. Parents who had the experience of feeling loved, feeling supported, and being made to feel special draw on these experiences, and these experiences shape the way the parents experience and interact with their children. Many parents are also clear that they do not want to repeat what their own parents did. Unfortunately, though, for many parents, these patterns do tend to be repeated as well, even in spite of efforts to avoid this—which leads to what we call "transgenerational transmission of relational trauma." Often, this repetition occurs because their own trauma has gone unattended to, leading to dysregulation of emotion or dissociation that interferes with the development of basic skills of curiosity and openness toward experiencing with children the challenging task of growing up.

A mentalization-informed approach to work with parents seeks to provide a new developmental experience, one in which parents can explore their relational pasts and the influence of their experiences on the way they organize their own emotions and their relationships with their children (as well as more broadly). When parents are "held" while they sit with their own early experiences and the current pain they feel, they develop a clearer picture of themselves and their children. Through this process, parents become not only motivated to provide a different experience for their children but also able to do so through mentalizing skills they obtain.

Facilitating the motivation to do this type of therapeutic work requires observation and validation of the unspoken pain many parents carry with them. In this chapter, we summarize empirical evidence regarding the impact of the "ghosts in the nursery," a term coined by Selma Fraiberg (Fraiberg et al., 1975) to highlight the impact that parenting can have on the socioemotional functioning of an individual who carries the legacy of relational trauma. We hope to illustrate how these findings, from rigorous research on the impact of early AREs, are resonant in our clinical work with parents. We propose a model of therapeutic work that helps unmask such ghosts and lift the cloud of intergenerational transmission of trauma and its impact on parents' ability to function, through a relational environment that enhances epistemic trust, reflective functioning capacity, and mentalized affectivity. As parents shift in their own stances with regard to these relational abilities, the relational environments with their children will also change, placing the parents in the position to break these intergenerational patterns.

We return to Cristina's case throughout the chapter, in order to keep our discussion clinically relevant and alive for the reader. We invite you to pause and recall your own clinical experiences and how they might look from this lens.

VISITING THE GHOSTS IN THE NURSERY IN OUR WORK WITH PARENTS: THE ROLE OF AN ATTACHMENT LENS

Attachment relationships and family systems constitute children's relational environments and play a fundamental role in the children's psychosocial development. Attachment theory has provided a model for understanding the importance of early childhood experiences and the importance of relational dynamics between parental figures and the child (Holmes & Slade, 2017). From the beginning of life, babies are able to recognize and anticipate their caregivers' responses to, and ability to regulate, their distress. It has been observed that from very early stages, babies adapt their behavior in accordance with these capacities of their caregivers (Ainsworth et al., 1978; Sroufe, 1988; van IJzendoorn et al., 1999). Stob et al. (2019) synthesized the ideas of Bowlby (1969, 1973, 1980), describing how the experiences of loss, threat, and separation impact the internal representations of oneself and of others, conditioned by the ways the parent responds to the demands of care, protection, and emotional support of the child in times of need (Stob et al., 2019).

Evidence shows that beyond early childhood, attachment style and relational alterations predict the psychological development of the adolescent and impact relational patterns with others, as well as the parenting practices of their own children (Bowlby & Ainsworth, 1951; Fearon et al., 2010; Fraiberg et al., 1975; Grossmann et al., 2005; Slade, 2014; Steele et al., 1996).

In the relational history of parents who have suffered AREs, these have led them to a narrowing or closure of the epistemic trust learning pathway described in Chapter 2, impeding their ability to learn through emotional experience with others and consequently being less flexible in the face of change. This is a fundamental obstacle that we face in therapeutic work, since it configures an initial scenario of the therapeutic relationship where the parents very often do not ask for help for themselves but for the symptoms their child presents. Because of their own histories, despite their desire to receive help, the parents will often have difficulties relying on others with their struggles as parents, as they do not have enough experiences that allow them to trust others as potentially helpful.

When we are securely attached, the strong emotions that interfere with our capacity to mentalize activate our search for an attachment figure who can offer us tranquility and confidence that can help us recover. If we had good-enough relational experiences during our early childhood, we could also resort to now-internalized good-enough relational experiences that accompany us from within and provide a certain level of containment that will facilitate the recovery of our mentalizing capacities, diminished by the anxiety experienced.

We all have more difficulties mentalizing in situations of high arousal; the ability to regain mentalization in these situations makes us more resilient. In the mentalization-based model, resilience does not lie within the individual—it is relationally constructed. In this sense, the main objective of the therapeutic process and the therapeutic relationship is to scaffold and support parents' development of better mentalization capacities in potentially destabilizing situations that lead them to risky actions, especially parents who have suffered AREs with worse mentalizing capacities.

Babies and young children cannot make sense of their emotional lives, so they depend on their parents' (a) interest in their subjective experience and (b) ability to draw meaning from the child's behavior and make it understandable by interpreting it in terms of underlying mental states. Fonagy, Steele, and Steele (1991) demonstrated that parents' abilities to mentalize their own early attachment experiences predicted their infants' attachment security more than 16 months later. Following this evidence, Fonagy and Target (1997) proffered that mentalization plays an important role in the transgenerational transmission of attachment, proposing an intergenerational pattern where mentalization and the parent's ability to imagine what the baby's behavior communicates about what the baby feels, needs, and wants underlies the sensitive response and promotes attachment security.

The links between mentalization and attachment are bidirectional. Parents' appropriate mentalization promotes secure attachment, and, in turn, the development of children's optimal mentalization capacities occurs in the context of secure attachment relationships, when babies discover their minds through a relationship with someone who treats them like a person with a mind.

Parents' mentalization capacity therefore promotes sensitive parenting by helping them look beyond behaviors, being able to imagine what the child may be feeling, and responding in an attuned way to these mental representations of the child's emotional states. At the same time, the mentalizing capacity of parents allows them to inhibit negative interactions with their children, enabling them to be observers of what is happening in the interaction and to be aware of their own emotional state and regulate their own negative reactions, thus focusing on the central task of helping their child in the process of regulating the child's emotional life. In addition, it has been shown that the parents' reflective functioning is associated with the development of reflective functioning in children (Ensink et al., 2014) and adolescents (Benbassat & Priel, 2012).

As we can see, parents' mentalizing capacities and interest in the child's subjectivity and mind are key factors in the development of the child's own reflective function and mentalized affectivity. Mental states arise in the context of early attachment relationships, where the child learns to mentally identify and begins to represent their own emotional life by virtue of the parents' interest in the child's subjective experience (Ensink et al., 2016).

AREs have an impact on the attachment style that parents establish with their children. A child who is raised in a family where chronic neglect, psychological abuse, physical abuse, and/or sexual abuse predominate will live in a relational environment where the necessary conditions for the establishment of a secure attachment style will not be met. Research has shown that parents with more than four ACEs are significantly more likely to show a lack of resolution with regard to loss and trauma on the Adult Attachment Interview (Murphy et al., 2014). Parents' unresolved states of mind are associated with their children developing disorganized attachment patterns, characterized by a breakdown in affect regulation and relational processes (Granqvist et al., 2017; Schuengel et al., 1999). A secure attachment pattern develops when parents can be sensitive to their children's needs and respond to help them in situations of anxiety and discomfort. In a secure attachment, trust in the availability of parental figures predominates.

In a recent systematic review of the scientific literature on the subject, Malda-Castillo et al. (2019) stated that mentalization is a mechanism that operates at a neurobiological level, that is influenced by attachment relationships and that affects the ability to reflect on oneself and others. These authors also reminded us that the difficulty of establishing a reflective dialogue about one's own, or other people's, emotions and thoughts—that is, the capacity for mentalization—is relevant for a wide range of mental disorders. We know that a good mentalization capacity is

- what allows the possibility of meaningful dialogues that facilitate taking different perspectives on external and internal reality, and

- what helps us cope with the daily demands of the social world, reducing the possibility of experiencing moments of emotional dysregulation or distorted thought patterns (Malda-Castillo et al., 2019).

We also know that a central element in all mental disorders is precisely the alterations in the mentalization capacity, which are evidenced in the difficulty to handle negative and unpleasant emotional states or that exceed the person's resources to modulate them.

From the child's repeated experience of an available and curious parent, capable of imagining what their child is experiencing, a sense of self will develop as being intentional, with the child's own thoughts and feelings (Malberg & Midgley, 2017). Therefore, the ability of parents to think about the internal experience of their child as separate, intentional, and contextualized in the child's evolutionary process will determine the ability of the child to function and manage properly in the world of relationships (Malberg & Midgley, 2017)—that is, in life.

ADVERSE RELATIONAL EXPERIENCES: PREVALENCE AND PSYCHOPATHOLOGICAL CONSEQUENCES

Cristina is feeling anxious because she has to do a presentation at school. She had difficulty going to sleep last night and called her mom every other hour to be close to her. Mom (Mrs. O) wakes up, tired and frustrated, to make breakfast and get both children ready for school. Cristina is not coming down for breakfast, and her brother is ready to go. Mom has patiently called Cristina several times and has now given her daughter her final warning. Mom goes up the stairs, stomping quite loudly to make sure Cristina can hear her. Cristina quickly puts all of her clothing inside the closet (she knows Mom hates the mess) and is rushing to brush her hair when her mother opens the door. Mom screams at Cristina, "What is wrong with you, Cristina?! Can't you hear that I have been calling you?!" Mom's face is tense and stressed, and Cristina feels afraid and covers her face. "Look at me while I am talking to you! You are so disrespectful!" Mom continues. Cristina begins to cry and throws herself on her bed. Mom tells her "There is no time for this!" Mom has a work meeting, and Cristina's brother needs to go to school. Mom grabs Cristina by her arm, does her hair in a rough way, and tells her, "Two minutes to be ready downstairs, or else!" Cristina begins to repeat, softly, "Right away . . . right away . . ." as she picks up her things and walks down the stairs. She is going toward the kitchen, but her mom tells her, "There is no time for food now!" While driving both children to school, mom continues to scream at her daughter, who is crying the whole way.

Parenting is an experience that encapsulates a complex web of subjective connotations. Relational trauma haunts parents when they are at their most vulnerable. As in the case of Mrs. O, the voices of her harsh and unforgiving parents awaken when she is feeling mistreated and ignored by her daughter. At this moment, her capacity to reflect on her own experience and that of her child is absent, and the familiar behavioral responses to stress emerge. Mrs. O is temporarily unable to see the fear in her daughter's face and to reflect on the emotional impact of her behavior on her daughter's sense of safety.

Mrs. O had managed to function in life by disconnecting often from painful emotions. Becoming a mother or a father inevitably implies having to be available to receive and tolerate the unpleasant emotional states of our children, something that challenges our affect regulation styles and adult relationships. Mrs. O was not able to offer a different relational pattern to Cristina, as Mrs. O had not had good-enough relational experiences that allowed her to trust that approaching unpleasant emotional states could not only be safe but also offer a real possibility of modulating these emotions. Instead, she was having to continue investing enormous amounts of effort and energy in psychological survival modes that impaired her relational life, especially when it came to parenting skills. This situation led to the very frequent—or even inevitable—transgenerational transmission of relational trauma, as Cristina was already suffering from the emotional isolation of living in a relational environment where approaching, identifying, naming, tolerating, and processing unpleasant emotions was experienced as threatening. The initial therapeutic task at hand in this context is how to create a safe space, in the therapeutic relationship with Mrs. O, that promotes connection leading to epistemic trust fostered by the nonjudgmental, genuinely curious, and patient attitude of the therapist—how to motivate Mrs. O to learn new ways of being with another, in the context of painful feelings, while experiencing a sense of safety and validation of her relational experience.

In this context, how Mrs. O sees herself internally in the world of relationships is one way in which the ghosts in the nursery will appear. Another way is how Mrs. O organizes and expresses her emotions. Selma Fraiberg (Fraiberg et al., 1975) famously asked why a mother she was working with did not seem to hear her baby's cries, and she concluded that the mother's own cries were not heard and responded to. Consequently, her own emotions and her baby's emotions were overwhelming her, and she was resorting to defense mechanisms (or coping strategies) that, on the one hand, helped her to ward off painful emotions but that, on the other hand, were causing problems in her relationship with her baby and preventing her from experiencing that relationship in full. Mrs. O needs to feel empathized with, her cries heard—and all of the emotions that often become loud noises when she is in the presence of Cristina's challenging behaviors. She needs to do this to be able to start to differentiate her thoughts and feelings from those of her daughter's.

INTERGENERATIONAL TRANSMISSION OF RELATIONAL TRAUMA AND AFFECT REGULATION

Reviews of the research on the intergenerational transmission of parenting indicate that "parenting in one generation predicts parenting in the next to a modest to moderate degree" (Conger et al., 2009, p. 208). It is a commonly held idea that parents who were mistreated when they were young are more likely to mistreat their children; however, studies show that the intergenerational transmission of parenting is more nuanced and that positive and constructive parenting is repeated across generations (see Conger et al., 2009).

While the number of subtypes of maltreatment experienced by children predicts their emotional dysregulation, so, too, does maternal depression and the number of subtypes of maltreatment the mother experienced. Research exploring mediators of this relationship across generations suggests that positive parenting predicts that the child will show greater academic and social competence at subsequent stages of development, which in turn predicts that they will show positive parenting characteristics with their own children. The editors of the special issue of *Developmental Psychology* where these papers were published highlighted that an important way to promote positive parenting and interrupt the intergenerational transmission of maltreatment and trauma is to support the development of children's and parents' competencies in general, rather than focusing solely on reducing externalizing or antisocial behavior (Conger et al., 2009). On a related note, longitudinal developmental research has illustrated that supportive and secure relationships later in development (e.g., through teachers, coaches, romantic partners, therapists) are integral to "breaking the cycle" of maltreatment (Egeland & Farber, 1984).

We must keep in mind that not only the degree, intensity, and number of adverse experiences suffered by the child, but also the good-enough and benign relationships that may also exist in the child's closest relational environment, will determine the consequences on a psychological developmental level. The concept of ghosts in the nursery coupled with that of "angels in the nursery" (Lieberman et al., 2005) provides us with containing metaphors that help us to work with parents on exploring the balance between the angels and the ghosts in the parents' relational past.

The metaphor of angels in the nursery is often helpful to invite parents to reflect on people who made them feel seen and accompanied when they were young, during good and bad times. In the process of exploring their angels, many parents realize that the qualities that these people had, and that made them special for the parents, are within the parents themselves. Furthermore, parents are able to make links between important characteristics of their personality and those of the angels, who often are described as being fun, always there, forgiving, and simply present. This is a wonderful way of exploring the relational past of a parent, highlighting their strengths but also inviting a dialogue away from symptoms and quick solutions.

Many young children who have already been exposed to the impact of AREs are often overlooked and classified under a myriad of labels and medicated to "help" them manage and function. Or, when parents are included in treatment, the focus is on guiding them through how to engage with or respond to their child, often in an attempt to create a more secure relationship, without addressing the underlying mechanisms of their own emotional dysregulation that stem from their own relational traumas. This would be the risk associated with a psychotherapeutic approach that dwells upon Cristina's difficulties independently from the relational dynamic that predominates in her family environment. When working with parents, we must always consider the effects of such early childhood experiences on adults' well-being and, particularly, parenting.

GHOSTS IN THE NURSERY AND THEIR IMPACT ON PARENTAL REFLECTIVE FUNCTIONING

Ensink et al. (2016) described how better awareness helps parents detect their own negative, intrusive, aggressive, and withdrawn responses that undermine the development of attachment security and organization. These authors stated that with better reflective function, there can be better filtering of parents' own affects of aggression, anxiety, and fear— protecting their babies from negative behaviors, because the parents are more aware of their own affects and can see themselves from the outside, as far as this is possible, and imagine the anxieties experienced by their babies. As illustrated by the following clinical vignette, mentalization also involves an implicit understanding that affects become less intense over time and can be changed through thinking and viewing situations differently, and this can help mothers with better reflective functioning to tolerate difficult feelings.

Mr. O has been silent most of the session; he seems very quiet and pensive. The therapist notices and names his unusual demeanor: Mr. O simply shrugs his shoulders. The therapist responds by looking puzzled. Mr. O looks uncomfortable, so the therapist chooses to observe, "I may be wrong, but it seems to me that you feel uncomfortable when I talk about how I see you . . . Am I right?"

MR. O: Actually, you are not wrong. It's just, I don't know what you are looking for when you do all this stuff about what we are feeling.

THERAPIST: I'm glad you told me that. It makes me curious to know, when you were upset or something bad happened when you were young, what did you do? How did those things go in your house?

MR. O: I mean, we weren't unhappy very often. When there was something wrong, we always cheered each other up, and like, we were always really busy with sports and stuff, so eventually we would get distracted. It was fine . . . this thing of paying attention to things so closely . . . Yes . . . it makes me uncomfortable.

THERAPIST: I am so sorry, I would never intend to make you uncomfortable. Perhaps I haven't explained enough what I do . . .

MR. O: Oh! You misunderstand me . . . I feel uncomfortable but I don't necessarily dislike it altogether . . . the thing is . . . my wife . . . well . . . although she had it rough . . . and trust me if you met her dad, you would understand . . . she has a reason of sorts to be doing badly with our kid . . . but me . . . I come from the family where everything was pretty good . . .

THERAPIST: I have to be honest, I would have felt a bit lonely in that family . . .

MR. O: How so?

THERAPIST: Well, only the good feelings were allowed, and we all have the other kind . . .

[*Mr. O pauses and is silent*]

THERAPIST: Can I ask what you're thinking and feeling now?

MR. O: I guess I feel kind of sad thinking that I demand of Cristina the same they demanded of me . . . to be happy, to be OK . . . I always thought of it as a good thing, or like, I never thought it was a bad thing.

THERAPIST: Kids do what they have to in order to survive and get what they need from their families . . . That is what you did, and Cristina is lucky she has two parents that want to do the difficult thing and actually pay attention . . . is not easy . . .

MENTALIZING WITH PARENTS: WHAT IS YOUR MYTH OF PARENTING? A SCRIPT THAT THE THERAPIST CAN USE WITH PARENTS

Considering your cultural and family history, what do you think is your ideal of a "good parent"? How does that ideal weigh on you at times? How do you think it was constructed? Can you think of experiences that set the foundations for what you consider the ideal of a parent? When do you feel you are being a good parent? And when do you feel you are being a bad parent? Do you experience pressure and criticism from members of your family in your role as a parent? Do you experience support and validation from members of your family in your role as a parent? If you could pick five words that describe your "myth of parenting," what would they be?

TRANSGENERATIONAL TRANSMISSION OF RELATIONAL TRAUMA AND THE CONCEPT OF THE ALIEN SELF

Mrs. O spoke of feeling badly about the way she behaved with Cristina. She said when she returned home after dropping off the children, she felt terrible despair. After a long pause, her husband responded to her silence by telling her that he knew she tried her best and that he was sorry he had left her alone with the kids for a whole week due to his demanding work schedule. Mr. O spoke of needing to work on that, and Mrs. O agreed that he could not be there to protect the children from her anger all the time. The therapist said that she imagined it must be so difficult at times, but she could tell that both Mr. and Mrs. O are able to work together and think of each other's experience, motivated by their love for their child. This comment seemed to surprise both of the parents, so the therapist noticed it out loud and wondered if she was correct in naming the shift. Both parents visibly relaxed and spoke of their shame and helplessness and their tendency to think of each other in conflict and not work together.

Parents' deficits in mentalizing capacity inhibit their ability to provide an experience of mutuality and reflective curiosity about the inner experience of their children's relationships. But their mentalizing impairments also interfere with their relationships more broadly, including with each other and also with other systems, such as schools. Parents' inability to regulate their own affective states fosters an unpredictable and inconsistent relational environment for their children to grow up in. The transgenerational transmission cycle of relational trauma becomes evident and facilitated in this context.

Too frequently, we find stories of relational trauma repeated through the generations. If a mother was abused in her childhood and this abuse was silenced, she will likely struggle to find an internalized, balanced, and mentalizing way to provide the "protective shield" necessary in parenting. In these cases, it is important not to get carried away by the external impression and the reality of whether someone is trustworthy or not, as it has nothing to do with the reality of the internal world, where there is no possibility of someone to trust (Tizón, 2019). If, in the internalized relationship experiences, compromise and endurance dominate and submitting to abuse is the only possibility, then the parents will not be able to cope with the repetition of that abuse on their children. To be able to protect, one needs to have reliable internalized relational experiences—one must feel hope that someone is going to take their side, the possibility of trusting someone who can help them. The development of this ability to trust others is also linked to the development of a sense of self.

As described in Chapter 1, we know that parents who respond to their children's manifestation of emotions with contingent marked affective displays (and this includes tone of voice, facial expression, bodily distance, and bodily motion) allow their babies to modulate their own emotional states; this practice, also referred to as *marked mirroring*, is thought to be particularly important when it comes to the management of negative emotions (Fonagy et al., 2002), because it permits the child to enter and maintain a mentalizing space. We know that early experiences of marked mirroring facilitate the development of mentalizing and what is known as the secondary representation of the child's experience in their own mind (Bateman & Fonagy, 2004). This gradually repeated experience contributes to form the child's nuclear self (Fonagy, 2000), which leads to an internal representation of themselves as intentional beings and as agents, which is generalized to the representation of others, leading to the development of a mentalizing model of the world. This model helps the child to perceive the relational world with meaning and in a predictable way and to respond to the complexities of social reality with resilience (Fonagy, 2000).

If this process does not develop in a minimally adequate way, it can lead to the development of what Fonagy (2000) named an "alien self." In a situation of a parent who is overwhelmed by their own suffering or unpleasant emotional states and responds in a hostile or fearful way to the child's discomfort, we could imagine the young child's experience could be described as follows:

> If my parent misperceives my internal state, if they get scared or angry about my discomfort, what I will see and experience is the fear or anger in the other. So, the experience that I incorporate and keep in my mind is the experience that my discomfort scares or annoys the other whom I desperately need, which leads to the internal experience that I am fearful or I make the other angry, when what is really happening to me is that I am alone and terrified. (Dangerfield, 2021b, p. 155)

When this adverse relational pattern is constant and predominates in the parent–child relationship, the child internalizes this dysfunctional relational pattern (neglectful or abusive relational experience) as a nuclear aspect of their sense of self as bad, frightening, or dangerous, when it is in fact a state of the caregiver that becomes an "alien state" of the child.

The child's real state is that they are alone and terrified, experiencing unbearable, overwhelming anxieties that cannot be processed. This concept of alien self refers to the process in which the caregiver's representations of the child are based on erroneous attributions, something that will promote the child's internalization of misadjusted representations of themselves. If the relationship with the caregivers is predominantly marked by repeated experiences of this type, there will be a situation where the child's mind is dominated by an alien self (Rossouw, 2012).

As Dangerfield (2021b) described,

> This highly pathogenic feature emerges as the child is experiencing a moment of emotional discomfort, when what will be triggered in their mind is the maladaptive relational pattern of a mean and hostile response to their moment of discomfort, something that will only increase the suffering and trigger an escalation of despair, loss of mentalizing and teleological and psychic equivalence modes in an extreme level resulting in high risk of destructive acting out. (pp. 155–156)

The internal experience of the alien self is similar to the experience of an internal tormentor: constant self-criticism, self-loathing, absence of internal validation, and expectation of failure. When the alien self is triggered and organizes the person's internal experience, the self is hated, and, through the projected lenses of the alien self, the external world can be perceived as potentially hostile, humiliating, and persecuting (Rossouw, 2012). At the same time, the internal representations are inconsistent with their own experiences. Representations of others will also be misadjusted and lead to the experience that the relational world is meaningless and unpredictable.

HOW TO WORK WITH THE GHOSTS IN THE NURSERY: AN IMPERFECT SCAFFOLDING PROCESS?

It is always a challenge to translate our theoretical and research knowledge into clinical practice. With the advent of evidence-based research and practice, however, the link between (a) what happens between us and our clients and (b) how it is informed by actual data is important. We conclude this chapter by making that link through clinical guidelines and highlighting the process of scaffolding in our work with parents, keeping in mind the influence of both ghosts and angels in their nursery—that is, the shadows of their relational past that inform parents' attributions; challenge their capacity for self and other reflective functioning; and feed fears, hopes, and expectations.

When we work with parents in psychotherapy—whether (a) it is their own individual treatment in which they are talking about their relationships with their children and experiences as a parent, or (b) the treatment is focused on the child or family—an appreciation for their own developmental history, namely, their AREs, guides our work.

ESTABLISHING EPISTEMIC TRUST

We begin this process in the assessment phase, which is described in detail in the next chapter. From this starting point, we set the tone that we do not see parents or children in isolation. Every child has a parent, and every parent was once a child. We approach this in concrete ways: for example, asking parents directly about their own AREs and those their children have experienced. Even without making the links explicit, parents often hear in their own responses the similarities and differences between their experiences and their children's.

Clinicians often feel hesitant to ask about trauma or early relationships at the beginning of treatment, believing that trust must be established before inquiring about these experiences. While it is necessary to be sensitive and attuned in the ways we introduce and delve into this material, this sequence may actually be the other way around. In asking parents about their experiences (and what they know their child to have experienced), we are showing our interest in them—not only what has happened to them but also the imprint that it has left internally. It is through precisely this process that trust is built.

While exploration of past experiences gives us a sense of what the ghosts in the nursery might be, it can also be a pathway for identifying the angels in the nursery; however, we usually need to ask parents directly about who the angels were, offering that these angels may not have always been angels but did provide moments when the parent felt loved, special, and safe. And in the therapeutic relationship—and particularly using our mentalizing stance—we position ourselves to create new developmental experiences with the parent. Although in Part II of this book we explore research tools and their clinical use in exploring these difficult issues in a contained and structured way, the following are important clinical principles to follow during the process of building epistemic trust:

- Show genuine curiosity for the values and expectations of the parent's culture of origin, naming moments of misunderstanding when they appear in the process of exploration, in order to promote openness and sending a clear message that any perceived judgmental attitude in the therapist can be addressed and mentalized together.

- Be brave, and ask questions regarding traumatic experiences in an open and clear way while keeping in mind the parent's psychological functioning and levels of social support.

- Communicate nonverbally your interest, and, when appropriate, display marked mirroring in the context of expressions of difficult emotions.

- Check frequently about the emotional impact of the conversation, and monitor your own reaction to the material being discussed.

TELLING THE STORY: THEN AND NOW

A new developmental experience is offered when we ask, at the beginning of the treatment, about parents' own histories. Rather than focusing on the facts of what happened, we demonstrate a curiosity in what the parents' relationships with their own parents were like and gain an initial idea of whether the parents are able to share that with us and invite us into what their world seemed to them, by giving specific examples of things that took place. One also gets a picture of the parents' mentalizing capacities, whether they can take different perspectives—for example, differentiate what they felt or thought when they were young from what they feel or think now. Also, what they do with our perspective as therapists—that is, whether they seem to feel the urge to convince us of their experience, or if they do not see the point in talking to us about it, or if they can take in and respond to our curiosity with openness not only to share but also to think together about their experiences. In the case of loss or trauma, do their emotions become overwhelming and cause their narratives about what happened to become confusing or disorganizing?

The process of retelling stories—whether it is what happened in the past or what happened this week with their child—repeats many times over the course of treatment and contributes to mentalized affectivity. It allows for an integration of cognition and affect that transcends mere regulation of emotions upward or downward. When we open our focus beyond the facts of what happened, we scaffold the parents' abilities to construct narratives and to communicate about their experiences in ways that build trust. In a gentle and curious way, we help parents to flesh out their stories—which are often, at the beginning, difficult to understand and follow or difficult to believe—so that we can both understand and believe them. When people feel understood and believed, we see their anxiety decrease and their capacity for mentalizing and playing with ideas (and, literally, with their children) increase.

At a more technical level, the use of familiar sounds (e.g., songs) and imagery (e.g., pictures, sharing visual memories) sometimes allows for an atmosphere of "serious playfulness," which promotes mentalizing difficult and painful memories. Cocreating a more coherent narrative of a parent's painful relational past is not an easy process and one that is often fragile. During the process of assessment, one must determine what level of exploration is realistic considering the psychosocial functioning of a parent and the potential consequences of opening up memories often guarded away in safely locked "emotional containers."

EMERGENCE OF SOCIAL LEARNING

The lens of developmental psychopathology—that is, an appreciation of parents' current functioning in terms of what they experienced in the past and how those experiences shaped them at a psychological and neurobiological level—underscores the therapist's view of the parent as having a mind with agency and intentionality, which are the foundations for epistemic trust. Furthermore, when a parent's story and history is seen and believed, it opens the channels for social learning within the therapeutic relationship and, in particular, the kind of learning facilitated by epistemic trust, where information is taken in and can be applied more broadly to other contexts.

However, particularly in the case of complex trauma, this process is not linear. The emergence of social learning and epistemic trust may be followed by what seems like a sudden backslide and a return to mistrust, heightened epistemic mistrust, and a constriction of the channels for social learning. Being able to understand these as traumatic responses that can be seen, acknowledged, held, tolerated, and thought about together, rather than a failure on the part of the therapist or parent of the patient, brings us back to opening the epistemic superhighway and the potential for epistemic trust with others beyond the therapist. For instance, it might really facilitate accessing social support from school or from other allied professionals and systems supporting the growth and health of children. It might also decrease social isolation and mistrust and facilitate a feeling of "not being so alone" with challenging parenting situations. Armed with mentalized affectivity, the prospect of well-being can be realized.

CONCLUDING SUMMARY

- Love—particularly the feeling that another human being is keeping us in mind and trying to understand our subjective experience—is a powerful motivation for change.

- AREs potentially impact generational transmission of relational trauma, and the implications for child and adult mental health have been shown in research and reinforced by clinical experience.

- It is not always easy to feel compassion and express genuine and loving empathy toward parents, especially when they awaken our own ghosts in the nursery.

- We often find ourselves the target of parents' frustration and helplessness, our mentalizing stance challenged and, at times, ruptured.

- Working in the here and now of the session by explicitly naming and noticing what is going on can be helpful and productive in creating an atmosphere of safety and trust.

- Alicia Lieberman's (Lieberman et al., 2005) concept of the angels in the nursery posits that early experiences are characterized by intensely shared positive feelings between parent and child in which the child feels fully understood, accepted, and loved.

- Exploring the angels in the nursery opens the door to reflect on the experiences through which the child develops a core sense of security and self-worth that can be drawn upon, when the child becomes a parent, to interrupt the cycle of relational trauma.

- Invite parents to self-observe in a more balanced way, looking at their relational strengths and weaknesses. Many times, parents discover that they have the same qualities as those people in their early life who made them feel seen and understood.

- Playfulness, flexibility, and genuine empathy are some of the ingredients that help to fight the shadow of the ghosts in the nursery and support the child—and, later, the parent—to connect in a relationship with a sense of safety and hope.

- Sometimes parents need a new developmental experience in order to value and embrace their own inner angel qualities. Sometimes parents need to be loved with genuine and compassionate inquisitiveness and empathy.

4 ASSESSMENT WITH PARENTS FROM A MENTALIZING APPROACH

As described in the Introduction to this volume, the articulation of this treatment model emerged from the awareness that therapists may benefit from a clearer framework for working with parents. In the context of assessment, for adult mental health care providers, training and clinical work tend to focus on the assessment of adults' personal difficulties, without a broader perspective of their relational and emotional life. Because many adult psychotherapists have not been trained in child, adolescent, and family therapy, they may feel less confident assessing the complexities and conflicts around parenting. Similarly, clinicians who work with children may find gaps in their approaches when facing issues related to parents' personality organization and attachment security that arise in the context of child or family treatment, not wanting parent work to become individual therapy or intrude on the child's therapeutic space. Therefore, our treatment model aims to bridge these gaps in patient care. We view our assessment approach as an integrative treatment of the parent as a whole person, which can be utilized within the framework of

https://doi.org/10.1037/0000341-005
Working With Parents in Therapy: A Mentalization-Based Approach, by N. Malberg, E. Jurist, J. Bate, and M. Dangerfield

individual adult or child treatment or work with couples and families. Throughout the remainder of this book, when we use the word "patient" or "client," it is to refer to the parent, even if the child is the identified patient for the treatment.

Consistent with evidence-based treatments (Eells, 2011), the therapeutic work starts with a clinical conceptualization or formulation, a dimensional picture, which will guide the intervention. In this section, we describe our method for conducting an initial assessment and how it leads to the development of a case formulation informing the treatment planning and overall process. Whether treatment is just starting or already underway, this framework is appropriate whenever attention to the patient's identity and experiences as a parent are indicated; this may mean that in an adult's or child's individual therapy or in couples therapy, there has been a shift in the work and this focus is now needed, or this may be the clinical focus from the start. The goals of our mentalization-informed assessment are as follows:

- to give the parent the experience of being listened to,

- to develop a case formulation centered on the mentalizing profile of the parent, and

- to introduce the parent to the experience of feeling mentalized by another.

A MENTALIZING APPROACH TO LISTENING

The initial assessment is as much about listening as it is about asking questions. We gain information from not only the content of what the parent says but also how they communicate the information. The purpose of the assessment is both to gather information and to learn about where we are starting from, what resources the parent has, and where challenges and difficulties currently lie, in order to identify treatment goals and a general sense of moves and shifts that may help the parent to achieve their goals.

First, we seek to get a full understanding of the problem(s) that the parent wants help with. In our thorough exploration of the problem(s) they are concerned about, we bring in the mentalizing stance, slowing down the process, asking the parent to give us specific examples and walk us through, moment to moment, how these interactions unfold. In other words, we begin with the patient's own sense and understanding, but we do not simply passively receive it.

HOLDING IN MIND THE MENTALIZING STANCE

In initial sessions, the therapist aims to elicit a full, detailed, and nuanced picture, keeping in mind the qualities of a mentalizing stance:

- curiosity
- not-knowing
- collaboration
- perspective taking
- developmental perspective
- looking past behavior to internal experiences
- genuine, authentic use of self—making your own mind transparent
- playfulness and humor

As Herb Schlesinger (2013) wrote in *Endings and Beginnings: On Terminating Psychotherapy and Psychoanalysis*, patients' reasons for coming to therapy are very often their "ticket for admission"; they may be their conscious reasons, or they may be what the patient thinks they need to say—but rarely do these chief complaints provide the whole story. We find the same to be true for many parents: The chief complaints are rarely the full story about their child or themselves, and the things that trouble them. Take, for example, a 45-year-old father who presents to therapy for "anger problems." While outbursts of anger are indeed a significant part of the clinical picture and causing him big problems with his family, the therapist comes to learn, through the assessment, about this man's early history of abandonment, his incarceration in a juvenile detention facility, and sexual abuse he suffered silently. Knowing this, the mentalizing approach to therapy helps this father link this anger to his trauma, opening up wells of vulnerability and providing an opportunity for the therapist to help him manage the feelings of shame he carries, as well as his attachment longings. Through this process, he becomes better able to recognize that the anger he experiences in the present is misplaced, he is able to step outside of it with curiosity, and he is not defined or controlled by it.

GOALS FOR ASSESSMENT AND CONCEPTUALIZATION

- Develop an understanding of the problems the parent is coming in for help with.
- Create a profile of the parent's temperament, personality, and attachment patterns.

(continues)

GOALS FOR ASSESSMENT AND CONCEPTUALIZATION (*Continued*)

- Assess the quality of the parent's relationships.
- Determine where the parent is on the developmental spectrum in the role as a parent.
- Assess the conflicts or struggles the parent is facing internally.
- Create a profile of the parent's capacity to mentalize, including (a) when and in what ways their mentalization breaks down and how to get it back on track and (b) which prementalizing modes of functioning seem predominant.
- Assess the parent's mentalized affectivity (identifying, modulating, and expressing emotions) and overall affect regulation profile.

Assessment, in general, provides a guide for understanding patients' chief complaints in a deeper way, to identify what the problems are and to give an idea of pathways forward. However, therapists must remember that assessment is not a one-time thing that is conducted at the beginning of treatment. A hallmark of a mentalizing approach is that each session—even each therapeutic moment—involves a microassessment of where the patient is, how they are responding and how treatment is progressing, the state of the therapeutic relationship and the alliance, and whether shifts in the approach are justified or necessary. In the spirit of making the implicit explicit, we strongly encourage supervision or consultation as a space where therapists can reflect on their implicit assessments and formulations and make them explicit. The formulation and insights from assessment are not, however, necessarily explicit in the treatment at all times. In fact, they should not be, because explicit assessment and formulation requires cognitive energy and attention that may bring the therapist out of the here and now of the present moment with the patient or may interrupt the genuine and authentic qualities of the interaction that are essential to a mentalization-based approach.

So, where do we begin our assessment and formulation? The assessment in this approach is semistructured. The therapist draws from psychodynamic approaches that advise beginning with an open invitation for the parents to talk about what is on their minds and what brings them in. The therapist is attentive to how parents respond to this openness and how they talk about themselves, their children, and their families. For example,

- Do parents launch into high levels of emotion and distress? Do they show low levels of emotion and distress, even where we might expect it?

- Do parents seem to place blame or fault?

- Are parents collaborative with the therapist, providing enough information for the therapist to understand what they mean?

- Do parents leave space for the therapist to ask questions or offer reflections?

- Or do parents seem to need structure in order to begin, as if needing to be drawn out?

BEGINNING THE ASSESSMENT WITH MR. AND MRS. O

Following is an excerpt from the first session with Mr. and Mrs. O, in which the therapist is exploring the chief complaint, while simultaneously working to establish epistemic trust and a mentalizing stance. The italicized notations in brackets indicate aspects of the mentalizing stance that the therapist is already implementing in their interaction.

THERAPIST: So, tell me, what brings you here and how might I be able to help? [*curiosity, collaboration*]

MRS. O: I don't know how much Cristina's school counselor told you, but she has OCD and it's been getting worse recently, especially at school. So, we'd really like to know what we can do to help her.

THERAPIST: The counselor did tell me about the OCD symptoms, but I'd like to hear more about them from the two of you [*marking perspectives*]. Before I ask more, is there anything you'd like to add, Mr. O, that you are concerned about or would like to get help with? [*collaboration*]

MR. O: No, I mean, I don't know what she could possibly have to be anxious about. Her life is a breeze, like any normal kid, just school and playdates. To be honest, I think she just knows how to get what she wants now. Everything has to be done her way, and she has a meltdown if we don't let her have it. I'm sure that's why she isn't socializing with her little friends anymore, because they probably won't have it and so she just wants to stay inside. I don't think we should be giving her even more attention.

THERAPIST: So it sounds like the two of you may have some different opinions [*marking perspectives*]. And it doesn't really make

	sense that she would be anxious, to you at least [looking at Mr. O] [*not-knowing stance*], but it sounds like there is some consensus that she has what you refer to as these OCD symptoms or some signs of anxiety [*reflection*]. Could you tell me more about what she says or does that you've noticed? [*curiosity, clarification*]
MRS. O:	Well like, the newest one is that I've noticed she is doing something where she seems like she's counting to herself and touches her fingers together like this [demonstrates tapping her fingers]. I tell her to stop and keep her hands still, and I tried getting her one of those things to keep your hands busy, what do they call those little toys?
THERAPIST:	The fidget spinners? [*collaboration, active participation*]
MRS. O:	Yes, yes. I got her one of those because I thought it might help.
THERAPIST:	Sounds like you have been working hard to try to resolve this [*looking past behavior, reflecting parents' strengths*]. You said that's been the most recent behavior you've noticed? When did it start? [*curiosity*]
MRS. O:	Probably like a month or so ago. Like, around the time they went back to school after the winter break.
THERAPIST:	Ah, so you noticed it seemed to be around the time of the break? Tell me, since I don't really know your family yet. What is life like in your home, and how are these breaks and things?
MR. O:	You can't possibly think it's actually linked to the break. We went skiing, she had a great time.
MRS. O:	She did not have a great time, she cried hysterically when we dropped her off at ski school. I didn't think she was going to make it through the day. It broke my heart.
THERAPIST:	Is it OK if we slow down a bit? [*stop and stand*] I need to do this in order to think [*use of self, simmering down*]. Mr. O, I know therapists have a reputation for trying to find these links really quickly, and I agree it probably isn't that simple. But it's just helpful for me to know not just about

the problems but also what things are like in general, even, or actually especially when they are going well. Sounds like the ski trip was in some ways good, but these separations were difficult [*multiple perspectives*]. Maybe, could you walk me through how these things go, when she gets anxious, like getting dropped off at ski school? [*curiosity, slowing down*]

MRS. O: How far back should we start?

THERAPIST: Wherever seems to make sense. Maybe the point at which she didn't seem so anxious? [*stop and rewind*]

MRS. O: Well in the morning everything seemed fine. She and her brother were playing, while we were sorting out the schedule for the day and figuring out where we needed to get the passes and stuff. So that was fine. But then she and I got into this thing because she was complaining that she didn't want to wear the gaiter I had brought her. She has two that go with her jacket, and I couldn't find one of them so I just brought the other. But she said that wasn't the one she wanted, that she doesn't like that one because it's itchy. And this is where things can get really tough with her, because she gets it in her head that she wants something else and she will just not let it go, even though I explained a million times to her that I didn't bring it and that I was sorry, but she would just need to wear the one we had. But she was refusing to wear it, so eventually I just gave in and said fine, you'll be cold, but have it your way.

THERAPIST: So before we even move on to what happened at the ski school, what was that moment like for the two of you? [*looking past behavior to feelings*]

MRS. O: For me it's dreadful! I felt terrible I hadn't brought the other gaiter, and there is no solution and she's being totally irrational. I don't know what I'm supposed to do!

THERAPIST: And Mr. O, what's it like for you? [*collaboration*]

MR. O: Oh, I wasn't really part of this. I had a work call first thing in the morning, so I wasn't involved. I just heard the shrieking . . .

In this example, the therapist is helping the parents to zero in on a focus and then using that focus to generate curiosity and explore alternative perspectives while staying close to reality. In addition, the therapist is validating each of the parents' experiences all throughout and displaying genuine interest in exploring and understanding the difficulties that motivate the parents to seek help.

ASSESSING FROM A DIMENSIONAL PERSPECTIVE

Throughout the assessment, the therapist inquires about the presenting problem, the parents' own history, and their relationship with their children, which provides us with data about the parents' mentalizing capacities. Assessment of mentalizing, like assessing attachment, is done through interacting, listening, and observing self and other in the here and now. Bateman and Fonagy's (2016) four dimensions of mentalizing, which facilitate the emergence of explicit mentalizing, help provide a structure for observation in the context of assessment. The therapist observes and listens to these in the context of the initial therapeutic interactions and beyond, in order to identify the areas where there is a lack of integration and balance, to promote a return to prementalizing ways of functioning.

- Implicit and Explicit: This refers to what kind of mentalizing the patient is using. *Implicit mentalizing* is the automatic mentalizing we all use moment to moment, to navigate the social world, and it operates outside of our conscious awareness; *explicit mentalizing* refers to the conscious mentalizing processes that we use when we slow down and think about an interaction and actively reflect on our own intentions or behaviors and how our interactions with other people are unfolding.

- Internal and External: This refers to the sources of information that we draw from in order to mentalize. When we are externally focused, we are attending to behavior, facial expressions, and other observable aspects of ourselves and others. When we are internally directed, we focus on the internal experiences that we or others may be having.

- Self and Other: This is often the easiest to recognize—since mentalizing is interpersonal, our efforts to mentalize can be focused on ourselves and our experiences or on other people.

- Cognitive and Affective: This refers to the balance between thoughts and feelings, and we may tend to emphasize or center one over the other.

WHY IS PAYING ATTENTION TO THE FOUR DIMENSIONS THAT FACILITATE MENTALIZATION IMPORTANT DURING ASSESSMENT?

Each of these aspects of mentalizing has a time and a place where it is adaptive; however, a balance between sides on each of these four dimensions is often optimal. In assessing mentalizing, we are taking note of what the parent is spending the most time on, per se. Our goal, then, is increasing the other side of the scale for each dimension during interactions, through what mentalization-based technique calls *contrary moves*. A contrary move means shifting the focus and attempting to increase the other side to restore balanced mentalizing that will enable the patient to have the fullest picture of their interpersonal world. With cognition and affect, there is a further possibility beyond balance—that is, integrating them, as occurs in mentalized affectivity.

In learning about the parent, and what is bringing them in, during the assessment phase, weaving in questions that prompt mentalizing helps the therapist evaluate the parent's capacity to work in this way and plants the seeds for a therapeutic environment focused on mentalizing. The therapist does this while holding in mind the therapeutic goal of achieving balanced mentalizing in terms of the four dimensions, thus assessing both parental strengths and weaknesses with the goal of creating a mentalizing profile of the parent.

- Self and Other
  - If the parent seems better able to articulate their own internal experiences than those of their child, the therapist might reflect on the parent's good assessment on what goes through the parent's mind and ask what they imagine goes through their child's mind.
  - If the parent speaks more comfortably about their child's behavior and internal experiences, the therapist might invite the parent to say more about what goes through their own mind or what they themselves do at certain moments.

- Internal and External
  - If the parent is focused on giving information that gives us an external picture of what happens—what things look like—the therapist might ask them about what they feel or what they think goes on inside of other people.

- If the parent talks more about internal states, the therapist might ask them to give examples or paint a picture so that the therapist can better understand.

- Cognitive and Affective
  - If the parent is able to recall their own or other people's thoughts or takes a more intellectual approach, the therapist may inquire about the emotions involved.
  - If the parent can identify and talk about emotions, the therapist could find out more about the thoughts that are connected to these emotions.

- Implicit and Explicit
  - Most parents tend to show more implicit, but less explicit, mentalizing, but the therapist must also keep in mind that too much explicit mentalizing can become overthinking or hypermentalizing, and not enough implicit mentalizing or going with one's gut or intuitions can also be a barrier for parents.
  - If a parent does not show much explicit mentalizing, we consider moments where we can experiment with slowing them down and going back over something together.
  - If a parent is highly cognitive and intellectualizing, this can seem overly explicit, and we can notice this and try to help them to move into speaking more freely and authentically.

It is of value to think of these approaches as subtle probes, while noticing where the parent seems to be able to move and where they seem to get stuck, thus contributing to the therapist's emerging understanding of the parent's mentalizing functioning.

HOW ATTACHMENT FINDINGS INFORM THE PROCESS OF ASSESSMENT AND DEVELOPMENT OF EPISTEMIC TRUST

To give the parent the experience of being listened to and facilitate the emergence of epistemic trust, we need to be able to trust the parent first. Therapists demonstrate our trust by listening, taking in, valuing the parent's perspective, and, ultimately, demonstrating our understanding. But not all parents (or patients in general) are easy to understand. To understand people, human beings need to have some idea about how they communicate. Depending on the therapist's own communication patterns, they may find certain parents easier to understand and communicate with than others (Petrowski et al., 2013; Rubino et al., 2000; Talia et al., 2020). So, as a therapist tries to understand what the parent is saying and put themselves in the parent's shoes, they are attentive to how the parent tends to communicate. Here are some possible examples:

- clearly, but with few details, leaving a lot of room for the therapist

- sparsely, without volunteering details, and reluctant to respond to the therapist

- difficult to understand and follow—lots of detail, as though they are making a case and enlisting the therapist

- collaboratively

These ways of communicating give us some initial cues to the parent's attachment style (Talia et al., 2017):

- Avoidant/Dismissing: clearly, but with few details or facts, leaving a lot of room for the therapist

- Resistant/Preoccupied: difficult to understand and follow—lots of detail, as though they are making a case and enlisting the therapist

- Secure/Autonomous/Balanced: collaborative, open, able to express interpersonal wishes and wants

Categorizing attachment patterns was created for research purposes. For therapists, it is more helpful to think of attachment patterns as ways of seeking proximity, particularly when in distress. It is important that the therapist recognizes the parent's unique communication style, because it can give them clues as to what the parent might be worried or anxious about. The parent who communicates clearly but with few details might not be sure if the therapist is interested in their internal experience or why they think or feel a certain way and may assume it is better if they keep things short, simple, and to the point, as in dismissing or avoidant attachment patterns (Talia et al., 2017). The parent who gives a lot of detail or tells long, seemingly irrelevant stories may be anxious that the therapist will not believe them and may think they need to convince the therapist or turn up the volume to make sure that they get their point across, as in preoccupied attachment patterns (Talia et al., 2017).

Most importantly, though, making note of a parent's way of communicating can help the therapist maintain their own mentalizing stance when they are having difficulty understanding. The therapist can appreciate the difficulties that come up between them and a parent as reflective of something about the parent's current internal experience, and not a deliberate attempt to thwart the therapist's efforts to help. So, in the end, it is about recognizing whether the parent's interpersonal communication style is collaborative or not and what might be making collaboration difficult. In recognizing this, the therapist can avoid making missteps that exacerbate the situation. For example, the therapist can avoid challenging or questioning the parent who is anxious about whether they are believed or not by the therapist. In these instances, instead of experiencing the avoidant parent as rejecting and uncooperative, the therapist can recognize the parent's struggles and demonstrate their interest and curiosity.

THE PROCESS OF ASSESSMENT

The main aim of a mentalization-informed-approach assessment is to learn about the parent's experience; their capacity to mentalize these experiences and the associated emotions; and their representations of their children, their partners, their own caregivers, other significant people in their lives, and themselves. Figure 4.1 illustrates the components of the mentalizing profile that is constructed by following the structure we describe here.

How Would This Look in Clinical Practice?

Imagine a parent who describes numerous anxious thoughts that they have as a parent and wishes that their in-laws would be more cooperative in listening to them when interacting with their child. The parent focuses on describing the behavior of their in-laws and how they laugh when the parent expresses their concerns but does not put words to the emotions of fear or anger. At the beginning of this part of the session, the mentalizing that the parent is already doing is likely to be automatic, implicit mentalizing, so we will be working to bring explicit mentalizing online, so to speak. We might do this by slowing down the interaction and asking if we could look at this together in a bit more detail. Since the parent appears to be focused on their anxious thoughts, rather than their own feelings, the therapist might try to help the patient to elaborate on the emotions that they are feeling. The therapist will remain empathic and validating of their experience at first and, in time, try to help shift the attention to mentalizing the experiences of others, including the in-laws, the parent's partner, and the child. Finally, the therapist might note the parent's focus on the behaviors (verbal and

FIGURE 4.1 Mentalizing Profile of the Parent Wheel

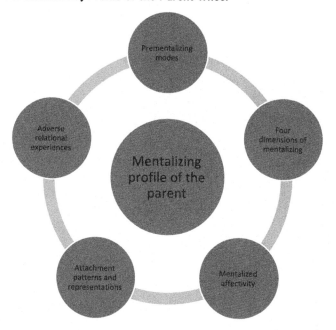

nonverbal) in the interactions described, which reflect an external focus, and attempt to guide the patient to paying attention to what is going on within themselves internally, as well as what might be internal and not visible in others. Highlighting the importance of observing and working through misunderstandings is also a way to direct attention toward awareness of opaqueness of mental states and encouraging curiosity in relational exchanges, rather than certainty.

Representations of Attachment Figures, Children, and Self

To efficiently assess the quality of parents' representations of themselves, their children, and the relationship with their children, it is helpful to use a set of structured questions such as those from the Parent Development Interview–Revised (Slade et al., 2004). The Parent Development Interview was developed by Arietta Slade and colleagues to assess attachment with regard to a person's own children, rather than with regard to their parents. Following are questions that clinicians may find useful:

• I'd like to begin by getting a sense of the kind of person your child is . . . So, could you get us started by choosing three adjectives that describe your child, something about his/her/their personality? What do you like the most about your child? What do you like the least about your child?

- Now I'd like you to choose three adjectives that you feel reflect the relationship between you and your child. Can you tell me about a time that illustrates how the relationship is like this?

- Describe a time in the last week when you and your child really "clicked."

- Now, describe a time in the last week when you and your child really weren't "clicking." What was that like for you? What do you think was going on inside for your child?

- How would you describe yourself as a parent?

- What gives you the most joy in being a parent?

- What gives you the most pain or difficulty in being a parent?

- Do you think your child ever feels rejected?

- How does your child let you know that they need attention from you? Can you tell me about a recent time?

- How does your child let you know that they need help from you? Can you tell me about a recent time?

- What are separations like for you both? Like going to school? Or going away to camp or for a trip?

- Do you think there are experiences in your child's life that you feel have been a setback for him?

Alternatively, the Five Minute Speech Sample (Adkins & Fonagy, 2017) has been found to be helpful clinically, particularly if it can be audio recorded. The therapist introduces this tool to parents by saying something like the following:

> I have a short activity for you to do, like an interview of sorts, that will help me to get a sense of your relationship with your child. But it's a little bit different, because I am not going to ask you the questions. I am going to give you this sheet of paper that you see has three questions on it. I am going to let you read them at your own pace, and then I would like you to just talk about your answers to each of them. And I'll give you 5 minutes. And in that time, I am not going to say anything. I am going to focus on just listening. And if it's still OK with you [we assume that you have already discussed recording with the parent], I will record it so I can type it up, and sometimes it can be helpful for us to look back on, like

where your mind was at and what things were like at this moment in your life and your child's life. How does that sound? Do you have any questions?

The four questions on the Five-Minute Speech Sample are:

• What is your child like?

• How do you feel about your child?

• How do you think your child feels about you?

• Tell me about a problem you had with your child recently and how you dealt with it.

When listening in the moment or reading back, this material can further elucidate the salient dimensions of mentalizing for the parent, how coherent their representations are of themselves and their child, and the quality of those representations. From this exercise, the therapist can learn how parents see their children and see themselves as parents, what they love about their children, how they tolerate negative emotions as a parent, and what internal conflicts they have.

While there is increasing recognition that finding out about parents' own histories and personalities can help improve child treatment, our assessment goes beyond what might be typical for most child intake assessments. For this, we draw on the Adult Attachment Interview (George et al., 1996) and use some or all of the following questions, which have been modified for clinical use:

• Who would you say raised you?

• Could you tell me a few adjectives or words that would describe your childhood relationship with your mother [or replace with primary caregiver], from as early as you can remember until about 12 years old? Can you tell me about a specific time or memory that would illustrate for me why you chose those words to describe the relationship?

• And now could you tell me a few adjectives or words that would describe your childhood relationship with your father [or replace with other primary caregiver], from as early as you can remember until about 12 years old? Can you tell me about a specific time or memory that would illustrate for me why you chose those words to describe the relationship with them?

• When you were hurt or upset as a child, either physically or emotionally, what did you do? Did you go to anyone?

- Did you ever feel rejected or hurt (physically or emotionally) by your parents as a young child?

- Did you experience any setbacks in your childhood? How did those effect you?

- Why do you think your parents behaved as they did during your childhood?

- How do you think your experiences being parented affect your experience of being a parent now?

- Is there anything that you have gained from having the kind of upbringing you had?

- When you imagine 20 years from now, and your child is all grown up, what do you hope they will say about what they learned from being parented by you?

When parents can hold their own and their children's minds in mind, there are increased possibilities for changes in their interpersonal interactions as well as other aspects of their life (e.g., role satisfaction). In our experience as therapists, we are better able to support parents when we have a sense of their own states of mind with regard to attachment.

So how do we understand parents' responses to these questions about their own histories? In order to do this, we rely on the coding systems developed for the Adult Attachment Interview and the Patient Attachment Coding System. The Adult Attachment Interview and Patient Attachment Coding System are complex research tools based in linguistics and relevant to therapy sessions and interpersonal contexts. Extensive training and completion of a reliability set is required to code. This overview is not meant to replace training in these coding systems, which is of clinical value. What follows is an explanation of common markers of different attachment patterns and their potential to inform the therapist's attention.

- Avoidant patterns
  - minimizing or downplaying emotional experiences, particularly overtly negative emotions (e.g., "But it wasn't that bad," "It's normal though, whatever")
  - idealizing—presenting only "good" picture
  - difficulty providing narrative examples when discussing child or own parents
  - lack of memory

- Therapeutic attention to
  - putting words to, and deepening connection with, emotional experiences
  - mentalizing around attachment relationships
- Preoccupied patterns
  - strong emotions, particularly anger or frustration, that seem to become absorbing
  - gives narratives but gets absorbed in emotions or details, or uses vague ways of speaking that convey the emotion but leave unclear exactly what happened
  - therapist feels pulled to agree with the patient, as if the patient is building a case for their perspective
  - Therapeutic attention to
    - support and validation of emotional experiences to facilitate attention and affect regulation
    - actively interrupting nonmentalizing and promoting collaborative exploration
- Secure patterns
  - balanced view of self and others—can discuss positives and negatives
  - valuing attachment relationships
  - uses narratives to communicate, making it relatively easy for therapists to understand
  - open and collaborative interpersonally
  - able to take multiple perspectives
  - can self-monitor and recognize internal conflicts and breakdowns in mentalizing
  - Therapeutic attention to
    - identifying contexts where mentalizing is difficult and activating mentalizing in those contexts
- Unresolved/disorganized patterns
  - displays freezing or dissociation
  - provocative interpersonally
  - marked incoherence when talking about loss or trauma

– Therapeutic attention to

- processing and constructing narratives around loss and trauma, with focus on how parent is impacted in the present
- mentalizing around traumatic experiences and losses

Discussing Attachment Histories With Mr. and Mrs. O During Assessment to Guide Treatment Goals

Mr. O—who reports believing he has undiagnosed attention-deficit/hyperactivity disorder—when asked about his own early experiences with his parents, responds, "I don't really see how that's important. It was normal, just like your average childhood." When asked if he might be able to recall any memories about how his childhood relationship with his parents felt normal or average, he is not able to. The therapist could begin to understand, from this presentation, that Mr. O is likely to have an avoidant pattern regarding attachment, and, as such, the therapist would be on the lookout that Mr. O might be likely to minimize his needs or emotions, as well as those of others. And, rather than be readily able to explore the thoughts, feelings, and intentions that underlie his own behaviors, Mr. O may be likely to shift into a pretend mode of mentalizing, relying on diagnoses and jargon to describe internal experiences and thus distance himself from them. The treatment goal, then, would be to help Mr. O find the words for his internal experiences that might be underlying his difficulties in attention regulation. Over the course of treatment, Mr. O would begin to describe challenges in his relationship with his own father, and ways in which he had long felt socially uncomfortable and not good enough. In acknowledging these feelings, his longing for more closeness with his wife could also emerge parallel to improvement of his mentalized affectivity in the context of overall family dynamics.

Mrs. O, when asked about her parents, goes into great detail, frequently jumping to speaking about their relationship in the present. Her representations are characterized by anger and frustration, and the therapist often feels like Mrs. O is making a case for how enraging her parents are. At the same time, she continues to want a relationship and hopes to be able to get them to see her side of conflicts and to change. This way of speaking and representing the relationship could be seen through the lens of a preoccupied attachment pattern and suggestive of a strategy for coping with emotions by getting absorbed in them. With Mrs. O, the therapist therefore may focus initially on emotional-validation strategies to help regulate Mrs. O's attention and emotion, before attempting explicit mentalization.

ADVERSE CHILDHOOD EXPERIENCES AND RELATIONAL TRAUMA

As described in Chapter 4, the fact of knowing whether parents were abused or neglected as children is essential for developing comprehensive formulations and effective treatment plans. Evidence shows that most people who use mental health services are never asked about child abuse or neglect (Read et al., 2018). The findings of John Read and colleagues' (2018) study show that

> the majority of cases of child abuse or neglect are not identified by mental health services. Only 28% of abuse or neglect cases identified by researchers are found in the clients' files: emotional abuse, 44%; physical abuse, 33%; sexual abuse, 30%; emotional neglect, 17%; and physical neglect, 10%. Between 0% and 22% of mental health service users report being asked about child abuse. Men and people diagnosed with psychotic disorders are asked less than other people. Male staff ask less often than female staff. Some improvement over time was found. Policies compelling routine enquiry, training, and trauma-informed services are required. (p. 7)

When working with parents, it is indispensable to ask about what has happened in their lives and to actively assess the presence of adverse childhood experiences (ACEs) in the past and in their own parents' childhoods—that is, the presence of transgenerational transmission of relational trauma and how it may be essential to understand their current situations and difficulties as parents. The fact of not assessing ACEs may lead to partial and superficial understanding of the parents we are working with, something that may lead to iatrogenic interventions that can be avoided only by asking explicitly about abuse and neglect.

It is essential to ask parents about the qualities of the relationship with their own parents, while also inquiring specifically about loss and trauma, and to make a point to ask the patient to consider how these experiences affected them at the time and continue to influence them now, in their relationships with their own children. In addition to asking what happened, questions for assessment include the following:

- How did you respond at the time?

- Do you think this experience affects you now? Does it affect your relationship with your own child?

Parents' responses to these questions give us some idea of whether they have been able to develop an organized story around their experiences, particularly traumatic experiences and losses, which plays an important role in being able to contain and regulate emotions that might be related to these experiences. Some parents become absorbed in details about what happened, while others might speak in ways that are disorienting, such as speaking about someone who is dead as though they are alive or reporting abuse and then saying that it was not abuse or that they deserved it. We pay close attention to markers like these, which are associated with an unresolved state of mind in adults and predictive of their children showing disorganized attachments with them.

The Adverse Childhood Experiences questionnaire can be used to get a clearer picture of the relational context in which parents grew up. It is preferable to ask the parent these questions verbally and use Murphy and colleagues' (2014, 2016) format, where the parent responds "never," "once or twice," "sometimes," "often," or "very often," instead of "yes" or "no." By avoiding the yes/no format of the brief questionnaire, we tend to get more nuanced information and a better understanding of the parent's experience. The last question, which asks about whether the parent felt special, loved, or supported by someone in their household, is an important one, and research shows that parents who did not regularly have this experience are more likely to be unresolved with regard to trauma or loss. If the answer is anything other than "never," we ask parents, "Who was that?" While we want to help parents make connections and understand why they are the way they are, considering their own attachment histories, it is especially crucial that we open up their access to their angels in the nursery, because these are the experiences and relationships that they will ultimately be able to use as resources to parent their children.

Finally, the therapist can ask parents about their children's adverse experiences. The primal aim of this is not to determine whether children are at risk, though one may learn information that leads the therapist to consider and/or make a referral to child protective services, and we must always be prepared to do this if needed, in accordance with the laws of our locality. But this is not the main goal. Rather, the objective is to understand the traumas that children may have experienced, to find out the meaning of these for the parent, so we can help them to resolve their painful feelings around those experiences. But, perhaps most importantly, by asking the parent first about their own ACEs and then about their child's ACEs, we reinforce the distinction between the parent and child and the past and the present, to separate and help them differentiate between what happened to themselves "then" and what is going on with their child "now" (Murphy et al., 2016). What we also often find is that answering these questions about their own child often brings to light that their child has not experienced, and has even been protected from, some of the adversity that they themselves experienced.

We should note that it is not to be expected that parents will always feel comfortable disclosing this information. It is best to discuss, at the beginning of the assessment, that the therapist wants to get to know them, and therapy tends to work best when they feel free to say, think, or feel anything in the here and now of the session. But we also want them to know that they do not have to answer or talk about anything that they do not want to talk about. Asking these questions directly is meaningful, though, because it lets parents know that we can speak about things that are difficult to speak about, and these are things that they (a) may try, on a daily basis, to push to the back of their minds or (b) may be overtly struggling with. So, by asking parents these questions, we let them know that we care and that we are available to listen and talk about whatever has happened in their lives, and we reinforce our stance of making links between behavior and internal experiences, as well as between the past and the present.

Taken together, these questions about attachment experiences and adverse relational experiences (AREs) give us a sense of the ghosts and the angels in the nursery of parents. We gain an understanding of what the parents learned from their environment about what emotions are acceptable, how those emotions can be expressed, and, specifically, how to manage painful emotions such as anger and sadness. Therapists can identify what parents tended to do in the past, and perhaps still do, with stressful emotions:

- Indicators of avoidant attachment: Do they tend to minimize or downplay their emotional experiences? Do they tend to ignore attachment cues that would signal who is available and go it alone?

- Indicators of preoccupied attachment: Do they tend to turn up the volume on expressions of emotion, particularly distress? Do they stay highly vigilant about the availability of other people—whether people are understanding them, connecting with them, available to them? Do they long for closeness in times of distress and tend to turn to others, but have difficulty actually taking in and feeling comforted by others?

- Indicators of fearful attachment: Do they show deep mistrust and avoid reaching out, because they are afraid of rejection, even though they also want proximity for reassurance?

- Indicators of secure attachment: Are they able to balance experiencing and expressing both positive and negative emotions? Do they recognize who is available to them, and are they able to use relationships to help them regulate their emotions?

- Indicators of unresolved loss and trauma: Are there indications that the experience of loss or trauma has been disorganizing for them and interrupts their ability to stay in the present and use attachment relationships for processing and regulating emotions? Do they appear to get flooded and confused in their speech or dissociate when talking about these kinds of experiences?

Recognizing a parent's pattern of attachment can help the therapist better understand what the parent likely expects from relationships and what their usual ways of processing and expressing emotions are. The therapist then considers how these apply specifically in their role and identity as a parent. What are their internal reactions to their own children's emotions? What messages might they be passing on about how emotional experiences are discussed and processed? How do these patterns shape their availability to their child? What are their expectations about how others would react to their emotions, which might be transferred to the therapist?

These are all questions therapists should ask themselves when considering the ghosts in the nursery—the needs the parent may have had when they were young that remained unmet and have left the parent with the options either to avoid acknowledging them or to cry out for help in ways that might seem inappropriate.

Attachment history and AREs interviews also provide information about the angels in the nursery—that is, someone who, for even a moment, gave the parent an experience of feeling special, loved, protected, and safe. These figures and memories should be noted and included in the case formulation. By prompting the parent to reflect on them, the therapist helps the parent increase their access to the positive resources that they have internalized. In remembering such moments, the parent is more likely to experience that "good-enoughness" inside themselves, which is an asset in parenting.

Multicultural Orientation

The mentalizing stance is aligned with a multicultural orientation. Multicultural orientation (Davis et al., 2018) refers to a way of understanding and relating to clients' cultural identities. It is a lifelong process that includes three central components: *cultural humility* (remaining other-oriented and maintaining a lifelong stance of learning and self-reflection), *cultural opportunities* (inquiring and initiating conversations that facilitate exploration of the client's identity), and *cultural comfort* (feeling at ease, calm, and relaxed with clients whose backgrounds are different than the therapist's).

Furthermore, the egalitarian positive of thinking together side by side with the parent—rather than being an expert offering interpretations, guidance, or advice—challenges traditional hierarchical and patriarchal systems that have historically placed patients, particularly those from non-White, non-Western, and low-socioeconomic backgrounds, in the position of "other" and implicitly supported the "White-savior complex."

Systems are created by people, so, like individual people, they include mentalization (Fonagy et al., 2021). When we watch the news or popular media, we can notice who is being mentalized and seen as three-dimensional and agentic, and whose thoughts, feelings, intentions, and behaviors are restricted to a one- or two-dimensional conceptualization. Next time you watch the news or your TV show, notice who is represented and how they are represented. Where are representations limited, and who is not represented and mentalized at all?

When we take a mentalizing stance, we mentalize not only individuals but also systems. We recognize that none of us can be completely free from being influenced by the systems in which we grew up and live. This is similar to the fact that we all lose our capacity to mentalize. But within the mentalizing stance, we can be a participant observer, make the implicit explicit, notice and name, and, in recognizing the systemic influences at play, offer a deeper level of understanding and empathy to our patients and reestablish our own agency and intentionality instead of being blindly driven or compelled by the systems we are embedded in.

What does this look like, clinically, though? Assessments should be conducted from a multicultural lens, including (a) questions about parents' and children's identities; (b) questions about their experiences related to their visible and nonvisible identities, such as racism or other forms of bias; and (c) an openness and curiosity about how the parents view things within their own cultural lens. The Cultural Formulation Interview in the fifth edition of the *Diagnostic and Statistical Manual of Mental Disorders* (*DSM-5*) provides useful guidance to incorporate into our assessment questions (Lewis-Fernández et al., 2017). Some sample questions—reproduced but with modifications made for an interview with a parent—include the following:

- How do you understand the problems that you are experiencing as a parent/ with your child? What do you think are the causes of these problems?

- What do others in your family, your friends, or others in your community think is causing these problems?

- For you, what are the most important aspects of your background or identity?

- Are there any aspects of your background or identity that you think have shaped you as a parent or your way of parenting?

  - Often, aspects of people's background or identity have shaped them as a parent, for better or worse. By "background or identity," I mean, for example, the communities you belong to, the languages you speak, where you or your family are from, your race or ethnic background, your gender or sexual orientation, or your faith or religion. What aspects of your identity do you feel have been most salient in shaping you as a parent?

- Are there any aspects of your background or identity that are causing concerns or difficulties for you? Are there any aspects of your child's background or identity that are causing concerns or difficulties for you?

- Often, people look for help from many different sources, including different kinds of doctors, helpers, or healers. In the past, what kinds of treatment, help, advice, or healing have you sought for these difficulties?

- Sometimes therapists and patients misunderstand each other because they come from different backgrounds or have different expectations. Have you been concerned about this with me today and is there anything that I/we can do to provide you with the care you need?

In addition to these questions, the therapist asks about the child's identities and the meanings of those for the parent. Certain aspects of identity can have various meanings for parents, including children's skin tones, style of dress, sexuality and gender expression, and disabilities—and ways in which their children's identities are different from or shared with them.

Exploring identity goes beyond asking directly about identities: It involves listening for what aspects of identity are most salient for the parent and their child at any given moment. Most importantly, the therapist remains curious about what it is like for parents to hold certain identities, or what aspects of their identity mean to them. Exploration of identity can include inquiries about what their social experiences have been, what certain identities or terms mean to them, how their identities intersect, and how they have been impacted by current events. A developmental lens is also crucial, recognizing that how people see themselves is likely to change over time. Therapists can also support parents in reflecting on how their identities have developed.

Weaving exploration of identity into the assessment is important to show that you are comfortable talking about various forms of identity and that you want to understand the parents' experiences. While it is impossible to avoid stereotypes and biases, therapists must (a) be aware of the assumptions they may be inclined to make and (b) focus on an open and curious stance. It is often helpful to be clear in explaining to parents that you are asking questions about their background because you do not want to make any assumptions about their experience. There are some parents whose cognition dominates their emotions, and, of course, there are some parents whose emotions drown out cognition. Mentalized affectivity represents the potential not just to balance cognition and affect but to integrate them. For example, a parent might choose to tolerate a negative emotion, as it allows them to learn from an experience. Some questions that a mentalization-informed therapist can hold in mind when considering how parents have been shaped by the cultures that they are embedded in include the following:

- Which emotions do the parents have an easier time mentalizing? Why?

- What are the cultural expectations around expression of emotion?

- How does it feel to explicitly mentalize and verbalize self-states? Is this allowed culturally, or should one prefer implicit subtle ways of mentalizing?

Finally, mentalization involves attempting to see yourself from the outside, and, as such, therapists must be aware of their own identities—both those that may be visible to a patient (e.g., skin color) and those that are less or not visible (e.g., religion, socioeconomic status). The choice to disclose aspects of your own identity as a therapist is one that we recommend approaching thoughtfully but cannot provide advice on. The choice to make disclosures to the patient about your identity and/or experiences should be done in the service of enhancing mentalization and in thinking together with a supervisor/consultation group and the parent, so that disclosures do not stand alone—their meanings are explored through the mentalizing lens of the internal experiences they bring up, as well.

Nevertheless, regardless of the "realities," all therapists should hold in mind how their patients may perceive them and how the therapeutic relationship may be shaped by their identity in relation to the patient's identity (e.g., trans patient with cisgender therapist, Indigenous patient with White therapist). Being able to invite discussion (without forcing it) is the foundation of the mentalizing approach.

MENTALIZING WITH PARENTS: "WHAT IS YOUR BIGGEST FEAR, AND WHAT IS YOUR BIGGEST HOPE, FOR THIS CHILD TODAY?"

Asking this simple question may begin to open the window into what is blocking, inhibiting, or challenging a parent's capacity for reflective functioning. It can also help the clinician explore parental expectations and understand who the child is to the parent—that is, what they represent from the past and in the present. For example, a child could remind a parent of their own parent or of themselves in the past, or a child could trigger feelings in the present, such as of incompetence—a representation of the parents' failures now.

CASE CONCEPTUALIZATION AND TREATMENT PLANNING

Having now thoroughly described the assessment process and our mode of listening and inquiring throughout, we present a model of case conceptualization. The reader will notice that while there is an emphasis on mentalizing and early experience, the case formulation includes a conceptualization of the parent's general level of functioning that one would consider in any mental status exam or initial intake assessment. Following is the outline guiding the proposed mentalization-informed case formulation:

1. The problems that are bringing the parent to treatment

2. Salient aspects of the parent's identity and the child's identity

3. General level of functioning
   a. Intelligence
   b. Capacity for reality testing
   c. Neurological or cognitive deficits
   d. Presence of symptom-focused disorder (e.g., major depressive disorder, generalized anxiety disorder, psychotic disorders)
   e. Level of personality functioning (including borderline, narcissistic, antisocial, paranoid, and histrionic personality traits)

4. The mentalizing profile of the parent
   a. What dimensions of mentalizing does the parent tend to use with ease?

b. Which are more difficult?

    i. Self–Other

    ii. Internal–External

    iii. Cognitive–Affective

    iv. Implicit–Explicit

    v. Identifying–processing–expressing

c. When mentalizing breaks down, what prementalizing modes does the parent tend to use?

    i. Psychic equivalence

    ii. Teleological

    iii. Pretend

d. How quickly do they recover, and how do they recover?

e. What level do you expect the therapeutic work to focus on?

    i. Attention regulation

    ii. Affect regulation and mentalized affectivity

    iii. Explicit mentalizing

5. Presence of AREs

a. Did the parent suffer AREs during their own childhood?

b. Impact of AREs on present functioning and parenting

c. AREs and trauma-specific reflective functioning

6. Attachment profile and object relations

a. Epistemic trust—open and balanced versus hypervigilant or overly trusting

b. Representation of self

c. Representation of others

d. Representation of relationships

e. State of mind regarding attachment

    i. Valuing of attachment relationships

    ii. Normalizing or minimizing of attachment needs

    iii. Idealizing of attachment figures

    iv. Angry preoccupation with attachment figures or attachment needs

    v. Vague preoccupation around attachment figures or attachment needs

7. Relevant cultural factors that shape parenting or parent–child relationship

TREATMENT PLAN INFORMED BY CASE CONCEPTUALIZATION

We now describe how the case conceptualization shapes the treatment plan. The first three items in the case conceptualization describe the parent in terms of all of the factors that might shape the work and their capacity for mentalizing. This information is important because it will shape the goals and what might be expected from the treatment process, as well as what other referrals might be necessary. For example, if a parent is on the autism spectrum, if they are currently exhibiting signs of depression, or if their thinking tends to be concrete and they have poor reality testing, these are all factors that play a role in what level of mentalization they will be able to achieve. While it is useful to know these factors, we also do not see them as a reason to not engage in a mentalization-informed treatment. We believe that most, if not all, parents can benefit from this approach and expand their capacities in ways that will benefit them and their children. But we also want to ensure that alongside the goals of our treatment, other supports are being engaged and utilized—for example, psychiatric medications, substance use treatment, or a more intensive individual therapy.

The heart of the case conceptualization is the mentalizing profile of the parent. The goal for the four dimensions of mentalizing is to achieve balance. While parents will shift between dimensions frequently, it is helpful to have a sense of areas of mentalizing that tend to be strengths for them, and areas where they could increase their abilities that could be a focus in therapy. We find it helpful to pick one or two areas on these four dimensions to target. We also pay specific attention to the capacity for mentalized affectivity and whether there are deficits in identifying, processing, or expressing affects that should be addressed. Finally, we do not expect mentalizing capacities to be uniform. We (a) expect that some content might be more difficult for parents to mentalize around and (b) are alert to trauma-specific reflective functioning and whether work specifically around the experiences of trauma is going to be necessary, because research shows that parents' trauma-specific reflective functioning predicted their children's attachment years later, independent of other factors involved in the actual traumas experienced. So, if a parent has experienced trauma, we want to understand their ability to mentalize around it and to address that experience in treatment if needed.

Generating an idea about which prementalizing modes parents are prone to shift to and, even more specifically, what that might look like for them is important to have at the outset of treatment, because nonmentalizing begets nonmentalizing, so being aware of what to look out for as signals that mentalizing has gone offline can help therapists to notice and address these moments. We also pay attention to the parents' capacities to restore mentalizing after these moments. Similar to rupture-and-repair processes in relationships, avoiding mentalizing breakdowns is not possible and likely not even therapeutic. The overarching goal of therapy is to help parents be able to identify, manage, and then restore mentalizing when their capacities have been overwhelmed or gone offline. We can think of this as working within the parents' zone of proximal development, so that their capacities are challenged enough to be able to grow, but not so overwhelmed that they cannot be brought back online.

As we have described in earlier chapters, the capacity to mentalize develops in the context of attachment relationships and epistemic trust, and the quality of the therapeutic relationship and the ability to establish epistemic trust are important determinants of the outcome. Describing the parent's attachment patterns and representations gives us clues about how the parent might relate to us and others, and what they might be expecting. Knowing these patterns helps us to understand their perspective, remain open and compassionate, and make therapeutic choices that could provide a corrective emotional experience by violating their expectations and offering them a different way of relating.

Finally, in addition to holding in mind identity, we note salient cultural factors that should also be held in mind so that treatment goals and processes are in alignment with the patients' cultural values.

TREATMENT PLAN STRUCTURE

The treatment plan not only includes where to start and the goals of the therapeutic process but also must consider the optimal structure of treatment. Parents may present to treatment requesting child therapy, family therapy, individual therapy, or couples therapy. The assessment serves to clarify for the therapist what the parents' current abilities are, where there are opportunities for gains to be made, and then, ultimately, what format would best support the aims. This aspect of the work may mean that the therapist explains to the parent that they recommend a different format than the one that the parent initially requested, and the therapist must be prepared to explain their recommendations by translating the formulation in a way that creates a motivation in the parent to pursue further sessions. In the context of a mentalization-informed treatment, the feedback session has as its primary aim to introduce the parent to a different way of thinking and understanding their child from a curious and collaborative stance with the therapist.

CASE CONCEPTUALIZATION AND TREATMENT PLAN FOR MRS. AND MR. O

As we described in Chapter 1, Mr. O and Mrs. O are the married parents of a 9-year-old girl, Cristina, and a 7-year-old boy, Jack. They presented to therapy because Cristina had been referred, by her school counselor, for treatment for obsessive-compulsive disorder. In the assessment phase, the therapist learned that Mr. and Mrs. O were discussing separating, though they did not believe that their children were aware. Mr. and Mrs. O have different understandings of their daughter's anxiety symptoms, but both are grounded in a sense of certainty. When Cristina's anxiety is high or she has a meltdown, Mrs. O is inclined to become more teleological and try to fix the problem, while Mr. O tends to take a position of psychic equivalence, where he cannot imagine that Cristina has any problem.

Emotionally, Mrs. O is open in therapy and can name feelings, but she has difficulty actually mentalizing affectivity for herself and others (e.g., Cristina), including both processing and expressing it. Mr. O has difficulty with mentalized affectivity as well, especially in terms of others.

The therapist developed the following case conceptualization:

1. Presenting problems

   a. Cristina's anxiety symptoms

   b. Conflict in the relationship between parents

2. Both Mr. and Mrs. O are neurotypical. Highly intelligent. Reality testing is generally intact. Mrs. O reported a history of depressive symptoms.

3. Mrs. O is White, cisgender, heterosexual, and left a fulfilling full-time career to work part-time after having children. Mr. O is Latin American, born in the United States after his parents immigrated to a "typical American suburb." English is the sole language spoken in the home.

4. Mentalizing profile of Mrs. O

a. What dimensions of mentalizing does the parent tend to use with ease?

    i. Self–Other—has greater difficulty mentalizing herself

    ii. Internal–External—balanced

    iii. Cognitive–Affective (mentalized affectivity)—cognition and affect not integrated, is able to identify emotions but has more difficulty with processing and expressing affects

    iv. Implicit–Explicit—difficulties slowing down and explicitly mentalizing, tends to rely on her connection with her daughter to mentalize

b. When mentalizing breaks down, what prementalizing modes does the parent tend to use?

    i. Teleological—wants to take action to help her daughter

c. How quickly do they recover, and how do they recover?

    i. With scaffolding, mentalizing can be recovered relatively easily.

d. Where do we expect therapy to focus in terms of the three levels?

    i. Attention regulation is well established.

    ii. Some difficulties with affect regulation, specifically a tendency to get overwhelmed by emotion

    iii. Mostly able to work in therapy at the level of explicit mentalizing

5. Mentalizing profile of Mr. O

    a. What dimensions of mentalizing does the parent tend to use with ease?

        i. Self–Other—has greater difficulty mentalizing others

        ii. Internal–External—focuses more on external aspects rather than internal experiences

        iii. Cognitive–Affective (mentalized affectivity)—cognition and affect not integrated, has difficulty with identifying, processing, and expressing affects

        iv. Implicit–Explicit—difficulties slowing down and explicitly mentalizing, tends to avoid explicit mentalizing

    b. When mentalizing breaks down, what prementalizing modes does the parent tend to use?

        i. Psychic equivalence—has difficulty comprehending the internal experiences of others, separate from himself

    c. How quickly do they recover, and how do they recover?

        i. Mentalizing can be challenging to restore, because it is underdeveloped

    d. Where do we expect therapy to focus in terms of the three levels?

        i. Techniques focused on attention regulation will be needed to establish epistemic trust.

        ii. Difficulties with affect regulation will need to be addressed through mentalized affectivity for himself.

        iii. May be able to work at the level of explicit mentalizing once attention regulation and epistemic trust are more established

6. AREs

    a. Mrs. O reported experiencing emotional maltreatment and neglect in her family.

    b. Mr. O did not report any significant relational trauma history.

7. Attachment profile and object relations, based in attachment

    a. Mrs. O is valuing attachment but experiences strong emotions in the context of attachment relationships.

    b. Mr. O is dismissive of attachment relationships and tends to minimize his own and others' attachment needs.

8. For Mr. O, there may be intergenerational trauma related to parents emigrating from Latin America.

Treatment Plan: In terms of parent work, the goal of therapy is to help Mrs. and Mr. O be able to come together—that is, think together—in order to support Cristina in the therapeutic work needed to address her anxiety symptoms. The mentalizing approach will target mentalized affectivity for both parents, but with Mr. O, focus first on establishing attention regulation and affect regulation. The therapist will need to pay close attention to moments when both parents are overly certain in different, often opposing, ways about Cristina's internal experience. In addressing these modes of prementalizing, the goal is to help Mr. and Mrs. O shift to a more authentic way of interacting with and relating to each other, as well as Cristina, and to feel more confident in their capacities to mentalize Cristina. A greater capacity for mentalizing others will help them to improve the quality of their own relationship, potentially reducing tensions within the home, and to improve their relationship with Cristina. In terms of attachment, the therapist will be aware of their tendency toward quite different strategies—namely, Mrs. O's strong attention to emotion (as a contrast to her own childhood experiences) and Mr. O's tendency to minimize or downplay attachment needs. The goal of therapy will be to help both Mrs. and Mr. O tolerate and stay present and connected with the emotions they and their daughter experience in challenging moments.

CONCLUDING SUMMARY

- Effective formulations and treatment plans for parents are always based on rigorous and comprehensive assessments of their past and present lives.

- These assessments must include an active exploration of ACEs potentially suffered by parents, their own parents, and their children.

- A mentalization-informed therapist will always try to keep a mentalizing stance when working with parents, and it is important to maintain this position from the intake interview with the parents: curiosity, not-knowing, collaboration, perspective taking, developmental perspective, looking past behavior to internal experiences, genuine and authentic use of self (making your own mind transparent), and playfulness and humor.

- The goals of parent assessment are as follows: Develop an understanding of the problems the parent is coming in for help with; create a profile of the parent's temperament, personality, and attachment patterns; assess the quality of their relationships; determine where the parent is on the developmental spectrum in the role as a parent; assess the conflicts or struggles they are facing internally; create a profile of their capacity to mentalize, including when and in what ways their mentalization breaks down and how to get it back on track and which prementalizing modes of functioning seem predominant; assess the parent's mentalized affectivity (identifying, modulating, and expressing emotions) and overall affect regulation profile.

- We must always keep a multicultural orientation, as a way of understanding and relating to parents' cultural identities.

5 MENTALIZATION-INFORMED TREATMENT WITH PARENTS

A Scaffolding Process

The goals of our work with parents are determined by the assessment and, particularly, our understanding of the parents' difficulties and strengths, their mentalizing profile, and that of their children and the larger family system. Therapists often feel a pull to work on explicit mentalizing prematurely. When a therapist is not attuned to where parents are, developmentally, in their capacity to mentalize, they risk creating a nonmentalizing environment where cycles of prementalizing functioning will emerge. Assessing and strengthening epistemic trust as well as parents' capacities for attentional control and affect regulation facilitates creativity and imagination in our work with parents, without the pressure of "knowing."

SCAFFOLDING MENTALIZATION: THE OVERARCHING FRAMEWORK

Scaffolding is thought of as working within the parent's own zone of proximal development with regard to mentalization and parenting, where the therapist avoids taking over the mentalizing processes as much as possible. Instead, the

https://doi.org/10.1037/0000341-006
Working With Parents in Therapy: A Mentalization-Based Approach, by N. Malberg, E. Jurist, J. Bate, and M. Dangerfield

therapist seeks to create a supportive environment that can serve as a secure base and safe haven for parents, so that they can develop their own capacities to provide a secure base and safe haven for their children across different developmental stages.

The concept of scaffolding of treatment requires a good assessment and formulation of the functioning of the parents during the initial phases of treatment. We attempt to create a preliminary formulation that will guide us in determining where to start working with parents (this chapter). Once we begin our work with parents, we embark on a process that begins with establishing epistemic trust (see Chapter 2, this volume) in order to facilitate the exploration of parents' relational past (see Chapter 3) and existing potential for mentalized affectivity (see Chapter 2). We approach the treatment with interventions that scaffold parents' existing and emerging reflective functioning capacities while attending to the intensity and frequency of nonmentalizing cycles in the here and now of the therapeutic work and the everyday life experiences of parenting (see Chapter 1). Informed by a developmental model, the treatment is framed by the three blocks that constitute "the mentalization line of development."

Sometimes when parents present with specific demands it is difficult to know where to start or how to intervene from a mentalizing perspective while maintaining the alliance. We often feel stuck and become quite teleological ourselves by giving advice or assuming the role of the expert. It is in this context that we find the proposed framework of intervention helpful. When epistemic trust and the capacity for mentalized affectivity are scaffolded and restored in parents, then we find that parents become able to gain from the therapeutic relationship, their relationship with each other, and their relationship with their child in ways that allow them to find sustainable solutions for problems and find rewarding feelings in the experience of parenting.

TAILORING TREATMENT TO THE DEVELOPMENTAL LINE OF MENTALIZING

From a developmental model of parental mentalization, the treatment can be guided by a fluid journey through a scaffold based on the three building blocks of mentalizing, which helps the therapist to track the developmental line of mentalization throughout the process of the session: (a) attention regulation, (b) affect regulation, and (c) explicit mentalizing. Following this framework seeks to guide and help the therapist's technique and the nature of their intervention.

All three of these blocks contribute to the unfolding of mentalized affectivity: While affect regulation is most obviously a source of processing emotions, attention regulation is a source of identifying emotions, and explicit mentalization is a source for expressing emotions.

Attention Regulation

Prior to the development of affect regulation, there is first the ability to regulate attention (which we refer to in Chapter 1). We do not often discuss attention regulation or control in the context of therapy, though it has been written about by attachment researchers like Mary Main (1996), as well as the parent–infant "baby watchers," such as Beatrice Beebe (2005). Attention regulation is most obviously present in joint attention and when we are engaged in a shared activity with a patient. Techniques for attention regulation include the following:

* Noticing and naming what is happening in the here and now, as well as creating moments for joint attention regarding a particular situation by inviting the parent to sequence the situation and slowly explore it from multiple perspectives, while paying attention to the affective shifts in the room—not only in the parent but also in the therapist.

* Attending physiological sensations and experiences is critical to mentalizing, and yet many parents have been ignoring their bodies and missing the affective cues—or worse, suppressing them. One aspect of attention regulation is therefore focusing attention inward and connecting with emotions in the body, even without naming them verbally.

* Nonverbal contingency can prove to be very powerful, particularly in the context of cultural differences: When working with parents, paying attention to posture, level of eye contact, and vocal tone can be very important in creating an atmosphere where epistemic trust can emerge. It conveys respect and genuine interest in the subjective experience of the other.

Affect Regulation

Affect regulation in parents is a difficult arena to manage and work on, particularly because it involves several important variables—among them, the parent's temperament and how they interact with the child's budding capacity for mentalized affectivity especially in the context of emotions that feel forbidden or are often avoided (e.g., feeling hatred and rage toward one's child). The following are important considerations in working from an affect regulation perspective with parents in their developmental journey:

- Awareness of empathic validation as a valuable and powerful tool conducive to motivation to share and learn. Consciously finding ways of "being with" the parent in their emotional state.
  - This is particularly true when working with parents functioning in a psychic equivalence mode, where their own internal experiences are so overwhelming and real that they cannot be observed and reflected upon.

- Drawing on an understanding of the parent's history to recognize and tolerate the childlike aspects of the parent's emotional landscape, keeping in mind that these are parts of the parent that may not have received the care that they needed.

- Rather than trying to move a parent away from dysregulated states, approach them with an understanding that they do not have the words, so we cannot expect them to use them; we must help them to find their own optimal level of regulation and play with finding the words when necessary.

- The focus is not only on downregulating emotion. Optimal emotion arousal and regulation is seen through a midrange model, where too much unregulated emotion interferes with the ability to mentalize, but too little emotion also blocks it.

- Supporting parents' integration of cognition and affect.

As with attention regulation, the therapist consistently attends to breakdowns in affect regulation in the context of parent sessions or when parents bring sequences that include their own inability to manage their emotions and those of their child. So, the therapist works at two levels: whate is happening in the here and now of the session and also what has happened at home around affect regulation.

The therapist addresses that dysregulation presents in moments of overarousal and acting out, while also paying attention to overregulation (where a parent is tightly controlled and holding everything in). At the more extreme end of the spectrum, a parent's emotions may even appear shut off, and flat affects predominate. Emotion-regulating techniques in working with parents aim to maintain an optimal level of emotional arousal and regulation, hence there is a strong focus on the development of mentalized affectivity in parents.

Several techniques can be used to increase or decrease emotional arousal:

- Marked mirroring and empathic validation are key components of enhancing affect regulation in psychotherapy. When working with parents at this level, the therapist may need to spend a lot of time validating difficult emotions without judgment or attempts to offer alternatives that might be misconstrued as corrections. *Marked mirroring* (Fonagy et al., 2002) is a specific form of empathic validation that refers to the capacity of the therapist to show the parent, verbally and nonverbally, that the therapist is trying to understand and interpret the parent's signals and expressions of emotion. Importantly, the therapist is not only attempting to provide an attuned and congruent response but also communicating to the parent that this expression being reflected back belongs to the parent's internal world. In other words, it is the parent's subjective experience that the therapist is attempting to represent, not the therapist's own feelings. Repeated marked mirroring seeks to reinforce the parent's sense of ownership and selfhood in the context of the parenting experience.

- Clarification, to bring the parent back to connecting with their experiences, is another technique. We inquire and challenge or confront, concerning what is unclear or seems disconnected from reality. This is done alongside empathic validation regarding the difficulties in facing and talking about some of the challenging situations and feelings around parenting. If a parent is giving an intellectual explanation that is difficult for us to follow or understand, we express our confusion and emphasize that our efforts to clarify are based on a desire to fully understand and to be authentic so that we can best help them to sort through the challenges. This is very important to avoid feelings of shame and feeling judged or to evaluate in the context of the therapeutic relationship. For example,

  > It is clear to me that you have read extensively about autism and worried about this with Joey. However . . . I am still a bit confused and frankly a bit curious about how difficult it has been for you to talk to your mom about what you perceive as cruel behavior toward your child because she dislikes his behavior . . . That must be so painful for you . . .

- The therapist and parent work together to identify triggers or moments when the parent's capacity for affect regulation—and, thus, mentalization—goes offline in response to characteristics of their child or specific behaviors, or something else in their environment.

- Practicing toleration of negative emotions through verbalization is very important in strengthening the parent's capacity to self-observe and regulate during moments of high levels of emotional arousal and activation. Most important, it seeks to help the parent to be forgiving of themselves.

- Creating a language of regulation, one that parents can practice during their own sessions, is helpful in learning new ways to respond to and play with potentially threatening relational interactions—for example, speaking of "high and low volume of emotions" when helping a parent retell the story of a difficult moment when both they and the child went offline, or identifying *bumpy roads* (sequences leading to nonmentalizing exchanges).

Inviting parents to recount how emotions were explored and expressed in their family of origin and their cultural environment is very important. This is particularly relevant when working with families emigrating from other cultural environments where expectations regarding children's behavior and parenting responses might clash with the new culture. As parents, we all want to offer the best to our children; however, sometimes it is difficult when we offer something better than what we had and we do not receive the response that we expect from the child. When a therapist shows curiosity and empathy toward a parent, there is a better chance that new social learning can take place. Putting ourselves in the shoes of the parent is often challenging, though, especially when we feel conflicted about our loyalty toward the child or when aspects of the parent's functioning trigger our own attachment style or relational history. Mentalizing our own experience of the parent is very important to regulating our own emotions, so that we can maintain a therapeutic stance, and highlights the importance of reflective professional consultation and supervision.

WAYS IN WHICH WE CREATE SPACES OF JOINT ATTENTION AND COREGULATION WITH PARENTS

- interacting with awareness about the impact of our nonverbal behavior (ostensive cues), attempting to maintain an open and welcoming attitude (e.g., tone of voice, posture, facial expressions) during sessions
- empathizing with and validating parents' experiences and explicitly "putting ourselves in their shoes"
- displaying genuine curiosity for aspects of their culture (expectations of parenting: What is their "myth of parenting"?)
- working clearly and explicitly in deciding the objectives of the treatment and providing psychoeducation regarding mentalizing
- explicitly asking questions that make parents feel understood in their fears, sufferings, and difficulties as parents (past and present) from a nonjudgmental and genuine stance

Explicit Mentalizing

When a parent's attention and emotion are regulated, then we have the foundations for engaging in explicit-mentalizing interventions. Such explicit-mentalizing interventions include linking mental states to behaviors, playing with different perspectives, noticing breakdowns in mentalizing and intervening to restore it, and mentalizing the therapeutic relationship.

A range of interventions to link mental states to behaviors prove helpful in this context. For example,

- Asking, "I have a good picture of what it looked like was going on from the outside, but can we think together about what was happening on the inside?"

- Suggesting hypotheses and checking with the parent. For example, "I am just wondering—because it stood out to me when we talked last week—do you think when your daughter screams at you, it reminds you of how angry your mother used to get, and that really gets your heart rate going?"

- Sequencing can help not to get the facts straight but to explore, with parents, how their internal experiences and behaviors interact with others' (particularly their children's). For example,

  > So she pulls away and withdraws, I can see how that may feel like she is rejecting you, particularly because of your hope you would have a mother–daughter relationship that was different from your own. It sounds like then you feel angry but work hard to keep it all in, but then end up being disconnected from the relationship. Of course, it sounds like you're doing this to protect her from your anger, you're trying to hang in there with her during this difficult time. But I wonder how she experiences it?

- Being attentive to stopping or interrupting prementalizing modes, when the patient is in teleological, psychic equivalence, or pretend mode. When the patient is in teleological mode, we interrupt this mode by being transparent about our mind and our urges to act—to think about this in the context of the relationship. When the patient is in psychic equivalence mode, we resist the urge to challenge or point out distortions, and instead validate their experience (e.g., "To feel like everyone is against you is just awful"). When the patient is in pretend mode, we address the detached quality and attempt to engage them in a more genuine exploration of internal experience.

- Mentalizing the therapeutic relationship represents the highest level of mentalizing and requires processing how our perceptions, internal experiences, and behaviors are impacting the parent—and vice versa—in the therapeutic relationship. It is the most challenging to do in therapy because the here and now of the interpersonal interaction is arousing or stimulating, thus making it difficult to think and feel at a slower pace and without jumping to action. When a parent's behavior changes in an unpredictable way during a session, for example, the therapist checks with themselves and tries to observe and understand their own reaction to what is going on in the room between themselves and the parent. Second, the therapist speaks openly about their own mentalizing process and invites the parent's curiosity to understand what is going on. Finally, the therapist tries to link it to what happens to the parent in other relationships, especially with their child.

• Explicitly mentalizing fears and hopes. Asking the parent, upon meeting them, about their biggest fear and their biggest hope for their child can provide an opportunity to observe the parent's capacity to balance the self–other dimension and to think about behavior as a communication, as well as their capacity for mentalized affectivity when discussing difficulties with their child. We also establish the foundations for epistemic trust as we listen, validate, and empathically respond to the parent.

Holding in mind the parent's attachment and communication patterns helps the therapist to notice ways in which emotions may be dealt with and how epistemic trust may be engaged. Then, the capacity for mentalization is addressed in different ways depending on the parent's attention regulation, affect regulation, and explicit-mentalizing capacities. Interventions are tailored to expand the parent's mentalizing, without overwhelming the system. The therapist may move back and forth, addressing each of the three developmental levels, depending on where the parent is at any given moment.

WHEN PREMENTALIZING MODES EMERGE

As described previously in this book, the prementalizing modes that characterize understanding (or lack thereof) of mental states early in development become integrated between 4 and 8 years of age and give rise to mentalization. Throughout the lifespan, however, children and adults alike may use prementalizing modes to make sense of the interpersonal world. Sometimes this is necessary. For example, if a parent has seen their child take a bad fall that's resulted in a gash above their eye, they need to jump to action, getting something to put on it and bringing their child to the doctor (teleological mode). The problem is when the interpersonal environment requires mentalization but the parent cannot access their capacities, either because they never developed them fully or because they have broken down in the face of heightened affect or stress.

The mentalizing stance is central for a therapist working from this perspective, as well as being aware of when and why prementalizing modes emerge in the therapeutic environment with parents. This focus helps the therapist to support the parent in identifying situations that inhibit their reflective functioning capacities. It is also of relevance for the therapist to make technical modifications to motivate parents to exercise their self-reflective capacities and identify emotions and thoughts that get in the way of effective and mentalizing parenting.

As therapists, we need to be mindful of our prementalizing responses in the context of our clinical work with parents. Often, nonmentalizing begets nonmentalizing, so when a parent's mentalizing goes offline, ours is more likely to do so, as well. We see these moments as opportunities to be observed and understood in the context of our growing therapeutic relationship. It is at these times, when the therapist can show genuine humility and openness about their own struggles with understanding and managing challenging situations, that the door to epistemic trust can be opened.

What do we mean by that? By accepting and accompanying parents in the context of behavioral manifestations of prementalizing modes and offering new ways of responding and understanding, we can create a "relational lab" where new social learning can take place. Paying attention to our own emotional and cognitive responses to parents in the here and now of the session is of the utmost importance in this approach. Prementalizing modes of functioning tend to have the effect of creating a certain feeling of loneliness and disconnection relationally that one must learn to pay attention to. In the same way that often parents send their children to time-out instead of staying close and help them "organize their feelings," therapists can leave parents in "time out" feeling misunderstood and judged.

CLINICAL ILLUSTRATION: ADDRESSING PREMENTALIZING MODES WITH MR. AND MRS. O

Teleological Mode: It Is Obvious You Just Don't Care!

Mr. and Mrs. O had a tough weekend with Cristina, as she was withdrawn and not very communicative. They emailed the therapist, expressing their frustration and asking for help. The therapist replied, thanking them for the communication and offering an appointment to discuss. Both parents seemed angry and defensive upon arrival. The therapist spoke openly about it, inviting both parents to express their concerns and their feelings. It seemed that they both felt that the therapist did not take seriously enough their difficulties with their daughter. Explicit discussion of those feelings and exploration of the worry and helplessness behind their anger were necessary to restore epistemic trust.

We tend to be in the presence of a teleological stance when parents are able to consider internal experiences only if they are visible and manifested through physical actions—for example, a parent feels loved by their child only if they give them a kiss every day when they come in the door. While for many people this might well be a nice routine that contributes to them feeling loved, the difference in teleological mode is that if they are not greeted with a kiss, the parent believes they are not loved.

The teleological mode may arise in how the parent relates to the therapist—for example, feeling that the therapist cares about them only if the therapist gives them extra time in the parent session after a tough time with their child. The therapist drawn into this mode may feel an urge to "do something"—as in, take action to solve the problem or try to improve the patient's situation. Rather than acting on this without thinking it through, a mentalizing-informed approach recommends that the therapist works to restore mentalizing in themselves and the patient by putting words to the urges they are noticing in themselves to think it through with the patient. For example, when working with a parent who reports that they are feeling totally alone and have no help taking care of their child, the therapist may find themselves beginning to brainstorm solutions or even making recommendations for resources. While these might be helpful to the parent, doing so without reflection will do little to help build the parent's mentalizing capacities in ways that will support their ongoing relationships with others.

As the therapist notices a tendency of going down the path of working in a solution-focused way, they may call attention to this and think with the parent about what is going on between the two of them, and the internal experiences that are not being attended to in this moment as they jump to finding solutions—for example, "We've gotten right into talking about solutions, I think because this is clearly very difficult for you and Cristina and we both want you to feel better. But I think we've skipped some important steps in this process." When we resist the urge to act in the teleological mode, through this exploration, we can help to restore the parent's own affect regulation, which increases epistemic trust—that is, the ability to take in and learn from our relationship.

Furthermore, we frequently find that parents are able to come up with solutions to their problems that previously seemed out of reach. For example, Mr. and Mrs. O got into a pattern with the therapist where, in each session, they would present the latest problem they were having with Cristina. Each week, the therapist would explore the problem with them, they would identify a solution together, and they would return the next week, reporting that it had been a success and then presenting the next latest problem. After several sessions of going on like this, the therapist brought their attention to this rhythm they were in together. When Mr. and Mrs. O reported the success of that week, the therapist said,

> So before we go much further, I actually want to point out something that I am noticing. We seem to be at a point where each time we talk through a problem we come up with a solution that you then try and it's successful and then we move on to the next problem. And that's good, of course, that things are working. But it makes me think that something is happening where we are moving from problem to problem and not looking at the links in a way that can help you in the longer term. You're left feeling like you need to bring the next one to me, and it's like whack-a-mole.

Mr. and Mrs. O agreed with this and elaborated, "Yeah, you're so good," to which the therapist replied, "I have the impression that it's as if you don't think you could be that good or you could do it, Mrs. O, am I getting it right?" Cristina's mother acknowledged, "Yes, I don't know how." The therapist then proposed, "So, would it be helpful if I told you more about what I do and what goes through my mind as we talk this through?"

When Mr. and Mrs. O indicated that they would like to know this, the therapist explained that when thinking through these situations, she thought back to her own experience of being a young girl, what her world had been like then, and what her relationship with her parents had been like—what she remembered finding helpful or longing for. This opened a new area of exploration with Mr. and Mrs. O, to not only think about their own childhoods but also examine what kept them (a) from looking back on them and (b) cut off from this pathway to better understanding their daughter.

This vignette is not meant to suggest that disclosure of the therapist's internal process is the technique that should be applied to build mentalizing. What this scenario illustrates is the process by which the therapist became aware that their mentalization as a dyad was in teleological mode. The therapist became aware of this by self-observing and noticing a tendency to continually engage in problem solving. Once aware, the therapist drew attention to the pattern and the dilemma it posed for her as a therapist—she wanted to be helpful but also felt that some important part of the process was being missed. This is a critical step in the process of restoring mentalizing. It is not a matter of pointing out a failure to mentalize and then redirecting to a mentalizing stance. The therapist instead took a descriptive and reflective approach to how the mother might be experiencing the pattern. By elaborating the parents' experience and bringing their awareness to the dependence and "stuckness" they were experiencing, the therapist helped to bring mentalizing back online, created a connection with the parents, and opened the pathways for learning within the context of the relationship.

Psychic Equivalence Mode: I Know My Child—I Am Her Parent!

Cristina's dad is convinced that his daughter does not like him. He says he can see it in her face and feel it. Nothing the therapist says seems to help. He is very angry at first, but the therapist just stays with his feeling and continues to validate his experience. Minutes later, Mr. O can speak about his confusion and frustration that he feels as his daughter grows up and as he perceives that he is losing their special connection.

Typically, we know we are in the presence of psychic equivalence when a parent is speaking about mental states but is taking a position of certainty and assuming that what they are thinking or feeling must be the only reality. It is tempting, when parents are in this mode, to want to challenge what appears to be a distorted thought—but, as Bateman and Fonagy (2016) suggested, we caution against this. To restore mentalizing when a parent is in psychic equivalence mode, we must first acknowledge to ourselves what is happening and recognize our own urges to challenge, and then shift to a place of empathizing with how it is to be the parent in the world, the way they see it. For example, as Mr. O is saying that his child hates him, we do not attempt to evaluate that thought with him. Instead, we roll with it and elaborate what it is like for him to have that experience, including his underlying longing to connect with his child. We use a similar approach when parents express with certainty something that they believe we think or feel about them. We do not immediately deny it but instead attempt to connect with what this is like for them—for example, "You are coming here to get help and have a therapist who you feel is judging you and ready to shut you down at every turn." Often, this will be enough to help restore the parent's regulation and epistemic trust.

Pretend Mode: I Am OK—My Child Is Just Obviously ADHD!

Mrs. O read an article online that she felt helped her understand Cristina. She said she could see how Cristina was very sensitive to many things and that this was the reason things were so hard for her and why she isolated herself. When asked for an example, Mrs. O began to quote the article and link it to her own observations of her daughter's behavior. However, there was no curiosity or mention of how Cristina might be experiencing things because of her sensitivity—just descriptions based on the article. Mrs. O spoke of her own sensitivity and her mother's and then spoke of how she felt that Cristina just needed some occupational therapy and that this might really improve her quality of life.

We might be in the presence of a pretend mode of functioning when the parent may appear to be exploring the world of mental states but is disconnected from "reality," which may include being disconnected from the reality of the present moment in the therapy room. Parents who are in a pretend mode may talk about their children or their own early childhoods using diagnostic terms and jargon, perhaps sounding as if they are repeating what they have read in a book or heard from another therapist. They may also present long, detailed stories that leave the therapist feeling bored and wondering what the point or purpose is. Bateman and Fonagy (2016) recommended interrupting pretend mode by gently challenging the narrative that the patient is presenting. Ways of gently challenging might include the following:

- "But what do you mean when you say that . . ."

- "I'm not sure I understand what the terms you're using mean for your child specifically . . ."

- "I must be honest—you've kind of lost me in this story, and I'm trying to figure out what might be escaping us here . . ."

- "I am trying to follow what you're saying, but I wonder if we might be going down this path because it's a bit easier or safer than thinking more about . . ."

One example of how this can come up is when parents, particularly those with preoccupied states of mind regarding attachment, talk about their own parents as though they are analyzing them. For example, Mrs. O described her own mother in this way:

> She was a total narcissist, I know that now. My friend pointed it out to me, and then I read about it, and she totally fits it. She is grandiose and manipulative, and she has been this way my whole life.

It would be tempting to be empathic here, but the therapist who notices that this is prementalizing and not actually mentalizing might instead say,

> So I certainly know what people generally mean by using the term "narcissist," and it sounds like that term really helped you understand her better. But it's a bit of a clinical term, and I wonder if you could tell me more about her and what your relationship was like?

IMPORTANT CONSIDERATIONS FOR NAVIGATING MENTALIZING AND PREMENTALIZING MODES IN TREATMENT

- maintaining and monitoring the mentalizing stance of the therapist
- keeping in mind the initial formulation and revisiting expectations considering new clinical material and the parent's functioning
- monitoring the parent's prementalizing moments and working with the parent in becoming aware of relational triggers
- being aware of aiming too high in our interventions, considering parents' ever-changing capacities
- always remembering that there is a child at home who is dependent on the adult(s) in the consulting room

EMERGENCE OF THE PARENT'S REAL FEELINGS ABOUT THE CHILD (AND THEMSELVES)

As we work with parents along the developmental line of mentalizing, and their capacity for mentalization becomes improved and more nuanced, the therapist begins to witness new emotions emerge in expression and gain a clearer picture of how those emotions inhibit parents' mentalizing capacities. For example, the mother of a high school adolescent placed high expectations on her daughter and was distraught about the ways in which her daughter was not meeting them—and, in fact, had no desire to meet them. The mother insisted to the therapist, "I will not be happy unless she goes to college and is successful." After several months of working together, the therapist noted that the mother wanted her daughter to have choices that the mother herself had not had.

After a few sessions, the therapist inquired,

I am struck by how you say that you will not be happy unless she goes to college. I am guessing that you want this for her because you imagine that she will be happy and feel more confident. I wonder if education meant that for you growing up and in your life?

To which the mother replied, "I gave up on my dreams way too quickly, and it's all over for me now, I can't change that, but I do want more for her." At last, the therapist had touched on the deep hopelessness that the mother felt about herself, which was interfering with her ability to see her daughter as a separate person and contributing to her desire to control her daughter. And now, the work around her sense of herself as someone who could still want things could be focused on allowing for a more balanced self–other and cognitive–affective balance functioning for the mom—and with it, a new openness toward imagining what her daughter needed and wanted separately from her.

CONSOLIDATION OF IDENTITY AS A PARENT AND PARENTAL REFLECTIVE FUNCTIONING

The final aim of working with parents is the consolidation of their identity as a parent and their capacity for mentalization, specifically in the context of parenting. Like the process of parental development, children's development consists of many stages. Just as scaffolding is useful in building a skyscraper, it is also useful in approaching both parental and child development. Each "floor" is unique—but, also, each has similar components that will need to be navigated: the child's separation and individuation; aggression and conflict in the parent–child relationship; the parents' own representations of themselves, as well as their representations of the child and the relationship; and how their own experiences are activated. As therapists, we provide the scaffolding as parents do the work of sharpening and putting to use their tools in building their relationship with their child at each stage of development. Each stage requires a reevaluation, a process of actualizing their understanding of their child and themselves. As the "building" gets further along, the scaffolding is no longer needed to support the work.

Of course, as much as we aim to end treatment with parents in a place where they are able to continue in a fulfilling relationship with their child without us, occasionally, new problems do arise in the future, or we discover that something we thought had been dealt with had not been fully resolved—and, thus, scaffolding needs to go back up, so that renovations or repairs can be made. As Daniel Stern (1995) explained, working with parents and their children requires "serial brief treatments" that are, perhaps surprisingly, best suited to the transitional nature of development. We see this repeatedly in our own application of this mentalizing framework. For example, Mr. and Mrs. O may require further support when Cristina starts approaching adolescence, not only due to the challenging moment that adolescence always is for parents but also because of their known difficulties in mentalized affectivity.

END OF TREATMENT

Children and adolescents tend to have a way of letting us know when they are ready to let go and say goodbye. Some children begin to remember things that you did with them, others begin to complain about wanting more time for friends, and so on. Parents also give cues showing that they are ready to end. First and foremost, we see that their mentalizing capacities have improved, and that they are more able to regain their mentalizing without using us. They have often connected or reconnected with people outside of the therapy who have become their supports in this, whether it is a change in the relationship with their partner, joining parenting groups, or engaging with friends in new ways. While problems or symptoms may have resolved, the reality is that parenting is challenging and a lifelong process that, as we describe in Part II, takes on new shapes at each developmental stage.

A good goodbye in psychotherapy with parents is very important because it sets the tone for future contacts, if necessary. It also allows the parents to experience the process of separation and loss while being guided by the mind and the heart of a mentalizing mental health professional. Often, the process of ending treatment activates the parents' difficulties with separation in a way that might get in the way of a good-enough farewell. It is during these moments that the epistemic trust built between therapist and parents becomes under pressure but also can prove to benefit the process of reflection and joint attention, to face the fears, in parents, about letting go and feeling alone again.

Working from a process-oriented framework also proves extremely helpful in the context of ending therapy, as it allows us to revisit the narrative of the treatment with parents, reflect on the gains, and discuss the feared losses. A mentalizing stance in the therapist where good reflective modeling takes place is crucial during this part of the process, as old concerns and teleological needs return and new challenges to parents' mentalized affectivity present themselves—as ghosts in the nursery make their voices heard during times of stress, such as the ending of a treatment, which hopefully has offered the family good-enough holding and containment.

Reflecting and Practicing the Language of Mentalization-Based Treatment Explicitly Throughout

All throughout the process of parent work, from assessment to treatment, we introduce new ways of thinking about the process of mentalizing. First, the therapist models and promotes attention regulation through phrases such as

"Did you notice how your face changed when you began to speak about your son's difficulties?" The language of mentalization is one characterized by doubt and curiosity—for example, "I am not sure, but I am just guessing here . . . I imagine your daughter was perhaps feeling a bit sad . . . ?" The word "imagine" is key here, as it indicates a lack of certainty but also places emphasis on the fact that nobody ever knows for sure what is in someone's mind.

As explored earlier in this chapter, the language of mentalization is also one of affect regulation. Our capacity to mentalize is influenced directly by emotional dysregulation. We seek to expand a parent's capacity to playfully name and notice affective or behavioral changes in themselves and their child—for example, "I can see your emotional volume is becoming higher . . . What do you think we could do to help it go down?"

The use of explicit sequencing of nonmentalizing exchanges in the room is also an important element of a mentalizing-informed intervention. It facilitates the activation of prefrontal regions of the brain and, with it, executive functioning, which facilitates affect regulation. Phrases such as "hot spots of interaction," "'organizing your feelings' moments," and "bumpy roads" are some metaphors that can be used to encapsulate prementalizing modes. To observe, describe, explore, and understand these sequences will help parents stay regulated and mentalizing during moments of stress with their children. During the end-of-treatment phase, we hope to witness a shift in the parent's capacity to use the mentalizing terms and the language of regulation in a way that allows the parent to place the "mentalizing oxygen mask" when the "emotional temperature" changes in the context of the relationship with their child.

Revisiting Fears and Hopes

Revisiting fears and hopes during the period of termination is important, as it allows us to observe changes and transformations in a parent's reflective functioning capacity. It also allows us to place joint attention on the losses and gains of the process and create a story of the treatment process with parents. In this way, we can highlight the strengths of the parents and "keep the door open" to future consultations.

Allowing and Mentalizing the Return of the Symptom

Parents often seek psychological support for their children, motivated by a symptom or difficult set of behaviors. In mentalization terms, they come with "teleological needs and requests"—for example, "Our child is controlling, the whole family is always being ruled by her moods, we need tools to help us manage her, can you help?" or "We have struggled with our son's sleeping issues since he was a baby, we have tried everything, and now he is not going to school because of them—we need strategies." Keeping a mentalizing stance is difficult when faced with parents' demands for solutions—particularly throughout the process of treatment, when we tend to be the recipients, alongside parents, of pressure from other systems such as school. However, when discussing symptomatology, we can offer a developmental (including expectations and realities) and transactional (what belongs to the child, and how does it interact with their relational context—for instance, the parents' own temperaments?) approach, which facilitates "mentalizing the symptom."

The following section presents a proposed scaffolding process of thinking about symptoms with parents throughout our work, but particularly when it appears during the ending phase of the work:

- historical understanding of the symptom from multiple perspectives (parent, child, and therapist). This will include impact on relationships, personal meaning of the symptom, and coconstructed mentalizing of the symptom.

- short-term and long-term concerns about the symptom, in the context of child's development and relational functioning

- revisiting parents' perceived contributions and reinforcing new social learning (strategies)

- explicitly discussing potential challenges to mentalizing now and in the future

In summary, the ending of a treatment is a wonderful opportunity to explore themes that might not have been explored previously or to revisit some that have been touched upon briefly but gently avoided. It is important to remember that it activates the attachment system of not only the parents and children but also the therapists. Different families represent different sets of emotions, moments of joy or rage, and satisfaction or frustration for the therapist. One of the many values of working from a mentalizing stance is the capacity to use one's own experience in helping parents grow and learn—as we do, too. The end of a treatment should be an opportunity for all involved to revisit, reexperience, and learn new ways of dealing with the emotions that leaving and letting go entail. It provides an opportunity to navigate through the building blocks of mentalizing and practice new skills learned in the context of a safe and predictable working therapeutic relationship between the parent and the therapist.

A Clinical Example: Ending Treatment With Mr. and Mrs. O

Mrs. and Mr. O have improved their mentalized affectivity capacities. In addition, they are able to accompany their daughter and appropriately send ostensive cues to promote a relaxed and safe relational experience during stressful times. They now understand the link connecting the tensions between the two of them and their daughter's difficulties. However, during the ending phase, it is important that the therapist helps them in constructing a coherent story of the treatment process, one that contains their gains and their vulnerable areas. Most significantly, it is important that they can use the ending phase as a time to mentalize both their fears and hopes for their daughter, through a lens that is informed by developmental understanding, playfulness, lack of certainty, and genuine curiosity for their experience and that of their child. Therapists, like parents, are there to be left—but how we say goodbye while facing the feelings that come with it is of the utmost importance in the process of consolidating the gains of a therapeutic process with parents.

CONCLUDING SUMMARY

- A mentalization-based therapeutic stance is characterized by genuine curiosity and a not-knowing and nonjudgmental attitude that fosters the emergence of epistemic trust.

- Over the course of treatment, the therapist continues monitoring breakdowns in trust and addresses these as needed.

- Mentalizing is thought of and worked with on a developmental line that goes from attention regulation to affect regulation to explicit mentalizing.

- The treatment process involves a scaffolding approach to support parents' existing capacities and work within their zone of proximal development, as they move along the developmental line of mentalizing.

- Mentalization involves balance and integration of self–other, internal–external, affect–cognition, and implicit–explicit.

- The therapist addresses moments where prementalizing modes take the place of mentalizing.

- Mentalized affectivity and, specifically, mentalizing affects related to ghosts and angels in the nursery is critical to parental mentalization.

- Termination is part of the therapeutic process and involves the reinforcement of mentalizing skills and epistemic trust.

- Development and change are not linear but involve "fits and starts" (Bowlby, 1980). A mentalizing approach restores parents on a developmental trajectory and sets them up with (a) new capacities that will help them in future difficult moments and (b) the knowledge and trust that they can return to therapy or turn to others for support if and when it is needed.

PART **II** MENTALIZING
PARENTING
ACROSS THE
LIFESPAN

6

PARENTING TODAY

Researchers have explored cultural and historical differences in parenting practices for many years (Bastaits & Mortelmans, 2017; Duflos et al., 2020; Krishnakumar & Buehler, 2000). In general, they tend to agree that three major factors often explain differences in parenting style: emotional warmth versus hostility (how loving, warm, and affectionate parents are toward children), autonomy versus control (the degree to which children are given a sense of control over their lives), and structure versus chaos (how much children's lives are given a sense of structure and predictability). For approximately 75 years, studies have been investigating how individual differences in general parenting practices might influence child development. The evidence regarding the fact that the emotional bonds (*attachments*) that children have with their parents or caregivers can have lasting effects is indisputable.

Indeed, attachment theory (Ainsworth, 1985; Bowlby, 1986) has influenced a cultural tide reflected in a profound movement toward a child-centered approach to parenting, which puts the needs of the child at the center of their learning and development. Bowlby's attachment theory emphasized the importance of an infant–caregiver bond—most exclusively with the mother or a

https://doi.org/10.1037/0000341-007
Working With Parents in Therapy: A Mentalization-Based Approach, by N. Malberg, E. Jurist, J. Bate, and M. Dangerfield

primary caregiver. In Bowlby's original formulation of attachment theory (Bowlby, 1982), one of the most important functions of the attachment system is its adaptation to environmental conditions. But despite Bowlby's emphasis on the attachment system's adaptedness, ethological attachment research has concentrated on just one model of early infant–caregiver relationships as the universal strategy—the independent model of Western middle-class families— thus neglecting the differential influence of sociocultural environments on attachment relationships.

Cross-cultural studies (Rothbaum et al., 2002; Trnavsky, 1998; van IJzen- doorn & Kroonenberg, 1988) have demonstrated that these early interactions are influenced by the ecocultural context within which they take place. When we consider cross-cultural research (Brassell et al., 2016; Fox et al., 1995), we find justification for a move away from a matricentric focus and toward a more collective view of attachment, informed by the understanding that the way attachments are formed (and with whom) can differ. As Hrdy (2009) argued, if one looks across the expanse of human history, attachment has been most often supported by the presence of allomothers who contribute to children's development.

Research in other cultures has revealed different ways of responding to the universal need for attachment security in infants. For example, a study exploring attachment patterns in 30 children from the Northwest Region of Cameroon's Nso community revealed some fascinating differences around attachment (Otto, 2008). Nso mothers tended to have very different beliefs about the value and importance of an exclusive mother–infant bond. In fact, they often discouraged maternal exclusivity, believing that in order to provide optimal care, many caregivers are best. As one mother noted, "Just one person cannot take care of a child throughout." It was important to Nso mothers that children did not develop an exclusive attachment to them and developed equally close bonds with older siblings, neighbors, or other children in the community: "Following only one person is not considered good, because I want her [the baby] to be used to everybody and love everybody equally." There is also anthropologist Susan Seymour's (1999) work on Indian parenting, where exclusive mothering is the exception.

In the contemporary Western world, beliefs about attachment and parent- ing have a strong connection to Bowlby's original framework. These ideas and beliefs have played a critical role in the move toward a healthier society for child development and well-being. We see their impact on decisions about child care, child protection policies, and divorce custody, to name a few. However, in the end, perhaps it is comforting to know that parenting is so diverse and that there isn't a one-size-fits-all model. The framework guiding our clinical work with parents is guided by this belief. A mentalization-informed approach to working with parents honors the uniqueness of each parent's experience and the way in which they choose to organize their parenting around their needs and values alongside those of their children. The mentalizing stance, which is based on a genuine, curious, and humble approach, is the best way to work with parents in a culturally sensitive manner, as it encourages an openness toward mutual social learning in the intersubjective space between the parent and the therapist. That is, when we approach our work with parents from a truly curious stance while aware of our own prejudices and expectations (which might obscure our capacity to mentalize), we have a much better chance to establish a relationship that promotes the emergence of epistemic trust.

Parents come to us usually filled with shame, rage, and helplessness. It is only natural that they would want to communicate these emotions, both consciously and unconsciously, to us. A mentalization-based approach requires that the therapist models "looking at themselves from the outside and imagining the other from the inside." This reflection includes not only what is being said but also the nonverbal communications offered in response to parents. In this way, as previously mentioned in this book, the therapist offers a "new developmental experience" in the context of a relationship with someone who is attentive, curious, respectful, and attempting to connect with the parents by responding to and learning about the parents' values, expectations, and fears.

Parents today are raising their children against a backdrop of increasingly diverse and, for many, constantly evolving family forms and complex environmental challenges such as emigration, poverty, and climate change. In this introductory chapter to Part II, we explore some of these family forms in the context of complex and/or difficult situations and illustrate the application of a mentalization-informed approach to working with these new ways of creating and organizing a family and the challenges that they can represent for a parent's reflective functioning. Our intention is to mark contemporary problems that our patients are bringing, but it is selective, not comprehensive.

PARENTING AND THE EXPERIENCE OF MIGRATION

As soon as she opened the door to her office and invited us in, a blast of cold wind from the air conditioner swallowed me in its gentle, westernized embrace. I took in a deep breath, and suddenly, America was inside my lungs. Next to me, my mother began to cry.

—Kien Nguyen, *The Unwanted: A Memoir of Childhood*

The literature (de Haan, 2011; Perreira et al., 2006) on immigrant parenting has traditionally stressed the problematic side of parenting in migration settings. Pointing to contrasting parenting traditions between the immigrant group's country of origin and the host country, studies have focused on parents' experienced stress, their loss of status, and their inability to develop effective parenting strategies in the new setting. For instance, Suárez-Orozco and Suárez-Orozco (2001) reported that Latino immigrants practiced more severe punishment methods (e.g., withholding meals, spanking) in comparison with American middle-class norms. Also, they reported that immigrant parents take a critical stance toward these middle-class norms, as they find that American schools lack discipline.

Reports describing the parenting practices of immigrants who emigrate from non-Western to Western-oriented communities have shown that after migration, support relationships in the family are reorganized, becoming more geared toward child support rather than toward dependence and mutuality between the generations. Delgado-Gaitan (1994), for instance, reported that for Mexican families who immigrated to the United States, independence—a value associated with the American school context and middle-class parenting—became more important as a socialization goal in the American context, at the cost of traditional values of mutuality and dependence. Parents started to invest more in the development of their children, which fundamentally changed the relationships between generations in the family.

Bacallao and Smokowski (2007) found that both first-generation Mexican immigrant parents and their children, in the United States, perceived that parental discipline had become more severe after migration, often causing conflict between adolescents and their parents. Both studies showed that severe discipline and vigilance was not a continuation of traditional parenting practices from the home country but was clearly a response to the new setting that demanded new strategies of child-rearing.

Since the turn of the century, transnational-migration studies have begun to focus on the phenomenon of families living across borders. Studies analyzing the effects of such family arrangements emphasized the negative effects of family separation on children's general well-being (Dreby, 2007; Parrenas, 2005). These studies identified important elements of children's family arrangements that influence their relationships with their migrant parents: the mediating role of the caregiver, the contact that the parents and children are able to maintain, and, especially when mothers migrate, the emotional suffering this causes for the children.

When reunited after a period of geographical distance, it can prove quite difficult for parents to reconnect with their children. Many factors influence the quality of the relationship—to name a few, the length of time apart from each other, the age of the child, the quality of the relationship before separation, the parent's capacity to mentalize the experience of the child as separate from their own, and their capacity to balance their needs with those of the child.

A mentalizing-informed approach takes a different stance toward parenting in the context of immigration: one that is nonpathologizing, aims to get to know the parents and the family from the inside, acknowledges strength and resilience, and fosters agency. It facilitates this process by helping the parent

- connect with the child from a developmental perspective

- feel mentalized, so that they can mentalize the children

- identify prevalent prementalizing modes of functioning in response to the stressful context of immigration or reunification

The following vignette illustrates the work with Sayid, a Turkish father of three, who had been away from his children and wife for nearly 5 years, working in a large North American city. His youngest, Tahir, was only 3 years old when his father left. At the time of referral, Tahir was 9 years old and had been reunited with his father for 1 year. Tahir's older sisters, ages 13 and 15, seemed to be adapting well, but Tahir was struggling with learning English and making friends and was constantly defiant toward his father. He was referred for treatment by his school after a fistfight with another boy. Sayid and his wife, Mira, seemed both embarrassed and extremely defensive when asked about Tahir's difficulties. Sayid did most of the talking, while Mira looked away. On one occasion, Sayid had to attend a meeting at work, and Mira came alone. The following is an excerpt from that meeting between the therapist and Mira:

MIRA: I am sorry my husband couldn't make it, he has been busy at work.

THERAPIST: How are you doing? Your husband mentioned that you were looking for a job? I imagine it's difficult. You were a teacher back home, right?

MIRA: I was, I miss the classroom.

THERAPIST: How was it for you to come here alone today?

MIRA: A bit scary, to be honest, but I learned English in my country, but people here speak fast . . . You don't speak so fast . . . [*both smile*]

THERAPIST: If I do, just let me know.

MIRA:	OK, I will do . . . Tahir had a good week; we were so happy. Then . . . the weekend he had a terrible fight with his sister over the TV . . . how do you say? . . . The . . . control.
THERAPIST:	The TV control, is that a frequent fight? Happens a lot?
MIRA:	Yes . . .
THERAPIST:	What happened then?
MIRA:	My husband came in and told him not to treat his sister badly. Tahir said he was a man and he had priority . . . My husband said it does not work like that in our home. Tahir said that he hated being here and that he liked Turkey better. He told my husband he did not like him. My husband told him to go to his room and tell him when he was ready to say sorry to his sister. He spit at my husband . . . My husband grabbed him by his arm and took him to his room, he was not mean, just firm. Then my husband went to our room and got very sad. He said he made a big mistake and Tahir is broken now; he worries a lot.
THERAPIST:	What do you think of all of this? It must have been so difficult for you to witness all of that. How do you imagine Tahir felt?
MIRA:	I think Tahir is a good boy, he is just confused and angry. Sayid is very kind and loves his children, but he does not understand why Tahir is so angry with him. I think Tahir is angry and sad, he misses his friends and our family. I do, too . . . but I am a grown up . . . I don't know how we can help him. I am worried that Sayid is giving up on his son.
THERAPIST:	It must be so difficult for everyone . . . What do you think Tahir's rejection means to Sayid?
MIRA:	It means he has failed, and it means all the effort to give them a better life is not appreciated . . . I worry one day he is going to lose his temper . . . or just stop talking to Tahir . . . He looks like a tough boy, but he is very sensitive. He thought he was the man of the house and now he is treated like a boy . . .
THERAPIST:	It must be very confusing . . . for everyone.
MIRA:	It is . . .

THERAPIST:	And I imagine it must be tiring for you . . . You were also used to being just you and the kids . . .
MIRA:	[*smiles*] Yes . . . I am happy to have my husband, but yes, everything is new . . .
THERAPIST:	I imagine it must be tough to tell him when you feel tired or angry after all he does . . . He seems to work hard . . .
MIRA:	It is . . . Tahir does, but he is a boy . . .
THERAPIST:	I wonder if together we can help Sayid see it from Tahir's point of view and help him see that Tahir does not have the right words, so his behavior speaks . . . Still . . . spitting at your father is not OK . . .
MIRA:	That is right . . . It worries me more that he does it at school . . . I don't want him to be a bad man in the streets . . .
THERAPIST:	That is a tough fear to have, especially in a country that is new for you . . .
MIRA:	It is, some days I just want to go back . . .

In this vignette, we see how the therapist begins by empathizing with Tahir's mom's stress and slowly invites her to look at the situation together. Staying in the attention regulation block, the therapist seeks to help Mira feel less alone in trying to make sense of her conflictual feelings and those of her son and husband. Mira's reflective functioning capacities are activated, and she can use her "grounded imagination" to try understanding what is behind Tahir's behavior. She is then able to express the fears that might be inhibiting her capacity to support her husband during difficult times with Tahir. In this way, a mom that feels disfranchised and alone can experience a sense of agency and validation, supported by a mentalizing therapist who explicitly invites her to share her voice, perspective, and fears. Having Mira's support in helping Sayid mentalize his experience and that of their son would maximize the possibility of social learning and, most important, of generalization of new ways of identifying, modulating, and expressing extremely painful emotions regarding (a) the lost years with his son and (b) the feeling of being far away, emotionally and physically, from him. This intervention would seek to restore the reflective capacity of the parental couple, which in turn would help them model mentalized affectivity during moments in which they are challenged by their child's behavior. A parental couple that can provide such a response will improve the sense of safety and predictability for the child and most likely help the child regain his own capacity to mentalize the painful experience of migration, as well as the restructuring of his family.

SINGLE PARENTHOOD

In modernized societies, many families feel disconnected from their neighborhoods and communities (Zahran, 2011). This has weakened the informal social support and safety net for a lot of families, requiring more families to assume full responsibility for their children's welfare, rather than relying on the extended family and community to join in the oversight, protection, and nurturing of children. This situation impacts single parents significantly.

Life in a single-parent household can sometimes be a bit tougher for the adult, as we try to describe. Both parental couples and single parents may feel, at times, overwhelmed by the responsibilities of juggling caring for the children, maintaining a job, and keeping up with the bills and household chores. However, there is an important difference between a parental couple and a single parent: the lack of support from the other member of the parental couple in the latter. We must remind ourselves that mentalization is relational and that we all lose our capacity to mentalize when faced with intense emotional impacts or in situations of high emotional arousal. We also know that the best way to recover our capacity to mentalize is in a relationship: in a trustful and good-enough relationship where we can feel adequately mentalized, something that will help us modulate the emotional dysregulation and move back into a more curious and perspective-taking stance. In the absence of the other member of the parental couple (or when the parental couple is dysfunctional or pathological), the single parent who is emotionally overwhelmed will suffer this situation in isolation. This is likely to increase the level of dysregulation and delay their capability to recover the capacity to mentalize. We would argue that from a mentalizing perspective, single-parent families must face higher levels of emotional overwhelm or moments when it is harder to recover mentalizing capacities, while parental couples may not face such degree of intensity, because the adults are not alone in their parental roles—not alone in the moments that every single parent faces quite regularly, when children manage to generate emotional impacts that interfere with their capacity to mentalize. In cases in which there is a high degree of conflict and/or violence, the presence of another might have a harmful effect.

In this context, a mentalization-informed approach to support single parents, for example, in the context of their home and community can prove extremely helpful. As clinicians, we are familiar with the high level of absenteeism in community mental health when working with at-risk families. Often, we find ourselves working with parents who understand the importance of early intervention and seek support as they wish to break generational transmission of trauma, for instance. However, due to the physical and financial demands of being a single parent, these parents find themselves unable to adhere to clinical hours offered to them and their children. It is in this context that home visiting programs (Dangerfield, 2021a; Stob et al., 2019) and group-based interventions within the community (Marvin et al., 2002) can both prove extremely effective in supporting parents' reflective functioning. This process often begins with letting parents know that we are aware of their desire to grow and to become more effective in their parenting but that we are also aware of and respect the limitations of their role as parents within communities where survival and protection of one's children can be an everyday struggle. By visiting families in their homes, we are sending a clear message: "I understand there are many obstacles in the way, and I am here to support you and your family and to experience an hour in your shoes, in your home, in your community." The impact of such a message can help the opening of the "epistemic highway" and the parents' desire to allow a bit of hope and playfulness into their lives, hence activating their capacity to mentalize their child. Furthermore, using parenting groups designed to help parents look at themselves from the outside with the support of other parents (via the use of video feedback or simply by providing psychoeducation, which promotes self-observation), we can create a mentalizing support system for the parent—one in which their fears and concerns (many of them based in reality) feel validated and contained by a community.

The following is an example of the application of a mentalization-informed framework working with a single parent in a home visit. We seek to illustrate the value of a focus on the here and now of the relationship and a curious stance when presented with a myriad of teleological needs and high levels of emotional dysregulation due to environmental and relational stressors:

Yolanda, a 26-year-old mother of two children (6-year-old girl and 10-year-old boy), moved to the United States from her native country in Latin America to escape a marriage dominated by domestic violence. Although Yolanda had finished her university studies in her country of origin as a primary school teacher, it had been difficult to obtain credentialing, and she was now working full-time and attending night school to acquire her certificate as a teacher's assistant. She lived in a modest two-bedroom apartment that she paid for with her salary and a small amount of money she received every month from her parents back home. She was referred to a home visiting program after she failed to engage with the local mental health services following a few initial assessment meetings with her son, Tomás. Yolanda had self-referred to the local mental health counseling clinic out of concern for her son's sudden angry outbursts at home and at school. She described Tomás as a sweet boy who had never caused any trouble until he turned 9 years old, 5 years after they had arrived in the United States. She thought that perhaps as he was getting older, he wondered why they had left his father behind, about whom he remembered only good things. Yolanda did not want to speak ill of her husband in front of the children but worried that they would someday be hearing a version wherein she took them away just to hurt their father. She felt stuck and scared every time she seemed unable to help Tomás manage his emotional storms. She wondered if he was becoming like his father. As a result, whenever her son was verbally aggressive toward her, she would freeze and cower as he escalated further, throwing chairs and objects all over the room.

The following is an excerpt from an early session, where the therapist is trying to mentalize Yolanda's experience:

YOLANDA: I had a tough week with Tomás . . . It is only Wednesday but I really look forward to the weekend because my friends come over and we can support each other . . .

THERAPIST: Your friends sound like good company.

YOLANDA: They are, we put music on and tell each other about our worries, now that I think about it, it feels like a support group . . .

THERAPIST: What do they say about Tomás's behavior? Does he get angry in front of them?

YOLANDA: He does, but I think I feel stronger when they are around because I am able to stand up to him in a calm and strong way. It is more difficult when we are alone, I get really scared of losing my temper, too, and hurting him with words or with my hands . . .

THERAPIST: I can imagine how difficult this situation is. I am also wondering if when you were a girl, you were hit at home?

YOLANDA: Yes and it made me behave better. I know we are not supposed to do it here, but I feel it made me more respectful of adults and less of a defiant girl.

THERAPIST: It sounds to me like you're talking about safety and how to achieve that for all, you, and your children . . . but I am curious . . . When your parents hit you, did you feel safe?

YOLANDA: Well . . . I felt like I knew what to expect . . . but I would not call that safety, I felt scared.

THERAPIST: I can imagine. Small children tend to feel afraid and angry when they feel helpless. Also afraid of the grown-ups, that they also trust . . .

YOLANDA: I never thought about it like that, I guess I figured out it was just the way it was and that I brought it upon me for being such a big mouth.

THERAPIST: That is an awful way of feeling for a child, for a grown up too . . . Do you feel afraid of Tomás, too?

YOLANDA: I do, it is terrible but his eyes . . . he has the same face as his dad . . .

THERAPIST: I can only imagine . . . But you said something that I think is important: that you felt supported by your friends. Could you tell me a bit more about how and maybe should we try to figure out what other ways we can think of in which you can achieve this safety when trying to find a balance between weak and mean in the presence of Tomás's anger?

YOLANDA: I think that is a good idea . . . but other than my friends I don't really have many sources of support . . .

THERAPIST: I am sorry, I am getting the impression you don't feel I understood how alone you are, am I right?

YOLANDA: Well . . . it is a little frustrating when people ask you to do things and they don't know enough about your life yet . . .

THERAPIST: I can see that; it seems I was going too fast and maybe you felt misunderstood or pressured?

YOLANDA: A little . . .

THERAPIST: I apologize, why don't we "stop and rewind" and maybe you can walk me through the last time you felt like that with your son . . .

YOLANDA: OK, sounds good . . .

In this vignette, we evidence the emergence of a relationship between an afraid and tired single mother and a therapist trying to connect and establish an environment where the mom's epistemic hypervigilance can reduce. The therapist rather quickly falls into a solution-focused mode, which ends up with Yolanda feeling misunderstood and perhaps a bit judged. Working from a mentalization-informed lens, the therapist acknowledges the possibility of a mentalizing impasse and takes the responsibility, followed by a curious stance, opening again the possibility of motivation for social learning and the creation of a safe therapeutic working space.

SECOND CHANCES: GRANDPARENTS AND EXTENDED FAMILY

In many families, caregivers other than parents take over substantial shares of the parenting task (e.g., grandparents, other relatives, neighbors, teachers). This is still insufficiently captured in parenting research, but research on this topic is evolving. The effect of grandparenting, for example, seems to depend on the caregiving roles, residence, and personal attributes of grandparents (e.g., age, health, personality), as well as their relationships to their grand-children and the parents (Duflos et al., 2020).

Caregiving, both formal and informal, performed by relatives is particularly common among African Americans (Scannapieco & Jackson, 1996). By the mid-1990s, 13.5% of African American children were taken care of by grand-parents or other relatives, in comparison with 6.5% of Hispanic children and 4.1% of Caucasian children. This prevalence of African American children in kinship care is closely related to an African American tradition of extended family structure and dense kin networks (Fuller-Thomson & Minkler, 2000).

In the context of children's protection services, we often come across the difficult question of placement after removal from a child's primary home and parent(s). In general, social services prioritizes kinship placement. The primary practice assumptions made by advocates for kinship care is that it helps children ease the pain of losing birth parents because it offers social relationships of extended kin networks and familial and cultural continuity. In addition, biological ties and established bonds between kin caregivers and children are expected to increase caregivers' commitment.

The following is an example of working with Joan, aunt of 3-year-old Ismael, who was removed from his mother's care because of severe neglect due to her substance abuse—namely, heroin. Joan was a 29-year-old single woman who had not had contact with Ismael since he was an infant. However, when she was contacted by social services, she felt moved to offer Ismael a home. Joan, the youngest of six children, was very close with Ismael's mom, the fifth child. Joan had suffered a lot when her sister ran away as a teenager but understood, as her sister had been sexually molested by their maternal grandfather and had not been believed by their parents when she asked for help. Ismael's grandparents had died in a car accident a year prior to his birth. The other siblings had moved elsewhere in the United States, and Joan was his closest relative.

Joan was not involved in an intimate relationship and lived alone in a two-bedroom apartment close to the college where she was a graduate student. She worked part-time teaching undergraduates and had two small dogs. She described her life as having been organized and predictable. Ismael was a little "hurricane" who had been placed in a foster home for a week prior to moving in with his aunt and was described by his emergency foster parents as "loving but quite a complicated little boy." He was extremely active and seemed to shift emotionally quite unexpectedly, which had caused some difficulties at the local day care. Joan sought parent support and guidance from the local mental health community clinic, as she felt at a loss on how to manage Ismael, who insisted on sleeping with her, refused to eat the food she prepared, and cried inconsolably every time he thought of his mom or when he did not get his way. Joan felt tired and "out of her waters," but the thought of Ismael going to a strange family haunted her. The following is an excerpt from a session with Joan after several months of work with her therapist. Ismael had been working with a child psychotherapist for about the same time, so Joan felt more supported and freed to slowly explore her thoughts and feelings away from a teleological stance (e.g., "How do I get him to eat and sleep alone?"). It had been important that the therapist responded to Joan's concrete (teleological) needs with psychoeducation on development and invited Joan to understand her nephew's behavior beyond what she could see. The next step for Joan, the therapist thought, once enough epistemic trust was established, was to explore more deeply the meaning of having such a little boy in her life.

THERAPIST: How is everything going with Ismael?

JOAN: He slept in his bed 3 nights last week and I made a big deal and bought him some ice cream . . . He is less hyper, the other day he was able to sit through a whole book after dinner. It is funny . . . I picked a book that my sister and I liked as girls . . .

THERAPIST: How did you experience sharing that with him? . . . It seems very intimate . . .

JOAN: It was both rewarding but also a bit sad that his mom can't read it with him . . . She is in a bad way . . . I get so sad sometimes . . . He has her eyes and her smile . . . We don't know who his father is . . . What would I do if he asks me?

THERAPIST: Those are a lot of feelings all at once, the joy of helping a small child feel safe but the sadness of the potential loss of your sister . . . It seems you're thinking of him getting older, how would you explain about his parents and who you are? That is a lot to sort out, suddenly your life and future look very different, too . . .

JOAN: That is right . . . I don't know if I am ready to be a mom now. I said yes to foster Ismael before I realized how ill my sister is. They don't even know where she is right now . . . last time they had news of her, she was seen downtown in the park looking for drugs. They want to move toward terminating her parental rights . . .

THERAPIST: I imagine this must be so scary for you . . .

JOAN: It is . . . If my parents were alive . . . They felt they let my sister down. You know . . . my grandpa tried with me, and I bit him and ran and told my dad, who went after him with a gun . . . It was awful . . . I moved out 3 months later. I was lucky, one of my great aunts took me in, but my sister was not so lucky. We had four brothers and they were spared but the two of us . . . he targeted her for some reason . . . How would I explain all of this to Ismael?

THERAPIST: What do you think he needs most right now? He is a scared 3-year-old. What do you need? What would help you?

JOAN: [*sobbing softly*] I think he needs to play; he needs to learn how to eat properly, he needs to know that I am not going to disappear like my sister . . . but it is a lot for me, because I am only 29 years old and starting graduate school!

THERAPIST: Do you think organizing a network meeting with social services and trying together to explain Ismael's needs and yours, and trying to get you some support might help? Help them to see beyond actions and behavior? You and I can continue figuring out what is realistic moving forward and how to integrate Ismael into your goals, your life.

JOAN: I think that would be helpful, just because I meet their criteria on paper does not mean I can become his sole caregiver . . .

THERAPIST: I agree with you, and I think and feel that we need to keep that option open if you feel you must, it is a big step.

JOAN: Yes, it weighs heavy on me . . . but I keep in mind what you said: When I play with Ismael it is good for me and for him!

This vignette highlights the importance of balancing the therapist's attention between the content and the process going on between therapist and parent. Foster parenting is a challenging role, especially when new attachments develop in the context of uncertainty. While kinship foster care is perhaps beneficial in many ways to the child, as pointed out by research cited earlier in this chapter, it does awaken the ghosts in the nursery in the family. For Joan, seeing the positive impact of her love, care, and predictability toward Ismael was rewarding but also bittersweet, as it reminded her of the experience of seeing her sister not being protected by the people she trusted the most. By giving a safe space to first explore the practical concerns of Joan, the therapist provided the experience of care and protection from a mentalizing stance for Joan. Following the emergence of epistemic trust in the therapeutic dyad, Joan was able to ask for help and explore her fears and ambivalent feelings regarding the possibility of becoming Ismael's primary caregiver at the age of 29. The potential loss of her sister needed a place in the work, as the work of mourning her beloved sibling had to be explicitly separated from the task of integrating a 3-year-old into her life. A mentalizing stance promotes expression of affect as well as increasing self-awareness in the context of stressful situations such as kinship foster care. This example also illustrates the value of attempting to *mentalize the system* (Fonagy et al., 2005)—that is, to introduce a common framework that encourages curiosity for the internal experience of both Joan and Ismael within the social services, so that the external needs of both are considered while keeping their emotional and developmental impact.

AND THREE MADE ONE: ASSISTED REPRODUCTIVE TECHNOLOGY AND PARENTING

These words—from a mother seeking support—exemplify what we hear often from parents who are experiencing reproductive issues:

> Sometimes I look at my child and I wonder about his personality; he is so different from me. I wonder if his silence and his difficulties relating to others have to do

with my own traumas or the sperm donor's biology . . . I feel awful and lost. What does he need from me? What am I doing wrong? Is this a punishment for having a child alone? My mother says it is a very selfish thing I have done, bringing a child into the world without a father.

Psychosocial aspects of fertility, infertility, and assisted reproductive technology (ART) can significantly impact parents' sense of self-identity and personal agency, mental well-being, sexual and marital relationships, reproductive efficiency, compliance with treatment, and pregnancy outcomes (Mundy, 2007). The psychosocial implications, on our society, of ART include a shift toward older maternal age at conception, the complexities of third-party reproduction, and consideration for the psychological and socioeconomic barriers to receiving care. Clinicians must understand, screen for, and identify couples struggling with the psychological and social aspects of fertility and ART. The psychosocial implications of ART can begin, for families, many years prior to the birth of a child. Any type of ART may be associated with long periods of parental stress, compared with natural conception, which could influence adaptation to the parental role, parental relationships, parent–child relationships, and children's socioemotional development (Stanhiser & Steiner, 2018). Moreover, the issues around this choice do not disappear with success and the birth of a child.

For example, Ehrensaft (2005) described the feelings and fantasies of parents in relation to having this "other," outside party involved in conception. She believed that the anxieties connected to introducing an outside person to the intimacy of conception leads to various psychological defenses, including denial. These anxieties and coping mechanisms can be responsible for the reluctance to tell children. Feelings about the conception then extend to the relationships with children.

The quotation opening this section is an example of the troubling and conflicting thoughts and feelings that parents who have benefited from ART might experience. Helping the parent(s) to mentalize their experience, with the purpose of increasing their capacity for self-observation and sense of agency as a parent in this context, can prove extremely helpful in facilitating parental reflective functioning. The following is a clinical example of work from a mentalization-informed framework with a couple, Daisy and Roger, who, after years of trying to conceive, decided to opt for ova donation. Daisy carried the twins successfully and seemed to have psychologically integrated the idea of the two boys as her children. Roger seemed pleased about finally being able to build a family with Daisy after 10 years of miscarriages and failed in vitro fertilization treatments. Both parents came from very small families, so they were thrilled with the idea of twins at first. However, once the babies were born, the new parents began feeling extremely overwhelmed by the amount of "parenting work" (in Roger's words) it took to keep the twins safe and well. Daisy and Roger had been married for 20 years and were both in their late 40s when the twins arrived. Daisy had chosen to quit her job and dedicate herself to enjoying the twins. Roger worked as a schoolteacher but had to supplement their income with tutoring college students after school hours. The multiple in vitro fertilization attempts had left the couple both financially and emotionally depleted. Daisy and Roger brought their twins to treatment when they were 5 years old, due to difficulties with emotional dysregulation and sleep. "The twins," as they were referred to by their parents, were two boys named Ed and Tim. When asked how they had chosen their children's names, Daisy and Roger said that they had waited until the children were born and then decided based on their looks and their personalities. The therapist thought this was a good indication of these parents' curiosity about their children's personality. However, it could also be understood as their reluctance to make these children "real" until they were in front of them, alive and well. The therapist tried to hold in mind both of these considerations. When the therapist wondered about the impact of having lost other babies, a wall of silence was raised. The therapist then apologized and said that it seemed as though her comment might have made them uncomfortable. Both parents became visibly relaxed, and the conversation resumed:

THERAPIST: OK, let me slow down and go back to the reason that brought you here today.

DAISY: The twins are very smart and loving boys, but the problems with putting them to bed and the major fights and tantrums are becoming unbearable. I think I have spoiled them too much.

THERAPIST: What do you mean "spoiled them"? Could you help me see how you have done that?

DAISY: I think I am too tolerant of some behaviors like their constant jumping on beds. They both have hurt themselves; they are just so active and we are not like that. We are quite sedentary, quiet people . . .

THERAPIST: That is very tough, having one child is challenging enough and two that are also active must be exhausting!

ROGER: It is! We love them but we don't have a lot of help and support. Other couples our age have older children, they aren't still in this phase. There are good reasons why people have children younger than we did, it takes so much energy!

THERAPIST: It must be tough to see your friends already with older kids, when you are just starting.

ROGER: I had not even allowed myself to think about it, but now that you mention it, yes, to be honest it's complicated!

DAISY: Roger, you make it sound like our children are a burden . . .

[*Roger looks down, looking a mix of frustrated and shamed.*]

THERAPIST: Roger, is that what you were saying? I wasn't so sure, it seemed to me that we were talking about different temperaments but also the clash of developmental agendas . . . The boys are 5 and you are about to be 50 . . . It is not easy to balance . . .

DAISY: Well . . . not everybody is lucky to be super fertile and to get pregnant just like that!

THERAPIST: That is so true and that makes me think of all the hopes and dreams you had for your kids, and that you still have, and how hard you worked to have them . . . have those hopes changed?

ROGER: I think they are still there but achieving them feels impossible these days . . .

THERAPIST: What are those hopes, and do they come with fears?

DAISY: I think I wanted to see the boys getting along and happy, I don't think that this is too much to ask for . . . I am afraid they are going to be like bad kids, grow up to be drug addicts or something like that . . .

THERAPIST: Drug addicts? They are 5 . . . Have you noticed some behaviors that make you see that in their future?

ROGER: I think we do worry about not knowing where part of their genetics come from . . .

DAISY: Well . . . not so much that . . . but more like how are they going to react when they find out that they share biology with someone else than us? And how about their difficulty managing their emotions . . . Where does that come from?

THERAPIST: Biology is not everything . . . but that is irrelevant right now, I think we need to start looking at Ed and Tim as separate from each other and from you, and try to understand what their behavior is trying to communicate about how they think of themselves and what they need. They are lucky to have parents that are willing to put themselves through yet another "expert examination of your parental functioning," because they love them so much and want the best for them. I can imagine it is not easy . . . What do you think? Can we start there?

DAISY: That works for me.

ROGER: For me, too, and thanks for understanding how hard this is for both of us!

In this clinical vignette, the therapist realizes quite quickly that she is being influenced by the way these parents speak about their children and by the need to support parents who have gone through so much. She models self-observation and explicitly speaks about her belief that her intervention has made the parents feel defensive and misunderstood. Both parents react well to the therapist's interaction and seem to be more open to dialogue. The therapist then supports the expression of difficult emotions and moves back and forth between the first two blocks of the developmental line of mentalization. The focus becomes twofold: first, to explicitly name the clashing developmental agendas of the parents and the children and, second, the exploration of the parents' hopes and fears. Rather quickly, Daisy can communicate her fears and link them to the "birth other"—in this case, the female ova donor. This is the beginning of a conversation that hopes to help these parents mentalize and integrate their experiences as a couple that endured infertility and are now the parents of Ed and Tim. The main aim is to activate and support these parents' reflective functioning in a way that would benefit a parenting style based on their understanding of themselves and that of their children. By mentalizing a painful experience for the parents, we are facilitating their self-mentalizing and fostering their capacity to mentalize their children's experience.

The experience of ART and how it is processed and integrated is influenced by many factors, among them social support, cultural values and expectations, and parents' previous psychological functioning. Feeling understood, and not judged, in the context of expressing painful and difficult thoughts and feelings regarding the experience of ART facilitates finding a balance in the mentalizing dimensions and a reduction of prementalizing modes of functioning. This is particularly important when parents are confronted with exhausting and frustrating challenging child behavior.

CONCLUDING SUMMARY

- As the concept of family and parenting has continued alongside sociocultural transformations, a mentalization-informed framework might potentially facilitate the level of openness and curiosity in mental health professionals.

- Cultural sensitivity, openness, and cultural humility are supported by a mentalizing stance in the therapist. As a consequence, the possibility of true engagement and a therapeutic alliance based on epistemic trust and social learning are maximized.

- When parents face stressful situations as a result of circumstances such as single parenthood or reproductive difficulties, their reflective functioning becomes challenged and possibly inhibited. A mentalization-informed approach plays an important role in creating therapeutic environments where parents can rehabilitate and restore their mentalizing capacities in a way that promotes their self-mentalizing and that of their children.

- Mentalization can prove to be an extremely valuable protective factor in the context of difficult circumstances, such as those present during and after the process of emigration.

- A mentalization-informed framework provides the therapist with a lens that helps them focus not only on the parent but also on themselves and the emotional impact of supporting parents who are under unthinkable stress. It reminds the therapist of the importance of empathy and validation and the need for teleological measures at times, with the goal of increasing epistemic trust.

7

JUST A TWINKLE IN MY EYE

Mentalizing and the Transition to Parenthood

Julissa was 31 years old when she presented for treatment for her depression. She had been in psychotherapy as an adolescent. She was not sure that she needed therapy, but she was, from time to time, concerned that she might not have the appropriate emotional reactions to things, especially since giving birth to her son, Lionel, who was 6 months old. Since returning from a rather short maternity leave, she had frequently felt irritable with her colleagues at work. She also reported feeling detached from her baby, her husband (Steve), and her extended family. Julissa, a Black woman, had been married for 3 years, and she and Steve had waited a couple of years to conceive, because of their careers. She said that conceiving had been easy but that pregnancy and giving birth had been very difficult for her. She worried about not looking as good as she used to and feeling tired all the time.

As Julissa's treatment began, she complained frequently about her husband, whom she described as being like a teenage boy. She felt frustrated that she was always picking up after him and that he spent weekends watching sports and staying out late with his friends often. He drank heavily, which worried her because his father had a history of substance abuse. Julissa noted, though, that

https://doi.org/10.1037/0000341-008
Working With Parents in Therapy: A Mentalization-Based Approach, by N. Malberg, E. Jurist, J. Bate, and M. Dangerfield

she felt she could not address this with him because she also liked to drink, and it was an important part of their social life. After a few months of treatment, she brought her son, Lionel, to a session. The therapist felt concerned for Lionel, who seemed very passive, almost sleeping with his eyes open, she thought. Julissa did not look at him for most of the session, as Lionel just sat in his mother's lap while sucking on his pacifier. Julissa spoke of Steve having really wanted to have a baby—he was a bit older, and his friends all had children, so he did not want to wait. However, she felt she could have waited a little more, as her career was just taking off after much effort. The therapist asked Lionel, in a playful voice, what he thought of all of this talk. Julissa said that he was OK as long as he had his milk and his toys and that she lamented the moment he would start understanding more, as she would have to be careful with what she said.

Julissa talked fast, often coming to sessions with a list of frustrations she wanted to address and explore. While she seemed highly engaged in the process—coming every week, eager to talk—the therapist found it hard to feel close to her. She rarely showed emotions, though she talked about her frustration, anger, and anxiety. But even happy emotions did not seem genuine—they came off more as a determination to be happy and to keep things moving. When her husband left things a mess, she cleaned them up, resentful. She was unapologetic about coming back from brunch with her girlfriends, tipsy from mimosas, having left Lionel with her sister. Julissa felt this kind of fun was deserved because of how hard she worked during the week, having to be "on" at work in a challenging job.

In an attempt to slow things down and make real contact with Julissa, the therapist spent some time reviewing Julissa's own history. Julissa was the product of both parents' second marriages. Her mother had stopped working when she was born, and Julissa resented how involved her mother was in her school. She recalled,

> It's like she was the one in high school. My friends loved her, but it always annoyed me how much she was around because she acted like they were her friends. And she was always making undermining comments about me, like about my weight, and commenting on how great they all were.

Julissa remembered her father as working all the time, and she saw her mother as someone who "just liked spending his money."

One day, Julissa came to the session and reported on a difficult moment with Steve the previous week. Work had been especially stressful for him recently, and she perceived him as always in a bad mood and on edge. On this particular evening, their dog had an accident in the house, and Steve blew up. Julissa told him that she felt scared, which alarmed him and caused him to fly into a self-deprecating outburst, suggesting that she did not understand him and did not want to be with him. She said that she felt bad afterwards about using the word "scared," and she was curious about why she had felt that way. The therapist encouraged her curiosity to examine further how she noticed that the term "scared" didn't quite make sense in this context:

JULISSA: Well, I don't know if this has anything to do with it. I was not usually scared of my parents, but I do have this one memory, I don't even know how old I was or what I had done, but we were driving, and my mother got so mad, and she pulled the car over and yanked me out of the back seat and screamed at me and threatened to leave me there and make me walk home. I don't remember anything like that happening any other time, but is it possible that that stayed with me? Like I do feel like he's about to do something in those moments and I don't know what he might do.

THERAPIST: Has he ever been violent or threatened you?

JULISSA: Not at all. Steve rescues spiders and ants instead of letting me kill them, he would never hurt anyone.

With safety concerns addressed, the therapist moved forward in "mentalizing the moment" with Julissa. The therapist empathically validated the fears that Julissa would have around anger, given that her parents had been unpredictable when they were angry, and how it left Julissa feeling completely unsure of what would happen next when someone was angry. Furthermore, there was a lot going on between Julissa and Steve recently. They were having difficulty learning how to be a working parental couple. This new developmental stage was demanding their capacity for interdependence, a challenging shift for a couple who was used to being two autonomous adults. They were now needing each other in ways that they had not before, and they were both aware of how much they were needed by the other; this increased dependence could be scary for them both.

Additionally, expectations around the experience of parenting were constructed and experienced very differently for Julissa and Steve. For Julissa, expectations were quite impacted and shaped by her own experiences of relational neglect while being parented by a mother with narcissistic traits, who needed to feel special and at the center, and a father who was largely absent. Steve, in contrast, maintained a somewhat avoidant expectation in which he had convinced himself that everything would be fine and that Lionel would help them become parents. Steve's naive approach bothered Julissa, because it felt like he could not see how painful it was for her not to feel passionate love for her child. From Julissa's perspective, this felt like a complete abandonment, from her husband, of both her and her child.

In exploring all of these themes over the course of the session, Julissa, toward the end, arrived at one more insight. The therapist realized that with all of the discussion about Julissa's experiences of other people's anger, they had not talked at all about her own anger. At that moment, Julissa reflected:

JULISSA: Yeah, I feel a lot of anger! And I think that scares me! I worry about what I might say or do, because I know I have it in me to lose my temper and go for the jugular like my mom.

THERAPIST: So maybe when you get scared in these moments, it's not only Steve's emotions that you're scared of, it's also your own. Like you said, you wish Steve would take a pause and stop himself in those moments and take a breath and just clean up the mess. But you and Steve are different people, and you approach things from opposite directions. But maybe you can even learn from each other.

JULISSA: Yeah, Steve is the first person I've ever met and certainly that I've ever been with, where I feel that I can be totally myself.

THERAPIST: And that's beautiful, because when you think about what you want for your baby and what you want him to learn about emotions . . .

JULISSA: Oh, I definitely want him to feel the acceptance that I get from Steve. I don't want him to experience us as unpredictable, but I don't want him to feel like his emotions don't matter and he has to put on a face for other people all the time like I did. I mean, it clearly doesn't work, I have issues with anger and anxiety now.

CORE ISSUES AND DEVELOPMENTAL ASPECTS OF THE PERINATAL PERIOD

The *perinatal period* is wide, spanning from the moment when parents begin to think about bringing a child into their family through, typically, the first year of infancy. But the term is also limiting, because it does not traditionally capture the transition to parenthood of a nonbiological child (through adoption, foster care, or kinship care). While aspects of this transition are similar—in terms of the relevance of internal representations; the activation of parental reflective functioning; feeling-states such as ambivalence, excitement, and loss; and physiological changes (with the production of oxytocin and other hormones)—there are also differences (Bick et al., 2013; Grasso et al., 2009). Children may not be infants, and the process of becoming a parent will have looked different, perhaps taking different forms at different times. While this section focuses on conception and infancy, many of the concepts are applicable to the transition to parenthood, however it happens.

We now have neurobiological evidence demonstrating the changes that happen not only in the body but also in the brain when one becomes a parent (see Von Mohr et al., 2017). While some of these changes have appeared to be linked to the biological process of carrying a child in the womb and delivering, we now also have evidence from research on nonbirthing parents (e.g., fathers) and nonbiological parents (e.g., adoptive parents) that there are neurobiological changes that occur, as well, when one becomes a parent.

From a psychological level, psychoanalytic and attachment theorists and researchers both have written about the psychic reorganization that takes place during the transition to parenthood (Raphael-Leff, 2019). Elements of this include the shift from being the child of one's own parents to being the parent of a child, an increase in one's own dependence on a partner or a community, and a shift in identity and accompanying feelings of newness as well as losses. Like any developmental period, the transition to parenthood is not one thing—there are multiple stages or moments of significance within the developmental process, which we describe in this section, and everyone's experience is unique. The topics we introduce here are often relevant in this developmental stage and represent subjects that are not commonly acknowledged or talked about. These are areas where the therapist's curiosity and interest can activate mentalization where it has not yet been activated. But the reader should not mistake the purpose of this section as saying what is "normal." Later on, we acknowledge "normalizing" and its place in a mentalizing approach.

Finally, you may notice that a common theme throughout this developmental stage is loss, which might seem counterintuitive in a chapter that is about having a child. There is, of course, a new addition to the family that is to be delighted in, but there are significant losses to be acknowledged and processed so that parents can delight in their child, who is now more than "just a twinkle in their eye."

Appreciation for Diversity of Experiences and Not Knowing

While every parent's experience will be unique, and generalizations or assumptions can be harmful, it is crucial that therapists working with women and men during the transition to parenthood have an appreciation for the developmental process and the themes that may arise. This is not about "knowing" the answer to parents' questions or being able to normalize or diagnose. This is about becoming familiar with the wide ranges of experiences that parents have during this developmental period, as one more source of knowledge that can support you in the mentalization of parents' experiences.

Imagining

As the title of this chapter indicates, the idea of becoming a parent or having a child enters parents' minds before they actually have a child. For some, this idea and the process of imagining began when they themselves were young (and may or may not have changed and evolved), while for others, this idea does not enter their minds consciously until later in life or after becoming pregnant. But there is always exploration to engage in with the parent about when and how they started imagining their child and imagining themselves as a parent. It is helpful to ask parents what their hopes are/were and what their fears are/were. Notice what shaped the parent's imagination—was it their own childhood? Was it what they saw in other families? We often call parents-to-be, during pregnancy, "expecting." What is it they are expecting? And importantly from the mentalizing approach, how are these expectations held? Is the parent certain, or are they able to hold a not-knowing stance? If they do not have any expectations, what is stopping them from being able to acknowledge expectations or wishes?

When faced with parents who have a difficult time imagining and reflecting about their role as parents, the therapist seeks to inquire and explore, not to get an answer. We are not often asked by others what we imagine or hope or fear—we are usually asked more concrete questions. This may be the first time that the parent has been invited to share their internal world and their fantasies. Through openness and curiosity, we invite parents to get in touch with and share their longings and wants, regardless of whether those are realistic or are likely to be fulfilled.

As we discuss later, therapists should pay attention to where on the self–other dimension of mentalizing the parent falls when imagining or talking about the ideas they have/had. If parents are focused on themselves and the idea of what they are going to be like as parents, then the therapist may ask questions that invite mentalization of the child, even before they are born. It is not uncommon for parents to have difficulty mentalizing the child early in pregnancy (or the foster or adoption process). This may be protective against potential loss through miscarriage or other sudden changes that can occur. For parents who have children through pregnancy, parents often begin forming representations (thoughts and feelings) of their child as having agency and intentionality—the foundations of mentalization—when they can start to feel the baby move. Parents may start to talk about what the baby's activity level is like, make inferences about what the baby likes or does not like, and put voices to what movements might be communicating.

It is important to know what parents imagined, in order to then help them with the transition from the idea of the child to the reality. This shift involves loss—the end of the imagined child and experience, which comes with meeting the actual child. This is the first step in the child becoming separate from the parent. They once existed only in the parent's mind, and they are now in the world, where other people can see and interact with them. Noticing, naming, and acknowledging the loss that occurs here can allow parents to experience the feelings around it and move through them, rather than holding those feelings of loss inside and unprocessed.

The Birth Story

Whether it is the labor and delivery experience or another process such as foster care or adoption, the birth story is a profound experience that needs to be put into words, narrated, shared, and witnessed (Callister, 2004). Those who support birthing parents (e.g., doulas, midwives) have long known this, although services in medical settings have largely failed at mentalizing parents and recognizing the need for narrative and sharing around this process and the medicalization of the birth process (Burcher et al., 2016; Puia, 2018). While every experience is different, it is helpful for therapists to be aware of some of the experiences that parents may have. For example, often birthing parents are not permitted to eat during delivery, and this can be extremely upsetting and unrealistic. Birthing parents sometimes describe feeling like doctors were focused on the medical data instead of listening to them. The presence of medical students can be objectifying during this personal process—it can feel like the baby is the focus of attention and the priority, rather than the mother who is delivering. There is documentation of racial disparities in non-White parents, particularly Black parents, being listened to and responded to, and the mortality rate is significantly higher for non-White mothers compared with White mothers, independent of socioeconomic status (Vedam et al., 2019). The second parent is also in a unique position—watching, perhaps feeling unsure or scared at moments (depending on the process), at times feeling helpless or out of control, at times feeling amazed and overwhelmed with emotions (Hughes et al., 2020). Their experience also needs words and expression.

A mentalization-informed approach discourages making assumptions about the parent's experience or even whether they want to share it, but having some knowledge can assist the therapist in noticing subtle cues about the parent's experience that they may be unsure about sharing. This information prepares therapists to be able to ask certain questions, which can implicitly normalize the range of experiences parents have. Furthermore, therapists should stay aware of certain cultural practices around the birth of a child. For example, in some cultures, the mother does not leave the home for a certain period (Han et al., 2020; Waugh, 2011), and there are cultural norms about who is present for the birth and the roles of different people after. Indeed, the extent to which birth experiences are talked about and whom they are shared with may be shaped by the culture of the family, ethnicity, or religion. Scaffolding the intervention in our work with parents so they can determine what they want or need to reflect on and express, without dictating what the process should be, is part of the mentalization-informed framework.

Finally, the birth story can be long and encompass many steps and stages. The increased accessibility of egg freezing, intrauterine insemination, and in vitro insemination, among other forms of reproductive technology, has increased the visibility of other narratives around bringing children into the world. It is important that therapists seek out knowledge about the processes their patients have gone through, while being open and listening to what their subjective experiences throughout these processes are and continue to be. For example, a mother who knows that, due to lifelong medical problems, she will not be able to conceive and carry a child selects an egg donor and surrogate. She reports both the joy that she has access to these resources and gratitude for the community that is making it possible for her child to come into the world, alongside acknowledgement that at times during the process, she has felt like a bystander and longed to be able to have a more active role. Or a woman in her early 30s who makes the decision to freeze her eggs, because she is in graduate school and does not have a partner and wants to maintain her sense of agency and choice, goes through a process where, after her egg retrieval, she learns there were fewer mature follicles than expected—and then has to go through a grueling waiting period, where each step of the process involves the report of how many eggs remain viable. Pregnancy loss through miscarriages are not uncommon, especially during the first trimester, but parents note the lack of sharing about the range of experiences of pregnancy loss that they have. The choice to not become a parent or to not bring a child into the world at any given point must also be acknowledged as complex and an experience that may take on new meanings over time.

A New Identity and the Parent's Body

Throughout this book, we hope to give therapists a way of thinking about parenthood and parenting as an aspect of identity that should be included in therapy, whether the focus of the therapeutic work is (a) an adult who is a parent, (b) a child, or (c) a family. The transition to parenthood marks a change in identity and roles. Parents' lives necessarily change, in many ways, around having children, and we describe several of these in this chapter, in order to help therapists work most effectively with them. These changes include changes in work life, the frequency and ways in which parents engage with their own friends, a new role within their own families, and even changes in personality (e.g., a mother who always considered herself pretty chill is actually more anxious than she expected).

An aspect of identity that must be acknowledged in this process is the body. It is perhaps most salient for parents who carry and birth children—we mentalize the experience of their body changing both internally (e.g., hormones) and externally (e.g., weight gain, hair growth or loss), what these changes mean, how these changes feel and are experienced, the experience of society's gaze, and the feelings of the body no longer being one's own but existing for a baby or a family. However, therapists must remain attuned to the ways in which the body is relevant for parents who do not carry and birth children. For women who are not able to conceive, there are experiences of the body as a failure, which must be reckoned with. Even if a parent does not carry a child by choice, the relationship with their body has likely been a part of that decision. Fathers or partners who are not carrying the baby have a new relationship with their partner's body. The mentalizing approach can be particularly helpful in this aspect of therapy, because mentalization involves making links between the internal and the external.

From the Child of Your Parent to the Parent of Your Child

As already mentioned, the transition to parenthood represents a shift from being a child to being a parent. In this shift in identity and position in the familial system, there is loss, often colloquially referred to bluntly as "the death of your own inner child," emphasizing that parents are not appropriately prepared for this occurrence.

The parent's "inner child" refers to the collection of memories and experiences that shaped their internal representations of themselves and other people. It is particularly helpful to recognize the needs that went unmet. These can be painful, so parents understandably shield themselves and cope in various ways; examples include focusing on the positives, rationalizing the way their caregivers were with them, and using anger to protect against vulnerable feelings. When parents can acknowledge both what they gained from the kind of childhood they had and what needs were not met, then they can also recognize how they are still coping with those unmet needs or trying to get them met. Often, adults are still trying to get those unmet needs from childhood met by their parents, and the mentalizing approach can help them to put words to the longings and also to examine what is realistic. This process is not only cognitive but also experiential. By exploring the long-standing unmet needs, therapists are very often providing a corrective emotional experience where they are meeting those needs— among them, the need to share, to have the internal worlds recognized and embraced.

But while parents may need support in nurturing their inner child, the mentalizing approach scaffolds the parent in stepping into their new identity and role, not as the child in their family but as the parent in this new family. Using the angels in the nursery exercises introduced in Part I can help support parents in accessing their own support systems and internal resources to inhabit their new role as attachment figures. It is not enough to know "I need to be a secure base for my child." Parents benefit from learning what gets activated from their own infancy/early childhood that actually shapes how they experience their child and themselves as a parent now, in the present. In terms of the ghosts in the nursery, those are important to recognize and to support parents not only in making cognitive links but also in mentalizing the affects that were not acknowledged around those experiences. One note about memory, though—therapists should keep in mind that these early relational experiences are not encoded in memory and able to be recalled in the same way that later experiences are, but they are remembered and carried within people's bodies and as forms of implicit relational knowing (Lyons-Ruth et al., 1998). When working within a mentalizing approach, we must attend to aspects of memory that are embodied, just as we do with those that are recalled.

MENTALIZING WITH PARENTS: LOOKING BACK AND FORWARD

Driving a car and checking the rearview mirror provides a helpful metaphor for parents to strike this balance between looking back at their own childhood and looking ahead at themselves as a parent with a child of their own. The therapist can explain to parents:

> When you drive a car, you have to sometimes check the rearview mirror to see if there is anything coming up from behind you that might get in the way, but you don't stare at the rearview mirror. If you did that, you wouldn't be able to see where you are going and all the other things on the road, so you check it and then look back ahead. It's similar when we look at the past here. We check our own rearview mirrors to see if there is anything that might be coming up from our past that we need to be aware of so that we can navigate it, but we don't spend all our time looking at the past, the focus is on where we are now and where we want to go. So, we look back but don't stare at the past.

A Change in Relationships With Parents

Parents need nurturance, because we all continue to need understanding and relationships long after childhood. New parents in particular are in a stage when they may feel like they are giving so much to their child (and others). Conflict between a new parent and their own parent (the new grandparent) is not uncommon, as the parent of the parent may feel pulled to parent the child themselves and may be unsure of their new place in the family structure. Therapists can help parents to get clarity on what they want and need from their own parents at this stage in life. A mentalizing approach can also support patients in considering their parents' perspectives and the impact of the change in the family structure on everyone, without being challenging, confrontational, or invalidating.

Parents are also seeing their own parents in a new light. Some parents feel they have a new understanding of their own parents. Others, however, may experience frustrations around seeing their parents either repeat patterns with their children or interact very differently with the child as grandparents, compared with what they were like as parents. Mentalizing how the patient sees their own parents now, what is stirred up in them when they see their parents as grandparents, can smooth out the edges on this sharp change.

A Change in the Partner Relationship

Nearly all new parents report difficulties with their partner in the transition to parenthood. Research shows that parents of young children report more marital dissatisfaction than couples without children, although when children are grown, these couples report higher marital satisfaction than couples without children (Doss & Rhoades, 2017). So therapists must be prepared to provide therapy that targets the couple relationship, whether they are working with an individual parent or a couple.

Both partners are experiencing changes in identity. Under the stress of pregnancy and needing to take care of an infant, or having a new child in the home, parents are dependent on each other in ways that they had not been previously. Parents are redefining themselves in new roles with new priorities and new responsibilities on their plates. They often wonder if they can speak to each other in different ways, thinking that if they find the right way of expressing themselves to their partner, their partner will finally hear and understand them. A mentalizing approach can help parents to better understand their own underlying longings and needs that are shaping their communication, and also how they are coming across to their partner and the role that they are playing in interactions (Johnson, 2011).

Some therapists may notice that when working with a parent individually, they find themselves empathizing with the other parent. While it may feel complicated to not be empathizing with the patient, the empathy the therapist has for the other parent can be a way of bringing the partner into the room, even when you are not working with the couple. The following example, from the case of Julissa, illustrates this:

JULISSA: Another week, another fight.

THERAPIST: Tell me, what happened?

JULISSA: I just feel like Steve is not accepting that our lives have changed, and I don't know how to get it through his head. It's when he comes home from work. He thinks that I've been at home all day, so he doesn't understand why the apartment is such a mess. It's like he thinks because I'm not working that my day is luxurious and relaxing.

THERAPIST: So what is the scene, when he comes into the apartment?

JULISSA: So yesterday, he comes in, and he takes one look at the laundry on the floor, and is like, "Are those clean clothes on the floor?" And I'm like, "Yes, I was meaning to get back to them, I was just getting them out to fold and then Lionel woke up early from his nap and I had to go take care of him, and I never got back to them." And he's got this look on his face like he doesn't believe me or something and he thinks that I am just intentionally making the house a mess.

THERAPIST: And that's gotta feel really bad, I imagine. Thinking that he sees you in that way, a mess.

JULISSA: Yeah, like I am a total failure in his eyes. And I'm working so hard, I'm even the one coming here. And he thinks this is like vacation time for me, too.

THERAPIST: You wish he would come to therapy to talk about these things together, I know. I mean, even though he's not here, I wonder if I could kind of play his role, and maybe that would help us get more into thinking about what's going on between you. Would you be up for that?

JULISSA: Yeah, I'd love to figure out what's going on.

THERAPIST: OK, so for a bit I'm going to try to put myself in his shoes and not in yours, I just don't want you to feel like I am taking his side, it's to try to help you two through this.

JULISSA: [*laughs*] Yes, I appreciate that.

THERAPIST: So he gets home, and remind me, what is his work like?

JULISSA: He loves his job, but it gets him really stressed. He's almost always in a bad mood when he gets home.

THERAPIST: OK, so he comes home and he's in a bad mood. He is having a hard time, and then he gets home and there you are, and you're doing what?

JULISSA: I'm giving Lionel a bath.

THERAPIST: I'm picturing bath time as maybe a sweet scene, is it?

JULISSA: Yes, he loves water.

THERAPIST: OK, so you're with Lionel and Steve comes in and sees you and Lionel but his mind is on this laundry on the floor.

JULISSA: Yeah, he's got a thing about laundry on the floor when it's clean. Like he thinks the floor is dirty, which is also insulting, because I work hard to keep it clean for him!

THERAPIST: So he's got a thing about the floor, it's not totally rational.

JULISSA: No, none of this is rational.

THERAPIST: Right, this is an anxiety of his, he thinks the floor is dirty, he sees the clothes, he knows that you know he doesn't like this. And he doesn't know the backstory, he's not thinking like that. He is in an irrational place and thinking maybe, what, "Julissa doesn't care about what's important to me? She's not holding me in mind?"

JULISSA: Oh my gosh, it's so funny you should say it that way, because he literally said that in another argument we got into this week about having sex. We were in bed and I was like scrolling through Instagram, catching up on all the stories from the day, and he starts trying to cuddle and like clearly wants to have sex, and I was like, "Not now, I really want to just relax." And he got so annoyed and rolled over and was like, "All you care about now is your social media." And I just didn't even have the energy to respond. I have a baby and I don't need my husband being a baby about this.

THERAPIST: I wonder if you just put your finger on something really important. There has been this huge shift. You are caring for a baby now, and I'm not saying he's in the right, but perhaps something is getting stirred up in him that you don't care about him anymore.

JULISSA: Well yeah, he's not the center anymore. He's not a baby! And like, what about me? Who is taking care of me?!

THERAPIST: Right, of course. So of course it's all-hands-on-deck focusing on Lionel, but you two still have needs, and the need to feel seen and loved and thought about. And whether it's rational or not, certain things, like the laundry for him or even him not being more chill about social media for you, leave you feeling like the other person doesn't see you and isn't thinking about you. And it's not anyone's fault, it's just, this time in life right now. But it can be really painful.

JULISSA: Yeah, I thought we would be this awesome team.

THERAPIST: Did you hear what I just said as implying that you aren't an awesome team?

JULISSA: No, I guess it's not what you said, but I am not really feeling like a team right now, and I really want to feel more like a team.

Six months later, Julissa began the session in a way that reflected changes that were taking place . . .

JULISSA: I want to tell you about this amazing realization I had; I think you'll be proud.

THERAPIST: I'm eager to hear, you sound proud!

JULISSA: So Steve was driving me nuts this week. He is complaining so much about his work. And it was making me so mad, because I couldn't figure out what the point of the complaining was. It felt like he was complaining to me so I would help him solve his problem. But then I had this epiphany! Maybe he doesn't need me to solve his problem. Maybe he just needs me to listen. I think I didn't realize how much he likes to vent. I hear it as something else I need to do. But I've had in mind all of our conversations about what we both need and I realized that he just needs me to listen.

THERAPIST: And maybe to connect in this way.

JULISSA: Yes, he actually needs so much more connection than I ever realized before.

THERAPIST: And this made such a difference for you to hear him in a different way, as needing connection instead of something else.

JULISSA: Yeah, I think part of me thinks, "Hey dude, I have a lot going on, too!" Like he's doing something to me or not seeing me. And then I just am like, "Oooh, he just needs me right now," and I can give that to him, and that feels really good! And then get this, he even asked for the name of the book you had mentioned to us, the *Hold Me Tight* one.

THERAPIST: Ah, so he's more open to you as well, it sounds like.

This vignette and the shift that took place in Julissa's mind over the 6 months of treatment illustrate one way that a mentalizing approach can be used to help couples navigate the significant changes they are going through together, even when only one partner is in therapy.

WORKING ON EPISTEMIC TRUST DURING THE PERINATAL PERIOD

During the perinatal period and/or the transition to parenthood, parents are entering into the unknown, and along the way, they are likely to receive a lot of information from different sources, depending on their sociocultural context. They will meet with doctors, nurses, and other medical figures; friends and family members may provide support, advice, or even warnings; and the media has a lot to offer, whether through parenting books, experts on television, or social media pages. As already discussed in Part I of this volume, epistemic trust is central to how we take in and apply information. Some parents might be inclined to listen to everything their own mother says or to follow guidance from certain experts without question, losing out on the chance of developing their own opinions and strengthening their sense of agency as a parent. Other parents may lean the opposite direction, trusting no one or not trusting any one person or source above others, based on their own assessment of how reliable and helpful the source might be—they treat all sources as relatively equal. There is a good chance that such parents are highly anxious and find containment in the "illusion of knowing." While these parents might be able to listen to themselves, they are restricted in their abilities to benefit from the knowledge and help of others.

Therapists can track where parents' epistemic trust is at any moment. Is the parent clinging to the voices of others? Then the therapist may work on helping the parent to access their own internal voice. Does the parent avoid or restrict taking in what others might have to offer? In this case, the therapist might help the parent relax their epistemic vigilance by bringing their attention to ostensive cues to help them be able to establish trust with others, so that they can get help and support when needed. This process can first be practiced in the context of the therapeutic encounter, particularly when parents bring issues they feel rather self-conscious and defensive about. The following is an example of Julissa's work with the therapist early in the process, while trying to decide when to stop breastfeeding:

JULISSA: I need your help thinking about something important and a bit charged for me.

THERAPIST: Yes?

JULISSA: I need to decide if I should stop breastfeeding and how.

THERAPIST: Lionel is 8 months, how did you decide that this might be the time to stop?

JULISSA: Do you think it is too early? I know everyone says you should do a year.

THERAPIST: I am sorry, it seems like my question made you feel perhaps judged?

JULISSA: No, it's OK, I am just so anxious about the whole thing . . . and yes, I get defensive easily.

THERAPIST: Well, you can always check and clarify with me if I make you feel like that. Do you think you could do that?

JULISSA: Honestly, I don't think so. You're the therapist, it doesn't feel right to say that.

THERAPIST: I tell you what, if you feel shy about doing so . . . just frown or something and I will be the one to ask [*makes a funny face*].

JULISSA: [*smiles, affective tone changes*] I wish Steve and I could find a way of doing what we just did . . .

THERAPIST: What is that?

JULISSA: Moving on with a bit of humor.

THERAPIST: What gets in the way?

JULISSA: I think when we are both stressed about failing at being good parents, we both get really defensive and that is it . . .

THERAPIST: How does it end usually?

JULISSA: Tense silence . . .

THERAPIST: That must be tough . . . I imagine you both feel quite alone . . . ?

JULISSA: Hmmm . . . "alone," well that makes me think of the breastfeeding question. I wonder when Lionel will be OK without my breast milk. I need my independence again . . . I am starting to feel like a cow . . .

THERAPIST:	It sort of feels like a chore?
JULISSA:	I am embarrassed but yes . . . I did not even want to breastfeed, there was a lot of pressure . . .
THERAPIST:	That must be tough . . . so you wonder if you are ready but Lionel is not . . .
JULISSA:	Yes . . . I think you can say that . . .
THERAPIST:	What does Steve think?
JULISSA:	He says it is really up to me, I don't think he understands the burden in terms of time and effort.
THERAPIST:	Is there anything about the experience you enjoy?
JULISSA:	[*smiles*] Yes . . . Lionel's little eyes looking at me . . . is magic.
THERAPIST:	That is great.
JULISSA:	It is . . . I guess that we could substitute the breastfeeding with another activity that keeps us connected.
THERAPIST:	I think that sounds great. Should we do some brainstorming, or is that something you think you've got a handle on and you want to move on to other things on your mind?

In this example, the therapist validates and empathizes with Julissa's shame over what she seems to perceive as an unmotherly desire. By doing this, the therapist gives explicit permission to Julissa to express herself and begin playing with new ways to connect with her developing child. The therapist respects Julissa's initial epistemic vigilance and invites her to consider the decision to stop breastfeeding from both a practical and developmental perspective but also a relational one. Julissa needs to gain some of her independence physically and emotionally. Parallel to her baby, she is also developing new thoughts and feelings about who she is and who she wants to be. Having a therapist who mentalizes her experience and helps her identify, modulate, and express her emotions will help her be able to do the same for her son. When parents feel understood, they become more open to learning from others, including their infant.

It may be challenging for the therapist to hear a parent either not taking in any information from others or appearing overly guided by what they are told or what they read. Identifying these ways of being as reflective of a lack of epistemic trust and the security to rely on others, while also remaining free to explore and make decisions for themselves, can help therapists remain empathic and then notice and name the difficulty the parent is having with trust.

WORKING BACK AND FORTH WITH PARENTS IN THE DEVELOPMENTAL LINE OF MENTALIZATION DURING THE TRANSITION TO PARENTHOOD

A feature of our mentalizing approach to working with parents is the conceptualization of the parent's mentalizing along the developmental lines of attention regulation, affect regulation, and explicit mentalizing. At any given moment in the therapeutic process, the therapist implicitly or explicitly assesses where the parent is on these developmental lines and utilizes interventions to target the appropriate developmental level. Here, we describe how these capacities may be uniquely at play during pregnancy, infancy and the transition to parenthood.

Attention Regulation

Attention regulation is the first capacity on the developmental line of mentalizing. It is what the new baby will be working on developing. How parents respond to their child's developing attention regulation, and parents' abilities to sustain their own attention, may vary based on their internal working models. Young babies do not sustain attention for very long. We watch their eyes move around a room, taking everything in. Novelty is more likely to capture their attention.

Face-to-face interactions are the basis of engagement and play for young children and are a context in which challenges with attention regulation may arise. Many parents may have unrealistic expectations for their child's attention regulation at this young age, and children's short attention spans can bring up strong feelings in parents as they attach meaning to the child's shifts in attention. When a baby stares for a long time, we often hear "Ooh, he likes you!" or "He likes that!" When the baby's attention shifts, we might see indicators of parents' anxiety. Their attention may shift, too, and they may lose or give up interest, or they may feel anxious and want to call the baby back and continue engaging them. Of course, there are numerous other ways parents might respond, but these are a few.

New parents are often fatigued, enveloped in the world of their baby. The changes in their own attention regulation may be noticeable to them. They may find it miraculous that they are able to sustain attention with their baby, but common phrases such as "baby brain" are indicators of the struggles with attention regulation that new parents experience in the haze of fatigue, hormones, and a huge life transition that can be all-consuming. Furthermore, parents' attention regulation is being reworked as they learn how to control their attention now that they have a child who they may feel is always on their mind, somewhere in there.

Depending on the context in which the parent is being seen and their capacities for attention regulation, in parallel with their experience of their children's attention regulation, the therapist may work with attention regulation in different ways. One of them is to help the parent discover and name aspects of the infant, such as their temperament and emerging personality. This is important, as it will provide the possibility of alternative explanations for their baby's behavior. Another way is to provide developmental information in order to help parents develop realistic expectations. Finally, it is always good practice from a mentalization-informed point of reference to model and elicit curiosity about the possible meaning behind an infant's behavior. This will promote a sense, in the parent's mind, about their infant as an "agentive self," with their own likes and dislikes and their own sense of intentionality in relationships. Working dyadically with infants and parents is a wonderful way to inject such ways of thinking about the infant and produce situations in the consulting room or during a home visit that promote moments of joint attention. Even if parents usually attend sessions individually, there are often times when parents bring the baby to the session because they need to, which can be used as an opportunity, and the therapist can even invite the parent to bring the baby for a session. The following is an example of such an intervention with Julissa and her son, Lionel:

Julissa brings Lionel to a session with her therapist, who happens to be a child therapist, as well. Lionel, 8 months now, sits on the floor playing with some soft building blocks his mom has brought for him.

THERAPIST: It is so nice to have you here with us, Lionel! [*Baby smiles while waving a block in the air.*]

JULISSA: [*with a tone of enjoyment*] Look at that, you are such a flirt, my son!

THERAPIST: Oooh! What do you have there in your hand, Little Man?

JULISSA: He gets really concentrated on those and can be sitting in the corner with them for almost 20 minutes. Do you think that is good concentration or should I be worried? Do you think he is autistic?

THERAPIST: I don't see any signs of that . . . Why don't we sit with Lionel on the floor . . .

JULISSA: [*sits on the floor, looking quite uncomfortable*] Oh man! If I knew, I would have worn more appropriate clothing . . .

[*Lionel reaches out to his mom and offers a block after having drooled all over it.*]

JULISSA: [*in a rather flat mode*] Oh my! Was that really yummy?

THERAPIST: [*in a more musical and playful way*] Lionel, Mommy is funny! Yummy? No! [*with a very funny face, and the baby responds with giggle*]

JULISSA: Let's build something [*Mom starts making a small tower while baby stares.*]

THERAPIST: What a great invite to play, Lionel!

JULISSA: Lionel likes destroying the things I make . . .

THERAPIST: That is very spot-on for a 9-month-old . . . [*gives some developmental information*]

JULISSA: That is a relief . . . I haven't been sure about that. His dad says I shouldn't let him do that, that we are teaching him to make a mess.

THERAPIST: But you notice that he enjoys this, and it's a game you're playing together.

JULISSA: Yeah, he's just so mean about it. [*Lionel knocks over the blocks.*]

THERAPIST: [*speaking as the baby*] Yes, Mommy, but I am my own little self!

JULISSA: [*while hugging her infant*] That is true. It is difficult sometimes to remember that! I feel like I fail Lionel all the time. And I am worried you are going to give me an F, too!

THERAPIST: Here, the only F is given by the same person that gets it . . .

JULISSA: I got it . . .

Affect Regulation

Developmentally, infants do not consistently have the capacity for independent affect regulation—they rely on others for self-regulation. Research
shows that the capacity for self-regulation and affect regulation develops
through a sequence where the child shows and physically expresses the
emotion that they are having difficulty regulating (through crying, fussing,
shrieking, pulling away, making a face, using their hands, etc.), and the
parent responds with marked mirroring, reflecting back what they think
their child is thinking and feeling and making clear that this is what they
imagine the child is thinking and feeling, not what they are feeling themselves (Gergely, 2018). Then the parent or caregiver makes a move to try to
offer comfort and alleviate distress. While this may involve concrete things,
such as offering food, a diaper change, a blanket for warmth, or removing
layers if the baby is hot, these actions are accompanied by subtle regulating
movements on the part of the parent or caregiver. They may hold the baby
close to their chest, where they hear their heartbeat. They may use their
voice and coo, making what Beatrice Beebe refers to as the "woe face." They
may offer a finger or a hand. They may stroke the baby's arm or back when
removing or adding clothes. These are all subtle ways of helping the baby to
regulate their emotions.

But what of the parent who does not seem to recognize and respond to the
child's cues that they need help regulating their emotions? This is the question
Selma Fraiberg (Fraiberg et al., 1975) famously addressed in *Ghosts in the
Nursery: A Psychoanalytic Approach to the Problems of Impaired Infant–Mother
Relationships*, where she concluded that when a mother does not seem able to
hear her baby's cries, it is often because her own cries were never heard. In
working with parents, we must attend to their affect regulation capacities
(Goldberg, 2011). As we have already discussed, the presence of a new baby or
child is likely to bring up all kinds of emotions as parents make the psychological shift from being the child of their own parent to being the parent of their
own child. The baby's presence and sounds may call to mind their own
experiences. These memories are not likely to be cognitive—that is, parents
are not likely to recall what happened when they were a baby. But feeling-
states may be activated from when they were younger. And these feeling-states,
though the thoughts and memories associated with them might be outside of
conscious awareness, can be dysregulating. A combination of attention regulation and affect regulation approaches can therefore help to reestablish affect
regulation.

Julissa and Steve have been referred to a colleague of Julissa's therapist to
work with them together on some difficulties they are having with Lionel, now

9 months, regarding affect regulation. The following example illustrates the therapist working mostly at an affect regulation level with both parents:

THERAPIST: Lionel you look so happy and excited today, listen to all that babbling! [*The baby responds positively to the therapist's marked mirroring.*]

STEVE: Lionel likes you so much.

THERAPIST: What makes you say that?

STEVE: He is usually so serious, but here, he has been so full of smiles!

JULISSA: Maybe he can tell we are more relaxed, too . . .

THERAPIST: That is interesting, I think that is a very valuable observation. How do you feel about being here, the three of you and me?

JULISSA: I don't know [*looks down*].

THERAPIST: What is happening right now for you?

JULISSA: [*shrugs*] I'm trying to find the words.

THERAPIST: [*noticing that Steve seems to be ready to talk*] Steve, it looks like you might have some idea. Do you want to try to help?

STEVE: Jessie is always worried she isn't feeling the "right" things. [*Steve uses his hands to gesture quotations*]

THERAPIST: Is he right, Julissa?

JULISSA: Yeah, definitely. This whole experience is like a rollercoaster ride, and I just can't figure out if it's normal.

THERAPIST: What do you think those feelings are? How do we know we have them?

JULISSA: You know . . . when you see a mother in the park and she is smiling with pride and she looks like she feels so lucky she got her kids and they are the center of her world . . . I love this little rascal but I don't feel bliss like that . . .

THERAPIST: The Hallmark version of motherhood . . . [*Both parents laugh with the therapist.*]

JULISSA: I mean, sometimes I feel really happy, but also, sometimes I just am like, "Oh my god, shut up and go to sleep!"

STEVE: I think you make a good point. I don't know how other parents do it. Like our friends are always posting on Facebook and Instagram the activities they are out doing with their children, and that's how I want us to be. But for us it's like exhaustion, frustration, and of course some precious magic moments, but . . . I always tell Julissa, everything is going to be OK, I was raised to be optimistic but . . . sometimes lately, we wonder if we were ready for this . . .

THERAPIST: What do you think, Lionel? [*as she touches the baby's hand*] I see you looking at Mom and Dad as they speak, and you look like a pretty loved and cared-for little baby . . .

[*The adults continue to speak, and then Lionel begins to cry after he seems to have hurt his gums. Julissa becomes visibly upset, and Steve seems to freeze at first, followed by a lot of singing and moving the baby around. The baby continues to cry for 2 more minutes and then succumbs in his father's arms*]

STEVE: OK . . . that is what we were talking about . . . This happens a hundred times a day. It makes it impossible to do and enjoy anything.

THERAPIST: What do you hear when Lionel cries?

STEVE: I hear unhappiness . . . that there is something I am not doing or giving him.

THERAPIST: [*nods empathically*] And you, Julissa?

JULISSA: I don't like the crying, it makes me feel very nervous and then angry . . . I hear it as saying, "You suck at this. I don't like you."

THERAPIST: Both of you experience it similarly, it sounds like. It brings up a feeling that you aren't giving him enough, and Julissa, you just articulated how you can then feel like accusations are tacked on—"You suck at this. I don't like you." Is that his voice, or is that someone else's voice?

JULISSA: Now that you put it that way. It's definitely my mom's voice. I have it kind of two ways. Like, that's how she responded to me when I was young, if I didn't do what she wanted, she got so angry and I can't remember if she actually said it, but she would definitely say things that would make me feel like I was an awful daughter for not doing whatever it was that she wanted me to.

THERAPIST: So there is a lot in there that might be helpful for us to go back and explore a bit later, but it sounds like you're noticing that those feelings come from you and your own experiences managing difficult feelings, and the experiences of your parents and perhaps others in your home having difficulty managing the difficult emotions and tensions in relationships, could that be? It is tough to imagine, as it sounds like it was hard for your mom to imagine, that maybe Lionel is just scared or surprised by the painful feeling in his mouth . . . especially when we are anxious or angry . . .

STEVE: I see where you are going with this . . . we understand him as adults, we need to learn baby thinking . . .

THERAPIST: I'm aware this could sound like I'm nitpicking language, which I don't mean it as, but I don't even think of it as "baby thinking." It's like, Lionel is feeling and thinking and you're trying to get into his mind and imagine all of the things that it might be—and so of course those voices from the past come up, but then when you look at him in this moment and try to see him as not connected to any of that, what's his voice like? And guess what, it takes a lifetime, because he will change and so will you.

JULISSA AND STEVE: [*laugh*] Oh god! We have a long road ahead.

THERAPIST: So what happens between the two of you at these moments? Let's look at that now, because I think then we can think about how you two can help each other through them.

The therapist is working with Lionel's parents in cocreating a story about their child and who he is as an infant. It's a story that includes where he is developmentally as well as relationally. It's a story that includes his temperament, his personality, and his attachment behavior. The therapist offers an alternative "normalizing" version of the baby's distress and links it with a lack of safety when he gets hurt. This is helpful, as the therapist and these parents are working within a therapeutic environment of epistemic trust. By speaking to the infant in the presence of his parents, the therapist is bringing the internal voice of the baby and creating a space in the parent's mind for the baby as his own separate self. Furthermore, the therapist is explicitly using humor and a developmental lens to maximize the possibility of positive attributions of the child's behavior. The baby's cry does not mean recrimination in this version—instead, it means a cry for help.

Explicit Mentalizing

The last block on the developmental line of mentalization involves explicit mentalizing. Children do not have these capacities during the first year of life. This does not mean they do not have early mentalizing. In fact, we see that their mentalizing takes the form of what, in adults, we call the prementalizing teleological mode. Almost from birth, children can recognize contingencies—"If I do this, then they do that." But this is as far as their mentalizing goes, that they can begin to predict what people will do based on contingencies they have observed repeatedly.

The baby's lack of explicit mentalizing may be a barrier to the parents' being able to activate their explicit mentalization about their child. Not infrequently, parents of infants will seem to refuse to mentalize their child, making statements such as "I don't know what she's thinking, she's a baby, probably just wants food" or "How am I supposed to know what's in his mind, he can't speak." To these statements, we might reply, "You're right, we can't know. But we can think about it and wonder and try to figure it out."

One technique that can generate explicit mentalizing in a playful way is to speak for the baby, exemplified in the previous section. When the parent has the baby in the room, the therapist can actually speak to the baby about their internal experiences and make links with their behaviors and the past, modeling for the parent a way of interacting that engages the child as someone who has a lively mind. For example, as a mother prepares a bottle for her baby, the baby, who is reclined on their back amid a pile of pillows, looks in the mother's direction, their legs churning and feet wiggling. The therapist describes, "Ah, you see Mommy. She's making your bottle. You look very excited, with those legs going, like you wish you could get over there and get it yourself. She's coming . . ." and then, turning to the mom, asks, "She likes this formula? I know you were worried she wasn't that interested in the other one." "Yeah, this one she likes," the mom answers, to which the therapist replies, "You have your hands full getting the bottle together, so I don't know how much you can see her right now, but she is watching you and looks like she is getting ready for it." These small questions subtly reflect that the therapist sees the baby as having a sense of agency (that she can have preferences, that her behavior is expressive) and also reflects the mom's experience (that she might not be able to see these moments).

At a higher, more complex level of mentalizing is a therapist who is working with a mother who had a traumatic delivery and who is quite tense and anxious and describes her baby as cranky and difficult to settle. As the mother is speaking, the baby is indeed fussy and crying. The therapist reflects, "You two have been through a lot together already. It's difficult to settle into feeling that you are both safe now after something so scary."

Explicit mentalizing requires a great deal of cognitive resources, which are heavily taxed during the perinatal period. Therapists must be sure that they have addressed attention regulation and affect regulation first, so that they are not trying to mentalize with a parent who is quite simply not able to get their mind online. As always, in one single session, we can go from one level to another—however, it is best to always begin at a basic level in order to reconnect with parents and help them connect with their infant.

We now go back to the example of Julissa: While she was excited to be a parent, it was difficult for her to think of her baby as a psychological being. One of the earlier days in session, Julissa described the weekend with Lionel, when she had brought him to a friend's birthday party: "I love putting him in cute outfits and taking him to parties and showing him off to all my friends. They always say he is the best dressed, and he is!"

The therapist felt a mix of anger and despair at Julissa's description of her infant as a doll. One of the challenges of working with very small children and their parents is how strong we can become with the infant and forget about the parent's needs as troubling, yet important, communications of the parent's internal world—how they see themselves and who this child is for them.

THERAPIST: It is so nice that you feel so proud of Lionel, he is a gorgeous and bright baby indeed. I am curious . . . are there times in which you see him as mean and ugly? I know that is such a weird question . . .

JULISSA: No . . . actually it is not . . . I think I try hard not to pay attention when I feel like that about him . . . but I do . . .

THERAPIST: That is an awful feeling . . .

JULISSA: Yes, it is . . . it really is . . .

THERAPIST: When do you feel like that about him?

JULISSA: Sometimes I feel he looks at me with contempt . . .

THERAPIST: Oh boy . . . that must be very upsetting . . . anyone else look at you like that . . . ?

JULISSA: My dad used to . . . he was a very proud man and nothing was ever good enough for him. He was disappointed that I wanted to be married and have children, being the only child in my family, I had to be the boy of my dad . . .

THERAPIST: That is a lot of pressure, and may I say, I would have found it confusing . . . Could it be that sometimes your mixed feelings have to do with Lionel being an actual boy . . . ?

JULISSA: Like . . . penis envy . . . ? [*smiles*]

THERAPIST: No . . . just complicated . . . yes, maybe kind-of envious feelings?

JULISSA: What kind of person feels like that about their child?

THERAPIST: Would it surprise you to know that most people do at some point? Many of us don't realize it and it comes out in feeling rejected, of imagining that the child is rejecting you . . . does that make any sense?

JULISSA: It does . . . Maybe that's why I want him to look perfect and I want him to be admired . . . then I think "Well . . . I am perfect and admired . . ."

THERAPIST: That is an amazing place you landed us in . . .

PARENTING AN INFANT: A BALANCING ACT

As this chapter has illustrated so far, becoming a parent, even if the experience occurs multiple times, has various and diverse meanings every time—as it finds the parent in different developmental and psychosocial circumstances every time. With each child, parents are confronted with the challenging and delicate task of creating a picture of their newborn that allows them to approach the challenges of early childhood to adult functioning in a mentalizing way (as often as possible). Caring for an infant is a dance filled with ruptures and repairs (Beebe et al., 2010; Tronick, 1989). It can be both exhausting and rewarding, like most stages of parenting.

So, how do we help parents to work on finding balance in the four dimensions leading to improved potential to mentalize? The following are some important considerations.

Self-Other Dimension

Julissa's example with dressing up Lionel illustrates the challenges in this dimension of parenting infants. Infants babble and express themselves with movement and other nonverbal behaviors. We can observe infants' capacities as viable relational partners during nonperfect contingencies that make up the relational dance between infant and caregiver. When well-choreographed, the exchange has musicality and rhythm (Monaci et al., 2021). As therapists working with parents from a mentalization-informed lens, we can help parents' reflective functioning through the use of videotapes or the retelling of sequences between them and their infant, where we bring attention to what was happening for both the self (parent) and the other (infant). Working in the joint-attention block with parents facilitates balance in the self–other dimension, as it allows us to help the parent begin to think about their infant as a subject with their own thoughts and feelings.

Because infants have no words and most adults rely on words, this is a difficult time at first. It is important to help the parent be aware of their body, and that of their infant, as holding memories of past emotional experience and as a container of current emotional states. This process and the exercise of the capacity to observe and listen beyond words are more challenging when parents are under duress psychosocially. Stress leads to a lack of safety, which inhibits parental reflective functioning.

Cognitive-Affective Dimension

During patients' transition to parenthood, it is helpful for therapists to be attuned to which aspects of internal experience parents are attending to and which are being excluded. An imbalance between the affective and the cognitive dimensions can be noted in a parent who is full of thoughts (cognitive) but has not expressed much feeling, or a parent who expresses a great deal of emotion (affective) but is not clear about what is going through their mind. When a parent is reflecting on their child's emotions, imbalances emerge, as well. A parent may be able to reflect on their infant's emotions but not put words to what they imagine could be going through their child's mind, or they may articulate the child's thoughts but not connect them to any feelings.

With babies, the affective dimension may be easier for some parents to mentalize, because babies express emotion (in the form of crying, smiles, etc.). The therapist can help increase mentalizing of cognition by speaking for the baby and putting words to the baby's experiences. However, some parents are quite intellectual about their children and imagine their minds as rich in thought but do not connect to the emotion. For example, Julissa enjoyed talking about Lionel's development, the things he liked to do, and what she imagined he was thinking, but she often did not connect these explicitly to emotions—such as when she said he liked knocking over towers she built, but did not note his joy and excitement. This example is mild and hardly pathological, but as described in another vignette, Julissa had difficulties with his expressions of emotions and affect regulation, and putting words to both positive and negative emotions may help with affect regulation.

Internal-External Dimension

Mentalizing necessarily involves looking at external cues and thinking about people from the inside. However, for 9 months of the perinatal period, there are not any external cues besides occasional movements because the baby is still in utero. So parents' mentalizing begins by being heavily weighted on the internal dimension.

Babies' external cues are unique because the only forms of communication they are capable of in the early stages of life can be quite intense. Before there are smiles, there are cries, shrieks, and head turns. A parent who is focused on only the external cues could feel like their baby hates them, is under great threat, or is uninterested in them. When a parent can balance reading their child's external cues with imagining what might be happening internally, then they are more likely to be able to regulate their own emotional and behavioral responses to their child.

For example, Beatrice Beebe and colleagues' (2007, 2008) research looked at parents and 4-month-old babies who were invited to interact face-to-face for 10 minutes. While most parents gazed at their baby the majority of the time, the infants tended to look away from time to time. Beebe et al. observed differences in how parents respond when their baby looks away, which may be related to their capacity to mentalize the baby's internal states alongside their external cues. The external cue when the baby looks away is important, and we want the parent to be able to pick it up, but it may be understood by the parent in a variety of ways. If taken concretely, the parent imagines "My baby does not want to look at me." But if the parent is able to mentalize the baby's internal state in a more complex way, they might understand "Something else just caught her attention," "That interaction might have gotten a little too stimulating," or "Hmm, maybe he wasn't so sure about that game." Being able to mentalize the internal state and link it to the external cues allows the parent to be able to respond appropriately.

Implicit-Explicit Dimension

Parents, especially new parents, come to treatment often with a great deal of self doubt and shame. It can therefore be helpful to recognize the ways in which parents are effectively automatically (implicitly) mentalizing much of the time; they do pick up on signals from their child and respond appropriately at many times. Where we see most parents have difficulty is when emotions are highly activated and the parent is in distress themselves. These are moments when automatic mentalizing risks slipping into a prementalizing mode, and controlled (explicit) mentalizing can help to restore balance.

Of course, not all parents operate in an automatic mentalizing dimension most of the time. We might consider some parents to be overthinkers. Some new parents, especially, may deal with the newfound lack of control they are experiencing by trying to find control through controlled mentalizing—"slowing everything down"—instead of going with their intuitions or their gut and allowing their automatic mentalizing to run smoothly.

PREMENTALIZING MODES IN THE CONTEXT OF THE TRANSITION TO PARENTHOOD AND PARENTING A NEW CHILD

New parents are especially vulnerable to breakdowns in mentalizing, as they are contending with high levels of emotion, alongside sleep deprivation, changes in hormones, and a host of anxieties and fears about keeping alive a new human who is in their care. When we are overwhelmed, whether it is with love or stress, mentalizing is prone to going offline. This section describes some of the cues therapists might look for when working specifically with new parents.

Teleological

The teleological mode of prementalizing is characterized by a focus on action and behavior, rather than reflection and thoughtfulness. Of course, there is a time and a place for this kind of jump to action—namely, when there is a real, significant threat to our safety—that is not a time to think, it is a time to act. However, teleological mode can be a way of operating that is used in place of mentalizing even when there is no (clear) threat. It is at these times that the therapist aims to identify the nonmentalizing and interrupt it, to guide the parent back to a mentalizing stance.

Welcoming a new child into the home is a huge change that brings a great many unknowns, particularly when it is a parent's first child. Teleological mode is one stance that parents may shift into in order to manage these changes. For example, parents may focus their mind on gathering information and trying to make plans. These actions are not pathological, and—certainly—doing research, making birth plans, and nesting are all important steps parents take during pregnancy. But therapists should be on the lookout for when the parents' focus on what they can and should be doing is taking over the space needed for thoughtful reflection and being in touch with their emotions. New parents tend to ask a great deal of therapists. Some of the questions might include asking for advice about sleep training, whether certain behaviors are normal, when milestones should happen, and so forth. Therapists who know a great deal about young children might be inclined to share what they know, while therapists who have less knowledge and experience with infants and young children might feel anxious about what they do not know and what they cannot give the parent. In this model, the therapist tries to pause before "acting" on what the parent is asking for. First, the therapist must internally acknowledge that even if they have ideas that could help the parent, they do not know the answer or know for sure how it will go. Having paused themselves, they can then explore what their fear is that is prompting a rush toward solutions—what emotions are being avoided?

Psychic Equivalence

Children do not enter the realm of psychic equivalence until later into toddlerhood, when they are aware that they are separate from the parent but still not aware that two different people can have different perspectives. But parents may be prone to going into psychic equivalence, having difficulties with separating their thoughts and internal experiences from their children's or those of others around them. Psychic equivalence is noticeable because even as the parent may be talking about internal states, they are speaking about them as though they are certain that they know what is in the mind of the baby or someone else.

Therapists should be alert to the parent's ways of speaking about their baby's mind in this way, because it can sound like mentalizing—and while it may often be benign, when the parent is under emotional stress, what they imagine is in their baby's mind might become more threatening or negative. This is illustrated in the following example:

JULISSA: So we just spent the week with Steve's parents, and I really need to talk about it! They were all over me about how quickly I respond to Lionel, they think I'm spoiling him. And it's at the point where I can't even trust them to watch him, because I just know that they are not going to be keeping a close eye on him.

THERAPIST: And what are your fears about that?

JULISSA: That he will need something and they will ignore it.

THERAPIST: And then what?

JULISSA: And they will just be caught up in their adult conversation and not really paying attention to him.

THERAPIST: And do you envision something dangerous happening?

JULISSA: Not necessarily, but more likely, he will be crying and no one will respond and he will feel like he's all alone, and no one cares about him, and I've abandoned him.

THERAPIST: So that gets really powerful really fast. He will feel alone, like no one cares about him, and like you've abandoned him . . .

JULISSA: Yeah, when you say it back, all the things I felt as a kid.

While Julissa is putting herself in her baby's shoes, she is imagining only one possible experience, which the therapist notes is quite tragic. The therapist notices that a psychic equivalence mode is possibly emerging here and interrupts it by leaning into Julissa's imagination, accepting it as a possibility, and empathizing with it.

This clinical example also points to another context in which psychic equivalence often arises: relationships with families of origin, particularly in exchanges between new parents and grandparents. During those moments when the grandparent is asserting their parental knowledge and experience—depending on the quality of the relationship between grown child and grandparent—the new parent can regress to a psychic equivalence mode of functioning. Following are examples of comments that reflect a psychic equivalence mode:

- "I ask my mom to take care of the baby, and when I pick them up after 2 hours, it is like she is the expert of my child and I know nothing . . ."
- "I feel so incompetent around my parents with my baby . . . everything I do seems to be wrong . . ."
- "My father looks at me almost with fear when I pick up my son, he believes I am a total idiot . . ."
- "I know my mother thinks she and my father were better parents . . ."

Therapists need to resist the urge to try to bring explicit mentalizing online too quickly when parents are in psychic equivalence mode. It is tempting to challenge these comments, bring in other perspectives, or offer skills for acceptance. But psychic equivalence is an indicator that there is an affective experience that the parent has not mentalized. So, mentalization needs to first be brought back online, often through empathic validation that helps the parent to regulate, before they can begin reflecting, reevaluating thoughts, or taking up behavioral changes.

Pretend Mode

Earlier in this chapter, we presented one version of pretend mode that Julissa went into during the early months of her son, when she was talking about bringing him to a party and the positive reactions of everyone. Later in that session, Julissa was discussing going back to work. She said, "Maybe I'll be able to work from home, and then I can work and take care of him." She continued describing the scenario of sitting on calls with her totally silent baby by her side. The therapist gently pointed out that Julissa had the expectation of a silent baby with almost no needs and then empathized that this thought seemed like a way to tell herself that she could do it all and that she would not have to make choices. Again, Julissa's wish was validated, and the therapist could easily empathize with this longing, but it was important that the therapist noticed that Julissa's statements were not reflecting wishes or longings—she was actually going into a fantasy space that was disconnected from the external reality. When parents become overly focused on books and intellectual understandings of their child or themselves, they are at risk of remaining disconnected from their emotional experience. The key to guiding parents away from a pretend mode is to help them connect with their fears and hopes. Provide a safe space where it is OK to say, "I did not like my baby yesterday when he was crying for an hour! I wish I never became a mom/dad!" or "I wish I could have all of these things—my baby, my freedom and independence, and my work!"

CONCLUDING SUMMARY

- The perinatal period is often overlooked as a psychotherapeutic opportunity to identify, modulate, and express difficult and painful emotions emerging out of the experience of a life-changing experience to come. When parents are able to explore their fantasies and fears before the arrival of the infant, it provides an opportunity to work on parents' reflective functioning.

- Parenting during infancy is extremely challenging, as it requires a parent's grounded imagination. A developmental perspective can prove extremely helpful in supporting parents in balancing across the four dimensions of mentalizing.

- A mindful consideration of the need to function at a prementalizing level in response to the increasing levels of interpersonal and psychical stress during this period would help the psychotherapist to maintain a mentalizing stance away from pathologizing of parenting. This is particularly important because it is easy to identify oneself with the helplessness of an infant.

- Creating moments of vitality when the infant's intentionality and agency can be highlighted is of special importance in the process of translating and creating awareness of the infant's internal world—what we imagine are their thoughts and feeling-states.

- Strengthening parents' capacities to self-mentalize in the context of non-mentalizing systems (e.g., family, medical, day care) is a powerful protective capacity.

- Cultural sensitivity, when working with parents of infants, is a challenging area, as it requires genuine curiosity and epistemic trust. For example, some parenting practices may at times awaken in the therapist emotional responses that may challenge this capacity significantly. This is particularly true in areas that encompass safety and care, such as feeding, basic hygiene, and caregiving practices. In this context, the use of supervision and collegial consultation is invaluable and enriching.

- Working with the ghosts in the nursery in the context of parenting an infant is almost inevitable. This situation often challenges our capacity to maintain a scaffolding framework and tends to elicit feelings of "fixing" too quickly, leaving parents often feeling misunderstood and alone. It is important that we meet parents where they are and at a level where they are capable of exploring difficult emotional realities while still being able to remain a functioning secure base for the infant.

8 LEARNING TO LET YOUR CHILD WALK AWAY AND COME BACK

Mentalizing the Toddler Years

CASE AND CLINICAL FORMULATION

Lorain was a willful 2.5-year-old girl. She was the second child of White, heterosexual parents who were both raised by single mothers who had children with multiple partners and struggled financially. Lorain's parents both wanted to provide a different kind of home for her and her 4-year-old sister, Sonia. Dad (David) was 29 and worked for a local grocery-delivery company, and Mom (Andrea), also 29, had not returned to work at a local bakery since having children, because they could not afford child care. Recently, Lorain had begun to show what a local early childhood specialist labeled as "oppositional behavior," and they were experiencing a lot of pressure from their extended family around her behaviors. David and Andrea expressed their frustration regarding the amount of blame everybody placed on them and with how little these others paid attention to Lorain's genuinely difficult character. Lorain's parents described her as always being unhappy and displeased with everything.

https://doi.org/10.1037/0000341-009
Working With Parents in Therapy: A Mentalization-Based Approach, by N. Malberg, E. Jurist, J. Bate, and M. Dangerfield

Lorain's aggressive and impulsive behavior had really affected the couple, and they hard resorted to blaming each other for the misbehavior. Both parents felt confused and at a loss for what to do—in their relationship with each other, with their families, and with Lorain. When asked what their biggest fear and hope was for their daughter, Andrea spoke of her worry that Lorain would have a tough life because of being so defiant and stubborn. However, she also hoped that Lorain would grow up to be a strong and independent woman. David spoke of his fear that Lorain could be misunderstood and labeled, but he also hoped that she would find people in her life path who would be able to see how kind and loving she could be. Andrea interrupted David and clarified that Lorain could be like that but only with people she chose to, ascribing a great deal of intentionality to her young child.

Lorain was described as a willful and highly verbal toddler; she seemed to have mastered most developmental tasks ahead of time. However, once the therapist was able to establish a basic level of epistemic trust with the parents, new information emerged—for instance, that Lorain could lose her temper easily when there were changes in her routine. An example was given by her mom:

> I try to stick to a routine but it's not always possible. And Lorain does not react well when things don't go as planned. Like, last week, the girls were having breakfast and I was trying to get stuff ready to go, because I had a lot of errands to run. We are planning this party for my mom's 50th birthday and I needed to pick stuff up. So I wasn't paying that close of attention and I gave Sonia the cup that Lorain likes and Lorain just "lost it." She began to cry, scratch her face, and hit her sister hard with a wooden spoon. I picked her up to put her in time out and she was flailing her arms and hit me in the eye. I must admit, I yelled at her when she did that. And it was difficult for me to not spank her. I know we are not supposed to do that anymore, but my mom did it with me and my siblings and we never behaved that way again. David just apologized to Lorain because he felt bad that she was "spooked" by the changes. I am sorry, but she is too small to be acting like that already, she thinks she runs the house, I feel she needs to be put in her place. Her sister was never this rigid and mean! She is OK most of the time, but when she does not get her way she becomes a little monster, truly another child!

As the reader, what did you feel reading this? You might have felt anger toward either of the parents, or maybe you felt that you identified with the mom's frustration toward her child. This case exemplifies how toddlerhood is both a time of gains and enjoyment and a time of loss, fear, and frustration for many parents. In this chapter, we explore how the normative development of a child during this period impacts and challenges the developmental process of parenting. We will return to Lorain and her parents to illustrate the application of a mentalization-informed model for working with parents of toddlers from a developmental perspective.

Because of Lorain's age, the psychotherapeutic work would include her parents in a very direct fashion. The modality used with older toddlers will be defined by the state of the toddler's *object constancy*, referring to their ability to hold the parent in mind and feel connected to them emotionally even when physically separate. A toddler's capacity for object constancy depends on many sociocognitive factors—namely, (a) the quality of their relationship with their caretakers and (b) their developing cognitive capacities. Around toddlerhood, children shift from experiencing the world concretely, where what they see is all that there is, toward a more abstract way of understanding the world, where they can "imagine" their parent and feel safe to explore and take "small, healthy risks" such as staying alone in a consulting room with an adult they do not know very well. So upon meeting a toddler such as Lorain, finding out about their capacity to stay alone with the psychotherapist provides a lot of valuable information and also determines the type of modality to be used (e.g, dyadic, family, individual). Most important, the therapist determines what type of work will result in working with Lorain's parents' mentalizing skills within their zone of proximal development, where they can practice mentalizing while emotions are activated.

During this developmental period, it is best to meet with parents first and get a sense of "who this child is in the parent's mind." This can be assessed in many ways during the assessment period of a therapeutic process, through our careful listening to evidence of reflective functioning in a parent (as detailed in Chapter 6, this volume). Asking the parent such questions as what their biggest fear and biggest hope for their child is allows us to evaluate the parent's capacity to see their child as separate from themselves—as someone with their own thoughts and feelings—and invites an explicit differentiation between their expectations and the reality of who their child is. Items from the Parent Development Interview (Aber et al., 1985) such as "Describe your child with three adjectives" or "Tell me about a time when you felt your relationship with your child felt like it was working" allow for *ports of entry*—that is, opportunities for intervention to explore the parent's thoughts and feelings in the context of their relationship with a rapidly changing child.

In the case of Lorain and her parents, we find a parental couple who values and understands the importance of their relationship and the impact it has on parenting. However, when Lorain's behavior seems to threaten their *myth of parenthood*—that is, the ideal they each have of "how things should be going at this stage," Andrea responds with a somewhat-rigid and harsh understanding of her child's behavior as being a threat to balance in the family and to her vision of what her child should be and how Lorain should manage her strong emotions.

Parents' questions and expectations about what is developmentally appropriate arise often during toddlerhood, and therapists must hold in mind and explore the expectations that parents have and where those expectations come from. Andrea seems to have very high developmental expectations for her 2.5-year-old, with a strong value placed on kindness and self-control. On the other hand, David seems to take a more benign view of his daughter's behavior. Perhaps trying to compensate for Andrea's stern stance, he seems to at times become guilt ridden and quite apologetic toward Lorain. This situation might cause a bit of "signaling" confusion for a child who seems to be struggling in her developmental pathway toward age-appropriate affect regulation (Yerkes & Dodson, 1908)

Parents and children respond to and impact each other, as they make up a family system. But parents and children are also separate individuals, and their behaviors and responses are shaped, as well, by their own internal qualities. The first step in working with this family would be to assess how much of the child's emotional reaction is in response to the adults' response to what seems to be a slightly rigid and willful emerging personality, and how much it really belongs to the child as a vulnerability hindering her capacity for joy and exploration, two important tasks of toddlerhood. A family meeting would be helpful, in order to observe the following:

- the interaction between Lorain and her sister

- the verbal and nonverbal communication between Lorain's parents in the context of a new and potentially stressful situation

- the impact of negative attributions on Lorain's parents' curiosity about what is going on for their child at that moment

- the family's capacity for playfulness and mutual enjoyment

- Lorain's capacity to seek support and receive help in the context of a new environment (e.g., her capacity to send and receive verbal and nonverbal cues)

During these meetings, the use of videotaping (Leyton et al., 2019) could prove extremely helpful during the feedback meetings with Lorain's parents, as it might open a door to a new way of self-observation in the context of parenting a toddler and a preschooler—a fast-paced period for parenting!

Additionally, a meeting with Andrea and Lorain would help the therapist observe their capacity for coregulation as a dyad and shed some light about the quality of the interactions between mother and daughter. Finally, understanding David's role and helping him to work through his ideas of his role at this stage of development would be vital to bring some balance and predictability to the messages sent to Lorain by her parents during moments of emotional distress caused by frustration, shame, fear, and guilt—all emotions that tend to block a parent's mentalizing capacities.

CORE ISSUES AND DEVELOPMENTAL ASPECTS OF TODDLERHOOD FOR PARENTS

While mentalizing during the toddler years presents challenges for parents, it offers therapists many opportunities. Therapists who implement a mentalizing framework in their work with parents of toddlers implicitly and explicitly invite parents to participate in mentalization. The implicit nature of this invitation includes conducting an effective family assessment; working with parents to mentalize the child as a separate, agentic being; and working with parents to foster joint attention. It also includes helping parents gain mentalized affectivity, epistemic trust, attention regulation, affect regulation, and explicit mentalization. Finally, effective implementation of a mentalization framework requires coaching parents through the prementalizing modes, which are particularly easy to slip into during their child's toddler years.

Mentalizing the Child as Separate: The Me and the Not Me

"What is your first memory of meeting your child?" Asking such a question might surprise a parent and open both the cognitive and the emotional channels. It can also give the therapist a sense of who this child is for this parent and the focus of the parent's investment. For example, some parents may answer, "She was so beautiful!" in contrast to "I thought she was a feisty one the moment I laid eyes on her."

As in the example presented in this chapter, the child's progressive development might mean many things for parents. One of the challenges to maintaining parents' reflective functioning capacity during toddlerhood is their ability to actualize who the child is becoming while away from them. During this period, a child's personality emerges more clearly as their verbal and motoric capacities develop. This can truly encourage parents' capacity to start seeing the child as separate physically and psychologically. However, it can also represent a challenge to parents' mentalized affectivity capacities when confronted, for example, with a highly reactive toddler or a slow-to-warm-up toddler. During these moments, the parent's capacity to think developmentally about the child is vital in order to separate what comes from the child as a result of the maturational process (e.g., learning to be themselves separate from their parents).

Toddlers are not small adults—they might speak increasingly more and climb higher chairs than they used to, but they still experience and face the stressors of the world from a psychic equivalence mode of functioning, meaning that they will still process, for example, along the lines of "When I am angry, I see Mommy or Daddy as angry and will act upon that impression." This is very important to explain to parents, as being faced with a raging toddler is bound to activate the parents' prementalizing functioning as well as awaken all the ghosts in the nursery. Take, for example, the 2-year-old who does not want to eat her food, or the 3-year-old who refuses to put on his seatbelt in the car. Both of these examples could be understood, from a developmental lens, as indications of the child practicing their sense of "being themselves" in the world, or they could be interpreted as defiance and stubbornness, which carry individual meanings for each parent. So how can we help parents with the process of separating the self and the other?

- Provide psychoeducation about the emotional world of the toddler.

- Explore parents' expectations of what they believe their child should be doing or not.

- Explore parents' fears.

- Ask parents to bring examples, accompany the parents in sequencing, and look at the difficult episode from the perspective of the child and the parents separately.

WORKING ON JOINT ATTENTION IN THE MIDST OF EMERGING AND FAST-CHANGING SOCIOCOGNITIVE DEVELOPMENT

Dyadic work in the context of toddlerhood is vital (Kwon et al., 2012; Wass, 2021). Working alone with a young child, without including the parent, excludes the opportunity of providing both caregiver and child a chance to experience each other in a new, alternative way. Moments of enjoyment when the child and the parent can experience each other away from the usual nonmentalizing cycles, such as tantrums over bath time or refusal of other routines, facilitate the expansion of how the child sees themselves in the context of relationships—as well as give the parent the opportunity of regaining the pleasure and joy of the early days, away from the negative emotions that challenge and inhibit their reflective functioning. This is particularly true in the context of potentially traumatic experiences, such as domestic violence, medical issues, and neuroatypicality. Dyadic work seeks to

- promote a sense of safety in relating, through mutual enjoyment

- facilitate or even enable the experience of looking and making sense together of a difficult experience

- help each partner to discover the other under a different light—one based on strengths

- discover self-strengths in the parent that are often overshadowed by feelings of guilt and shame

- recreate early experiences of marked mirroring and imperfect contingency, where rupture and repair can take place and be reflected on

The following is an example of this in the work with Lorain and her mom, Andrea:

Andrea and Lorain enter the consulting room. Lorain (just over 2.5 years old) likes to play in the sandbox, so she grabs her mom's hand and directs her to it. The therapist remarks on how much Lorain wants to share this activity, which she likes so much, with her mom. Mom smiles and says she is honored.

LORAIN:	Come, Mama—now!
ANDREA:	[*looking at the therapist*] Somebody knows what she wants . . .
THERAPIST:	I agree, she wants to play with Mama—right, L? [*Lorain ignores the therapist and shows her mom all the toys in the sand.*]
ANDREA:	Lorain, Dr. M spoke to you . . .
THERAPIST:	Excitement makes our little manners disappear. I think that will be OK, Mama.
ANDREA:	Alright . . . I don't want her to think that is OK to do . . .
THERAPIST:	Your mom wants you to have good manners, Lorain. I respect that, but today, we are going to focus on having fun, like we can do in here.

ANDREA: I think that message is more for me than Lorain.

THERAPIST: Probably . . . [*smiles*]

Lorain invites Mom to make a small castle, Mom works hard on it, and then Lorain breaks it in delight. Andrea shrugs her shoulders. Lorain looks on with anticipation as Andrea adds, "I guess I will have to do another one." Lorain smiles with discernible relief and bounces up and down in excitement. Andrea touches her on the back and softly asks if Lorain can help her—to which Lorain says "no" and walks away.

THERAPIST: What do you think just happened?

ANDREA: She always wants it the way she likes . . .

THERAPIST: [*as Lorain starts taking some blocks from a shelf*] Is that the whole picture?

ANDREA: I guess not . . . Lorain, come, don't leave Mama alone, I need your help [*with a very funny facial expression*].

                  [*Lorain runs to Mom and holds on to her neck quite tightly. Andrea tickles her a bit to loosen the grip, and it works. Andrea tells Lorain it is time to destroy the castle. Lorain breaks it a little but leaves the rest intact.*]

THERAPIST: That is a surprise! I think you figured out that Mama really likes her castle.

LORAIN   Let's make a bigger one!
[SMILING]:
                  [*Andrea gives Lorain a big kiss as the child sits on her lap. Lorain helps Andrea, with her little hands, and, suddenly, the room feels different—less tension.*]

THERAPIST: Sometimes it takes a bit of time to figure out how to work together.

ANDREA: Indeed.

Following this session, the therapist and Andrea meet to explore the feelings in the room and think about what happened to each of the people involved, including the therapist. It provides an opportunity to explore the impact that Lorain's unpredictable responses have on her mother and how to understand and manage the emotions clouding Andrea's reflective function. In this sequence particularly, the use of nonverbal behavior is key—as in many sessions with a toddler–parent dyad. This is particularly important for a mom such as Andrea, who places a lot of value on what is said. This example takes us to the next challenge of working with parents of toddlers—that of maintaining the capacity to identify, modulate, and express emotions as a parent, when working with a young child who is still experiencing what psychodynamic theory calls *primitive emotions*— that is, emotions without too many words attached to them, not having been understood away from bodily experience (i.e., felt and expressed through the body via actions).

COREGULATION IN MOTION: WORKING TOWARD MENTALIZED AFFECTIVITY DURING EXPRESSION OF A TODDLER'S UNMODULATED EMOTIONS

Tolerating, staying present, and figuring out what to do during tantrums is one of the biggest challenges that parents describe facing. It is important to differentiate between parents who have not had access to parenting resources, and so do not have any strategies for responding, and those who know what the books say or who have gotten strategies from other therapists but are struggling in these moments of huge, confusing emotion. As we touch on later in this chapter, these "What should I do?" moments can indicate that the session is headed away from mentalizing and into a teleological mode. The therapist's first response to this question might be something along the lines of "Well, before we go into what you can do, let's talk a bit more about what her tantrums are like—for you and for her."

ANDREA: It is just wild. Like, totally bonkers.

THERAPIST: Is there a recent one that comes to mind?

ANDREA: Yeah, so last night, we're getting read for bed, and I don't even know how it started but she was laying on the bathroom floor pretending to be sleeping, and then when I said it was time to go to bed, she was like, "No, I'm sleeping here." So I took a deep breath, because it's been a long day, and in my calmest voice, I'm like, "Lo, sweetie, you can't sleep here, this is where people need to come to use the bathroom, and they might step on you. You need to sleep in your bed like a big girl." And then I don't even know, I can't even describe it. It was like some back-and-forth and just progressively she's like coming undone. She's flailing her arms and kicking at me to get away. And I'm like trying my best to stay calm and just repeat it to her that she cannot sleep there. But it's so hard!

THERAPIST: It is so hard! I think I can picture what you're describing, and it's the end of a long day . . . [*The therapist begins by empathizing and then noticing and naming the factors in the situation, to ensure that both participants are in a shared space of joint attention in this moment, now, in the therapy session.*]. You said what you were trying to do, but what was going through your mind?

ANDREA: Well, I'm trying to keep in mind like "Stay calm, breathe." But no offense, that stuff is kinda BS.

THERAPIST: Yeah, sounds like you were working really hard to do all the things parenting resources talk about. But I have a feeling there might be some other thoughts in there, because there often are for parents.

ANDREA: Oh, you want like the real thoughts.

THERAPIST: [*smiling*] Yes, I am curious about the thoughts that you might not feel like you should be thinking or saying outside of this room.

ANDREA: Honestly, I see so much of myself in my daughters sometimes, but I was just like, "When I was a little girl, I would have never been allowed to talk back to my mom in that way!" And I don't know if it's something that David and I did that she thinks she can be like this.

THERAPIST: So I think the blame you start to feel is something for us to note and come back to, but I also noticed something really interesting and important, I think, in how you just said, "She thinks she can be like this." It made me curious if it seems like she is thinking in these moments.

ANDREA: That is a really good point. I don't think she is.

THERAPIST: Yeah, that was my sense, too, but since you were the one there, I wanted to check it out.

ANDREA: I think she's super tired, we'd had a long day, all of us. And it has been so hot. I think all of us kind of felt like collapsing on the bathroom floor. I even did, after she went to bed, and just cried.

THERAPIST: So you could really connect to that feeling. Of course, I'm imagining you weren't flailing, but you could relate to that internal state.

ANDREA: Oh yeah, totally.

This vignette illustrates some of the techniques that can be helpful in working with parents around children's tantrums. In the beginning, it is hard to even imagine what you might be able to offer the parent, because tantrums are so difficult. But if the therapist can maintain their own mentalizing, they can notice the signals for a teleological or psychic equivalence mode and intervene in ways that rebalance the parent's mentalizing.

WORKING ON EPISTEMIC TRUST DURING THE TODDLER PERIOD

Parenting is a process of gains and joy and losses and mourning. Toddlerhood is a period when many parents mourn the level of physical closeness and dependency of the infant. For other parents, though, it signifies the emergence of their child as a person. Exploring this meaning is very important, as it opens the door to parents' "myth of parenting" and how it impacts how they self-evaluate and how they interpret their children's behaviors.

Toddlers tend to bring back feelings of frustration and rage in adults, which surprises and baffles them. On one hand, toddlers retain the physical "cuteness" of the young age (e.g., chubby hands, little features and voices), which promotes caregiving. On the other hand, verbal and motoric development brings the toddler forward as a more active and, at times, challenging partner. Returning to Lorain for a minute, for instance, she is described as a highly verbal and precocious toddler. This has different meanings for her parents, and exploring the thoughts and feelings that accompany those meanings can prove to be the door to the "epistemic highway."

The following is an example of how exploring a parent's values, expectations, and beliefs about a toddler can facilitate the emergence of a parent's belief that the therapist is truly interested in understanding the difficulties the parent is experiencing. This belief in the parent will help in moving away from the need to ask for concrete solutions as their main request and will hopefully give the parent a new motivation to learn to "be with" their child from a mentalizing stance, which, during their interactions with the psychotherapist, they have received.

David and Andrea come for their second parent session. During the first session, they explored their own experiences as children managing their emotions in the context of their families of origin. The therapist offered empathy and validation, as well as some basic psychoeducation about the toddler's emotional world. Andrea begins this session by reporting that Lorain enjoyed their meeting with the therapist and talked about being a big girl because she played alone with the therapist while Mom went to the toilet.

THERAPIST: How did you experience seeing Lorain so proud of herself?

ANDREA: I was surprised, to be honest, I thought she was going to cry when I had to go out of the room . . .

THERAPIST: By looking at your face, I am not sure if you felt that was a good thing or not?

DAVID: [*laughs a little*] I think Andrea is having a hard time with Lorain's "I am grown-up girl" attitude [*makes a funny hand gesture*].

THERAPIST: That is a fun-looking gesture, what does it mean?

ANDREA: It is a way of David showing that I am a bit "sensitive."

THERAPIST: Ah! I see . . . What would you be sensitive about?

ANDREA: I think . . . about the girls growing up so fast, you know?

THERAPIST: I think I do. What does "grown-up" mean for each of you?

DAVID: For me, it means being able to be alone in the world and survive . . .

ANDREA: I think of "grown-up" as . . . loss of fun and innocence . . .

THERAPIST: I must confess "loss of innocence" catches my attention, don't you think, David?

DAVID: I think what Andrea means to say is, you start understanding things that make you feel worried and less free as a child . . .

THERAPIST: Is that it, Andrea?

ANDREA: Hmmm . . . I think, yes, it is . . . it just makes me sad . . .

THERAPIST: When was a time that you realized that it happened to you?

ANDREA: For me, it was my parent's divorce when I was 6 . . .

DAVID: For me, it was when my grandmother died, I was 8 and I remember everything about the last day I saw her . . .

THERAPIST: She was someone important for you . . .

DAVID: She was . . . When my mom wasn't around and was out doing whatever she did, I would call my grandmother, and she would tell me funny stories to distract me . . . She was a very good cook and taught me to make good chicken . . .

ANDREA: He does make good chicken . . . [*all three laugh*]

THERAPIST: It seems that maybe not all the innocence and hope is gone from the two of you . . .

ANDREA: I see where you are going . . . but it is difficult when you see them grow so fast . . . you want to protect them from everything, and Lorain is just a bit stubborn and is not easy to help and protect sometimes.

THERAPIST: That would make any parent a bit worried, but she also seems to know that even when you are not physically there you are close, that you would do your very best to protect her, does that make sense?

DAVID: It does and it makes me think of when Andrea has gone out with friends, and Lorain goes to our room and lays in Andrea's spot in our bed for a bit and then goes off and plays. It's like, she wants to get close to Andrea and then she is OK.

THERAPIST: That is such a nice example, David. What do you think, Andrea?

ANDREA: I agree babe, that is a sweet example.

DAVID: Well, well . . . who is the psychologist now?

ANDREA: [*touches her husband's hand*] Don't let it get to your head [*laughs*].

THERAPIST: I think we have gotten to a good place together from which we can start understanding that the challenges are not only coming from your daughter but also from the feelings and

	memories and fears they wake up in you, does that make sense?
ANDREA:	It does, it really does. I know I am too "hot and cold" . . .
THERAPIST:	Did you hear me say that? I am sorry if you did.
DAVID:	[*hugs his wife*] She's always ready to hear a criticism . . .
ANDREA:	I do . . . I think Lorain is a bit like me . . .
THERAPIST:	I think that is a very good topic to explore, how about we start there . . .

Overall, as a society, we have the tendency of ignoring the emotional life of infants and toddlers. As a result, when a parent seeks help for a child under the age of 5, the source of motivation is often a concrete difficulty being experienced by the child, which disturbs the family's functioning. Working from a mentalization-based approach, we seek to help parents make the connection between the child's specific difficulty and the quality and functioning of the relationship in the context of the parent's own early childhood experiences. However, not all parents are like Lorain's, who were ready to talk about their own histories. Most mental health providers ask the question "Is there any history of mental health issues in your family?" While this is an important question, it may not be answered honestly and fully unless some basic epistemic trust has been established between the therapist and the parent. In the same fashion, when we ask parents too quickly about their own relationship with their parents, they might respond in a dismissive or defensive way. In our example of Lorain's parents, starting with the child's behavior in the here and now of the session and then following it with a positive attribution of her behavior (e.g., "She has good object constancy") sets the tone for a nonjudgmental environment focused on the child's and parents' strengths and not weaknesses. This framework sets the emotional tone, in the session, of collaboration, where the therapist lends their capacity to look at things from the outside and imagine them from the inside, with the help of the parents and vice versa. The parent session becomes a relational laboratory wherein to play with thoughts, feelings, and imagination.

As illustrated by our example, the use of humor and constant checking ("Did I understand that correctly?") and noticing and naming ("I wonder what that facial expression is trying to communicate") creates a dynamic, coregulating system where mentalized affectivity can be practiced in the service of the parents–therapist relationship. The hope is that parents discover here a motivation to learn from the therapist, and, most importantly, a different way of "being with" in the context of difficult and painful emotions—in this case, from their own past. By working this way, we can slowly make the connection between (a) the parents' own history and relational experience and (b) how it impacts their behavior. This insight can then be generalized to their understanding of their young child—that is,

> When my young child behaves in a certain way, they are communicating a thought, a feeling, a need, a conflict that they cannot put into words or play. What can I do to help them do that? What does my child need?

This attitude is very different from "My child can't sleep—tell me what to do."

WORKING BACK AND FORTH WITH PARENTS IN THE DEVELOPMENTAL LINE OF MENTALIZATION DURING THE TODDLER PERIOD

In this section, we apply the three blocks constituting the pathway toward explicit mentalization to our work with parents of toddlers: attention regulation, affect regulation, and explicit mentalization. We return to the case of David and Andrea, Lorain's parents, to provide clinical illustration of working in each of the three building blocks of mentalizing. Once a mentalizing profile of a parent has been developed, the therapist can get a sense of "where to meet the parent." In one single session with a parent, the therapist can navigate the developmental line of mentalization back and forth, going from a focus on attention regulation to one on affect regulation and back. It is helpful for the therapist to have this framework in mind, particularly in the context of parents' nonmentalizing stances.

Attention Regulation

During the toddler stage, the integration between what the child is feeling in their body and what they think and feel at a more abstract level is occurring. This is a time in which focusing attention on helping parents to use their "imagination based on reality" is paramount to avoid projection of their own experience. By working on providing the experience of feeling seen and heard to parents, we help them to develop the awareness of their own emotional functioning in a way that facilitates their own capacity to help their child in the same process. Moreover, the parent's awareness of the toddler's nonverbal communications can help the parent to avoid falling into a state of mind blindness, such as, "My child is fine, I don't know what you mean, he cries a lot usually, that is all" or of hypermentalization, such as, "I think my child is very depressed . . . he is probably like my sister who is bipolar" (both are examples of pretend mode). We help parents to work on their capacity for attention regulation by

- focusing on noticing and naming affective changes in the context of the session, which may indicate the emotional impact of something discussed

  Clinical example: *Andrea is speaking of Lorain's stubbornness at dinnertime. Andrea begins to talk loudly, and her face turns into a frown as she continues to describe the last "bumpy road" with Lorain. Minutes later, Andrea stops speaking and visibly relaxes and then looks out the window and says, "She does not like me, my child does not like me!" The therapist reflects out loud, "Andrea, I noticed that you seemed first somewhat angry or stressed, but now, I think you are suddenly sad, your shoulders are completely inwards. Am I perceiving the way you feel correctly?" Andrea smiles and says she feels so sad but also so tired. The therapist replies, "Tired of feeling like you always fall short with Lorain?" Andrea answers, "Yes, but most people just see the very confident Andrea as a mom, I hide the frustration and sadness well . . ."*

  - In this example, by noticing and naming a parent's affective shift based on the observable, we are showing the value of doing so before drawing conclusions about the motivations behind one's behavior. This is an important mentalizing skill that prevents negative attributions or avoidant parental behavior.

- bringing attention to a specific nonmentalizing sequence between the parent and the child in the context of dyadic work and inviting all involved to "stop and rewind"—trying to understand how the parent and the child "got where they are," feeling far away from each other and often at a loss as to what to do next to reconnect

  Clinical example: *David is sitting with Lorain, playing with memory cards for toddlers. They are really enjoying each other. Suddenly, Lorain becomes a bit fussy, and David tries to keep her engaged in the game, making funny faces and asking her what is going on. Lorain gets increasingly angry, gets up, and hits her dad with her fist and goes under the table. The therapist uses a calm but clearly confused tone and asks David, "What is going on with Lorain, she went 'poof' under the table!" David plays along and replies, "I think she got angry with me, because she hit me." The therapist responds, "I agree, but I don't know why she got angry" and hands a puppet that Lorain likes playing with to David, who gets under the table and uses it to speak to Lorain to "tell the story," meaning sequencing what just happened. Lorain smiles and tells the little puppet that she does not like to play too long; it gets too difficult. David tells Lorain he is sorry he did not know. Lorain comes out, they pick up the game, and daughter and father decide to play with the play dough.*

– In this example, the therapist helps the parent to redirect the focus of the child by using an explicit curious stance, which proves holding and facilitating to both parent and child. Both the therapist and the parent keep the dialogue with the child in the play by using the puppet to help the child regain the capacity to coregulate, which helps the process of affect regulation.

Affect Regulation

During the toddler stage, parents are presented with the daunting task of trying to help the child regulate emotions, by using both their bodies and their words in explicit ways to help the child feel safe. Safety is very important for the establishment of secure attachment—that is, the belief that there will be someone there to help when the child feels afraid, stressed, or under threat. When a child gets the signal (verbal or nonverbal) from their parent that their negative emotions are not received or are rejected or punished, the child struggles to find ways in which to express them and make sense of them. This is often the source of toddler's symptomatology such as sleeping and eating difficulties, which result in nonmentalizing battles between the child and the parent(s). Affect regulation requires some level of joint attention leading to attention regulation and the feeling of being seeing and heard by the other—in this case, the parent. Working with parents in learning how to identify, modulate, and express emotions (*mentalized affectivity*) for the child and themselves is the work we do when we are focusing on the block of affect regulation. Our work with parents of toddlers in this block requires practicing the following in a scaffolding way from 1 to 4, back and forth:

1. Checking: "I think you are feeling a bit judged by me, am I right?"

2. Stop and rewind: "Can we stop for a minute; I think something just happened to you when I started speaking of Lorain's angry outburst at day care . . . you seemed a bit angry with me and then you changed topics and I felt like I was being a bit mean."

3. Naming emotions and exploring how they are spoken or shown by both parent and child, beginning with what is observable, on our way to explicit mentalizing, which entails the use of imagination based on reality: "I have

noticed when you speak of Lorain's tantrums you look sad, but I am not sure if it is sadness or helplessness and frustration . . . How do you feel about her tantrums? What do you think she sees in your face?"

4. Working on parents' mentalized affectivity capacity during toddlers' unpredictable and contagious emotionality.

Explicit Mentalization

To work in the explicit mentalizing block, a capacity for collaboration and epistemic trust is necessary, as it requires the exploration of both the parent's perspective and the child's perspective through "grounded imagination." Furthermore, working at this level requires a parent's capacity to "observe themselves from the outside," as well. For this, parents need to have explored ways in which to "simmer down" their emotions and maintain their capacity for mentalized affectivity by identifying links with their relational past in the context of their young child's puzzling behavior. Working with parents of toddlers requires a developmental lens that helps the parent remember that they are in quite an uneven partnership, in which the young child is still depending on them for safety in very real ways—not only emotionally. Sometimes this is difficult to remember, especially when faced with stubborn and seemingly defiant behavior.

CLINICAL EXAMPLE: WORKING WITH THE PARENTAL COUPLE

Andrea comes with David to a session, after 3 months of working with the therapist, looking quite frustrated . . .

ANDREA: I can't take it anymore, we are going crazy with Lorain, she is out of control, and she is almost 3 years old . . . This is just not working, we need more specific guidelines on how to respond to her. I swear, someone is going to call protective services on us because of the way she cries. We are the ones who need protection!

DAVID: Here, look at this video we took of her yesterday . . .

[*The therapist takes David's phone and observes the video quietly. Then she wonders if they could all look at it together and have a conversation about it. Both Andrea and David agree, and the three adults look at the video.*]

THERAPIST: How were you feeling right there? [*pauses the video in a part where Andrea's face looks frozen and afraid*]

ANDREA: I think I was thinking "Are you kidding me? We are really trying here! It is not OK for a small child to have so much power!"

THERAPIST: What "power" does she have there and then? She looks a bit out of control, must have been very exhausting for both of you, this tantrum seems to never end . . .

ANDREA: It took almost an hour to calm her down . . .

THERAPIST: My goodness, I can feel the frustration involved while watching . . . I want to do something to help her . . .

ANDREA: That is the thing . . . I don't want to help her; I just want her to be quiet and be a good girl . . .

DAVID: Don't say that . . . You want to help her . . . That is your anger speaking . . .

THERAPIST: This terrible tantrum was yesterday . . . perhaps you are still feeling it inside of you?

ANDREA: I think so . . . I feel bad for feeling I wish she would disappear sometimes . . . she looks at me with those angry eyes . . .

THERAPIST: What do you see in Andrea's eyes, David?

DAVID: I see fear and sadness . . . not anger . . .

THERAPIST: Does that surprise you, Andrea?

ANDREA: A little . . . but he is right . . . I am afraid of what I feel like doing to her when she gets like that over not wanting to have her dinner . . . It is ridiculous . . .

THERAPIST: Not necessarily . . . what does her behavior here mean to you? What does it say?

ANDREA: "I don't want your food, I don't want you . . ."

THERAPIST: Just like when she was little, and you had a hard time breastfeeding her?

ANDREA: Yes . . .

THERAPIST: It has been a tough road for the two of you. What do you think she saw in your face here?

ANDREA: Maybe . . . that I am afraid of her . . .

THERAPIST: Tough for such a little person out of control . . .

DAVID: It's true . . . it is tough for everyone

THERAPIST: I agree . . .

THE BALANCING ACT IN THE TODDLER YEARS

As the toddler begins to move forward developmentally, this becomes a challenge, both cognitively and affectively, for the parent. Mentalizing is a sociocognitive capacity—not a unitary unidimensional capacity but a dynamic and transactional one that emerges in the context of relationships. Neuroscience findings have been particularly instrumental in defining mentalizing as being organized around four polarities, with each polarity having relatively distinct underlying neural circuits. These four polarities are (a) automatic versus controlled mentalizing, (b) mentalizing regarding self and to others, (c) mentalizing based on external or internal features of self and others, and (d) cognitive versus affective mentalizing (Fonagy & Luyten, 2009; Luyten et al., 2012).

Keeping these four dimensions in mind during our work with parents helps us to restore the capacity of mentalization to the interaction after prementalizing modes emerge in the context of stress. Thinking of the four polarities of mentalization allows us to structure and guide our technique. Furthermore, it allows us to model a new set of strategies for parents that hopefully they can learn and generalize in their child-rearing practices. This is particularly valuable in the context of early childhood, when the seeds for the development of mentalization are planted in the context of the interactions between child and parent.

In this section, we return to Andrea and David and illustrate the clinical application of the four mentalization dimensions to a therapist's way of responding and managing stressful situations in the work with parents, which we described in Part I of this book.

The therapeutic goal here is to try to notice when there is an unbalance, in one of the dimensions, that is causing a way of functioning, in the parent, that is impacting their capacity for reflective functioning. Usually, an unbalance in one of the dimensions manifests itself when the parent is experiencing strong emotions and feels threatened from internal feelings or perceived external threats. As indicated in the MBT adult model (Bateman & Fonagy, 2012), the therapists engage in contrary moves—that is, if a parent is strongly focusing on emotion, the therapist brings up something that balances that by activating more cognitive functioning: for example, a valuable piece of psychoeducation. In the following example, we illustrate the different technical moves of the therapist to help the parent in the process of regaining her reflective functioning capacities. We see how the therapist moves the mom from a state of certainty and lack of curiosity regarding her daughter toward a more curious and reality-based view of her child. We see how the therapist helps the mom move from a high level of affect to a more balanced state by introducing some psychoeducational aspects regarding toddlerhood. We also witness how the therapist helps the mom to distinguish between which emotions belong to her and which ones belong to her daughter. Finally, we observe the therapist inviting the mom to make more explicit her thinking out loud, in order to create an environment where both implicit and explicit mentalizing can take place and where the therapist can help as a source not only of validation but also of support for exploration of alternative ways of understanding the child's behavior.

CLINICAL EXAMPLE: WORKING WITH ANDREA (LORAIN'S MOM)

Andrea came to a session alone, after 6 months of working with the therapist. Lorain seemed to be doing better at school but continued to struggle with managing her feelings at home, despite her family's efforts. David had to be out of town for work, so he asked Andrea to come alone to the session.

ANDREA: I can't take it anymore . . . Yesterday, Lorain was so mean to Sonia, I became enraged and hit her on her legs with my hand . . . I felt terrible afterwards . . . I have never hit one of my girls . . . I swore I would never do it, but she really pushed my patience to the limit . . .

THERAPIST: I probably would have felt frustrated if I saw one of my children being that mean . . . [*validates and invites focus on self–other dimension*]

ANDREA: The thing is . . . she is getting older and stronger, and I am worried about the future. She just does not seem to have any empathy for any of us. I can't believe I am saying this but yesterday I thought "Why didn't we stay with one kid?" . . .

	She is such a manipulating little shit sometimes . . . I am certain she does not care that she makes all of us so stressed.
THERAPIST:	How do you know that? That must be terrible for you to see that in her, I am so sorry [*self–other dimension*].
ANDREA:	I don't know . . . it is the way she smiles . . .
THERAPIST:	What happens to you when she smiles like that . . . what does it say to you? [*cognitive–affective dimension*]
ANDREA:	It says, "You piece of shit mother, you are messing me up, I don't love you, you failure."
THERAPIST:	That is a very painful thing to imagine and feel . . . [*self–other pole*]
ANDREA:	It is . . .
THERAPIST:	I wonder if that thought was the one that made you cross that boundary of physical punishment you avoid so much, it must have hurt you deeply . . . [*cognitive–affective pole*]
ANDREA:	It did . . . and I don't know how she understood it . . . [*return to uncertainty, curiosity*]
THERAPIST:	What do you think?
ANDREA:	If I had to guess . . . probably . . . "Why is Mama hurting me? That makes no sense." [*explicit–implicit dimension*]
THERAPIST:	Sounds like there is a possibility that you were both pretty confused on your own, in your own islands but without being able to build a bridge, does that make sense?
ANDREA:	It does . . . How do we build a bridge? [*return to a sense of "we-ness" and togetherness*]

PREMENTALIZING MODES IN THE CONTEXT OF PARENTING A TODDLER

Toddlers function primarily in teleological and psychic equivalence modes of functioning as they further develop their sociocognitive capacities. This is very important to learn how to explain to parents in ways they can understand and in order to support their mentalizing efforts. It is also important to think about how to respond to parents' own prementalizing functioning and how it may be impacting the quality of their interactions with their children. Often, we find ourselves trying to balance the mentalizing poles in order to help parents exiting a prementalizing response to their children's behavior. The following are examples of this process in the context of Lorain's case.

Clinical Examples

Teleological: David and Andrea complained that Lorain was always asking for things—they were worried that she was greedy and not considerate. The therapist explained that 2.5-year-olds understand expressions of love that they can see, which includes gifts but also hugs and smiles. However, children this age are often trying to establish their sense of agency and intentionality, and this can take the form of what could be interpreted as spoiled and stubborn behavior (*focus on the child*). The therapist invited both parents to reflect on what thinking of their daughter as greedy felt like (*from cognitive to affective*). Andrea spoke of feeling worried that Lorain would not have friends at school and wanting to see Lorain invited to playdates, like her sister. Andrea said that she would like the therapist to help her child become more empathic (*teleological need*). The therapist spoke about the importance of this for Andrea and explored her disappointment regarding the speed of the therapeutic process. Andrea shyly agreed, and David said he was trying to be patient but felt frustrated not seeing enough change in their daughter. The therapist spoke of her understanding of Lorain from a developmental lens (*from affective to cognitive*) and spoke of seeing a true capacity to connect and a curiosity about others. However, she explained, she understood that it was difficult to keep that in mind when Lorain behaved in a spoiled and stubborn way (*focus on the parents' teleological stance while linking behavior to emotional impact*).

Psychic equivalence: David explained that he had a very bad afternoon with Lorain the previous Sunday. He had been feeling positive about closeness between him and Lorain and had come up with a "Daddy and Lorain" cooking project. Together, daughter and father had gone to the supermarket to find all of the ingredients to make a pizza. David thought it would be fun for Lorain to do something sensorially, as they had discussed her sensory integration profile in therapy and realized that applying pressure helped her calm down. David and Lorain had anticipated their "cooking date" for days. However, when the time came to begin working together, Lorain did not want to do anything—she seemed interested only in playing with the pasta roller. David tried being playful, putting the pizza dough in his hand and showing it to Lorain, who simply ignored him. After 20 minutes of failed attempts to get her engaged, David felt his anger come up, took away the roller, and told Lorain that he did not want to play with her anymore if she was not going to help with the cooking and sent a tearful and upset Lorain to her room, where she cried in despair. David spoke of feeling defeated and resentful that Lorain had been so mean to him—proof, he thought, that she did not like him (*psychic equivalence*). The therapist asked him what thoughts gave way to those feelings (*focus on mentalizing Dad's teleological need to feel loved and played with*). David explained that he thought Lorain did not like him because he always is the one to discipline her when she is mean to her sister and mother. He said that she would not ever hug him and seemed to enjoy playing with other family members, including his dad, much more than him. The therapist asked David about his own dad, as he seemed surprised that Lorain appeared to prefer him. David said his dad was a good father but that he had not ever had time to play with David, nor had he been warm toward David, as a child. David spoke of always wanting to be a different kind of father to his daughters—and how now he could tell he had failed (*ghosts in the nursery*). The therapist showed empathy nonverbally in her facial expression. David responded by saying that he did not need the therapist's pity (*psychic equivalence*). The therapist said that she was sorry if he had gotten the impression that she was pitying him and that, in fact, she was impressed with his insight and his honesty, adding that she felt sad that both father and daughter really wanted to connect but it was difficult. David looked moved and became visibly sad (*balancing cognitive and affective*); he said he knew Lorain was just a little girl and spoke of feeling guilty about disliking her so much sometimes (*self–other differentiation*). Toward the end of the session, David did not speak with such certainty of his daughter as disliking him—instead, he was more curious about understanding what had happened so that she had become so stubborn and he had become so distressed.

Pretend: Andrea was speaking of Lorain's progress positively and then explained that the area where she still worried a lot was that of Lorain's capacity to be kind and generous with her sister and with other kids. She spoke about understanding that developmentally, Lorain was different from her sister, Sonia, who was ahead of her peers in so many ways. Andrea added that she understood that Lorain was a different person from her sister and that Andrea had to be careful not to forget that. Andrea spoke of having read Dr. Brazelton's (1992) book and realizing she had been using developmental standards that were not realistic. However, she wondered whether Dr. Brazelton's work was gender sensitive (*pretend mode*). The therapist said that that was an important question, but she wondered how they had gotten there in a conversation that had begun with Andrea's worries about Lorain's difficulties being kind (*sequencing promoting the move from cognitive to affective*). Andrea paused and spoke of her difficulty accepting how different Lorain was from her, and she also talked about feeling guilty of not liking her (*self-mentalizing*). The therapist replied that maybe she was wrong, but it seemed to her that for Andrea, the difference was daunting and painful, and perhaps Andrea worried about how the world might respond to a girl who was different than what she thought was more accepted (*differentiating self–other*). Andrea visibly relaxed and added, "That is my main task, I guess—learning to live with that fear."

CONCLUDING SUMMARY

- Toddlerhood is a period of rapid change, both physically and emotionally, that requires a great deal of flexibility and grounded imagination from parents.

- Toddlers are often struggling with learning how to integrate their love and hate, and, because of that, sometimes they can prove quite challenging for parents.

- Parents' mentalized affectivity capacities are required in the context of a toddler's dysregulated emotions and the behavior it promotes.

- Parents' own relational pasts are often triggered strongly with the emergence of intentionality and the need for agency often experienced by toddlers.

- The shift from primary attachment figure toward a more "refueling" role can feel like a deep loss for parents, promoting, in this way, the reemergence of prementalizing ways of functioning.

- Very real fears regarding the child's future functioning inhibit parents' reflective functioning during this period of development, as the child's emerging personality traits become more visible as the child explores the world.

- Keeping in mind the balancing of the mentalizing dimensions during our work with parents can support the therapist's own mentalizing when presented with highly teleological demands from parents. These demands often emerge from stressful situations, such as sleeping and eating difficulties with the young child.

- Identifying nonmentalizing cycles between the parent and the child is vital during this period. Working dyadically and using video feedback with parents can help to activate a parent's self-mentalization and begin the process of differentiation from their child.

9 WORKING WITH PARENTS OF SCHOOL-AGE CHILDREN (5-12)

CASE PRESENTATION AND FORMULATION

Joe was a White 7-year-old boy referred to therapy by his school due to concerns with his capacity to relate to other children and his difficulty managing his emotions in class and on the school's playground. Joe was described by his school as a very sweet, yet unpredictable, boy. He would often hit other children over the head with balls and his hands without warning and often engaged in simulations of war scenes on the playground. Whenever a peer did not want to do what he wanted, he would lose his temper, cry, and punch adults and children. The school had resorted to placing him in a "calming down room," which worked only temporarily, frustrating the school personnel. A special assistant was assigned to Joe to facilitate his transitions and help mediate the peer world with which he seemed to struggle. A formal evaluation showed that Joe had significant difficulties with social pragmatics as well as with overall social situations in which he seemed to misunderstand others and react.

https://doi.org/10.1037/0000341-010

Working With Parents in Therapy: A Mentalization-Based Approach, by N. Malberg, E. Jurist, J. Bate, and M. Dangerfield

Joe was the youngest of three children; his siblings, Rose (age 13) and Richard (9), were doing well in school and in general. Marleen (44) and Sophie (47), the children's parents, had been together for 17 years. Marleen was the biological mother of Rose and Richard, and Sophie was Joe's biological mother. Marleen was a high school biology teacher, and Sophie was a tennis coach at the local college. Both parents felt that Joe was misunderstood at school—and, at times, scapegoated—but agreed that Joe had seemed to struggle with making sense of the social world since a young age. They spoke of Joe's early years as challenging, as he had had difficulties with feeding and regulating his sleep. Neither of his siblings had had such difficulties, so Sophie felt concerned because Joe's biological father had been a different sperm donor than that of Joe's siblings. Marleen was extremely supportive of Sophie and would often try to reassure her that it was nobody's fault that Joe was different—it was just because "that is who he is." Both Marleen and Sophie affectionately called Joe their "little unicorn," which often enraged Joe, as it seemed to signify his role as the "different one" in the family. He got along well with both of his siblings, who were extremely patient and accommodating with him during his moments of dysregulation at home.

Joe was given special accommodation at school, he was seen by a speech therapist to work on social pragmatics, he received occupational therapy privately to work on his clumsiness, and he was now attending individual psychotherapy once per week. As a result of the complexity of the case, due to the involvement of the school and other special therapies, two therapists shared the case: One worked directly with Joe, and the other worked with his parents and the professional network. However, both therapists would meet with Joe's parents and Joe together, once per month, to review the focus of the work. This chapter focuses on the therapist's applications of the mentalizing framework in the work with Joe's parents. Working with parents of a child, such as Joe, who presents with unpredictable emotional dysregulation and displays significant difficulties in his theory of mind functioning, is challenging for mental health providers because it requires one to mentalize not only the child and his parents but also the school system and other support systems.

Joe presented with quite atypical ways of dealing with normative peer conflict. The only time he seemed to feel at ease with other children his age was when he played video games and spoke to them online. This often confused his family, because they wondered if he had the capacity to understand and relate to others and was just choosing not to. However, during the classroom observation, Joe's therapist could observe evidence of genuine difficulties in relating, as Joe seemed truly perplexed and lost in the context of the usual "peer politics" characteristic of this age group. Joe's parents explained that at home, everyone "spoke Joe"; however, it was more difficult for other adults to understand him. As a result, Joe's parents felt they had, perhaps, overprotected him. Joe did not speak until he was nearly 4 years old—he had learned that signing with his hands and pointing was enough, in his home, to get what he wanted and needed. Both siblings had learned how to appease Joe, so his tantrums were largely avoided due to the whole family system being extremely mindful of his need to feel in control. Unfortunately, this was not an environment that was easy to replicate anywhere else, so kindergarten proved quite a challenge, with the school calling his parents every other day for him to be picked up at 11 a.m. for "not being safe in his behavior" or "being out of control and impossible to soothe." By the time Joe reached second grade, he had learned by heart all the regulations of the school and was able to function better inside the classroom if no major changes occurred. Whenever a new and unexpected transition was asked of him, he would become visibly anxious, flapping his hands and turning in circles many times, which would lead to some of his peers making fun of him and Joe becoming offended and aggressive in response. Joe's school psychologist had given him a diagnosis of autism after several assessment tools had shown marginal autistic functioning. This was important for getting support services in the school system but had a catastrophic impact on Joe's family. Both parents felt devastated and scared by the diagnosis, and his siblings seemed to coddle Joe even more.

Both Marleen and Sophie entered parent work filled with fear and anger. They both came from what they described as broken homes and had worked hard at building a home and a family together. They feared for Joe's future, as they were both already in their mid-40s and worried about having a child with special needs and no family support. However, a recent psychological assessment had shown Joe to have an above-average intelligence, despite his socioemotional difficulties, and this had brought great relief to both parents. Joe seemed caught in between two realities: At home, everybody mentalized him and sometimes hypermentalized his needs and wants, often anticipating what was necessary to keep him calm and unintentionally robbing him of the opportunity to practice at home the skills that did not come naturally to him. At school, much was demanded of him, regardless of his clearly anxious constitution and documented socioemotional neuroatypical functioning. As a result, Joe often felt afraid of taking "small risks" at school, finding refuge in his social and behavioral rigidity.

MENTALIZING WITH PARENTS OF SCHOOL-AGE CHILDREN: A WORD ABOUT MENTALIZATION-BASED TREATMENT FOR CHILDREN

Before describing the applications of the mentalizing framework to working with parents of school-age children, we want to explain how this chapter is different from, but can be integrated with, mentalization-based treatment for children (MBT-C). As described in Part I of this book, the mentalizing approach we discuss here is conceptualized as a way of thinking about the content and process of therapy, rather than a structured therapeutic model itself. For those who are not familiar with MBT-C, it is a time-limited and structured therapy designed to target mentalization in school-age children, working from a developmental perspective. Meetings with parents and family work is often part of the treatment, but, as with most child therapies, the work with the parents is considered an adjunct to the individual child treatment, and elaboration of how to work with parents is limited. The framework we present is for therapists who are looking for more

CORE ISSUES AND DEVELOPMENTAL ASPECTS OF THE SCHOOL AGE FOR PARENTS

Many parents look forward to their children entering school, as it signifies, in their mind, the beginning of a new phase, one in which children expand their sociocognitive horizons. It is a developmental stage that demands much from both the child and the parent(s), as it means getting outside the safety of the family and beginning to practice new ways of being in relationships away from the nonperfect, yet rewarding, contingency of the parent–child relationship (when things go well).

For children, this period represents new demands in the context of peers and adults in the environment of school and extracurricular activities. Traditionally, the 5-to-12-year-old cohort is somewhat challenging for psychotherapists, as it is characterized by intense interest and investment in hobbies and other specific pursuits. As a result, it is not uncommon to hear colleagues concerned about spending hours playing UNO or listening to a litany of details about Pokémon or a beloved YouTube video or show. The school-age period is one that demands a consolidation of capacities such as frustration tolerance and behavioral flexibility. Presenting difficulties during this period range from the usual peer difficulties to more severe affect regulation difficulties at home and school, which lead to more complex psychosocial difficulties. Mental health difficulties during this period have important implications for every aspect of children's lives, including their ability to engage in learning, make and keep friends, engage in family relationships, and find their own way in the world. During this period, mentalization consolidates through the relational experiences of rupture and repair offered by the expansion of the child's social sphere. Good reflective functioning serves a powerful regulatory function, supporting children in the process of making sense of their own and others' behaviors, thoughts, and feelings and, in so doing, creating an environment in which emotions are viewed as predictable, meaningful, and controllable. This is where working with parents and, when possible, teachers, becomes pivotal, as it maximizes the child's experience of feeling mentalized by significant adults.

The school years require the exercise of many qualities that foster reflective functioning in children and parents (Borelli et al., 2016) Reflective functioning may be important for parents of school-age children in that it may enable them to understand the changes that children experience as they progress through development and their own emotional reactions to these changes (Benbassat & Priel, 2012). A new significant adult, the teacher, comes into the life of the child, as does a new system: the school, with its demands and sources of support. Behavioral flexibility and curiosity regarding other thoughts and feelings in this context serve as protective factors for both parents and children. Additionally, other personality characteristics such as frustration tolerance and playfulness are conducive to an openness in learning from others, which facilitates the child's exploration and growth in a wider sociocultural context.

For parents, this is both an exciting and scary time, and it is one when self-reflective functioning is necessary to keep the self–other dimension balanced in the context of the child's normative desire to "hide" in their interests and hobbies—leaving the parents feeling, for the first time, far away and, at times, in a merely utilitarian relationship: one of being the chauffeur, the cook, the nurse, and so on. It is a time when the internal–external dimension becomes threatened by parents' feelings of loss of closeness and intimacy, as they see themselves substituted with heroes and friends. However, it is an exciting time for parents when the child's pathway toward interdependence and healthy autonomy is on the right track and the parent sees the fruits of the nurturance of the early years in the child learning to ride life and bicycles. In the following pages, we explore how to work with parents when constitutional aspects of the child seem to be getting in the way of the process of growth and development, as in Joe's case.

WORKING ON EPISTEMIC TRUST DURING THE SCHOOL-AGE PERIOD

We now return to Joe and his parents, Marleen and Sophie, who began working with the MBT-based therapy team after an evaluation period. A feedback session took place, in which both therapists discussed the focus formulation with Joe and "Mommy" and "Mama" (as Joe called his parents). The team spoke about Joe's wish to learn to play and have fun like his siblings and the other kids in school. They explained that there are different ways to play and be, with family and friends, the same way that there are different kinds of families and ways to make babies (a theme that had emerged in Joe's assessment sessions). Joe agreed and told his parents that he enjoyed making stories about different kinds of families and different kinds of kids.

The team explained that they thought of Joe as "the little prince" (one of Joe's favorite books), but he seemed a bit tired of being alone on his planet and wanted help learning how to "make his big feelings smaller" with the help of his family and his teacher. The formulation spoke of Joe's need for things to be predictable—but, also, learning to cope with times when "the story changes" and controlling the stormy and scary feelings was what Joe had to practice with his new doctor and all of the other nice people who wanted to help him succeed and be more like the other kids and not a lonely and scared prince. The therapeutic team checked with Joe and his parents and asked if this sounded like something they could all work on with Joe's help. Everyone agreed—however, Marleen wanted to know whether they were going to apply a specific method. Joe's therapist said that more than applying a method, everyone was going to practice thinking and responding differently to Joe's behavior, always keeping in mind the interaction between what they felt and thought and what he felt and thought. The parents' therapist added that it was an attitude, a way of being that helped families to work better and feel less alone with their worries and fears. Marleen smiled and added, "So you will help us to be good parents and fix our little Joe . . . give him new strategies?" The therapist replied,

> Well . . . good enough, let's start by agreeing that it helps if we know how to ask for help from others to get it back, especially when you are a little prince or really loving parents in distress. It is difficult to help anyone when you are worried and angry . . . and it is difficult to learn new strategies when our emotions are too big.

Following the feedback session, the parents' therapist began working with Marleen and Sophie every other week. Occasionally, Joe's siblings would join a meeting, when family issues were concerned and as a way of creating a common language that could be modeled by all at home and school. However, Marleen stayed skeptical of the work, as she felt that a more concrete and clearer plan was necessary to help her son. In response to this teleological need, the therapeutic team created a small table with some examples of how to apply some MBT skills in helping Joe to learn and practice how to interact socially. For example, the family was invited to systematically stop moments of dysregulation (*named bumpy roads*) and invite Joe clearly to "stop and rewind" and sequence with him what had happened before, by making small cartoons. This activity was practiced during his sessions with his therapist, as well. Additionally, the therapeutic team worked with the speech and occupational therapists in providing the family with light homework in the way of playful activities that fostered Joe's self-confidence and promoted his executive functioning (Shaheen, 2014).

When working with parents of children presenting with externalizing behaviors stemming from a neuroatypical profile, exhibiting signs of exhaustion and helplessness, it is important to respond to their teleological needs. It is often only in this way that parents can feel more regulated and contained and that the basis for epistemic trust between parents and therapist (in this case, a therapeutic team) can be established. Interdisciplinary collaboration is a must when working with children who have neurodevelopmental disorders, and a mentalization lens can be conducive to a common language and understanding of the child, which can prove extremely helpful in modeling a way of interacting that promotes theory of mind (Wang, 2015).

The following is an example of working on epistemic trust with Joe's parents after a foundation has been established:

MARLEEN: Joe is very happy with the new paraprofessional in the school, she is much better than the other person he had.

THERAPIST: What is so different about her?

SOPHIE: I think she gets him; she understands that he is smart but not relationship smart.

THERAPIST: That is important, you are right . . . It must give you some relief that he is not so alone in school? I imagine it has been very tough for both of you to be able to go to work and do all the things one has to do as a parent and adult while worrying about when the next meltdown at school will be.

MARLEEN: Indeed . . . it is a terrible thing when you begin to resent your child because you might lose your job and peace of mind because of him.

THERAPIST: It is a tough feeling indeed and one that parents often feel ashamed of admitting . . . as though parents are not allowed to want things for themselves . . .

SOPHIE: Exactly! Marleen and I speak about that all the time, especially because we are a same-sex couple, things have changed but we are always worried about people judging and drawing conclusions . . .

THERAPIST: Like what?

MARLEEN: Well, like the obvious . . . "They are two women raising a boy without a father, of course he is going to be inept and out of control" . . .

THERAPIST: Did I say something that annoyed you a bit? I am asking because it seems you feel I missed the obvious . . .

MARLEEN: I am sorry . . . I think I am fed up with explaining these things.

THERAPIST: No need to apologize, it is important that you let me know if my naive questions sometimes miss the mark or make you feel misunderstood. You have gone through a lot to build your family, and Joe's difficulties have impacted everyone, it is very tiring, and I imagine enraging at times.

MARLEEN: It really is . . . thanks for saying that . . . like Joe, I am tired of having to be the understanding parent and take all the looks and the smug comments . . .

SOPHIE: Marleen cares too much about what people say . . . but it is true it has been tough for us since Joe started school . . .

THERAPIST: I wonder if we need to spend some time thinking about the loss you feel and truly expressing how you feel about raising Joe and dealing with a judgmental and insensitive world.

MARLEEN: I would welcome that . . . being able to say what you really feel . . . sometimes I envy Joe's capacity to do just that . . . and wonder who is wrong—him or the world?

In this vignette, we observe how the therapist invites Marleen and Sophie to explore their feelings about having a son such as Joe. The therapist explores how it must feel to be called at work and to be worried about Joe all the time. Marleen responds defensively, which causes a momentary mentalizing impasse. The therapist stops and observes and takes responsibility for the emotional impact of her intervention. Thanks to an already-existing relationship between Marleen and the therapist, the exchange results in exploration of Marleen and Sophie's experience as a same-sex couple parenting a neuroatypical child. One can say that the door for learning from each other has been opened, as the therapist's nonjudgmental and genuine approach has helped Marleen to feel understood and contained emotionally.

The therapist is offering Marleen and Sophie an opportunity to mentalize their experience, rewrite their hopes for their child, and openly look at their fears in company. Epistemic trust is the intersubjective process through which we help parents regain hope in learning, about their child and from another—in this case, the therapist. The experience of feeling understood is extremely healing, facilitates increased behavioral and emotional flexibility, and opens the door for parents to understand the power of simply being with their child during difficult moments, surviving painful emotional and behavioral experiences.

WORKING BACK AND FORTH WITH PARENTS IN THE DEVELOPMENTAL LINE OF MENTALIZATION DURING THE SCHOOL-AGE PERIOD

Attention Regulation

Marleen and Sophie need to learn how to connect with their child in a way that is developmentally appropriate and that explicitly models mentalizing skills. It is a different way of parenting, one with which the parent does not rely on the implicit—that is, the parent does not take for granted that the child (a) is able to connect with another and (b) understands automatically. Making explicit the steps to connect with another is important when parenting a neuroatypical child.

Working at an attention regulation level with parents helps them understand the importance of jointly looking at an emotion or a thought and creating a "mentalizing think tank." The following is an example of such interaction:

SOPHIE: We have a bit of a problem understanding Joe's behavior recently with video games, and we are worried.

MARLEEN: We think he is becoming a video game addict. When we ask him to stop, he becomes really mean and he does not want to stop. It's like because he is turning 8 years old soon, he thinks he can do whatever he wants. We are kind mothers with all our kids, but we have rules in our house and we are not going to change them for him. He has 30 minutes of screen time after homework and that is that! You are probably going to tell us that we are being too rigid or something?

SOPHIE: Marleen, stop reading minds my dear and let the therapist speak . . .

THERAPIST: Wait, wait. I feel that the emotional temperature is rising here . . . am I right? What is going on?

MARLEEN: You are right, you know . . . I am always waiting for criticism . . . but I am worried about this one.

THERAPIST: I would be, too, if I thought about it as him becoming a video game addict. May I give you another version of this, with your support? Would that be OK? If at any moment I am getting it wrong or you feel I am being judgmental, please stop me and let me know.

MARLEEN: OK, will do.

SOPHIE: Sure thing.

THERAPIST: Well, why don't we walk through the last time this happened and first pay attention together at what was happening to you and then collectively imagine what we think might be happening to Joe . . . Might help us to think about how to deal with this situation in a way that might take into consideration the different perspectives and needs involved . . . What do you think?

Affect Regulation

Working on a parent's mentalized affectivity is particularly important in working with the demands of school and the overall psychosocial pressure that comes from other parents and extended family. Working at an affect regulation level can be thought of as a developmental line itself, as it can go from (a) the noticing and naming of nonverbal affective states (identification) to (b) the in vivo practicing of modulating and containing emotion to (c) being able to express the emotion while retaining one's capacity to reflect cognitively. The following is an example of such a process:

MARLEEN: I am fed up with the new teacher, she just does not get it. She keeps sending those stupid notes home. They really upset Joe and are bad for his self-esteem. How are you supposed to foster his self-confidence as a learner when you have a stupid cow undermining it?

THERAPIST: I heard from my colleague that Joe was angry with her . . . he kicked her?

MARLEEN: Yes . . . I would, too, if I could . . .

SOPHIE: See . . . how am I supposed to manage two out-of-control . . . nice example my dear . . .

MARLEEN: Don't start with me . . . I am the one that must pick him up every time . . .

SOPHIE: It is a reality . . . your work is next to his school, Marleen . . . I work 45 minutes away . . .

THERAPIST: Wait, wait . . . before we go into a place where we lose the connection with each other and find who to blame and who to kick, can we slow down for a bit? You both work so hard to translate Joe to everyone, I can see how it must be frustrating when someone just wants to keep speaking her own language to him . . . she does sound very behaviorally based, am I right?

MARLEEN: She is . . . what about that?

THERAPIST: Well, do you agree that trying to start by speaking a bit of her language might be helpful before we try to convince her there is another way? What makes you feel so strongly, Marleen?

MARLEEN: I think it is that . . . she is concrete and lazy and does not try . . . reminds me of my oldest sister. She was like that and still is, always gets away with murder . . .

SOPHIE: We are talking about Joe . . . Marleen . . .

THERAPIST: Yes, we are, but also, I think Marleen is trying to understand why she is experiencing such a strong emotion with this

	teacher when she has had to endure a lot of school stress before. Am I getting that right, Marleen?
MARLEEN:	Yes, I feel stupid feeling so angry with the teacher, she is just doing what she knows. I know Joe is challenging.
THERAPIST:	I think understanding she has personal qualities that trigger your dislike is important to manage your emotions when dealing with her. Your family has a very strong value of working hard and trying your best . . . seeing her not try with Joe is difficult.
MARLEEN:	Well . . . it reminds me that in the end, it is just us with him, we can't trust people will be fair and kind to him . . .
THERAPIST:	It is exhausting . . .
MARLEEN:	It really is . . .
THERAPIST:	How do you feel right now?
MARLEEN:	I am calmer, but I still don't like that woman . . .
THERAPIST:	Do you think Joe can tell you don't like her?
SOPHIE:	Oh yes! Marleen is not good at hiding how she feels . . .
MARLEEN:	I see your point . . . I want to kick her, but he does . . .
THERAPIST:	We are only human you know? [*All three laugh.*]
THERAPIST:	I am not going to lie . . . when I hear about the way she talks to your child, I am not particularly crazy about her . . .

Explicit Mentalizing

Parental mentalization has two dimensions: self- and other mentalizing. A parent can't mentalize their child's experience unless they are able to mentalize their own experience. Working along the developmental line of mentalization does not mean always getting to the point of explicit mentalizing. Sometimes, all a parent can manage is to work on the first two blocks to strengthen their capacity to manage a difficult situation by increasing their reflective functioning capacity. Explicit mentalizing might feel too overwhelming, especially when parenting a child whose capacity for relatedness is different than what the parent expects. Explicit mentalizing, for that parent, might be a source of regulation and facilitate mentalized affectivity, but it could also represent a source of distress, as the parent might be too overwhelmed by guilt or shame to achieve this level of functioning. However, that does not mean that the therapist can't provide and model the experience of feeling mentalized for the parent in a way that provides support and companionship with a difficult task: "mentalizing the unmentalizable" (Slade, 2009). The following is an example of such circumstances:

SOPHIE: I am sorry Marleen could not make it, she does a lot and has been getting in trouble at work because of missing time to pick up Joe.

THERAPIST: That must have been tough for you . . .

SOPHIE: It is . . .

THERAPIST: I feel like you and I don't get to speak too much, there are a lot of needs in your family . . .

SOPHIE: You mean . . . lots of noise . . . yes . . .

THERAPIST: How is that for you?

SOPHIE: I am used to it . . . does not mean I like it . . .

THERAPIST: How do you imagine it is for Joe?

SOPHIE: You may not get this, but I do try to see things his way, but I try not to think too much about how he feels because I can't make it better and that is tough . . .

THERAPIST: I get that . . . How do you think he understands the noise in your home?

SOPHIE: I think he is used to it . . . I know I am not . . . I came from a very broken home and when we are too disorganized or too demanding in our family, I immediately worry that we are becoming my family . . .

THERAPIST: That is a bit scary?

SOPHIE: Yes . . . it is frustrating. I love Marleen but her intensity scares me sometimes and I think it scares Joe but I could never say that to her . . .

THERAPIST: She does so much . . .

SOPHIE: That is right . . .

THERAPIST:	Well, perhaps you already understand naturally how Joe feels, more than you realize . . . you can provide a quiet and safe island when you both need it.
SOPHIE:	If he only took my hand . . . figuratively that is . . .
THERAPIST:	I get that . . . I'm just trying to think about why he might not, and wondering if maybe you offer your "hand" shyly and he gets confused?
SOPHIE:	[*smiles*] I probably do . . .
THERAPIST:	Who offered you their hand when you were young and you needed support?
SOPHIE:	My aunt, my mom's sister. She was a nice lady. She always smiled when I did something to get attention and she would hug me when my mom was mean to me. She seemed to really like being with me.
THERAPIST:	Listening to you I get the feeling that it was not something you were used to . . . am I right?
SOPHIE:	You are . . . My mom was a single mom and there were four of us, all from different dads . . . it was normal where I grew up . . . I am not proud of it, but it was the way it was . . . so I know my mom loved me but she was always too tired and stressed to show it. It always felt like I was ruining something for her . . . you know? I don't ever want my kids to feel like that . . .
THERAPIST:	Hmmm . . . it occurs to me that you know more about how Joe feels than I realized, but I am also understanding how difficult it must be to make that link and remember . . . what was the one thing you liked to do more with your aunt?
SOPHIE:	She taught me how to play tennis, you know? She is the reason I managed to get a scholarship to go to college . . .
THERAPIST:	She believed in you, saw your strengths . . .
SOPHIE:	She did . . . I like doing that for Joe and my other children, but it is more difficult to embrace their weaknesses . . .
THERAPIST:	I can understand that, I really can . . .
SOPHIE:	Thanks, it is tough for me to speak about this . . .

PARENTING: KEEPING THE BALANCE WHILE RIDING THE UPHILL ROAD OF RELATIONSHIPS DURING THE SCHOOL YEARS

During this period, children's emerging personality is being influenced for the first time by experiences and people outside of the home environment, as children spend a significant amount of their day at school. This can prove quite challenging for the maintenance of parental reflective functioning. Parents might find themselves having difficulty keeping a playful and curious attitude when faced with the rapidly changing individual personality characteristics of their child. This process demands a readjustment from the parents, regarding the level of access they can have to their child's private thoughts and feelings. During this period, parents need to become aware of the explicit and implicit messages that they might be sending their child about the meaning that their child's desire for exploration has for them.

Quite often, we hear parents commiserate with each other about the day their child stopped holding their hand or when suddenly their usual ways to redirect or calm down the younger child stopped working. Other parents speak of finding themselves at a loss when they ask their usual "How was school?" and the child simply shrugs or says, "OK." As children integrate their two realities—home and school—the space between parents and child may feel abyssal to some parents while holding tightly to their child in fear of losing the closeness they once treasured. For other parents, the child's newfound independence feels like a sign that they have done a good job, and they feel free to start reengaging in their adult interests and relationships. Whatever the meaning of their child's growth and development, this period, as all the others, requires a revisiting of hopes and fears in the context of increased complexity.

This process becomes more laborious psychologically when a child is experiencing significant difficulties—like Joe, the boy in our case example in this chapter. As reflected in the Introduction to this book and reiterated in the example in this chapter, today's family structure has expanded into new versions. Although this is a sign of social progress and expansion of equality and freedom, it brings with it new complexity and challenge to the role of parenting. For example, new ways of conceiving via assisted reproductive technology bring with them new realities, which need to be explored and integrated in our work with parents. A mentalization-based model of working with parents fits well with this emerging need, as it is both developmental and ecological in nature. Working clinically, attempting to balance the four dimensions that influence the capacity to mentalize new realities is a helpful way of approaching, clinically, topics that are usually difficult to deal with, such as the biological origin of an adopted child or a child conceived through surrogacy or semen or ova donation. The following example seeks to illustrate such a process. The italic phrases in brackets indicate the technical focus of the intervention, in regard to working on balancing the four dimensions of mentalizing.

MARLEEN: Yesterday, Joe asked us where his dad was . . . We knew this time would come and we have tried to slowly share the story like we did with our other two children, but Joe is different . . . he needs specifics and evidence.

THERAPIST: What did you feel when he asked you that? [*cognitive–affective*]

MARLEEN: I felt a terrible stomachache . . .

SOPHIE: Me, too . . . we held hands . . .

THERAPIST: How tough . . .

MARLEEN: What should we say? As always, we see ourselves lost in a new territory, we thought we could manage but with Joe it's all new, like the first time you become a parent.

THERAPIST: But you are not a first-time parent . . . what did you do when your other children asked? [*implicit–explicit*]

SOPHIE: It's different, they never asked like that, it was like . . . they absorb the fact that their biological father was a kind person who lent us the special material that is necessary to make babies.

THERAPIST: Do you think they have other questions? [*self–other*]

MARLEEN: I am sure they do, but they are worried about taking care of us, which Joe is not—he wants what he wants when he wants it.

THERAPIST: You sound pretty sure that it's like that. But I wonder if there is more to it, like, could it be that he wants to understand why he is different? Or is there something he does or says that makes you believe he just does not care? [*external–internal*]

MARLEEN: I know that is how he is, but we always submit to his questions [*becoming visibly angry*]

THERAPIST: This topic brings a lot of feelings into our conversation and brings a new person, too, someone that had something to do with Joe being here . . . [*cognitive–affective*]

MARLEEN: Are you saying that we don't want to give answers to Joe? All we know is that the sperm donor was tall, blond, and had green eyes. He enjoyed sports and was a college graduate . . .

THERAPIST: Since I've known you, it is my impression you do everything you can to give your son everything he needs and wants to avoid feeling alone, scared, or different. This is one thing that is not easy to explain or give in a way he can digest easily, being who he is . . . that must be so difficult and perhaps painful? [*implicit–explicit*]

SOPHIE: It is tough to know how much our guilt is behind it and how much he really needs to know. [*self–other*]

THERAPIST: I think that is a very good point, maybe we can think about this by trying to think like him?

MARLEEN: [*sarcastically*] That will be fun . . .

THERAPIST: Or not, but we can try . . .

SOPHIE: I think being scientifically accurate is the best thing for Joe, he loves those shows where they explain things with science.

THERAPIST: What do you think Marleen, how do you feel right now? [*cognitive–affective*]

MARLEEN: He will have another question and another . . . he always does . . . I feel lost and tired . . .

THERAPIST: So, it feels like an impossible mission, failed from the start?

MARLEEN: My fear that he will get really angry, and I would get angry, too, would make it a failed mission. [*self–other*]

THERAPIST: Why would you feel angry?

SOPHIE: Because she would understand it as she is failing him . . .

THERAPIST: Is that true?

MARLEEN: Yes.

THERAPIST: How about if you start by saying something like, "There are some things we just can't have full answers for, but this is what I know—are you going to be OK with an unfinished story?"

MARLEEN: I think he would probably find it frustrating, but I can make it into a funny story, and he would go for that. The truth is . . . I would like to know if this guy was also on the autistic spectrum . . . If he were, I would have someone to blame.

THERAPIST: Not yourself.

MARLEEN: Yes . . . aren't I fun?

THERAPIST: You are a mom struggling to give the best answer to her son about something complex, nothing fun about it, just tough and a lot of work. But we don't really know what he thinks, maybe it would be a good idea to ask him if he has any ideas about who his dad is before you say anything?

SOPHIE: He told me his dad is an alien, like him.

THERAPIST: Different . . . ?

MARLEEN: Yes, different, not like the others.

THERAPIST: I wonder if there is a value in exploring that with Joe, like a window into how he sees himself? [*implicit–explicit*]

SOPHIE: I like that, so while we are stuck in the specific story, part of it he wants to understand himself.

THERAPIST: Maybe?

MARLEEN: [*much more relaxed*] That sounds a lot like our Joe. [*cognitive–affective*]

PREMENTALIZING MODES IN THE CONTEXT OF PARENTING A SCHOOL-AGE CHILD

While the prementalizing modes are part of development and characterize the way infants and then young children think about the links between mental states and behavior and self and other, by middle childhood, children begin to develop the capacity for more mature mentalizing. Slips into nonmentalizing modes, however, may occur when children or parents become emotionally dysregulated. When this takes place in sessions, therapists' mentalizing stance facilitates reengagement of parents' mentalizing capacities. Occasionally, therapists may need to help parents recognize when they, or others in the family and social system, were not mentalizing and think together about how mentalizing was or could have been restored.

Teleological

As illustrated in Part I, a teleological mode of functioning is characterized by a jump to action or a demand for action. In earlier chapters, we gave numerous examples of parents' requests for parenting advice and skills, as illustrations of teleological mode. As children grow, the questions parents bring to therapy also change: When children are in infancy, therapists often get questions about eating and sleeping. When children are in toddlerhood, the questions are often about how to respond to emotions. When the children are in their school-age years, the questions become broader and more complex, as they often include other systems, peers, and other significant adults. The pressure felt by parents from other adults—regarding a child's behavior, for instance—can prove a powerful inhibiting force of mentalizing. Therapists must also recognize another important signal of functioning in a teleological mode: their own urge to take action. Of course, there is a time and a place to call a school, suggest a team meeting, refer a child for a psychoeducational evaluation, and so forth. As parents are feeling less in control of their children and their children's lives, the therapist may also feel more helpless and end up trying to aid the parent in thinking about what they can do. When therapists notice these urges and can question them, both in consultation with other professionals and sometimes even in thinking out loud with the parent, it can lead to a restoration of mentalizing and more meaningful therapeutic work.

MARLEEN: I need help figuring out how to explain to Joe that he needs to show empathy sometimes.

SOPHIE: I keep telling her other kids also need to understand he is different.

THERAPIST: Did something happen?

MARLEEN: Yes, they were on a visit to the zoo and one of the kids hurt himself and Joe started to laugh. The teacher told him that his friend was hurt and wondered why he was laughing. He said it was funny. The girl cried more and called him mean and Joe got upset and started to scream and covered his ears saying, "You are not my friend!"

THERAPIST: A bad misunderstanding altogether . . .

SOPHIE: You can say that.

THERAPIST: How do you think he could calmly be open to learning from the experience?

MARLEEN: Maybe saying something like "When we see people crying, even if we think it is funny, it is better to show that we see they are hurt, makes everyone calmer . . ."

THERAPIST: I think that is good because you are putting it in absolute and clear terms.

MARLEEN: Really?

THERAPIST: Yes, I think that is good. You see, I think you forget that you have been speaking to Joe longer than anyone else . . . and I understand, it is easy to forget your expertise when everyone keeps complaining . . . too much noise, makes the emotional volume go up and the thinking go down.

SOPHIE: Just like Joe . . . that is exactly what happens to him.

MARLEEN: Yes, but his volume is much louder.

THERAPIST: Exactly . . . I am curious, though, why did he think it was funny?

SOPHIE: He hates the zoo, he feels bad for animals in cages being hurt and thought it was funny that a human felt hurt like the animals . . . I guess his own kind of empathy . . .

Psychic Equivalence

MARLEEN: I am taking my child out of that school, they are always waiting for him to fail.

Psychic equivalence involves the parent's being certain that what is in their mind is also shared by others and is the only reality. There is a lack of curiosity regarding the child's thoughts and feelings that is quite characteristic of parents functioning at a psychic equivalence level. When parents of school-age children are prone to psychic equivalence, it can be especially challenging, because the level of emotional intensity is quite difficult to manage—easily becoming contagious for the therapist. We often deal with parents functioning in this way when they feel threatened or shamed by adults whose behavior and emotional responses have a direct impact on their functioning and that of their children. For example, when a parent gets called to school several times per week to collect their child early because their behavior is not being "safe," and no specific information is given regarding how the child's behavior was managed or understood, most parents will react in a nonmentalizing way, leading quite often to nonmentalizing responses from the school. It becomes a cycle that significantly impacts adults' capacities for curiosity and flexibility, leaving all involved feeling judged, alone, and misunderstood. The following example illustrates this:

SOPHIE: They are starting with the calling and the "not safe behavior" stuff again.

THERAPIST: What happened?

MARLEEN: The speech therapist was late and went to get Joe from the playground. He was following some of the girls, who thought it was funny that he was trying to catch them, pretending to be a lion. Joe missed the first break because of speech so he was delighted to get more playground time. When Mrs. J asked him to come with her, he said, "No, thank you." Mrs. J told him she understood but she needed to do her job and teach him, he then tried to negotiate with her for 5 more minutes and the teacher in charge of the playground came and told him he had to do as he was being told. Mrs. J tried to intervene, but it was too late. Joe was already running around, and he made a girl fall by accident. The teacher said it was unsafe behavior and asked him to come with her. He ran away as he often does. It took two teachers to restrain him and sit him in the nurse's room until I arrived. They are all assholes!

THERAPIST: I am so sorry, Marleen, what an awful thing for you and Joe . . .

MARLEEN: Mrs. J was so upset, too . . . but really . . . she could have just waited, she knows him. Aren't people like CBT trained or something?

SOPHIE: The problem is that this is going to happen anywhere we take him.

MARLEEN: He does not belong in a mainstream public school, I am looking for jobs in private schools with special ed classes.

	There is one an hour away, we could move, it is closer to Sophie's job.
THERAPIST:	I think that is a good idea. In the meantime, shall we try to think what I can do to support you and Joe better with the school?
MARLEEN:	Nothing! They are assholes; they just want to see Joe fail.
THERAPIST:	I agree that the school might not be the best for your child, but I am not sure they take pleasure in his failures, I think they are just not trained and don't have the openness to think about him in a different way.
SOPHIE:	I agree with that and maybe I need to find a way of being the one that comes at least once every week when they call, would that help a little, babe?
MARLEEN:	[*sobbing*] I think so . . . I can't take it anymore . . .
THERAPIST:	I think nobody could, Marleen . . . nobody. This is a very difficult and painful situation.

Diagnostic labels can sometimes be useful for parents, as these help them feel "they know" what is going on. However, they can often inform a parent's curiosity and motivation to become involved in the process of self-mentalizing and mentalizing their child. It is a comfortable place for both clinician and parents, when they find each other in the knowing realm of symptomatology and diagnosis. Exploring the meaning of the diagnosis for the parents and how it informs their view of their child, their fears and hopes, and their own role in the child's life will promote the restoration of a mentalizing stance for both therapist and parents.

THERAPIST:	My colleague tells me Joe had a great week at school and he seems to be doing well practicing small risks socially and checking with peers before reacting. How do you feel about that?
MARLEEN:	I have read kids in the spectrum are like that, good weeks and then really bad weeks, so I try not to keep my hopes up. After all, who knows if autism is really his pathology, maybe he is biologically predestined to be bipolar or something . . .
THERAPIST:	Why bipolar?

SOPHIE: Because he is so moody.

MARLEEN: Or simply unpredictable . . . we never know who he will wake up as and how he will respond to the help. Then again, autism is, after all, an anxiety-based disorder isn't it?

THERAPIST: I was wondering . . . Do you feel that my colleague does not see how much work it takes for him to have one single good week?

MARLEEN: Truth? I do. I think it is a dangerous game to be too hopeful, I just can't anymore.

THERAPIST: Do you think it changes the way you respond to Joe's behavior and your capacity to mentalize him?

MARLEEN: I do, but I must protect myself, too, you know?

THERAPIST: It sounds as if you heard me say that you are not allowed to do that, I am sorry if you heard that. You are tired and stressed and nobody can mentalize anyone in that state. Shall we think together about things you could do to take care of yourself?

MARLEEN: I would like that very much, I am tired.

Pretend Mode

Sometimes a parent faces painful and difficult feelings, such as shame and anger, toward themselves and others. When those moments emerge in the context of a session, one of the ways to manage them is by engaging in a pretend mode of functioning. It is challenging to be able to discern, as a therapist, when a parent is functioning in this mode, as it often feels like insight and engagement. However, one way in which therapists can identify it is by paying attention to the way they feel in the context of the interaction. For instance, when a parent goes on and on about their understanding of their child, using very jargon-heavy discourse, we often feel bored and disconnected. That feeling of emotional disconnection is a very important sign of pretend mode functioning. Professionals often join in with the parent on this way of functioning, especially if there has been an uncomfortable exchange in the room or a painful memory has been explored. The sudden shift to a very cognitive functioning, to the point of nonsensical association of thoughts, is very often a sign that something has changed—as illustrated by this example:

MARLEEN: I am feeling a bit fed up with all of this, I may have to quit some of my social activities because, honestly, I don't have any more energy, Joe takes it all . . .

THERAPIST: How do you feel talking about this to me?

MARLEEN: I feel like I am able to explore my true feelings and begin the journey . . . one that is very important for me and my kids . . .

THERAPIST: That sounds like an important goal . . .

MARLEEN: It is, I feel parents need to work on themselves to help their kids, I often read things, my mother never reads stuff . . . I was reading a survey the other day online and it is amazing how unaware people are about how to parent . . .

THERAPIST: You know, I wonder about what you were saying before, about the feeling of "I've had it!" . . . What about that . . . ?

MARLEEN: Ugh! I don't know . . . I just . . . it is embarrassing . . . I just wish sometimes . . . that I knew how to be a better mother . . . a good one . . . I always end up going around in circles about this . . . I read in a local magazine that it is normal for mothers to feel fed up . . . then again maybe it is just part of the process, you know?

THERAPIST: Yes . . . sorry to interrupt you again, but I noticed that we keep sort of changing the topic away from the feeling of you being fed up . . .

MARLEEN: I don't know that there is anything more to say . . . I am feeling a bit stuck in this conversation . . . Can we speak about Joe?

THERAPIST: Did my comment make you annoyed?

MARLEEN: A little . . . I am tired of feeling under the microscope because my kid is a pain . . .

THERAPIST: Not fair . . .

MARLEEN: Indeed!

As shown in this vignette, the pretend mode can serve as a shield from potentially painful emotional realities. However, when it is noticed and named, it can open the door to genuine and honest exchange. The mentalization-informed therapist has to walk a fine balance between challenging the pretend functioning and remaining empathic and validating of the parent's experience. This might require navigating some stressful interpersonal exchanges in order to arrive at a balance that facilitates coregulation and mentalization.

CONCLUDING SUMMARY

• School-age children and their parents find themselves negotiating new ways of interaction that include the outside world.

• The child's psychological and physical exploration in the real world, away from the parent, may trigger feelings of loss and anxiety in some parents and a desire to avoid the developmental reality in others.

• Parents' mentalizing capacities become tested by their interactions with school and the wider community.

• Parenting a child exhibiting internalizing or externalizing symptomatology becomes increasingly more stressful for parents under social pressure and by the increasing normative closing down of the child's communication with the parent. The sense of loss, guilt, and shame can prove quite a powerful inhibiting force of parental reflective functioning.

• Parenting a child with a developmental disorder or who is suffering from a chronic physical illness challenges the reflective functioning of the parent. There is a need for support in helping the parent make sense of the often-contradictory feelings they experience and the strong teleological needs those feelings trigger.

10 ADOLESCENCE

Redefining Boundaries

CASE AND CLINICAL FORMULATION

Michael was a 15-year-old who had dropped out of school about 1 year before he was referred for services through a home visiting program. He spent most of his days at home, playing video games for long hours, and occasionally would leave to hang out with friends in the evenings. He had been a reasonably good student until he reached the eighth grade, when his academic performance started to decline. This triggered his parents' concerns, as they were high achievers and expected their son to also be successful in his academic and professional careers. Michael was an only child, as his parents thought that having one child was as much as they could handle, due to their demanding professional lives. His parents had met soon after finishing college and had been together for over 20 years.

Michael's parents described him as a smart and happy child, although this had significantly changed over the last couple of years. They said that they were concerned and upset because when he reached the eighth grade, he gradually

https://doi.org/10.1037/0000341-011
Working With Parents in Therapy: A Mentalization-Based Approach, by N. Malberg, E. Jurist, J. Bate, and M. Dangerfield

began to lose interest in his schoolwork and behavioral problems started to surface—especially at home. His parents didn't understand why he had changed so much and why he was not reacting to their firm disciplinary measures, which consisted mostly of cutting back his privileges. Disagreements between the parents were also emerging, as they had different ideas about what it meant to cut back their son's privileges.

Michael and his parents had been seeing various mental health professionals over the last couple of years. These specialists had diagnosed Michael with attention-deficit/hyperactivity disorder and oppositional defiant disorder and started him on different psychological and pharmacological treatments, which had not been very successful. Michael was now refusing to see any other mental health professionals—that was what led his parents to contact a local home visiting team.

Michael's parents were desperate, as nothing seemed to work and situations at home were escalating to high levels of tension and confrontation. They reported that fights were now daily, between them and Michael and also between each other. Michael's mother accused her husband of not doing enough and said that she was the only one who was really committed to showing their son that his life was not going to be easy if he continued not making any effort to build a future for himself.

The family felt trapped in a relational dynamic that seemed only to reinforce their despair and also in a lack of understanding of each other's perspectives and feelings. They all felt very alone and misunderstood by one another—situations that led to mutual accusations, certainties about others, and higher presence of conflicts. As a result, an honest availability to be open and keen to understand, from a different perspective, what another member of the family could be feeling or thinking was rarely present during family interactions.

However, despite this dysfunctional family dynamic and the major dis-agreements between the parents, they had both agreed that the main problem was Michael's school refusal and lack of studying. They both accused him of being lazy and wanting only "the easy way out." Understandably, this parental stance increased the conflicts and tensions within the family. Michael seemed to expect to be financially supported by his parents, as they had both done quite well professionally and financially. However, according to his parents, Michael chose to ignore the fact that their successful professional careers were built on hard work and long hours of commitment to their professions. Both parents were worried because Michael had recently started smoking cannabis—in what seemed, to the therapist, to be an effort at managing the unpleasant emotional states that often overwhelmed him.

During the initial interviews with both parents, what caught the therapist's attention was the fact that both had personal histories of relational trauma: Mrs. H had been brought up in a very tough and emotionally abusive environment, and Mr. H had lost both of his parents in a terrible accident during his adolescence. They both had high cognitive capacities, which had helped them cope with life and organize their identities around their academic and professional achievements. Unfortunately, this meant not enough time and space in their lives to approach and deal with their emotional lives, especially when it came to painful emotions. Both parents had been brought up in relational environments with insufficient support and lack of containment of unpleasant emotional states. They had always been left alone in these situations, and they had both found a way to survive psychologically by over-investing in their very competent cognitive capacities. They both had significant difficulties in identifying, modulating, and expressing emotions (Jurist, 2005, 2018), and this had obviously affected the relational style that predominated with Michael.

The parents' difficulties in managing their emotional lives had a clear impact on the family relational dynamic, especially after the death of Mr. H's uncle 3 years prior to the therapist meeting Michael and his family. Michael had been very fond of this great-uncle but had not been allowed to attend the funeral, which the therapist understood as—given Michael's age and willingness to attend—his parents' difficulty in offering emotional support during such a challenging moment, rather than as an act of protection.

Similarly to Cristina (whose case was presented in Part I of this book), Michael's symptomatology could be understood in terms of avoidance of potentially stressful and dysregulating social and academic activities. Michael felt incapable of managing the stress and pressure derived from attending school and engaging in academic work, because of (a) his limited resources to manage his emotional life and (b) his limited mentalizing capacities. He also felt overwhelmed by what growing up and becoming an adult implied. He seemed to inhibit aspects of his developmental process by retreating from the world, finding safety in his virtual environments and in just hanging out with some friends from time to time. Cannabis helped him deal with the anxieties he lived with in this high-psychopathological-risk situation.

No matter how concerned both parents were about Michael's circumstance, and how much they suffered, all of their efforts in trying to help their son seemed only to increase the difficulties and move him further away from them. They were both quite desperate when they sought help, feeling that there was no way out and very worried about what could happen to their son.

One main issue was the impact of the parents' own challenges in managing their emotional life on their capacity to offer support and empathy to Michael. His behavior and difficulties seemed to be communicating his feeling that he could not live like they did—investing enormous effort into developing a life from an intellectual, academic, and professional sphere but dissociating from emotions and not developing the "emotional muscle" (Novick & Novick, 2005).

Both parents displayed an avoidant-insecure attachment pattern of behavior resulting from having suffered important adverse relational experiences in their childhoods. Michael's parents' behaviors and limitations in parenting were perhaps the consequence of the transgenerational transmission of relational trauma, as described in Chapter 4. In this family, emotional needs felt overwhelming and unbearable, something that led to avoiding and dissociating mechanisms as well as the hyperinvestment in organizing themselves and their identities around their cognitive and professional skills. Paradoxically, with his symptomatology, Michael was also offering his parents a possibility of exploring another way of approaching life. We return to the case later in this chapter, but first let us explore the developmental issues that parents of adolescents face during this developmental stage, in order to contextualize our exploration of parenting.

CORE ISSUES AND DEVELOPMENTAL ASPECTS OF ADOLESCENCE FOR PARENTS: REDEFINING BALANCES AND BOUNDARIES

Aside from the first years of life, adolescence is probably the stage in which the most marked changes occur in the shortest amount of time. Adolescence is a period of both great vulnerability and valuable opportunities. Kessler et al. (2010) reviewed epidemiological research on age of onset of mental disorders, focusing on the World Health Organization's World Mental Health surveys. They found that half of all mental disorders in most studies start by the mid-teens, and three fourths start by the mid-20s.

Adolescence is also a period of opportunities for growth and resilience and is associated with marked plasticity (Luyten et al., 2020). We know also that strengthening mentalizing increases resilience (Fonagy et al., 2017a), so the idea of helping parents navigate this period with their adolescent offspring, with a focus on helping parents improve both their capacity to mentalize and their mentalizing stance toward the adolescents, can be a very important task for any mental health professional.

Both physically and psychologically, all adolescents experience enormous changes that trigger intense and very diverse emotional reactions: from (a) the excitement, curiosity, and real interest in what the adult world can offer to (b) the fear of not being adequately prepared to face what are perceived as high demands of this adult world—and from the wish to be recognized as a grown-up to the need to still be taken care of as though a smaller child. These situations may also be very confusing for the parents, as the situations imply holding a balance between (a) allowing the child to explore their new physical and psychological capacities in a more autonomous way and (b) still being present to offer support and containment.

It is relevant to emphasize how important it is to focus on mentalizing the parents of adolescents. Parents often feel confused and annoyed when confronted with the dilemma of their teenager saying both "You just don't care about me!" and "Leave me alone, get off my case!" at the same time. On the other hand, we can imagine what the adolescent might be feeling, although they are not always capable of expressing it this way: "I need you a lot, and I feel that you don't understand me," while simultaneously feeling something such as "I can't stand needing you, because it reminds me of how unprepared I feel to face the demands of the adult world."

When working with parents, we must also remind ourselves of the mourning processes that facing adolescence implies, both for them and their children. They all must face a tough transition that implies mourning the loss of childhood. This means being able to identify, value, and integrate the new, developing young adult capacities that will be crucial to facing the demands of this changing and challenging world while holding a balance between (a) tolerating and (b) supporting the infantile aspects that always remain present and need to be contained. Here, we can exemplify with a comment that parents typically make: "Our child is sometimes capable of doing things on their own, but then they behave like a small child, asking us to do this or that for them."

SURVIVING ADOLESCENCE AND SURVIVING ONE'S CHILD'S ADOLESCENCE

When working with parents of adolescents, therapists must keep in mind that this is a very demanding time for them, too. Parents must also mourn the loss of the child who was generally happy to see them, needed them, appreciated them, and celebrated their presence. Suddenly, they are no longer appreciated in their role as parents. Instead, they are the annoying ones who "really don't get it."

A key aspect of this developmental stage is "What supports do parents have?" How does the parental couple comply with this function of supporting each other through the daily emotional impacts and emotional turmoil? Here, we must remind the reader of how fragile mentalizing is and how easily everyone loses this capacity in situations of higher emotional arousal. Being a parent of an adolescent is not an easy task. It is one that inevitably implies being hit by unexpected and rather shocking comments, responses, situations, and moments of interaction that leave the parent slightly overwhelmed and with a sometimes-urgent need of some support to recover their capacity to mentalize. When the parental couple has a good-enough relational dynamic, this process can be more feasible and facilitate a de-escalation of the tension that may have engaged the adolescent and one of the parents in a cycle of inhibition of mentalizing. The parent coming from the outside can have the very valuable function of rescuing the other parent and helping find a way to diminish the risk of things just getting worse—and of even having to call the police, in some extreme cases. Obviously, this process is not easy and doesn't always unfold in the desired way. Often, the parent coming from the outside can contribute to increasing the emotional dysregulation and make things even worse or intervene in a way that doesn't validate the other parent's experience, with the usual outcome of triggering conflict in the parental couple—something that won't be at all good to try to help modulate the adolescent's emotional turmoil.

In other situations, the other parent is simply not present, which leaves the present parent engaged in a tense or conflictual relational moment with the adolescent, quite alone and with no support to recover their mentalizing capacities and address the specific situation in the best possible way. This is especially challenging for single parents, as they don't have another parental figure with whom to count on in order to feel supported when needed. Being two in a parental couple can have some tough sides and require frequent efforts, by both parents, to try to make things work. Having to deal with their offspring's adolescence is something that tests their healthy aspects as a parental couple. However, when things go well, the parental couple can support each other in ways that can be very helpful in managing the daily situations that they encounter with their adolescent son or daughter.

For a single parent, finding support from one's partner is just not an option, leaving the parent with a higher risk of living in an increased degree of isolation—especially when hit by situations of high emotional impact in the relationship with the adolescent. As we know, we all lose our capacity to mentalize in situations of high emotional arousal, and we all need a relationship with a partner or a friend that can help us regulate and recover in order to be able to recuperate our capacity to mentalize and not get trapped in cycles of inhibition of mentalizing. Consequently, it would be very helpful for all single parents to have an available close friend or family member to whom they can turn in case of need, especially during the adolescence of their children.

When thinking of the importance of primary prevention in mental health, we must highlight the importance of the need that all parents will have for a trusted other (the other parent or, in the case of single parents, someone else), no matter how competent and adequate they may be in their parental functions. We know that isolation is a risk factor for emotional distress and emergence of psychopathology. Suffering in isolation increases this risk exponentially. Therefore, one of the main recommendations that the therapist should explicitly make is to always have someone "holding our rope," as parents of adolescents. Parents can't intend to face this intense and thrilling developmental phase for themselves and their children on their own. An effort should be made to minimize the levels of emotional and relational isolation that a parent may have, as one of the main ways to help them navigate these times.

The coexistence of child and adult aspects is a central characteristic of adolescence, as is the fact that holding an adequate and realistic balance between them is a key task that may determine the outcome of this intense, but interesting, time. Adolescence can be understood as a transition stage between the childhood that is being left behind and the adulthood that is being approached. It is defined by changes, in the body and mind, that entail not only the grieving processes for what one loses but also the challenges of what one is gaining: everything new that appears. Nonetheless, this implies a capacity to face and deal with the emotional demands of this change. One of the most central challenges is that of maintaining one's own identity and interests throughout this pivotal developmental transition. Changes in the adolescent's body and mind cause significant turmoil, as they imply a challenge to what sustains the young person. This is what has been classically understood as a period of crisis: a crisis in the sense of change and seeing this change as what triggers a crisis, due to how it forces the young person to lose the system that holds them together. It is not a crisis in a pejorative sense; it is the articulation between the new and what is left behind.

Adolescence inevitably generates anxiety, fear, high degrees of worry, and so on, both in the adolescents and in their parents—painful and unpleasant emotions that may have to do with these changes and shifts in the young person. We often witness a movement from the fear of being trapped in childish or dependent aspects (claustrophobic anxieties) to the fear of not being prepared to face the demands of the adult world and the fears of leaving the family world (agoraphobic anxieties), as described by Feduchi (2016). Any change worries the young person because it can intensify their uncertainties and their fear of not having control over what is happening and, therefore, make them lose their capacity to mentalize. At this point, we must remind our readers that a crucial aspect of the outcomes in these intense times is how the environment is able to respond:

- Is the adolescent sufficiently supported and contained, while also being helped to identify and integrate their capacities and strengths?

- Is the adolescent sufficiently accompanied in this transition?

Following the developmental perspective described in previous chapters, the way in which the adolescent develops resources to be able to manage this exciting and demanding moment will depend on how the previous stages of their life have been. As described in Chapter 4, here is when the ghosts in the nursery and the angels in the nursery will show their impact on the way the adolescent starts to confront, deal with, and adapt to the challenges and opportunities of this developmental stage. There is strong evidence of the relationship between having suffered childhood adversities and a higher psychopathological risk in adolescence (Dangerfield, 2020), as well as evidence that, sadly, shows that these adversities are not detected by mental health professionals, often because psychological and psychiatric assessments don't systematically include asking people about what has happened in their lives (Dangerfield, 2020; Read et al., 2018).

When things go well, there are three aspects to consider (Feduchi, 2016) that may help understand some of the changes and readaptations that the young person is going through:

- **Privacy:** The young person defends and claims this privacy. This covers aspects of their life that are experienced and lived as something more of their own, away from the parents' view or control.

- **Testing new capacities:** There are new aspects developing at different levels—changes in the body (e.g., conditioning from sports, new physical activities, sexuality), social-affective (e.g., new social activities, parties, going out, meeting new people, intimate relationships), intellectual (e.g., interests, what catches their attention), and affective action. The adolescent begins to experiment, deploy, and confront the world with their new capabilities in different spheres.

- **Leaving groups that have always accompanied them during childhood and finding new ones:** The young person begins not being as involved with the family group, the primary school group, or the neighborhood that have been present since their childhood. This implies socialization in new groups of young people of the same age—through new friends, the exchange of new hobbies, new interests, new opinions, and so on. Love and sexuality also appear. Intimacy is strengthened, and aspects of the new are verified in the body and in the emotional and intellectual spheres.

Parents need to remain present, supporting and taking care of what the adolescents still can't handle on their own. However, this is tricky, as it implies being able to trust the adolescent's need to explore and test their developing capacities, while being available to support the adolescent in what may sometimes seem like a regressive way of being by their side or responding to childlike demands. This will be important in order to facilitate an experience where parents straddle the often-gray boundary between (a) helping to acknowledge and validate the young person's developing capacities and identity and (b) validating and supporting the young person's fears, anxieties, and limitations.

All adolescents may feel capable and competent for some things but not for others: to go out and experience new things is great, but at home, the young person occasionally functions as though they were still a younger child: messy room, annoyed about food ("There is never anything good to eat in this house!"), and so on. They have needs that we, as adults, must continue to address. There is a risk of either leaving them too much on their own or overprotecting them, which prevents them from being able to show that they can move forward.

It is also important to acknowledge and support the adolescent's initiatives and interests—to recognize and validate healthy aspects in development. Creativity expressed in whatever possible way (music, art, sports, etc.) is also something that parents should accept and stimulate.

Curiosity in parents is a key aspect of their mentalizing stance toward adolescents. Showing the adolescent that the parent is interested in knowing about their life, their interests, their fears, their passions, and so on and available to learn more from them in a nonjudgmental way is a valuable means by which to foster curiosity and facilitate an experience where the adolescent feels mentalized—and thus improve the relationship between parents and adolescents.

WORKING ON EPISTEMIC TRUST DURING THE ADOLESCENCE PERIOD

How can we contribute to helping parents develop a stance that is more characterized by a way of being with their adolescent son or daughter, that facilitates perspective taking, curiosity, and learning from each other?

No matter how much our therapeutic identity moves us to start sharing our understanding of the specific situation, as well as the emotional and relational dynamics that we observe in the parent or parents with whom we are working, we must first try to find a way to be available enough and explicit in our understanding of their suffering.

As described in Chapter 2, epistemic trust is a fundamental concept to understand therapeutic work (Fonagy & Allison, 2014). In the therapeutic work with parents, this trust is based on—or stimulated by—the knowledge that the parents have about the fact that the therapist has connected with them in a manner marked by authenticity and empathy, fundamentally understanding their suffering. This empathic connection, which we can understand as the fact that the parents have felt adequately mentalized, is what allows them to feel that they can trust what the therapist will offer in terms of knowledge. It is what will allow the patient to learn about themselves through the mind of someone they trust. So, first, we must join them in their despair.

As Bateman and Fonagy described (2016; Fonagy & Bateman, 2008), nonmentalizing can't be addressed with mentalizing. We must first try to help modulate the levels of emotional arousal, in order to attempt to facilitate the recovery of the capacity to mentalize. We must offer a relational experience wherein parents feel seen and understood, an experience through which they feel validated in the emotional impact that they are living and that is overwhelming them. By doing so, we can facilitate the development of epistemic trust with the therapist, modeling this way of "being with the other" that facilitates a repairing approach to the damaged or conflictual relationship the parent may have with their adolescent son or daughter. From a mentalization-informed framework, the therapist's main goal is to help parents generalize this different way of being with the other, toward their children.

Clinical experience validates the belief that what helps improve trust in a relationship and improve the quality of attachment is feeling understood. This is precisely the main goal in mentalization-informed work with parents: to help them understand the value of this way of being with the other in a relationship, by offering them a relationship in which they feel mentalized. Therapists can't do this in a rational or intellectual way—we must offer an emotional experience wherein parents can feel the transforming value of being adequately understood, that can facilitate perspective taking and learning from each other, in a way that improves their mentalizing capacities and, as described in Chapter 1, will invite them to take a more genuine interest in what lies behind their child's behavior. This will better serve their child's social and emotional needs and improve their relationship. The therapist's capacity to mentalize the parent seeks to facilitate this new attitude, which is characterized by higher levels of flexibility, curiosity, and genuine openness toward their children.

The following vignette seeks to illustrate the initial part of the therapeutic process when working with parents. This is an excerpt from the second home-based interview with Michael's parents, Mr. and Mrs. H:

MR. H: He just won't do anything! We saw you last week and told you about this situation. Another week has passed, and he hasn't left home except for going out to meet with that bunch of losers he calls friends!

MRS. H: And the cannabis, because I notice that he has been smoking when he comes back home, because I can see it in his eyes. I know my son, and I can tell when he is stoned! But what my husband says is correct, we can be sitting here with you week after week and this kid will be doing the same: nothing but contributing to ruin his life and his future!

MR. H: And ours, too, by the way! Because I am really fed up! I have been doing some research and I have found some of these therapeutic schools. I have been talking about it with my wife and we are considering this as the only option we have. We just can't have him home with us if he just wants to ruin his life. You need to help us find a way to get him back to school, because if things continue like this the only solution will be to send him to one of these therapeutic schools.

THERAPIST: Yes, we must think of ways to help Michael, and we will. But I am also thinking that this situation with your son Michael is very difficult. If I were in your shoes, I would be very distressed, very angry and probably very scared. Is this close to what you think is happening to you?

Here, the therapist is aware of the intensity of the despair that the parents are experiencing and how it interferes in their capacity to mentalize. Also, it is moving the parents to try to find a teleological solution, through the idea of a therapeutic school that they want to send their son to or through a very concrete demand for a magical solution from the therapist. It is common for therapists to get trapped in these teleological demands, responding with things to do—potential concrete solutions to something that is always more complex. This doesn't mean that a therapist should never give advice to parents, telling them what they should or shouldn't do, because sometimes it might be necessary. What we argue is that the therapist must be able to assess where the specific demand of the parent is arising from: whether it comes from a teleological demand, where the therapist should try to address this prementalizing mode before giving a concrete response, or whether it is a result of a mentalizing process, where the parent may need some specific help with a concrete answer of suggestion on how to proceed—what can be understood as psychoeducational advice.

Let us return to the clinical vignette: The therapist's main task there was to offer an emotional experience to the parents, wherein they felt seen and understood in their suffering. Because of the parents' difficulties in identifying and expressing their underlying emotional states, the therapist chose to share his own emotional reaction as a way of modeling how he approaches his own emotional states—imagining what he would be feeling if he were in their shoes. It is important to remember that, from a mentalizing perspective, it is important to always finish an intervention like this by checking with the clients about their reaction to what the therapist has just said.

The parents replied as follows:

MR. H: I am very angry, yes. I don't know if I am scared, but I am definitely very angry.

MRS. H: I am angry, but I am also scared. I am very scared because I don't see a way out. I just think that he has entered a path that is very dangerous, and I am afraid that there is going to be a moment in which there will be no turning point. You know Mr. H and I have both struggled a lot to make it where we are in our professions. It hasn't been easy, and the world doesn't make things easy for anyone, even less nowadays. There are lots of kids with a good education, so you must be very good at what you are doing to really make it.

THERAPIST: Thank you for this, it is helpful, because what I am understanding is that you have worked very hard to build your professional careers, and you both have managed to be successful in them, but with a lot of effort. And I imagine that now, to see your son not fighting for his future, not seeing how important it is to really invest in building a career, must be very frightening and probably very painful to witness. What do you think about this? Does it make any sense?

The therapist is focused on facilitating this experience in which the parents feel adequately understood in their important and understandable concerns about Michael. As this is the second time they are all meeting, it is important to work on establishing a good-enough and trustful relationship, in order to contribute to the development of epistemic trust, and also on modeling a new way of approaching relational interactions, in which the main purpose is to mentalize the other.

MR. H: Yes . . . I think that this is quite close to what is happening to me. I just can't stand seeing him day after day in his room only interested in his video games, I can't take this anymore. And it is true that his future worries me a lot. He has no options if he continues living this way, and we are witnessing this at home every day: our only child, and he is not wanting to accept our help. We've both tried to talk to him hundreds of times about the importance of his studies, but it is absolutely useless, he just doesn't listen, or even worse, he gets really unpleasant and nasty, something that is totally unacceptable.

THERAPIST: Yes, I can see how unbearable it must be when you are trying to help Michael and he just responds in a mean way. And Mrs. H, I am also very interested in your perspective about this that I said before, about how you and Mr. H have both worked so hard, and now your son, Michael, doesn't.

It is also important to keep a balance between both parents when working with a parental couple. The therapist does it here by showing curiosity about Mrs. H's reaction to the previous intervention.

MRS. H: Well, it is also something that is very hard to witness. It is true that I always thought Michael would do fine, and we even thought that he would be able to get into one of the Ivy League colleges, but that thought has completely gone now . . .

THERAPIST: And I imagine that having these expectations of your child and now seeing him having dropped out from school and spending day after day just sitting at home with the video games must be very painful.

MRS. H: It is, yes, very painful indeed. And you know, what I just don't understand is what has made him change and show no interest at all in going back to school. Because he is a smart kid and his performance at school was always excellent, always straight As . . . but now . . . I just find it so hard to understand.

This initial part of the session shows how the active role of the therapist, in trying to validate the parents' perspective, manages to help contain the level of despair they were experiencing. This increases the parents' capacity to approach their own underlying emotions and start building a narrative of the situation, which ends with this very interesting moment in which Mrs. H, in a genuinely mentalizing way, can leave the psychic equivalence mode—or certainty mode—and tolerate a not-knowing stance, showing explicit curiosity about how to understand her son's shift and increasing difficulties. The therapist highlights this in the following way:

THERAPIST: Well, this is a very good starting point of what our work together can be: How can we understand what is happening to Michael? Because we know what he is not doing and what he is doing, but the question is "What is it that makes him behave this way?" Maybe this is something that we can try to think together about.

MR. H: I am in the same position as my wife in this because I just have no clue about what on earth made him start changing. Because he has a very comfortable life. We both work extremely hard, and we are very lucky to have this very comfortable life. Look at this place, and his room, the very expensive school, and great teachers that he had . . . he has been given lots of help, and for what? I just get very angry when I think about it, just can't . . .

THERAPIST: I can totally understand, Mr. H. It must be very tough to have done so much for him and now see him stuck in this situation, with the risk of dropping out of a professional future.

MR. H: Yes, this is very tough indeed. [*Mrs. H nods in agreement.*]

Mr. H can join his wife in tolerating this valuable not-knowing stance, which is an important aspect of the mentalizing process. However, he also immediately shows signs of escalating emotional arousal, although he remains capable of a higher degree of self-observation of his emotional state, as he can identify, name, and communicate his anger. The therapist continues with this important technique of offering an experience wherein they feel mentalized, that—as we can see—is contributing to the main goal of creating mutual curiosity, which we know is a building block of epistemic trust and mentalization.

Seeing that it has been possible to help modulate the parents' despair and increase their curiosity and trust toward the therapeutic process, the therapist decides to take a further step, inviting them to mentalize their son, as follows:

THERAPIST: But now that you say this, and that you have both helped me see how this situation is affecting you, I was wondering if you could possibly help me with this: Do you think Michael can notice some of the things he makes you feel? I mean, when you feel angry or scared about his situation, do you think he can tell?

MRS. H: Well, I have never thought about it this way . . . but I am pretty sure that he does. In fact, now that I think, he has told me more than once that he knows we are very disappointed. And I imagine that he sees that I am very sad about this and very worried.

MR. H: But we can't get stuck in this. We must move on and find a way to get him going.

THERAPIST: Yes, Mr. H, I think this that you say is very important, because I imagine it is very important for both of you to find a way to help Michael move on, and that you have seen lots of therapists like myself asking the same questions, or getting stuck in talking about the situation, and probably not feeling it was helpful.

Mrs. H can follow this invitation to mentalize Michael, but Mr. H finds it harder, so the therapist must go back to offer validation of what Mr. H seems to be feeling, including here the acknowledgment of how difficult it may be to have to see another therapist—that is, including here a recognition of the emotional impact that the therapist may be contributing to produce. This intervention seems to facilitate Mr. H feeling appropriately seen and understood by the therapist, which helps to modulate the emotional reaction and increase the level of epistemic trust.

Mr. H replies in a way that confirms the usefulness of the therapist's intervention, as it helps him to make explicit his mistrustfulness—a valuable step in the process of developing epistemic trust:

MR. H: Exactly, yes, this is quite true. Because we have seen lots of colleagues of yours and things have only been getting worse in the last couple of years . . . so yes, I am not really very confident about just sitting here and talking.

THERAPIST: I would feel quite the same in your shoes: Like "having to see another shrink and talking about the same things again doesn't seem to take us anywhere."

MR. H: Well, but there is something different with you and your team, because you are here in our house, and this never happened before. It does make a difference.

MRS. H: Yes, and I think that we do need to understand what is going on with Michael.

Mr. H shows more confidence in approaching his understandable reluctance to start another therapeutic process, to which the therapist responds again with validation and some self-deprecating humor, which can be helpful when used appropriately. This approach has a beneficial effect, as Mr. H can then acknowledge some positive feedback on the session—feedback that Mrs. H also supports.

As mentioned in previous chapters, our main concern as therapists, when working with parents, is "How can we facilitate the emergence of parents' belief that the therapist is truly interested in understanding the difficulties they are experiencing as parents?" Because of the intensity of adolescence, and the tendency that adolescents have to act out, it is quite common for therapists to be asked for very specific solutions to very concrete difficulties either of the adolescents or in the relationship with them. That is, parents come to therapeutic sessions with teleological demands, many times understandably triggered by the logical concerns and anxieties resulting from the situation that they are living at home. It is also frequent for therapists to get trapped in these prementalizing modes and respond in a teleological way, giving concrete indications about what to do with their children.

From a mentalizing perspective, we would argue that often such predictable responses by therapists are triggered by the anxiety that parents communicate to them and how this anxiety interferes with therapist's capacity to mentalize, moving them to join the teleological mode. Teleology invites teleology—although, at other times, the therapist might show signs of functioning in psychic equivalence mode, when their stance is dominated by certainties, or in pretend mode, when they get too dominated by theories about the adolescent and move into an intellectualized understanding of the situation (something that happens often among therapists). It is more comfortable to feel that one has control of the situation, in the position of the expert that has knowledge to offer the parents. This may be important sometimes, from a psychoeducational perspective, but we must monitor and self-observe whether it is really coming from a conscious decision of helping parents understand aspects of their adolescent child from a developmental perspective or whether it responds to the therapist's loss of mentalizing. This can be caused by the impact of what the parents are communicating, because of the pressure felt, by the therapist, of solving a worrying situation—or any other situation that is inhibiting the therapist's capacity to mentalize and moving him to prementalizing modes as described.

WORKING BACK AND FORTH WITH PARENTS IN THE DEVELOPMENTAL LINE OF MENTALIZATION DURING THE ADOLESCENT PERIOD

Therapists must remember that mentalization is fragile and that human beings are not very good at mentalizing, since we lose this ability continuously. It is a capacity that is very easily overwhelmed and is never entirely stable, consistent, or one-dimensional. When human beings receive an emotional impact that disturbs their capacity for mentalization, they turn (a) to an attachment figure who gives them tranquility and confidence, to recover, or (b) to reliable good-enough relationship experiences that they have internalized and that accompany them from within.

Everybody has more difficulty mentalizing in situations of high anxiety, while the ability to regain mentalization in these situations makes us more resilient. To facilitate this process when working with parents, a mentalization-informed framework proposes an approach based on the three building blocks of mentalizing described in Chapter 5, which we now go through using examples of Michael's parents' case to illustrate each section. This approach helps the therapist organize their interventions within a clear developmental and process-oriented structure. This can prove extremely helpful at moments of high emotional impact, for both the therapist and the parents, during the session. It helps balance the cognitive–affective dimension for the therapist.

Attention Regulation

During the initial assessment meetings with Michael's parents, the active role of the therapist, aimed at fostering the development of epistemic trust, facilitated a certain improvement of the parents' openness to describe aspects of their own lives—more specifically, their own adolescences.

It is important to mention that the three building blocks of mentalizing can overlap with each other during a session and that their functions feedback to each other in an interdependent way (Midgley et al., 2017). However, it is technically valuable to be aware of how to use each one of them to facilitate the mentalizing process when working with parents.

Let's first focus on the block of attention regulation, in which our main interventions or technical resources can be noticing and naming what is happening in the here and now of the session, in order to contribute to increasing moments of joint attention. We must also pay attention to parents' nonverbal communications, especially when we understand those as expressing emotions that may be very difficult for them to identify, tolerate, and verbalize. As described in Chapter 5, this way of being attentive and close to parents' emotional reactions in a curious, respectful, and validating way can contribute valuably to the development of epistemic trust—and, thus, to better outcomes in the therapeutic process.

The following clinical vignette from the third meeting with Michael's parents illustrates the work in the first block—attention regulation:

MRS. H: Things started to go wrong quite a while ago, and I remember that it all started soon after your uncle passed away.

Mr. H moves in his chair, looking upset and uncomfortable with his wife's statement. She continues:

MRS. H: Because soon after that, the school contacted us with concerns about a shift in Michael's work that had significantly affected his marks.

The therapist interrupts Mrs. H, to notice and name what he has perceived of Mr. H's affective shift expressed through nonverbal behavior, which Mrs. H seems not aware of or ignores.

THERAPIST: I would ask you to pause here for a minute, Mrs. H, because I am noticing that Mr. H might be a bit uncomfortable with this that you are saying. I am not sure about this, Mr. H, but I have the impression that now that your wife has mentioned the loss of your uncle, your body posture has changed, and you seem to express some discomfort. I would like to check with you if this is the case.

MR. H: [*visibly moved*] Well . . . this is something that I would rather not talk about . . . [*barely holding his tears*]

THERAPIST: I am so sorry, Mr. H, I don't want to make you feel uncomfortable.

MRS. H: Well, this was a great loss for all of us . . . his uncle was like a father to him, and like a very loved grandfather for Michael. But we had to move on . . .

THERAPIST: I can see that this is a very painful memory, that understandably one wants to move away from, because I imagine that it hurts a lot.

MR. H: It was a terrible loss . . . [*visibly moved*] . . . and yes, we all had to move on, as my wife says.

THERAPIST: I understand that you have both done the best you can to cope with these extremely difficult and painful losses and very tough situations throughout your lives. However, maybe we can try to find ways of approaching how they are still probably affecting you, in order to make you feel a bit more supported by each other, especially in this difficult period that your son Michael is going through and making you live. Because I have the impression that you are both a bit alone with the number of painful memories and current difficulties that you are experiencing.

In this example, the therapist decides to interrupt Mrs. H when he observes the nonverbal reaction of Mr. H, after the loss of his uncle is mentioned. Mr. H seems to express discomfort and unpleasantness that the therapist notices and names, checking with Mr. H about whether this is how he is really feeling. The therapist then validates this unpleasant emotional state, also apologizing for his contribution to this painful moment, as he has made Mr. H stop and look at what is happening in the room in the current moment. This is an important part of the intervention, as it is a way of facilitating epistemic trust again, through the honest acknowledgment of the therapist's role in triggering painful emotions and memories. However, the therapist also introduces a different perspective on this when he invites them to consider what is happening in the here and now of the session—and, in what we could also see as a moment of psychoeducation, he describes it as one of the main goals of the work that the parents and the therapist can do together, while validating the usual pattern that seems to have predominated in this parental couple to manage painful emotions: Move on, and dissociate from those emotions.

Affect Regulation

This second mentalizing block is a valuable reminder of the importance of helping parents to approach, observe, and reflect on emotions. The main goal of this block is to help parents improve their capacity to identify, modulate, and express unpleasant emotions. The therapist must be available to receive and tolerate these painful emotions, offering a relational experience that supports the parents in increasing their own capacity to tolerate them in the here and now of the session. This is an important step in the process of helping the parents to improve their capacity to develop what we sometimes refer to as the "emotional muscle," which process has a very valuable role in helping parents to enhance their capacity to mentalize themselves and others and, consequently, to improve their parental skills.

From a developmental perspective, we understand emotional well-being related, to a large extent, to the capacity to tolerate and modulate painful emotions. Michael's parents had both organized relational dynamics that promoted dissociation and denial of these emotions, as the only way to cope with life and move on, as they usually said. This pattern had limited their capability to help their son develop better ways of managing his own emotional life, as they were implicitly asking him to follow their own way of surviving emotionally: organizing and sustaining one's own identity through academic and professional achievements but with no space or time for processing emotions. Michael couldn't follow their steps and felt overcome by the demands of life in the onset of adolescence, retreating from the world that felt overwhelming to him and closing himself off into the safety of his room, his video games, and a reduced number of friends who shared his limited interests.

In the following vignette, we exemplify the use of affect regulation as a way of helping parents approach their emotional life from a different perspective. Following our framework, the idea is that parents can generalize this new way of approaching emotions with their adolescent children as a way of improving their capacity to mentalize.

Two months after we started working with Michael's parents, Mrs. H called the therapist for help, due to how desperate she felt after having a fight with her son.

MRS. H: I called you yesterday because this just can't continue! I knew we were going to meet today, and I apologize for my call yesterday, but the situation at home is totally unacceptable. If Michael doesn't change, we will have to send him to this therapeutic school that my husband found. When I arrived home yesterday evening Michael was lying on the sofa, with all that mess around him and plugged into his video games. He had been sitting there all day, eating pizza he had ordered and playing that lousy video game. We had a terrible fight because I just can't accept this behavior. It is not acceptable! I got so angry that I started screaming at him in a way that I understand wasn't helpful, because he totally lost it. But I was so angry, so much!

THERAPIST: I can imagine that it must have been really upsetting to find him lying on the sofa, as you describe, and how it can make you want to find a way to end this, like thinking of sending him to the therapeutic school. However, you are telling me about how angry you felt yesterday, and I wonder how you are feeling now?

The therapist validates Mrs. H's emotional experience—although not by trying simply to move her away from the emotions that contribute to the dysregulation but by inviting her to approach and observe her current emotional state, in order to try to offer support to approach it in the here and now of the session.

MRS. H: Well . . . I am so angry with him . . . so much . . . and I just couldn't control myself and I screamed at him, and it was a complete disaster. I should control myself better and probably just try to ignore him, because he started screaming back and it was just so bad.

THERAPIST: I think that I would feel quite the same if I were in your shoes. I imagine that it is very difficult to come back from a tough day of work and find your son there, seeing him lying on the sofa. But I would want to stop here for a minute and ask you to help me understand this anger you are sharing with me. I think that it will help me understand better the situation you are living at home with Michael.

MRS. H: Well, as you said, returning home from a tough day of work and finding him there just doing nothing! I just hate that! It is really something that infuriates me . . . he can't do that to himself! He is ruining his life! We have always told him how much effort both his father and I have invested in our work, and how we have achieved so much professionally because of that. Our parents didn't help us financially, it has all been thanks to our work.

Mrs. H can develop further understanding of her current emotional state, describing how she sees her fear connected to not seeing her son capable of doing as she has done: develop this successful professional career that can hold her together. She also includes aspects of her own personal history—something that can help develop mentalized affectivity, through observing and reflecting on emotions while considering past history and also tolerating emotions without being propelled to act on them, as described in Chapter 3.

The therapist intervenes, making a hypothesis on how both parents' hyper-investing in intellectual and professional achievements can be also understood as a way to survive the loneliness and emotional isolation in which they both seem to have lived, providing a sense of safety that they are terrified to leave.

THERAPIST: You just said that you hate seeing your son in this state, not attending school and spending his days at home. I think it would be important for us to understand together these painful feelings you are sharing with me: how you feel angry and see that you hate seeing Michael like this. You also mention how your parents didn't help you financially and that all that you have achieved is because of your own work. I think of how alone you have probably felt throughout your life and how building your professional career has helped both you and Mr. H feel safe. Does this that I say make sense?

MRS. H: Yes, we do feel safe because of all that we have achieved professionally. And we had to do it on our own. I have always been terrified with the idea of losing my job, of failing professionally. Now I am more confident with this, but then Michael doesn't do anything. This is what terrifies me and makes me very angry. Seeing that he is not doing anything to build his own safety.

THERAPIST: We must help Michael organize a professional future, but as we have been saying in our previous sessions, we must also help him feel safe in other ways, that have to do with developing confidence in facing one's own fears and anxieties. And you are now talking about your own fear of losing your job, what you feel supports you, and it makes me think of your own difficulties in trusting the possibility of facing painful emotions, as if there is no place for that in life.

> However, you are telling me about your anger and your fear related to your son's situation. Painful emotions that you are now capable of identifying and sharing.

Here, the therapist describes the reluctance toward, and fear of, approaching painful emotions among the family functioning, although also highlighting how, in the here and now of this session, Mrs. H is showing valuable signs of mentalized affectivity.

MRS. H: I am yes . . . but the thing is that before, I had no other option. When I was Michael's age things at home were very difficult. My father was very abusive—he never hit us, but he was always angry and very mean to us. Also, to my mother . . . and she never did anything . . . I found a way to survive in my books, always reading and studying. The library was my favorite place, and I was also lucky with the good teachers I had at school. They were very supportive because they saw I was always very committed to my work. But it is true that I never talked about my emotions . . . never! And I found a good partner with my husband, as he is the same. But I suppose this has affected our relationship with Michael, as my husband and I have moved on and have our way of living this way, but Michael doesn't.

THERAPIST: You are helping me see how your way of surviving in such a tough environment was to find shelter in your books and studies, and how that was your safe place. But you are also capable of seeing how it has had an impact in your family life. How at home this seems to be a bit unbalanced: a lot invested on the cognitive, intellectual, and professional pole, but not much time and space for the emotional one. Although, as we are seeing today, you are being able to think in a way that does show that there is more space for emotions, more capacity to be in touch with them, despite how much they may hurt. And this is what I think you all need more of at home, the possibility of feeling that this that you are doing now is possible between you, your husband, and Michael.

As we also highlighted in Chapter 1, a central aspect of our approach is to help parents retell their story and their child's story in a way that their self-observation increases and, with it, their capacity to "play with ideas" of what might be going on for the adolescent and themselves.

The therapist must keep in mind the parents' relational developmental path and how it is inhibiting their capacity to mentalize in the current relationship with the adolescent. We want to offer a relationship in which parents can experience being with a therapist who is trying to keep his mentalizing stance—a therapist who can tolerate a not-knowing stance and be genuinely open and curious toward the parents' emotional state, a therapist who can be humble and flexible in his understanding. The main goal is to offer this different relational experience in which parents can, hopefully, feel adequately mentalized and through which they can learn to take a different perspective on their adolescent child—a new perspective characterized by a more genuine interest in what lies behind their child's behavior, which will better serve their child's social and emotional needs and improve their parent–child relationship.

Deficits in parents' mentalizing inhibit their capacity to provide an experience of mutuality and thoughtful curiosity about their children's internal experience of relationships. The parent's inability to regulate their own affective states creates an unpredictable and inconsistent relational environment for them to grow up in. The cycle of generational transmission of relational trauma becomes evident and is facilitated in this context (Dangerfield, 2021b), something that Michael's parents dramatically portrayed. However, they are showing consistent signs of improvement of this capacity. This process has been facilitated through the process of building epistemic trust through joint attention and affect regulation (Midgley et al., 2017), as the first step in the process of helping reestablish mentalizing.

Going beyond the observable external behavior and seeing that there can be a way of understanding Michael's school dropout beyond what his parents see as "he is just not wanting to face the demands of growing up" was a crucial part of the work with Mr. and Mrs. H.

Explicit Mentalization

A common mistake that therapists make is to try to address prementalizing modes by use of mentalization. When someone is not mentalizing, we should not force them to mentalize, because they cannot listen to us. All therapists do it rather frequently, with the risk of contributing to increasing dysregulation and inhibiting even more the client's capacity to mentalize. There is also a risk of engaging with the patient in empty speeches, dominated by the prementalizing pretend mode. The two previous blocks, of attention regulation and affect regulation, are crucial in helping to achieve a certain level of containment, contributing to facilitating a recovery of mentalizing. The therapeutic process can continue with interventions that invite explicit mentalizing.

Another example of the work with Mr. and Mrs. H exemplifies this block:

MRS. H: We seem to be a bit stuck after the first interview with the school. We were very happy to see Michael interested in wanting to meet with his tutor, and we think the meeting went very well considering all that has happened in the last months, but as I say, we think we are a bit stuck now . . .

THERAPIST: I would appreciate if you could help me understand what being "stuck" means.

MRS. H: Well, Michael agreed to go to the meeting, listened to what the school offered as a plan to return there and get back to work, but it seems that he hasn't made up his mind about when to start. He said he will, but he is not getting back to the tutor with a response to what they offered and to set a date.

MR. H: And we think that it may be going back to the known behavior of closing himself off into his room. We are both concerned about this possibility, and afraid that this move toward school might be only something to calm us down . . . so that we don't bother him anymore and let him stay in his safe zone, away from all the demands and challenges that he is still avoiding.

THERAPIST: Well, this could be a possibility, Mr. H, of course. I do understand your concern, because the idea of Michael not following the plan to go back to school after all your efforts with him and all our sessions here, is quite annoying and worrying, indeed. However, we can probably think of other ways of explaining his behavior, don't you think? I mean, do any other possible explanations come to your mind that can help us imagine what is going on in Michael's mind and make him delay his response to school?

MR. H: I suppose so . . . [*to Mrs. H*] What do you think?

THERAPIST: I see that you are interested in what your wife may think, Mr. H. It makes me think of what we see is improving among both of you, this collaborative and supportive way of addressing the situations that you must face with your son.

MR. H: True, we do work together, and I also think that she is better than me in this mentalizing thing, because I do tend to go into my certainties quite often.

THERAPIST: As we all do, Mr. H. Also shrinks—we also do it rather frequently, especially under stress. But look, you are also showing your own capacity to mentalize, as you are observing how you sometimes fall into certainties, which is a good example of valuable self-observation. But going back to your question, Mrs. H, what do you think about Michael's behavior?

MRS. H: Well, I think that he is probably afraid of taking this last step of returning to school. He does have a different attitude toward us, we have all managed to improve things at home, as we are much more capable of having conversations, and also talking about how we feel. I think Michael is afraid, yes, and we should probably just understand that it makes sense that he feels this way. After all, it has been a long time away from school.

THE BALANCING ACT IN PARENTING AN ADOLESCENT

Mentalization will be effective if parents can maintain a balance across these dimensions and if they apply them appropriately, depending on the context—holding a balance between the different dimensions of mentalizing, between the internal world and the external world, between oneself and others, between what happens here and now and what happens at other times, between what parents think and what they feel, between what they imagine the other thinks and what they imagine the other feels, and so on. When working with a parental couple, we must also find a balance between interventions of both members. It requires a very active role for the clinician, who intervenes when mentalizing disappears because this balance is lost.

Family interactions are an ideal relational context to induce loss of mentalizing daily (Fonagy & Allison, 2011), especially because of the intensity of emotions. Also, adolescents are in a developmental stage where loss of mentalizing is more likely—and additionally from a neurological perspective.

Holding a balance in such circumstances is always harder—and even more so in families with a history of relational trauma or in families who are suffering current difficulty, such as serious financial strains, divorce, and so on.

PREMENTALIZING MODES IN THE CONTEXT OF PARENTING AN ADOLESCENT

When mentalization capacity is lost, there is a reemergence of ways of experiencing oneself and others that have parallels with the ways in which young children behave before they have developed full mentalization capacities. The prementalizing modes, which have been described extensively throughout previous chapters, are the result of imbalances between the dimensions of mentalization and imply the inability to be curious and available toward the adolescent's mental states. They also trigger inappropriate or harmful attributions about the adolescent's behavior. When the parent's minds are dominated by these prementalizing modes, their curiosity, acknowledgment of opacity of minds, and capacity to consider and accept different perspectives are inhibited or absent. This usually has an important impact, increasing the risk of dysregulation and lack of awareness of the effect of the parents' own mental states on their children. This happens reciprocally, as adolescents who also are dominated by prementalizing modes will not be very aware of the emotional impact that everything they say and do has on their parents. It is important for the therapist to be able to recognize and understand these prementalizing modes in order to treat them when they appear during the sessions. This is an important part of the therapeutic process, as the prementalizing modes tend to be the cause of significant interpersonal difficulties and may result in acting out (Bateman & Fonagy, 2016).

Prementalizing modes are better understood from a dimensional perspective. This implies that, for example, we would understand severe self-harm, addiction, or a suicidal ideation as extreme forms of teleological ways of dealing with intense anxieties, such as the very pronounced despair secondary to the experience of these anxieties. In a similar way, we can also understand a paranoid state as an extreme form of psychic equivalence mode. We must also keep in mind that every single human being, including all therapists and parents, falls into prementalizing modes on a daily basis—but, obviously, not always to the same degree or with the same intensity.

Prementalizing modes should also be seen as necessary under certain circumstances. It is important, for example, to be able to go into teleological mode and run away from a dog that is wanting to bite us, or to jump off our chair to stop a child from sticking his toy into a plug.

Psychic Equivalence Mode

When Mr. and Mrs. H asked for help, they were completely certain that Michael's behavior had to do with the fact that he was very lazy and wanted only "the easy way out." It was initially difficult for them to see beyond Michael's observable behavior. They were certain about the fact that he wanted an easy life and was fine with the idea of just sitting at home playing video games.

Mr. H's description of his son's problem is a good example of a thought process and discourse dominated by psychic equivalence mode:

> We have always shown him the importance of hard work, but he just doesn't care about his future, he is happy sitting at home playing video games and thinks that life is only that, having fun, enjoying himself, going out with those losers he calls friends. It is a complete disaster; he has such a lack of commitment and no interest whatsoever in any academic work. He is so profoundly wrong with this, because he thinks that the world is so easy and that he will be able to continue living like this . . . He just doesn't care about anything else and wants to get the most out of us. That's what I am convinced that he wants: to be able to use our money and laugh at us, as the ones that must continue working hard and provide all that he needs. I think that he is really getting abusive with us, and that the only way to make him reconsider this is being very firm with our boundaries: We must send him to the therapeutic school as soon as possible.

A few months after starting therapeutic work, Mr. H showed a considerable difference in his approach to Michael's difficulties, evidencing a shift that illustrated how he was much more able to mentalize both his son's situation and his own emotional experience:

> I am so worried about his future, and this worry has had such an important impact on the way I have been seeing things. Because I have just been pushing him back to school, but now I can see that he is overwhelmed and afraid. I imagine that it must have been very difficult to live with his mother and me, only focused on our work and asking him to do the same. You know, in a way I think that this situation has helped us all realize that we must give ourselves time for other things . . . the problem is that I have always found it so difficult to talk about feelings . . . I suppose that I am also quite afraid of them, not only my son . . .

Pretend Mode

The following clinical vignette shows how Mrs. H's discourse was predominantly in pretend mode during one of the meetings in the initial assessment phase:

> We talk to Michael very often about how fundamental it is in the current world to have an excellent education. A professional career is everything in life, and this is what he needs in order to have a good life. My life is very successful at all levels because of my efforts in building a profession. It is easy to see all that my husband and I have achieved because of our efforts, and this is what we are asking our son to do: to focus on what is important. Our concern is the fact that Michael has dropped out from school, and this is the only source of worry in our lives. Thanks to our effort, we have been able to build a very happy and stable life and, if it wasn't for Michael's difficulties, we would be a very happy family as we had always been until he dropped out from school.

After a few months of the therapist working with the parents, with an important focus on addressing their difficulties and suffering, Mrs. H's use of pretend mode to understand her family's situation had significantly diminished, as the following vignette shows:

> Michael was probably right to feel overwhelmed . . . What seemed to work for us didn't really work for him, and I don't blame him. It is true that neither Mr. H nor me had an easy life before we met. We both had quite a hard time with our families, due to the different circumstances that we have discussed with you, and funnily enough we coped with our difficulties in the same way: just moving on and working hard in our professions . . . It is still so painful for me to remember the fights between my parents . . . and how mean my father was to me . . . [*visibly moved*] Hiding behind my books was what saved me from all that horror!

Teleological Mode

Another clinical vignette exemplifies this prementalizing mode, where Mr. H understands that the concrete situation of not cleaning his room is clear evidence of Michael's defiant and threatening attitude toward them—without Mr. H being able to consider any other perspective nor imagine how his son may be feeling, as there is no space in his mind to hold his son's own mind and emotional experience:

> He just wouldn't clean his room, so there you have the evidence again of how he is just wanting to hurt us. We haven't been telling him to go to school every day, but we did ask him to clean up his room. And he hasn't! So, he is just wanting to go against us in this defying and threatening way.

The following vignette shows how different Mr. H's discourse can be after being contained and helped to develop his capacity to mentalize:

> I just find it so hard to understand why my son has collapsed the way he has. He doesn't even care about his room, when he has always been so tidy and organized with his things. It really worries me because I imagine that he must feel down and out... I don't know what is troubling him so much, but he is giving a clear message that he just can't cope with life. I can now see that we really need help to talk to him in a different way . . .

CONCLUDING SUMMARY

- The therapist must carry out a comprehensive assessment of family dynamic and case formulation, based on addressing family relational patterns.

- The underlying principle is that behavioral difficulties and family conflict are very frequently a result of a mentalization failure in the interaction between parents and adolescents.

- We know that mentalization is relational, so mentalization failure in one member of the family rarely exists on its own: It is often generated by, and affects, the whole family dynamic.

- The primary aim of a mentalization-informed framework is to improve parents' awareness of their own mental states and to facilitate an improved capacity to imagine the mental states of their adolescent children.

- As mentioned in Chapter 1, the main goal of our approach is to try to help parents improve the most valuable skill of all—that of imagining, in a curious way, what is motivating their behaviors and those of their adolescent children, especially during moments of stress.

- Therapists must mentalize parents first. Epistemic trust will be established if the parents feel adequately seen and understood, especially in their suffering.

- The way to facilitate a change is that adolescents can be open to listening to their parents. But this will happen only if they feel understood by them.

- When epistemic trust is established, adolescents will be open to learning from parents. If adolescents cannot trust parents, they will never be able to learn from them.

- Setting clear rules and boundaries with adolescents is important, but a control system only generates more rejection. What is important is trust.

- Help parents identify the cycles of inhibition of mentalization and how to stop them and facilitate recovering mentalizing.

- Psychoeducation for parents can help reduce negative attributions, specifically on developmental aspects of adolescence and the brain development and characteristics that also interfere with the capacity to mentalize.

- Value of repair in parenting: Parents get it wrong two times out of three. What counts is the stance of the parent—their way of being with the young person. Encourage a not-knowing stance, safe uncertainty, and capacity to repair.

- If parents can acknowledge that they were wrong in a specific situation or comment and that they know that this hurt the adolescent and are able to apologize for that, this is the experience of repair in the attachment relationship. It can increase epistemic trust and attention regulation that can facilitate mentalization. It makes it possible to diminish the defensive stance of the adolescent and increases the capacity to mentalize.

11 DAVID AND GOLIATH
Mentalizing Young Adulthood

CASE AND CLINICAL FORMULATION

Linda was a cisgender White woman in her early 40s who sought out therapy, for the first time, in the aftermath of a divorce. Linda grew up in an Irish Catholic family and attended Catholic school throughout her education. She was no longer a practicing Catholic, but some of her values derived from that background in ways that therapy helped to articulate and explore. The divorce had been a long time in coming, as Linda and her husband, David, had arguments about his lack of contribution to the family (he was a musician who traveled often, and so he did not hold up his end of the work at home). Linda and David had one child, Tina, a daughter who was 19 at the time of the divorce. Linda and Tina had a close relationship, although they had gone through a rocky stretch as Tina's adolescence progressed.

When Linda began therapy, she was preoccupied with stabilizing her life. She had a demanding job and wanted to be the best mother to her daughter. Her style was simply to turn the page and get on in her life. Thus, in sessions, she focused on finding her way to a new partner and plunging back into internet dating. Her therapist was struck by the quality of her determination to move ahead, which included making efforts to limit her involvement with her ex-husband—in particular, minimizing his role in Tina's life. She was rigid in this, and she reacted to the therapist's efforts to get her to reconsider whether this was in the best interests of her daughter by tensing up and questioning why the therapist was not more concerned with her, Linda's, feelings.

Rowen and Emery (2014) affirmed that interparental conflict predicts adjustment problems in young adults. They explored "parental denigration," rather than the widely used construct of "parental alienation," finding that it occurs more in divorced women—but occurs between both parents and results in fewer close relationships with children. This is especially true for the parent who is identified as the denigrator parent. Parental denigration backfires as a strategy and suggests a preoccupation with the partner, rather than an adaptive focus on the well-being of the children.

Linda began to initiate greater concerns about her relationship with Tina—her now-23-year-old daughter who was also now in graduate school—following her return home as the result of the COVID-19 pandemic. It was not that Linda did not bring up issues about her daughter before then; however, in interactions with the therapist, she was now looking for specific advice, and the therapist's efforts to encourage her to sort out her own feelings and values was construed as an unwillingness to help. Problems between Linda and Tina exploded to the surface as soon as Tina returned home. They had moved beyond the usual antagonisms that occur during adolescence, and Tina's being away had had a salutary effect on their relationship.

Linda was able to appreciate that the pandemic was causing upheaval in many families, but she seemed remarkably indifferent to rethinking her approach to Tina, such as refraining from monitoring her daughter's time spent on the bed instead of at her desk. Although Linda had been happy to welcome Tina home at first, she also resented the intrusion on her personal space. Dating had not been going well after one brief relationship, which Linda had hoped might work out. It did not, partially because she told her boyfriend that she had no interest in meeting his twin daughters, who were 5 years old, which he felt was insulting and a dealbreaker. Linda overtly expressed negative associations to young children and to babies, and she referred to her own experience of early mothering in a way that seemed cynical. Although her feelings, in part, were a result of not feeling adequately supported by her husband, the therapist imagined that there was more of a story to explore with her. The issues between Linda and Tina were a springboard for exploring her own history beyond some of the facts and data with which the therapist had become familiar.

Linda came from a family of six children and was far and away the most successful. Her siblings lived in or near the suburban town they grew up in. Linda moved away to go to college. She was a social activist in college, where she met David. They were friends for a long time before starting a romantic relationship, culminating in marriage. Linda saw herself as an outlier from her family of origin, observing that her other siblings maintained a closer relationship with each other.

Linda's parents both worked. Her father was a union electrician, and her mother worked in an antique store. Linda was the second-oldest child and shouldered the burden of caregiving to her younger siblings while their parents were at work. Linda self-identified as the mature kid who did not need to be asked in order to help in the family. She was a hard-working student and was well-liked at school. Retrospectively, she was aware of how much energy it took up to be the way others wanted her to be. Linda and the therapist were able to explore how her wish to please others was triggering considerable anxiety— especially, social anxiety. Linda had friends but not close ones, and she had limited experience with boys until college.

Linda's father was from a large extended family. He was a gregarious man to whom people warmed, which Linda contrasted to herself. They bonded over talking about politics but did not always agree, as Linda saw herself as more liberal. Linda felt that she was closer to him when young and that they each kept their distance from the other as she became a young adult.

Linda's relationship with her mother was hard to get a read on. She portrayed it without color or detail, as if it were part of the background furniture in her life. The therapist was curious to hear more about her mother's history, while attempting to mentalize Linda's experience as a mother herself:

THERAPIST: Tell me more about your mom, I do not feel that I have much of a sense of her as a person.

LINDA: My mom held down the fort. You could count on her to come through, even though she was completely exhausted.

THERAPIST: What kinds of things are you referring to?

LINDA: Like the time she stayed up late sewing a costume for a performance for me . . . when she had to get up at 5:30 a.m. to take care of things for the family.

THERAPIST: Maybe this is far-fetched, but did you ever wish that she could be more available to you, kind of, on an everyday basis?

LINDA: She was! And she had five other kids to worry about, not to mention a brother with mental health issues.

THERAPIST: Your uncle had mental health issues?

LINDA: Yup . . . I mean I only saw him a few times . . . but my mother felt bad for him. She remembers when he was made fun of as a kid. You know how kids can be.

THERAPIST: Your mom sounds like a caring person.

LINDA: She worked herself to the bone, day in and day out. My dad . . . well, he came home, sat in his chair, and watched TV until he went to bed.

THERAPIST: Did this bother your mother?

LINDA: No, you don't understand, she was a fucking saint [*laughs raucously*].

The therapist's mentalizing stance was important during these early stages of therapy, in order to create a safe environment where epistemic trust could develop. This was especially important in this case, as Linda's code of ethics interfered with her being able to look back and think about her relationship with her mother. Her basic physical needs were cared for. To some extent, she received as much attention as was reasonable to expect in such a large family. Nevertheless, it is revealing that Linda lacked clear memories of her mother being curious about and recognizing her emotions. Over time, it emerged that Linda never felt deserving of commanding her mother's full attention. Linda could not recall a single time when her mother asked her about her feelings. This impacted the development of her own parental reflective functioning capacities—specifically, her curiosity toward Tina's internal experience.

The focus in therapy had centered primarily on exploring and settling Linda's feelings about the divorce and warming up to be comfortable with dating. One day, she surprised the therapist, when referring to clashes with Tina during adolescence, by recalling that she and her mother also had lots of conflict during her adolescence. This contrasted with the predominant image of Linda as a long-suffering, dutiful child, and Linda's first thoughts reflexively made her feel guilty about being a self-centered adolescent. The therapist suggested to Linda that she might be minimizing the complexity of her feelings—that maybe she had been trying to engage her mother on a different channel in order to get what she needed. Linda grew quiet and slowly became tearful. As she left the session, she said that she appreciated how the therapist made her more aware of her emotions and that she hoped that this would become incorporated more in their work together. She looked the therapist directly in the eye as she said this, which was unusual. She had felt mentalized and understood by her therapist, thus allowing herself to travel back and forth down the developmental line of mentalization, with her therapist's support.

When the therapist first started to address the mounting conflict at home, Linda's inclination was to suggest that Tina was spoiled—about which Linda expressed frustration—and that she contested her mother's authority with everything from big issues to miniscule ones. Objectively, Linda was under more stress at work, forced to agonize about meeting with clients in person or just remotely. Tina, too, was under pressure—from having to be a Zoom student—and was disappointed to no longer have the opportunity to work at a research laboratory at school. Tina had been thriving in graduate school and, like many other young people, was forced to deal with the unexpected adjustment of losing personal freedom. The expectation that young adulthood entailed taking on greater responsibility had been universally marred by the restrictions due to the pandemic.

Linda's insight about conflict with her mother was fruitful because, in her mind, she felt insulted that Tina did not try to please her—as Linda had done in her family of origin. Linda was able to see that this strategy had worked in some ways (e.g., giving her privileges within the family) but also came at a heavy price (e.g., ignoring her own feelings). Linda had viewed the conflicts with her daughter as insults to her authority; now, she began to see that her daughter was resisting the kind of compliance that she herself had relied on and could identify as a source of her own private suffering. This was relevant in helping Linda identify the patterns that formed the nonmentalizing cycles of interaction between her and Tina.

Linda evolved as a parent through therapeutic work. She came to understand that although she had experienced a dearth of being mentalized about, she could try to do better with her young adult child. As a result of the experience of feeling mentalized by her therapist, her capacity to mentalize her daughter emerged. This led to a change in which she accepted that Tina wanted to have a relationship with her dad, which she had previously not encouraged and even opposed. Ironically, the pandemic had curtailed her ex-husband's traveling, and he was receptive to forging an adult relationship with his daughter. Linda found that having a coparent alleviated some of the burden of being a single parent, and mother and daughter established a respectful, if sometimes difficult, new relationship.

CORE ISSUES AND DEVELOPMENTAL ASPECTS OF YOUNG ADULTHOOD

Young adulthood marks the transition from childhood to adulthood. It is a relatively recently identified stage of lifespan development, roughly from 18 to 25 years old, that may well reflect phenomena that pertain to Western, educated, industrialized, rich, and democratic (WEIRD) culture and thus may not be universal. There is some literature on gender that suggests that men struggle with young adulthood more than do women (Miller, 2017; Nelson et al., 2007).

There remains some uncertainty around the defining age of young adults, with older literature claiming a broader age range (Colarusso, 1992: 20–40 years old; Erikson, 1994: 18–40 years old). Bonovitz (2018) proposed a slightly older range—22 to 28 years old, as opposed to the standard of 18 to 25 years old introduced by Arnett (2000, 2015)—that has now become widely accepted. We adopt the 18-to-25 age range, although it does seem to be the case that young adulthood is leaning in the direction of expanding beyond 25 years old. Ongoing research is necessary in order to specify the parameters of young adulthood with more confidence. Young adulthood is distinctive as a stage in pointing forward to full adulthood while remaining tied to earlier stages of development.

Like adolescence, young adulthood involves a reexperiencing and renegotiation of previous stages of development, such as separation and individuation. Young adults typically complete (or are near completing) their education by this time and move on to become more independent, increasingly more invested in finding their way in the world. Certainly, there tends to be less direct parental involvement at this point, although this can be affected by the decision to live at home rather than on one's own, as well as other economic and psychological factors. The negotiation of separation and individuation can take on different forms—from too much dependence on the family to a renunciation of dependence.

In contrast to earlier chapters, where work with parents may occur in either their own individual therapy or as part of their child's therapy, when we work with young adults, we do not typically have involvement with parents. There are, however, relevant case examples in which including the parents becomes necessary and helpful—such as the case described by Scharfman (1990), reported in Jacobs and Chused's (1987) account of a panel presentation, where the parents threatened to terminate the treatment because of the therapist's recommendation that the patient take a leave from law school, and a joint meeting occurred that allowed the work to continue. Jacobs and Chused drew attention to the crucial issue in working with young adults, about who is actually paying for the treatment: the parents, the patients, or a combination of both.

Benbassat and Shulman's (2016) study of 65 young adults, a follow-up study from the sample of 105 adolescents, found that parental reflective function, rather than parental warmth and control, predicted better adjustment regarding symptoms, self-perception, self-description, and romantic relations. In this study, adult children whose own reflective function had benefited from their parents' reflective function were better off in their self-description and romantic relations, although they had more internalizing problems and less positive self-perception. Thus, there seems to be a cost, as well as a benefit, to reflective function.

Research on parenting emerging adults suggests that the goals of this developmental period for the young adult themselves are autonomy, competence, and relatedness. Having already addressed the aspect of autonomy that is critical in this period, we turn now to the development of competence, which is closely related to self-efficacy—which is crucial to functioning in social and work environments. Studies have identified helicopter parenting and autonomy supportive parenting as two styles of parenting that may impact these developmental outcomes (Reed et al., 2016).

WORKING ON EPISTEMIC TRUST WITH PARENTS OF YOUNG ADULTS: DIFFERENTIATION OF SELF AND OTHER AND REBALANCING EPISTEMIC TRUST

Separation and individuation are best understood not as forming a single stage but as an ongoing process. For young adults, it occurs with higher stakes—living away from home (and not regularly returning home for holidays), finding jobs with genuine responsibilities, and cultivating important relationships. Young adults follow a path of their own choosing and are often less influenced by parents in everyday life. This allows them to view their parents in a new light—recognizing them as people, with gifts and flaws, and being less inclined to do battle with their adults, as adolescents often do. As Bonovitz (2018) observed, young adults begin to acquire a more nuanced understanding of their parents' and their own psychology as people in the world.

A certain courage, no doubt, is required to break free from the family of origin; it is hard to imagine that this separation can occur without some will and capacity for self-assertion. It is debatable whether and how much aggression toward parents is requisite. Perhaps, aggression becomes more likely when parents refuse to recognize the legitimacy of young adults' aspiration to become adults. Some caution is appropriate, too, in recognizing that the language of breaking free from the family may be a bias of WEIRD culture and, therefore, should not be assumed to be universal.

We believe that invoking the concept of epistemic trust in this context is helpful. During developmental stages leading up to adolescence, relying on the input from parents is crucial for gaining social knowledge that will allow people to thrive in a particular culture. Young adults face the challenge of relying increasingly on others outside of the family system and, as mentioned, developing close relationships with people beyond the family. Knowing whom to trust, how much to trust, and when and why to distrust are issues that necessarily come to the fore. Young adults must be able to draw on their own resources, a combination of being self-reliant and depending on others with whom there is mutual trust. So, parents need to be able to keep their distance but not abandon young adults. It takes time for a young adult to become a full adult; it is not automatic, and, realistically, some amount of failure seems inevitable. If you have learned how to swim—that is, if you have experienced some degree of epistemic trust as a child—crossing the large body of water that is adult social interaction can be envisioned and regarded as not beyond the realm of possibility. If you have never swum, the experience can be terrifying, overwhelming, and dangerous.

Epistemic trust has its source in the early parental relationship and then generalizes to other relationships. Epistemic trust is not an "either/or" category; it can occur to various degrees and also be contextual, depending on different circumstances. What stands out about Linda's epistemic trust is that she was able to rely on others—especially, teachers as mentors—although she experienced it less with her mother. Moreover, Linda did not experience abuse; she was neglected emotionally but not in other ways. It is less that her mother failed to provide opportunities for epistemic trust to develop than that she struggled to have the mental space to prioritize it. Linda was able to benefit from some exposure and had adaptively sought out more from where it was more readily available.

MOVING ALONG THE DEVELOPMENTAL LINE OF MENTALIZATION WITH PARENTS OF YOUNG ADULTS

Attention Regulation

An adult's state of mind with regard to attachment is closely related to attention regulation. The Adult Attachment Interview, described in Part I of this volume, directs the interviewee's attention to their early relational experiences. Secure states of mind are associated with flexible patterns of attention, able to shift back and forth from past to present and to consider painful or negative emotions as well as more positive feelings. Preoccupation is characterized by a lack of attention regulation, where the interviewee becomes absorbed in their memories or in their own state of mind, losing track of the interviewer and the questions that were actually asked. Avoidance, on the other hand, can be thought of as a turning away—a shifting of attention away from the emotions of early relationships (toward idealization or minimization).

When working with parents of adults, observing the extent to which they can engage, focus, and shift their attention to various topics and emotions is highly relevant. Linda's attachment pattern fits the avoidant style in some ways, although what surfaced in her relationship with her daughter seemed more like the preoccupied style. It was as though in her attachment needs being suppressed when she was a child, they returned with a vengeance to her as a parent of a girl. The attention that she lacked from her own mother was repaid in abundance to Tina. Linda and Tina had a symbiotic relationship—which, during adolescence, Tina rebelled against. Linda's struggle to accept this was challenged anew when Tina returned, out of necessity, to live at home. The conflict they experienced occurred for many families, due to the pandemic. There were already too many sources of both internal and external threat for Linda and her daughter: the normative fears around separation and individuation, the fears around being a single, divorced mother, Tina's frustration and fear about her academic and social future—and all organized around a terrifying global experience. In this context, the capacity of both mother and daughter to observe together their interactions and reflect on them in a productive way was inhibited further, leaving both mother and daughter feeling alone and afraid. Because of this, the mentalizing stance of Linda's therapist was central to helping this mother to recover her mentalizing capacities—her capacity of looking at herself from the outside and imagining her daughter from the inside, jointly with someone she trusted and who she felt understood by most of the time. This could be achieved by following a scaffolding process in which both therapist and client observe the interactions from the outside and attempt to understand them from multiple perspectives.

Affect Regulation

Linda had never sought out psychotherapy prior to her divorce. She was passionate about, and successful in, her career as an immigration attorney. She had steered her daughter to be successful academically, only to be contending with the less-than-ideal situation of a young adult's budding autonomy being interrupted by the extrinsic force of the pandemic. Linda had confidence in reading her own mental states. It was not that she was unreceptive to others, but she struggled to be able to interpret their mental states. This happened at work, not just in her relationship with her daughter, especially when she sensed that a client wanted something from her beyond legal advice.

At first, being in therapy meant that Linda would put her divorce behind her and move on to have a happier life. She did not want to trouble herself about her feelings regarding the divorce, although it was evident that divorce was not supposed to have been an option, given her religious upbringing. Consistent with this was that Linda could identify her emotions but was not absorbed in plumbing their depths. For example, in response to the Brief-Mentalized Affectivity Scale (B-MAS) item "I try to put effort into identifying my emotions," she said, "Not really," which is somewhere in between *disagree a little* and *disagree moderately*. In response to the B-MAS item "I try to understand the complexity of my emotions," she said, "Um, not sure," which is closest to *neither agree nor disagree*.

Processing emotions was not a natural activity for Linda. Early in the therapy, she rigidly stuck to prementalizing modes. She and the therapist had multiple interactions in which the therapist asked her for examples of her relationship with her mother. Her responses were bland and uninformative, like the examples in previous sections, in which she says that her mother "held down the fort" or emphasizes that Tina was "just so spoiled." Linda became more engaged in fathoming her relationship with her mother in connection with understanding her relationship with her daughter.

In response to the B-MAS item "When I am filled with a negative emotion, I know how to handle it," Linda hesitated and said that she "disagreed moderately." Indeed, Linda's style of handling emotions was to push aside and minimize negative ones. Her perspective on the divorce was initially stated in factual terms; eventually, she was able to acknowledge her sadness, even if she never wavered on that it was what she wanted. Linda also made some progress in appreciating her own sadness about, and difficulty with, her daughter growing up. She was proud of Tina, but she also missed being needed by her as much as when Tina had been young.

The primary associations that Linda had to expressing emotions were around danger. Through her family and culture, she imbibed a sense that emotions belong in private life and should not see the light of day. The therapist wanted to respect that and, at the same time, to urge her to consider that if emotions dwell in private, it is hard for others to have any idea what you might be feeling. Linda had a latent, underlying sense of being bad, despite her determination to be a virtuous, decent person. This was a legacy of her history and occasionally plagued her, even if it did not fit with her current values.

Explicit Mentalizing

As the therapy continued, Linda reported that conversations she had with Tina had shifted; she even acknowledged to her daughter that she had been threatened by the idea of Tina having a relationship with her father. Tina's response was to be reassuring, which Linda appreciated, as she had been deeply embarrassed by the immature wish to have her daughter for herself. Linda was able to remain in touch with her anger at her ex-husband for the past, while becoming open to having him reconnect with his daughter in the present. Linda burst out with the declaration "I love this damn pandemic!" Tina let her mother know that it made a big difference that she voiced support for the budding relationship between her father and herself, which she regarded as independent of her relationship to her mother.

Linda's mentalized affectivity improved significantly in therapy. She could make connections between her upbringing and her style of parenting. This allowed for adjustments, so she was not simply trying to recreate the past. She made strides in being able to acknowledge how difficult it was for Tina to be living back at home and not blame Tina or construe her struggles as a rejection of her mother. Linda did not resume dating, as the pandemic put up a formidable obstacle. However, the time and effort that Linda put into improving her mentalized affectivity will help her as she moves forward.

INTEGRATING AND BALANCING THE DIMENSIONS
OF MENTALIZING

As described in Chapter 10, parents' mentalization will be effective if they can maintain a balance across the different dimensions of mentalizing:

- Between the automatic and controlled, or implicit and explicit, where "automatic" refers to a nonconscious, unreflective, procedural function, and "controlled" happens when the parent is capable of reflecting on what someone else might think or feel of their own thoughts and feelings. It is important to note that explicit mentalizing can be considered genuine and productive only when the link between cognitions and emotional experience is strong (Bateman & Fonagy, 2016).

- Between the internal world and the external world, where "internal mentalizing" refers to the capacity to focus on one's own or others' internal states—that is, thoughts, feelings, and desires—and "external mentalizing" implies a reliance on external features such as facial expression and behavior (Bateman & Fonagy, 2016).

- Between oneself and others, where an excessive concentration on either the self or the other leads to one-sided relationships and distortions in social interaction, interfering significantly in the quality of the relationship that parents can establish with their young adult daughter or son.

- Between what parents think and what they feel, where an integration of both cognitive and affective processes leads to higher levels of mentalizing and improved social interactions, due to a better balance between cognitive and emotional processing and between rational or intellectual processes and mentalized affectivity.

If we are working with a parental couple, we must keep in mind the importance of also balancing interventions of both parents, as this will also contribute to improve the quality of the couple's parental reflective function.

In the context of working with parents of young adults, the self–other dimension is particularly important, as this is a period in which a great deal of factors potentially facilitate or inhibit this dimension. As the adolescent becomes a young adult, both parent and child contend with a change in their relationship. While the love, care, and concern the parent has always had for their child likely remains, the parent's role—specifically, their responsibility for the child—often shifts as the child becomes a young adult. Parents reactions to their children leaving home vary and often involve mixed emotions. Unlike an infant who needs their parent to mentalize for them because they are not yet able to make sense of and organize their own experiences and do not have the language to express their internal worlds, young adults have developed these capacities. Yet, all social relationships rely on the people involved being able to mentalize themselves and each other. The significant changes and, particularly, losses that mark the transition to young adulthood may make mentalizing especially challenging at these points. When parents can reflect on their own internal experiences as well as their young adult child's internal world and process how each might be impacting the other, they are more likely to be able to maintain a positive and secure relationship with each other. The use of italics is used to help the reader identify the application of a mentalization framework to the technique working with parents.

LINDA: So apparently Tina has a new boyfriend, and she introduced him to David. They got dinner last week when David was in town.

THERAPIST: I'm curious about what you are thinking about that? [*cognitive–affective*]

LINDA: I just don't understand why she would introduce him to David and not to me.

THERAPIST: I see, and I'm also imagining you had some feelings about that, her introducing him to David. And not to you, yet. [*cognitive–affective*]

LINDA: Well yeah, of course. I think any mother would feel hurt by that. It's not like I'm hurt by her not introducing him to me. She's an adult. I don't really need to meet anyone unless it's serious. But if she's introducing him to David . . .

THERAPIST: You said you feel hurt . . . [*cognitive–affective*]

LINDA: Yeah, it's hurtful. She is hurtful!

THERAPIST: Do you think Tina is doing it to hurt you? [*self–other*]

LINDA: I mean, I don't know about that.

THERAPIST: Ah, OK, that's a good point. But when you said, "She is hurtful," I heard that not just as how you're feeling, but also like that was her intention. [*internal–external*]

LINDA: I mean, I don't know why she would introduce someone to David and not to me. It's not like David has ever been around. But she still wants him involved in her life.

THERAPIST: So, there is some sense in your mind that Tina sees you and David in certain ways. And that she wants David in her life, but not you? [*self–other*]

LINDA: Well, I think I just always have been there and, in her life, so she doesn't ever want me.

THERAPIST: That seems tough for you. So, like she's pushing you away. You've always been there, and she doesn't want you? [*self–other*]

LINDA: Yeah, and it's fine. That's what mothers do. Show up and be there for their children, without expecting anything in return. Right?

THERAPIST: Well, I think that's the thing; Tina is your child, but she isn't a child anymore. I think the way you raise the question to me, it's like, there is a question about how to be there for your child who is a young adult? [*automatic–controlled*]

LINDA: Yeah, I don't really know. I guess by not being there, like David.

THERAPIST: I mean, let me ask you this. Do you have any sense of how Tina experiences you being there for her? [*self–other*]

LINDA: I mean, I think she's always appreciated it. But also, I know she really wants me to have my own life.

THERAPIST: In what way?

LINDA: Like, she thinks I should date, like join one of those dating websites or something.

THERAPIST: It's interesting, because you have told me you want that, too, if I've understood you correctly. And now she is going out and dating. How is that for you, to see her dating, as an adult? [*cognitive–affective*]

LINDA: I just can't believe she is really an adult. I mean, I know she is. But it's weird to think that she is at an age where she could meet someone and get married. I mean, I was younger than she is now when I met David, and I was probably around her age when we started dating.

THERAPIST: So not only are you navigating her dating, and her choices about involving you, and thinking about dating yourself. But this maybe also brings up the early days of you and David? [*automatic–controlled*]

LINDA: Yeah, and it makes me sad. I always thought we would be together seeing our baby grow up. Meeting her boyfriends together. Divorce is really sad . . .

The above vignette shows how the therapist closely tracks where Linda is in terms of the dimensions of mentalizing, making interventions that will not only balance but also integrate the two aspects of each dimension. Most obviously, the therapist prompts Linda to consider herself and her daughter. And at no point does the therapist challenge Linda's thoughts or cognitions, for example, but rather inquires about the emotion to help her integrate them. Similarly, the therapist does not explicitly stop to interrupt Linda's automatic reactions but, over the course of this exchange, scaffolds Linda's automatic mentalizing (her assumptions and reactions) to deepen the understanding of her internal and interpersonal experience with her daughter and arrive at more controlled mentalizing.

PREMENTALIZING MODES IN THE CONTEXT OF PARENTING A YOUNG ADULT

As we have conveyed throughout this book, a parent's developmental journey is influenced significantly by that of their child. Just as we await, with high expectations, fears, and hopes, an infant, many parents look forward to the coming of age of their adult children. Young adulthood is a period when, ideally, the process of separation and individuation becomes consolidated. New challenges to a parent's ability to mentalize their experience and that of their child emerge with the advent of their child's still-emerging identity in so many areas. Once again, both sociocultural and individual expectations influence and challenge the parent's capacity to find a balanced way to mentalize this stage of their child's development. Following are examples of situations in which Linda's sociocognitive capacities were challenged and led to prementalizing ways of functioning.

Accepting and integrating the idea that one's child is now an adult is not an easy process. This might be particularly true in managing conflict and disagreement regarding clashing ideas about how to conduct one's adult life.

Letting go and accepting the way in which their child chooses to live their life might bring strong fear of loss and anger for parents. Sometimes the child's developmental agenda clashes with the parent's own needs and wants. It is during these times that prementalizing ways of functioning might appear. Such was the case between Linda and her daughter Tina.

Clinical Example

Some of the three prementalizing modes of functioning—teleological, pretend, and psychic equivalence—will be presented in italics, in order to draw the attention of the reader to their appearance in the here and now of the therapeutic exchange. Learning to identify these modes of functioning guides the level of intervention. In the context of Linda expressing frustration about the conflict between Tina and her, since Tina returned to live at home, the therapist and Linda had the following interaction:

THERAPIST: Sure, I can see that it is a big adjustment to have Tina living at home, after she had been away.

LINDA: It is an unexpected adjustment, because I assumed she would have gone somewhere else and got a job. It's just like her, to expect me to be here to take care of things, and she is already in her 20s! When am I going to get a break?

THERAPIST: It is very difficult to have to readapt to having to live and take care of your daughter, especially at this age, and at this time of your life when you want things to be different.

LINDA: Yeah, but you are not listening, she doesn't care about other people, she is selfish, just like her father! [*psychic equivalence mode*]

THERAPIST: I am sorry, I have the impression that you are feeling misunderstood by me. [*mentalizing stance/use of self*]

LINDA: It's OK, I'm used to it! Especially now with Tina back home, as it's always me being the unreasonable one [laughs] . . . It is just the nature of parenthood, you know, I remember reading an article that spoke about that a while ago and thinking . . . "Why didn't I read this before?" [*pretend mode*]

THERAPIST: No, it's not OK, it is important that you feel supported and understood here . . . and I am getting the feeling that it is

difficult to go beyond the books, and into the feelings that
you are feeling here and now. What do you think?

LINDA: I am tired . . . when am I getting a break? Who takes care
of me?

THERAPIST: I have the impression that you are worried about her . . . and
tired of being worried and doing the right thing. Are you?

LINDA: She does not see that . . . everything she says conveys that I
am a nagging bitch!

THERAPIST: That is so hurtful . . .

LINDA: And infuriating . . . she is just so spoiled . . . she has no
empathy, does not care about my feelings, she hates me!
[*psychic equivalence mode*]

This interaction occurred when Linda was adjusting to Tina's being back at
home. She was stressed by this, and the therapist's attempt to make her aware
of this backfired. Linda's anger blinded her in this situation, with her becoming
critical of her daughter. The therapist was trying to validate Linda's emotionally
painful experience, although probably moving too quickly to using interventions that invited her to mentalize. Instead, the therapist's intervention might
have been more effective in facilitating modulation of Linda's unpleasant
emotional state if the therapist would have focused on interventions in the
attention regulation and affect regulation blocks. We know that we cannot
address prementalizing modes with active mentalizing interventions, as these
will not be received when the patient is in a prementalizing state of mind. Here
is where our proposed model of a scaffolding approach that will move back to
stay at an attention regulation and affect regulation level can be a helpful
technical resource.

For some parents, young adulthood signifies the end of a period of close
intimacy with their children. For others, it might mean a new opportunity to
redefine their relationship with them and make up for lost time, as sometimes happens with divorced parents. Whatever the meaning, it often
signifies managing difficult emotions of regret, hope, and fear all at
once, parallel to the excitement and pride many parents feel during this
period. However, there are many reasons why a young adult may be
experiencing what colloquially is known as "failure to launch." Serious
emotional disturbance might stop this process in its tracks, leaving parents
feeling at a loss and filled with great amounts of emotional pain and
helplessness at the sight of a young adult stuck in a pattern of dependency

and despair. The adjustment, when Tina returned home, added a stressor to Linda and Tina establishing a relationship, based on Tina's shift as a young adult.

The therapist and Linda made progress when the therapist asked Linda to recall what her relationship with her daughter was like when Tina first went off to college. Linda reported feeling needed by her, as Tina texted her frequently, throughout the day, for advice. Linda was delighted to offer it on any subject, drawing from her own history. At the time, she was disappointed if Tina did not turn to her, which she realized now but speculated that she was not aware of back then. Linda relished the role of the wise confidant. She struggled to accept Tina's eventual pulling away to be grounded in her own experience. Linda spontaneously remembered that she felt threatened when Tina told her about joining an Ultimate Frisbee team, as she had never shown interest in sports and had not told her mother anything about this. Although Linda lacked the ability to recognize this when it happened, it was evident to her that given the symbiotic quality of their relationship, she might have appreciated this as a positive sign of growth in Tina.

One of the most challenging realities of being a parent all throughout the lifespan is seeing one's child suffer and not being able to dissipate or reduce this suffering. The desire to "do something" is often strong even when we know that it is not necessarily conducive to growth and a sense of agency for the young adult child. Issues having to do with monetary support are often spoken about by parents of young adults when asking for therapeutic help. Linda wanted Tina to be more active in seeking employment, but she also was pushing Tina to extend her social life, given the artificial circumstance of Tina moving back home. Linda worried that Tina seemed to have withdrawn from the social world she had at college. Linda's anxiety about this led her to introduce ideas for how Tina might try to socialize, such as having regularly scheduled group meetings. Tina did not act on this and, in fact, seemed to isolate herself more rather than less. At one point, Linda recommended that Tina contact one friend she knew was an extravert and liked to organize events. Initially, the therapist's effort to encourage Linda to talk about how she was feeling seemed to fall on deaf ears. However, Linda was able to come to see that her intervention failed because it was driven more by her own anxiety than by her daughter's need. Linda could sit with the legitimacy of Tina's reaction—that Tina was sad and not too motivated and that listening to Tina, rather than pushing her, was helpful during this difficult time. As an experiment, Linda backed off, and, at an admittedly slow pace, Tina did show signs of being interested in her social life.

INDIRECT WORK WITH PARENTS VIA THE YOUNG ADULT

We just outlined a way of working with parents of young adults. Parents talking about their children in their own therapy is a subject that deserves greater attention than it has heretofore received. In general, as Benbassat and Shulman (2016) reminded us, there is a paucity of research about parenting beyond childhood.

Unlike therapy with children or even adolescents, once patients are considered adults, therapists will not work directly with their parents at all. Therefore, it is necessary for us to address, in this chapter, indirect work with parents of young adult patients. What we mean by "indirect work" is even though we do not work with the parents themselves, the parents are very much part of the young adults' lives and are "in the room," so to speak. We include indirect work with parents in this chapter on young adulthood, but, really, indirect work with parents is part of therapy with adults of any age, whether looking at the origins of core beliefs in cognitive behavioral therapies or the impact of early life experiences in psychodynamic treatments.

We do this with a second case—a young man, in therapy, named Zeke. With this case example, we look at parenting through the lens of the young adult. Although we are not privy to the parents' perspective here, we will be exploring the evolution of a young man who uses therapy to come to terms with how he was parented and who is on the way to becoming a parent himself.

CASE AND CLINICAL FORMULATION: ZEKE

Zeke was a 24-year-old cisgender, biracial, heterosexual young man who sought out therapy for the first time when he found himself partying too much and not feeling that he was making progress in his life plans. He had graduated from college and was living with three roommates in a newly gentrifying part of Brooklyn. Zeke worked for a small bank that demanded long hours, leaving him with little energy for other activities—such as going to the gym, which he enjoyed doing. He had been at the same job for over 2 years and had been promoted once, but he had recently been struggling to sustain the motivation to work so hard. A significant piece of personal history was that during his sophomore year of college, Zeke had an accident, breaking his leg in several places and necessitating a medical leave, at which point he returned home to live and to receive treatment. Growing up, Zeke had asthma—which limited his participation in athletics—and was often ill. The therapist noticed that he became animated when talking about this history, and at least part of it seemed to have to do with the relief of not going to school and with receiving extra attention at home.

Zeke was not the easiest patient to engage. He expected to get things done quickly and efficiently, which often interfered with the therapist's effort to get him to think about things as he presented with strong teleological needs. Here is a brief example from early in the work, in which we can observe his difficulties in establishing attention regulation with the therapist.

THERAPIST: You said that by the end of the week, you were exhausted and feeling too tired to meet up with friends.

ZEKE: Yeah, I know . . . I went out anyway. I said to myself that I would go home early. At 11ish, I thought about leaving the bar, but didn't end up going.

THERAPIST: Can we take a closer look at what happened at that moment?

ZEKE: There really is nothing more to say . . .

THERAPIST: Hmmm . . . not sure I am convinced about that.

ZEKE: I am not hiding anything, and the same thing pretty much happens every weekend.

This pattern was common, as the therapist had many interactions in which Zeke seemed to be on the verge of revealing himself and then backed away. In terms of his family, Zeke was the middle child and had an older sister, with whom he was close, and a younger brother. His father was an attorney who made a good living for the family; he himself came from a working-class Italian family, receiving a scholarship to play lacrosse in college. Growing up, Zeke's father had a large extended family that over time he distanced himself from, and Zeke's family had little contact with them. Zeke's mother was a Caribbean American of African descent who also grew up in a large extended family. Zeke's mother trained to be a teacher but stopped working in order to care for her children. Zeke's parents met at a concert and started dating. Both of them enjoyed smoking marijuana and continued to smoke nightly at home throughout Zeke's childhood. Both of his parents' families expressed skepticism about having a relationship with a person who was racially different. Zeke was the most successful of his siblings, academically. His older sister had been involved in his caretaking, and Zeke felt close to her. His younger brother was "a computer nerd," and Zeke never felt much of a connection with him.

Growing up, Zeke felt that his father was disappointed in Zeke not being an athlete and that he could be harsh, less in overt expression than what Zeke inferred from his countenance. In general, Zeke said that his mother was naturally empathic and could easily tell what he was feeling. Exceptions occurred when she had lapses in caregiving—such as in one memory in which Zeke came home from school and had to wait several hours outside of the house, alone and cold, before his mother returned with his brother. Later, Zeke realized that his mother was intoxicated—not a regular occurrence but an occasional one that happened, he estimated, several times a year.

The confluence of substance use in the family and in Zeke's fast-paced professional life in finance led to him feeling that his life was spinning out of control—but it also led him to seek out therapy. About 3 months into therapy, Zeke started to embrace it in a blustery, if positive, spirit: celebrating accountability, challenging himself, and voicing his wish for the therapist not to hesitate to push him ahead. The therapist's response of wanting to continue to get to know him and not being sure how they might best be helpful remained baffling to him. Zeke presented with a studied sense of self, which, to some extent, seemed to benefit him at work but did not benefit him in his personal life. So, the therapist's initial stance was based on perceiving Zeke's reliance on the pretend mode of functioning. However, his enthusiasm in seeking help gave the therapist hope that they would be able to make progress.

Prior to starting therapy, Zeke had tried to use an app to record, monitor, and alter his consumption of alcohol. This helped to some extent, but it also caused his drug use to bulge in new, unexpected ways. Both therapist and patient tried to address this as a priority, and it helped to establish the alliance—where Zeke could see the therapist as an expert who would reduce harmful substance use. The therapist saw this as a collaborative process; Zeke was inclined to understand his therapist as instructing him what to do. This dynamic created a bit of tension, but it also lent some useful insight into his relationship with his father—who could be domineering, although he also expressed love and affection to his son. Zeke felt secure in his love from his mother. He experienced her as being low-key and with a good sense of humor but occasionally remote and unresponsive to his needs.

Although epistemic trust was built during the initial phase where Zeke's substance abuse was moderated, he was reluctant to see any link between his parents' casual, but persistent, substance use and his own struggles. Zeke was more comfortable acknowledging his stress from work and the obligatory quality of after-work binges with his colleagues as contributing to his escalating substance use. The therapist agreed with this and also tried to convey the point that his family history was a factor, to which Zeke was not so responsive; he was more comfortable acknowledging his capitulation to peer pressure in using substances. He did change, though, in becoming open to looking closely at his mental states that he at times felt overwhelmed by.

Zeke was able to utilize epistemic trust, with a slight tendency to be overly self-reliant. This propelled him to have success as a student and, initially, at work. However, he was better at going off by himself and getting things done than he was forging relationships. He had begun to be aware that other, less talented young people had success at work by tying their coattails to their bosses, something he was averse to doing.

As Zeke's substance abuse shifted to more occasional substance use, he experienced more dissatisfaction at work. He struggled to have the motivation to work the long hours and short weekends. He began to entertain leaving his job. He wanted to choose a lifestyle in which he would not just work and sleep, interspersed with consumption. Once again, the therapist could tell that Zeke had the wish that they would supply the answer for him, and he expressed frustration at the therapist's hesitation to do so. He thought about business school but was reluctant to commit himself in this direction. He considered an alternative such as teaching but ultimately decided that he did not think he would be content to live under the modest conditions such a lifestyle change would entail. He seemed concerned about himself: What did it mean that in giving himself the freedom to choose anything, he stalled and could not figure out a path for himself? His therapist encouraged him to give himself the liberty to try out a direction, without the pressure that he would be committing himself fully in that direction.

As Zeke became more comfortable identifying his state of mind as being uncertain, the therapeutic process began to widen the scope, focusing on how to think about moving ahead. The therapist asked him to talk about things he had loved to do as a kid. He had liked to paint. He had enjoyed sports, despite his asthma, but eventually had given them up, as he had felt a bit too pressured by his dad. Zeke had played the piano and violin as a child; he had always wanted to learn to play the guitar, and so he decided to sign up and take lessons.

Another activity that Zeke recalled from his younger days was writing, and he had even imagined a career in journalism for himself. He had written a few articles for his college newspaper but then had become swept along by the challenge of a career in the world of finance. He began to read widely—partly as an effort to explore new career directions and partly as an end in itself. Zeke became fascinated with the work of Malcolm Gladwell, whose books he had encountered as an undergraduate and whose style of evocative storytelling that was based in interpretation of research findings seemed to hold a special prominence for him. He read everything Gladwell wrote. He was especially taken by *David and Goliath: Underdogs, Misfits, and the Art of Battling Giants* (2013) and *Talking to Strangers: What We Should Know About the People We Don't Know* (2019)—the former resonated because of its sensitivity to underdogs, and the latter resonated because of Zeke's awareness of not being able to communicate to others well. His therapist was struck by the relevance of Zeke's relationship to his father and his mentalizing issues.

Zeke realized, too, that he shared an aspect of identity with Gladwell, as the son of a Jamaican mother of African descent and a White father. Zeke decided to give journalism a try and began to write and submit articles for publication. He quickly had some success writing reviews of music performances he attended. However, he also resolved to write about the business world, which was more difficult but potentially more rewarding in terms of a career direction. The therapeutic process was geared toward helping Zeke to curtail the direction of his life and to reorient himself in an admittedly more precarious but fulfilling path. Working from a mentalization-informed framework, Zeke also came to terms with his inhibition about dating. As a party animal, he had ample experience with casual sex, but he was chagrined about his lack of experience in dating and/or relationships. As part of the therapeutic work, he also explored his complex emotions about his biracial identity, which emotions he had tended to underestimate. Although Zeke's skin color was light enough for him to be able to assimilate as a White person, he recalled some painful moments, during his childhood, when race came up as a topic among his friends—and when, on one particular occasion, a friend expressed shock and anxiety in realizing that Zeke's mother was not White. Zeke's growing awareness about race also became an issue between him and his therapist, as Zeke wondered whether a White therapist could really understand his experience. A mentalizing stance was extremely helpful here, restraining the therapist from trying to prove or convince Zeke of their ability to fathom this aspect of his identity.

ZEKE: I realize that in my family, and in school, and in our culture, I was encouraged to identify as White.

THERAPIST: So, others wanted you to think about yourself in a certain way.

ZEKE: "A certain" . . . spoken like a White guy.

THERAPIST: Yes, you are going to have to tell me about your experience, as I do not know what it was like. If I sound clumsy, I hope that will not prevent you from telling me about your experience.

ZEKE: Fair enough . . . I fit in, but there was always a part of me that maybe did not. I just pushed this aside.

THERAPIST: I am glad that you feel ready to think more about your identity, on your own terms, not those of others.

Zeke's choice to explore his biracial identity was a positive development, as it also included his perception of his and his therapist's differences, which he could explore in the context of a new and safe relationship. His dawning recognition of how it was easier—but also disingenuous—to pass as a "White guy" was appropriate as part of his struggle with relationships in emerging as a young adult.

Zeke and the therapist worked together off and on for 5 years. During that time, he underwent a job change, pursuing a new career trajectory. He met a woman, also an aspiring journalist, and they had been together for over 2 years at the time therapy ended. It is, of course, always tempting to define successful treatment in terms of such changes and accomplishments. However, it is even more accurate to define how Zeke changed in terms of his understanding of himself; his relation to his own emotions; and his relationships with his parents, his girlfriend, and others in his life. He surprised his therapist, for example, by voicing an openness to not only deepen his relationship with his girlfriend but also contemplate having a family. Quite literally, he moved from saying that he was not sure whether he wanted to have children to imagining, with some degree of pleasure, having children. He shyly acknowledged having had a conversation with his girlfriend about their shared hopes together.

One could say that a mentalizing-informed approach helped Zeke to tolerate, integrate, and reorganize around the emerging differences between himself and his parents and feel as more of an agent of his life, his choices, and—most important, perhaps—his emotional life in the context of relationships. He was not ready to start a family, but he could envision this as part of his future.

MENTALIZING THE PROCESS OF SEPARATION AND INDIVIDUATION

When Zeke began therapy, he resisted any link between his own substance use and his family's casual, but persistent, use. Toward the conclusion of his work with the therapist, the two had the following interaction:

THERAPIST: Have you discussed with your parents that you do not use substances excessively?

ZEKE: Nah, why would I do that . . . Um, no, I haven't, not sure why . . . maybe it has to do with that I know they might be sensitive and feel that I am accusing them.

THERAPIST: But at some points, they did express concern about you on this matter, right?

ZEKE: There's something else going on here.

THERAPIST: OK.

ZEKE: It has something to do with my relationship to my father . . . I am not sure that I believe that what he wants for me is based on what I want for myself.

THERAPIST: I wonder about that . . . you are getting to that stage of life where it is important for you to determine what's best for you. Is that fair?

ZEKE: Yup, I mean, I don't even know how my dad would react, really.

THERAPIST: That seems like a great insight.

In this short vignette, Zeke demonstrates his awareness of being fearful of hurting his parents by reducing his dependence on substances and his additional worry that his father would just see things from his own perspective, not Zeke's. At the same time, he is venturing to develop his own perspective and to have confidence about this. He is actively mentalizing his emotions here—his and those of his father. Most importantly, a focus on perspective taking allows for the emergence of more awareness of the emotional impact of one's thoughts and feelings and the actions they informed on the other and vice versa.

WORKING WITH YOUNG ADULTS TO MENTALIZE THE PARENT-CHILD RELATIONSHIP

Regardless of whether parents are directly involved in therapy, helping young adults to better understand and to mentalize about their relationship to their parents is a critical part of the work. It has long been a part of the psychoanalytic literature to appreciate that the challenge of young adulthood requires distancing oneself from one's parents in order to facilitate the process of differentiating the self. Related to this is the importance of paying close attention to the vicissitudes of how this plays out in the therapeutic relationship, as idealization of the therapist (as other than the parents) can serve positive and negative functions. As Miller (2017) discussed, the therapist often serves as a new relationship, providing an alternative to the relationship to patients' parents. Idealization can serve to foster the process of differentiation, or it can be primarily a negation of the parental relationship. Von Below's (2017) dissertation study of failed therapy experiences with young adults—a valuable topic, given how often young adults drop out—found that metacommunication was a key to ensuring better outcomes. She proposed that successfully monitoring young adults' mentalizing can prevent failed cases, a point that syncs well with the perspective. The MIT Young Adult Development Project, a valuable overall resource for information, stresses the point that the quality of thinking changes along with changes to the brain during young adulthood.

Von Below's (2017) unpublished dissertation uses grounded theory in interpreting three studies of young adult patients who were unsatisfied with their therapy. The first study, of seven patients at termination and at 18 months after treatment, found that patients felt abandoned by their therapists (although the therapists did not concur). The second study, of 20 patients at termination and at 36 months after treatment, found that patients felt they had been "spinning their wheels" in therapy and that there had been too much focus on the past. The third study, of 17 depressed patients at termination and at 18 months after treatment, found fear of change as a factor and also lack of activity on the part of the therapist. Von Below speculated that ongoing assessment of patients' and therapists' own mentalizing is crucial to avoid negative outcomes.

Young adults are anxious to be treated as adults; at the same time, adulthood can seem like a daunting status for them to pursue. Clinicians—not just parents—must be sensitive to the wish that young adults must be respected. This means that questions about their development can be misconstrued as undermining their current identity. It is important, therefore, for the clinician to make sure that the young adult patient understands that it is in order to help them in the present that the clinician is curious to hear about their history. If the young adult patient does not feel that the clinician is helping them in the here and now, there will be an elevated risk that they will leave treatment. A crucial role for therapists is to keep track of and mentalize patients' response to therapy.

The challenge of young adults is to rebalance epistemic trust and to embrace epistemic vigilance. However, the more that epistemic trust fluctuates or has been only partly established (or when the ongoing exposure to relational trauma reinforces epistemic mistrust), the more that the work of therapy will have to aim to restore it as a priority. Let us return to the case of Zeke, not only to illustrate some of the issues that we have introduced but also to address more specifically how therapy served to help him to contend with young adulthood while keeping his parents symbolically present in the room.

Zeke came to therapy because of a mounting crisis, where his use of various substances had increased, and he was struggling to find meaning in the career path he had chosen. He was inclined to judge himself harshly for not feeling satisfied with his choice to become a banker. The therapist encouraged him to view this situation in terms of being a struggle that might well be positive, both as a process and as a result. The therapist also encouraged Zeke to reflect on his overwrought self-criticism. He immediately associated this with his father, although he stressed that his father was as demanding to himself. Zeke was not receptive to the therapist's effort to get him to think about the relation between his parents' substance use and his own.

It was evident that Zeke embraced the challenges of young adulthood through therapy, as he became more interested in understanding his parents as people. He was able to identify the pressures his father was under in an immigrant family of origin, and Zeke even started to talk to his father about planning to slow down and enjoy himself more. In creating the grounds for a new adult relationship, the David–Goliath paradigm haunted him to a much lesser degree. Zeke's relationship with his mother was also affected, as they had conversations in which she acknowledged her own weaknesses as a parent (and surprised him by telling him that she had wanted to be a journalist, a fact that he had not known). Indeed, the therapeutic work deepened, as he became more curious about how his past history continued to impact his life in the present. His career change was influenced by his growing epistemic trust in his relationship to his therapist—but also by his adoption of Malcolm Gladwell as a new identification model.

As Zeke was impressed that Gladwell had struggled as a student and had taken time to evolve to forge the groundbreaking style of presenting and interpreting research for a popular audience. Zeke's epistemic trust increased, and he embarked on his first real intimate relationship; significantly, so did his epistemic vigilance, as he began to distance himself from friends who consumed drugs and alcohol immoderately. Epistemic trust, defined strictly in terms of the parental relationship, is mediated in young adulthood by other kinds of relationships—those with mentors, friends, and romantic partners.

MENTALIZED AFFECTIVITY: ASSESSMENT AND TREATMENT

In order to have a more detailed picture of Zeke's therapy, we need to focus on his relation to his emotions, as they are explored through the assessment of mentalized affectivity. Mentalized affectivity is about making better use of emotions, which is facilitated in young adulthood by the more sophisticated capacity of cognition. There are three components of mentalized affectivity: identifying emotions, processing emotions, and expressing emotions. Questions from the Mentalized Affectivity Scale were used at the beginning of the therapy, and the therapist compared Zeke's responses then to things he said later in the treatment, which were telling in terms of the progress he made.

Zeke was able to identify a fairly wide range of emotions, and he was comfortable expressing his emotions, as his parents were. He was not adept at processing emotions, but this is not surprising. Few young adults do this well, as they are just entering the realm in which processing emotions begins to matter and supports their emergence into adulthood. Moreover, insofar as young adults do not have much history to draw from and are just starting to reflect on family narratives about themselves and others, processing emotions can be arduous and a source of resistance if the therapist pushes the patient too hard.

Although Zeke was able to identify emotions, he was uncomfortable being able to tolerate not knowing what he was feeling—what we have termed "aporetic emotions." In remembering an incident from childhood, a Little League baseball game when he was 6 or 7 years old, in which his asthma acted up but he was fearful of communicating that to his father, Zeke had the following interaction with the therapist:

THERAPIST: Can you tell me a little more about what you remember from that experience?

ZEKE: I told you, I didn't really know what was going on . . . I was starting to panic—no, that's not it exactly . . . I was, um, like "I don't know what to do . . . if I tell my dad, he probably will be pissed" . . . so I tried to ignore it.

THERAPIST: It must have been uncomfortable to feel distress of some kind but not to feel that you could expect your parent to help. Can you describe the symptoms that you were having?

ZEKE: I told you, just confused, a bit dazed, upset . . . that's it . . . it was awful, and it seemed to last a long time, as I recall.

THERAPIST: OK, I see—by the way, what ended up happening?

ZEKE: The coach noticed something was wrong . . . he walked around with me . . . my dad did not ask about it and I never discussed what happened with him.

Zeke's discomfort with aporetic emotions had implications for how he identified emotions. He exhibited a wide range of basic emotions but did not readily acknowledge mixed, complex ones and was reluctant to link past and present experiences. For example, in the initial inquiry, Zeke responded to the therapist's question, based on the B-MAS item "I often look back at my life history to help inform my current emotional state and situation," by stating that he "moderately disagreed." Three years into therapy, Zeke was talking about how he would handle asthma attacks when they occurred: He always carried his inhaler and told his therapist that he tried to submit to the experience, noting that the feeling of terror, and often embarrassment, would pass. He then contrasted how he handled such attacks compared with the past. He returned to the incident that had occurred while playing Little League baseball, and speculated about how terrified he must have been—afraid that his teammates would ridicule him and feeling pressure to handle things on his own. He even wondered whether he was projecting a lack of empathy onto his father: Although Zeke's father had wanted his son to be an athlete, this was because playing sports had been formative for him—and not because he was an ogre. It is important to appreciate here that Zeke could enumerate his emotions in a granular way and understand how it took time for him to be able to contend with asthma attacks in an optimal way. His insight about his father marked his evolution from being an adolescent to being on his way to becoming an adult.

Research suggests that processing emotions is at the heart of psychotherapy (Greenberg et al., 2017). In its most basic form, processing is akin to regulation, where emotions are modulated upward or downward, depending on the circumstance. In its more advanced form, processing entails a comparison of whether we are living up to our ideals. In order to make such an assessment, someone must have acquired—or at least be invested in seeking—self-knowledge. For young adults, this has to be a tall order. In the beginning of therapy, Zeke was quite aware of falling short of his ideal self, in becoming intoxicated every weekend and frequently even during the week. However, he could be short-tempered in response to the therapist encouraging him to stay with his feelings. For example, his response to the B-MAS item "When I am filled with a negative emotion, I know how to handle it" was to state that he "strongly agreed." Zeke's self-confidence wavered, and he went through a difficult time as he entertained and embarked on the pursuit of a new career. Once again, his capacity to process emotions improved through the influence of

Gladwell's appreciation of the elusiveness of understanding the mind. By the time therapy ended, Zeke was able to engage in processing, more open to the therapist's input, and much more interested in what others thought. It was interesting, for example, that in the exchange about talking to his parents regarding his moderate use of substances, he first assumed how his parents would react but then recognized that he did not actually know. Zeke's path to adulthood is revealed both in his taking on of his own way in life and in his ongoing receptivity to others.

As the middle child of three, Zeke was used to asserting himself and expressing his emotions. He recalled, with pleasure, lively dinner table conversation at home. Zeke's response to the therapist's use of the B-MAS item "If I feel something, I will convey it to others" was to "moderately agree."

Zeke was able to express himself comfortably, especially with male friends. As an adolescent, he experienced some inhibitions with women. He was bothered by this more than he cared to acknowledge; however, it changed as he came to terms with his relationship with his mother. Growing up, she was loving and had a good sense of humor that could rouse him from negative affect states, but she could be absent in unpredictable ways that seemed to be tied to her drug use. Zeke's career change ushered in a time of experimentation, when he put more effort into Internet dating and eventually met a woman who shared his interest in journalism. Zeke started out being more expressive than many young male adults, and he became more articulately expressive over the course of therapy.

LAST THOUGHTS

The case of Zeke documents a young adult who rose to the challenge of moderating his substance use and reliance on peer pressure, reviewed and undertook a new direction with his career, and formed a new relationship that has developed over time. This process was abetted by his facing his parents as people—seeing the impact of substance use on their lives and striving to differentiate himself and relate to them as adults. The case of Linda documents a single parent of a young adult, compounded by the pandemic in which the daughter found herself living back at home. Linda struggled with establishing boundaries with her daughter, according more respect to her as an emerging adult, and stretching to be more accepting of her daughter's wish to reconnect with her father.

Zeke's therapy helped him to differentiate himself from his family—in particular, to own his identity in new ways and to pursue a vocational path of his own choosing. Linda's therapy helped her to differentiate herself in the way that she altered her response to others (her daughter and ex-husband). Linda would like to look for a romantic partner when the pandemic makes that easier to pursue. Meanwhile, she has become motivated to work on building friendships.

In both cases, the therapist's mentalizing spurred the patients to heed and cultivate mentalization. This does not ensure happiness, but it enables patients to feel equipped to cope with life, regardless of what happens to them. Let us conclude with a humble reminder that young adults and their parents are a challenging population to work with and that quick exits from treatment are a common problem. Even when that occurs, the experience can serve to make it easier for young adults to return to treatment at a later point. Mentalizing is the tool that enables therapists to anticipate quick exits, to reckon with them, and to take steps toward the best possible outcome.

CONCLUDING SUMMARY

- Working with young adults can be difficult because they can so easily experience therapists as being parental, so a mentalizing stance is particularly helpful in establishing a different role for the therapist.

- Working with young adults can be highly rewarding, as they embrace the road to adulthood, finding their own way and relying on their unfolding mentalized affectivity.

- It can be challenging to parent a young adult, as it requires giving them space to develop, yet being available when they are in need of support and empathy. This is particularly true when parents are attempting to move forward in their developmental journey, which includes the feeling that they can now start focusing on their own needs and wants, away from those of their children.

- Cultural expectations regarding the process of separation–individuation during this period play a significant role in the attributions parents make of their children's life choices. Therapists working from a mentalizing stance should explore these issues from a place of curiosity and genuine interest during the process of assessment and formulation.

12 COUPLES THERAPY WITH AND FOR PARENTS

A mentalizing approach to child therapy welcomes parents to be part of the process, and it often happens that such work leads parents to reconsider their roles and relationship and sometimes, as a direct consequence, to seek individual or couples therapy for themselves. It is difficult to imagine couples therapy with parents not addressing parenting issues; indeed, even in couples therapy with people who do not have children, future parenting style will come up as an issue or concern.

There is not yet a wealth of literature on mentalization and couples therapy. We expect this to change, though, as couples therapy provides a unique opportunity to witness and encourage mentalization, because therapists are in the position of not only hearing about interactions with others but also witnessing those interactions as they occur (or do not occur). This allows for timely, fruitful interventions. So, let's turn to see how our model can be applied to couples work.

https://doi.org/10.1037/0000341-013
Working With Parents in Therapy: A Mentalization-Based Approach, by N. Malberg, E. Jurist, J. Bate, and M. Dangerfield

CASE AND CLINICAL FORMULATION

Henry and Lan were an Asian American couple in their early 40s who decided to attend couples therapy as a last resort. It seemed as though they were leaning strongly toward a mutually agreed-on divorce, with joint custody of their two daughters, ages 11 and 7. Henry and Lan no longer had sex, and they argued frequently and destructively. However, from the beginning, the therapist noticed that they took turns speaking and that they seemed to function quite well at some moments. At other moments, the therapist could see Lan being turned off by Henry's "mansplaining," as Lan called it, and also observed Lan overlooking Henry's vulnerability and sensitivity in talking about her and their children. The mixture of being dysfunctional and functional at the same time was striking.

Henry grew up in an assimilated Korean American family on the East Coast and was a high-achieving student who had realized his dream of being an emergency room physician. He was 3 years older than his brother. Lan was an only child who grew up in a mixed Chinese Korean family on the West Coast. Her father, who was ethnically Chinese, had emigrated from Taiwan; her mother had emigrated from Korea. Her family was working-class, while Henry's was solidly middle-class. Lan had also been a high-achieving student who had become a dentist, but she had always been ambivalent about this career choice and had reduced her workload to part-time in order to take care of their children. Although they were comfortable financially, money was a divisive issue, as Henry enjoyed and liked to buy expensive things (he had a collection of fancy watches that he was especially proud of), while Lan was more frugal.

Both Henry and Lan recalled their courtship (after meeting at the hospital where they had both interned) as the best time in their relationship, when they had less responsibility and enjoyed activities together, such as going to the gym and having dinner with friends. Their conflicts deepened after the birth of Sarah, their first daughter, and they started to argue about everything from breastfeeding (which Lan struggled to be able to do) to decorating her room (Henry disdained IKEA; Lan thought it was fine for an infant). Both concurred that Sarah was not such an easy kid—extremely sensitive and hard to soothe. Henry was quick to blame Lan, according to her; she acknowledged that she was inexperienced but was trying her hardest (and did not have much support from her family). Lan felt that Henry's predisposition to criticize her was unfair and made her even less confident. Both also concurred that they were both quite anxious—fearful that as Sarah grew up, she would have serious problems and, perhaps, be at risk to harm herself. Both confirmed that they started to grow apart with Lan becoming shut down (a combination of being (a) exhausted and (b) furious at Henry) and Henry stepping up his expectations of what parenting should be like (imagining that he should have the same high standards at work and at home and readily devaluing Lan as a parent).

The birth of their second daughter, Ji-a, briefly seemed to improve their relationship. Ji-a was always an easygoing child, and they were able to make some progress in compromising about their different preferences—for example, Henry had wanted to buy a house, but they agreed to rent a bigger apartment for a year in the same neighborhood and delay a decision about what to do. Nonetheless, conflict erupted between them and escalated rapidly—to where their daughters had to try to intervene and ask them to stop, which was humiliating for them. Things did not get physical, but there were threats, implied aggression, and even greater disappointment in each other.

Henry and Lan's sex life fizzled out with their second child. Henry was especially aggrieved about this. He would bring it up, and although Lan agreed to reserve time for intimacy, it never ended up happening. Neither party had affairs, although Lan's friendship with a male parent at the playground had briefly become a source of jealousy for Henry. In a session, Henry avowed that he remained attracted to Lan; she did not reciprocate and was reluctant to discuss their sex life further. As they both pointed out, it was not part of either of their cultural backgrounds to seek help from a therapist. However, both felt desperate and regarded the choice as consistent with their respect for the health professions. Other couples they knew had been helped by going to therapy.

Over approximately a year and a half, Henry and Lan met with the therapist two to three times a month, depending on their schedules. They accorded respect to the therapist as an authority figure. Thus, they experienced the therapist's original feedback to them as surprising, as he took a mentalizing stance and told them that he thought slowing down the process might be a good idea and adopted a nonknowing perspective regarding whether they should move ahead with the plan for a trial separation. The therapist added his honest impression: "What I had heard so far did not lead me to conclusively feel that you should move in that direction." In fact, in meeting with them separately, the therapist began to understand more about their differences, why they often missed each other in frustrating ways, and why they found it impossible to redirect the relationship to be more satisfactory.

Incorporating mentalization into couples therapy is a work in progress, and there is not yet much supporting research. There is one qualitative study by Target et al. (2017) that focuses on an intervention with high-conflict couples in the postseparation or early divorce stage. The intervention has roots in the psychoanalytic approach developed at the Tavistock clinic, emphasizing the role of the unconscious in each member of the couple. Its main emphasis is on taking a mentalizing stance, staying in the present, and, most importantly, keeping the child in mind in all parental interactions. Parents are also urged to realize that they will make mistakes and to try to refrain from being too hard on themselves or their partner (Hertzmann et al., 2016).

Prior to the research just mentioned, Nyberg and Hertzmann (2014) devised a weekly workshop aimed at developing a model of using a mentalizing approach to couples therapy, based on 20 hour-long sessions for couples with high conflict (with one or both having a personality disorder). The model seeks, first, to provide a safe environment and, second, to identify a problem formulation that centers, in particular, on the characteristic affect that is shared by the couple. Once the problem formulation is identified, the therapist writes a letter to the couple, detailing it and then discussing whether it fits the couple's own understanding. Establishing a collaborative agreement provides a foundation for the work, and it can be revised as the work unfolds. In Nyberg and Hertzmann (2018), this model was updated and clarified in relation to older psychoanalytic models, stressing the more active role for the therapist.

Asen and Fonagy's (2021) recent book, *Mentalization-Based Treatment With Families,* addresses family therapy rather than couples therapy per se, but it is still relevant and provides copious wisdom that has informed our model and approach. Mentalization-informed systemic therapy (MIST) has developed strategies, for working with families and groups, that offer specific points about how to maintain and restore a mentalizing stance in the face of high arousal. Indeed, Asen and Fonagy stated definitively that effective mentalizing is incompatible with high levels of arousal, and they provided rich descriptions of the prementalizing modes that occur when mentalization is displaced. They showed us how to teach families to mentalize, without being too didactic. They encouraged a balance in mentalizing self and other, internal and external, cognition and affect, and implicit and explicit. They recommended staying with current thoughts and feelings, rather than fishing expeditions into the past. A most helpful point is their focus on "mentalizing the moment"—that is, drawing attention to times when the parties benefit from engaging in mentalizing. Ultimately, Asen and Fonagy wished to stress that the aim of systems work is not mentalizing in and of itself. Instead, mentalizing is the means to improve the capacity for trust in social communication.

Here is Asen and Fonagy's (2021) useful list of signs of effective mentalizing with families:

- openness to discovery

- empathic stance

- not-knowing position

- humility

- perspective taking

- playfulness and self-deprecating humor

- turn taking

- focus on mental states and ability to distinguish between thoughts and feelings

- reflective contemplation

- inner conflict awareness

- managing affect and arousal

- impact awareness

- capacity to trust

- capacity for collaboration

- belief in changeability

- assuming responsibility and accepting accountability for words and actions

- forgiveness

- autobiographical narrative continuity/developmental perspective

This wide-ranging and comprehensive list can be utilized in thinking about how we would like to help couples, and we will demonstrate how Henry and Lan moved in this direction (Asen and Fonagy also provided a list of what ineffective mentalizing looks like). Our framework and approach is consistent with MIST; however, our inquiry aims for detailed attention about emotions: not only distinguishing thoughts and feelings, managing affect and arousal, and balancing cognition and affect but also striving to help patients to be able to integrate cognition and affect—what we have termed *mentalized affectivity.*

We would also like to acknowledge the contributions of others that have influenced our approach to couples therapy and that will be evident in the work with Henry and Lan—such as Fraenkel's (2019) work on "last chance couples," where he discusses encouraging couples to develop new practices that experiment with pleasure, often beginning with humor; Gottman and Gottman's (2015) well-known work—in particular, the recommendation of strengthening couples' friendship and intimacy; Fishbane's (2013) work that urges couples to adopt a more generous benefit-of-the-doubt perspective toward each other; and Lebow and Rekart's (2007) work on keeping high-conflict divorced couples from getting stuck in past grievances.

CORE ISSUES AND DEVELOPMENTAL ASPECTS OF COUPLES WORK

The core issues in Henry and Lan's relationship centered on the alienation that unfolded after the birth of their first child and that continued thereafter, deepening to the point where they were contemplating the end of their marriage. Both members of the couple were highly intelligent, sophisticated people, and it was not clear to the therapist why they were stuck—all the more so because they seemed to be quite competent in negotiating some practical things well, such as schedules and kids' activities. Meeting with them separately helped the therapist understand the situation better, and so we turn to describe what the therapist learned about them.

Henry was someone whose life was defined in terms of striving for and achieving goals. He brought that intense spirit to parenting, which did not work as well as it did in his professional life. Lan felt under pressure and on the defensive, especially in the face of dealing with Sarah, their first child, who was difficult to comfort and continued to have adjustment problems. Henry's family had emigrated from Korea before he was born, and he was designated in the family as the one who would become a medical doctor and make them proud. Fortunately, this synced well with Henry's ambitions. Henry sped through school and was well-enough liked but did not make much time for socializing. He suggested that he hit every developmental milestone early and reported feeling periodic stress and anxiety as a student but not having any other symptoms. Henry had one younger brother who had become an attorney. Their parents pushed their children to be successful and had retired and moved to the South, where life was less expensive but where there was not the sense of community that they were accustomed to.

Henry reported disappointment that Lan did not share the same driving ambitions. At the end of the night, she preferred to watch mindless shows, exhausted after a full day of child care, whereas Henry liked to watch serious documentaries or even instructional videos on the latest ideas about parenting. While Henry was good-willed and affable, he did not seem to be too aware of the response that others had to him. This did not seem to be a problem at work—although in an ER, interactions are often limited and not deeply conversational. At home, Lan felt that she was invisible and a receptacle for Henry's ideas, unmediated by her reactions or preferences. He did not understand why Lan got fed up with listening to his overflowing ideas and plans, which, according to her account, often occurred at inopportune moments when she was immersed in the labor of everyday life.

As a father, Henry was present, although he worked long hours and was often away from home. He felt proud that it was his idea for Sarah to take dance classes, which she embraced after first rejecting them and which had helped her to become calmer and make new friends. His relationship to his younger daughter had been fraught as she had grown up, with her resisting his efforts to encourage her to be passionate in her pursuits. While Henry could be engaged and expressive as a dad, he had a harder time being relaxed and playful with his children. There would be repetitive fights with Lan when he came home and found the girls hanging around or wasting time on their iPads. Henry did not approach psychotherapy with a willingness to change and was inclined to try to convince the therapist that if Lan was more like he was, they would not have found themselves in this morass. Henry's perspective was one-sided, but he possessed the quality of earnestly saying what he thought, which the therapist appreciated and hoped would help them with the work.

Lan presented herself as motivated by common sense and pragmatism, but she also brightened considerably when talking about their daughters. In response to questions, she could easily become tense. Her childhood was rougher than had originally been disclosed: Her father's family had several upheavals, and he experienced bouts of untreated depression and psychosis, including one suicide attempt. Because Lan's mother had to work long hours to support the family, Lan was exposed, from an early age, to his unpredictable and frightening mental states. The more the therapist got to know Lan, the more it seemed that there were ghosts in the nursery and that she had experienced trauma as a child. The emphasis on education in her family of origin allowed her to develop and focus on a direction outside of the family, and she thrived in school; however, her internal identity was fragile and shut down. There was a gap between her intellectual and emotional development.

Lan had lived at home while attending a public university. She lived with roommates during medical school, at the same university, and then moved across the country for her internship. She did not recall having developed a wish to go far away, but her choice reflected this, as she did have options to stay closer to home. She had very little previous romantic history before Henry, having dated only a few men and without developing a relationship. Lan did not have close friends, which was in keeping with her family, who were suspicious of others (and sought to keep her father's problems under cover). It took time for Lan's issues to emerge, and she was reluctant to engage in a process in which they would see the light of day. Still, Lan was a determined person who understood that ending the marriage would not result in life becoming easier or calmer.

So, while Henry seemed to be the one setting the fires in their relationship, the therapist came to see that the couple had a dynamic that was also influenced by a kind of unresponsiveness in Lan that interfered with building connection. Henry believed that Lan's refusal to change doomed the relationship; Lan retreated from what she saw as his craziness, blaming him for their problems. Each of them tended to hold the belief that the problems in the marriage stemmed from the other party. Without being able to mentalize themselves or the other person, it was questionable whether the relationship would survive. Neither of them wanted the suffering to continue, and both expressed love for their children and were duly concerned about their children's welfare.

EPISTEMIC TRUST

Considering epistemic trust in couples therapy depends on the respective histories of the individuals. Couples tend to seek out couples therapy in the context of a crisis in epistemic trust—often when there has been a violation of such trust. Although there was no such acting out in the relationship between Henry and Lan, there were breakdowns of cooperation and collaboration that were harming the family. It was clear that in order for the relationship to survive, epistemic trust would need to be restored.

Henry was groomed to be self-confident and to work hard to have a successful career. According to his testimony, his family of origin was devoted to facilitating his development. Epistemic trust was valued, perhaps regarded more along the lines of being a means to an end rather than an end in itself. In recounting his history, Henry explained that he had sought out mentors whom he could hold in high esteem. This manifested itself in his relationship with his daughter, as his story about encouraging Sarah to take dance lessons included that he was taken by the mastery of her teacher, who had had a successful professional career. Henry had idealized his wife when they met, too, but, over time, developed more contempt for her, as the therapist witnessed in their interactions.

Self-esteem was a big issue for Henry, and he could be sensitive in the face of small injuries. Henry was aware of having dominated his younger brother, growing up, which his brother brought to Henry's attention as adults. When his self-esteem was impinged on, Henry could become strongly aroused, thus jettisoning his mentalizing ability. The prementalizing mode of psychic equivalence was evident in Henry's insistence that his wife's preferences ought to be the same as his own and in his rigidity in demanding for things to be on his terms. It was also revealing to keep in mind that Henry's wish for himself to become a doctor happened to coincide with his family of origin's wish for him. Henry also had moments of using the prementalizing mode of teleology, becoming preoccupied with things and unable to engage in perspective taking—which, at other times, he was able to do.

There was something confusing in assessing Lan's epistemic trust, as her mother valued it, and so it was a part of their relationship. However, as Lan's father became more dysfunctional, Lan's mother had to pick up the slack, working more and doing everything at home, and thus was often stressed out and exhausted. From Lan's father, she received the opposite of epistemic trust, as his thinking and behavior were unpredictable—and, at times, bizarre, frightening, and flagrantly antisocial. It was not that Lan lacked epistemic trust, but it was fragile and could be lost in the face of aggression, which happened in interactions with Henry. Under stress, Lan used the prementalizing mode of teleology, as she would become consumed with the material necessities of her daughters, losing sight of their feelings and thoughts. Lan's reliance on the prementalizing pretend mode, also, occurred in the way she projected a healthier image of herself, distancing herself from her traumatic history.

Henry and Lan reported an emblematic incident that became the catalyst for the conclusion that they were unsuited for each other and were causing harm to their daughters. Their mutual concern for their daughters was something that the therapist noted to himself as a positive sign. In their first session, they each had a chance to tell the therapist about the incident. Henry went first: He had asked for a day off so that the family could go apple-picking. He had found the perfect orchard, which had eight varieties of apples—including Honeycrisp, his family's favorite. It fell to Lan to plan further details for the day trip. Things did not go well from early on, as Sarah felt a little under the weather, and Lan was distracted with tending to her and packing at the same time. Sarah and Ji-a argued. The family got a late start. Then, when they arrived, it turned out that the orchard no longer had Honeycrisp apples to pick. Henry wanted to leave and see if they could find somewhere else. He laughed as he recounted this and acknowledged that it had been ridiculous. They decided to stay, and the girls even seemed to have a good time—until on the way home, when the fighting began. Lan's version of the story was that the whole day was typical—that they were all being forced to follow doing something in the way that Henry wanted it done, that she had intended to call to confirm that the orchard had Honeycrisp apples but forgot, that no one in the family really enjoyed the day except Henry, and that the fight they had on the way home proved to her that this was the way things would always be.

The fight on the way home began with Henry disdainfully telling Lan that she should have called first to find out what apples they had. Lan replied by saying that it did not matter, if the idea was spending the day together as a family. Lan criticized Henry for insisting that they buy 12 pounds of apples— much more than they would be able to consume. Henry exploded at this and recalled seeing that both of his daughters had become frozen with fear in the back seat. Still, he could not control himself and cited numerous times that Lan had proven to be "incompetent" and "wasted his time." Lan drifted into silence as Henry spoke (later in his work, the therapist established that Lan would enter into dissociated states at such times). In the consulting room, things quickly burst out of control, and both were drawn back into the fight, exchanging hostile, attacking comments and blaming the other person for the failed marriage. The therapist's attempt to intervene did not work; eventually, it was briefly received as a temporary pause, and they immediately resumed the fight, oblivious to the therapist's presence.

The following illustrates the affective tone of the exchange:

THERAPIST: Time-out! Can we please stop for a minute? This is not heading anywhere good . . . both of you are now too upset and angry at the other person . . .

LAN: This is what happens every time we try to talk. He's a bully, and a jerk, and if only his colleagues could see what he was really like.

HENRY: [*looks at the therapist in outrage*] You can see, my wife disrespects me because she can't face the truth, she can't see herself accurately, and she refuses to be open to my attempts to help her.

THERAPIST: OK, we need to pause for a moment. Do you know what I am thinking? I am thinking how disturbing it must be that when you try to talk about a fight, you go right back into the fight.

LAN: This happens every time, as I just said [*looking angrily at Henry*].

THERAPIST: Let's take a moment here: You are both trying to convince me that the problem is with the other person . . . and . . . that's not what I see . . . Rather than seeing one party at fault here, I see a dynamic in which—

HENRY: The dynamic is that my wife is kind of a loser.

THERAPIST: Henry, I realize that I don't know you well, but when you respond by insisting that Lan is to blame, I do not feel that you are open to hearing what I am trying to say. Can we experiment with giving "the other guy" the benefit of the doubt?

HENRY: OK, prove me wrong.

THERAPIST: I can't prove you wrong. All I can do is to urge you to consider that if both of you don't listen—really, if both of you don't try to understand how things look from the other's point of view—the fighting will continue . . . Lan, what's going on with you, now?

LAN: I am [*for a brief second, looks like she is going to cry and then pulls herself together*] done. I am so done. I am pretty sure you must be thinking "These guys are heading right for a divorce."

THERAPIST: Well, I can see why you would say that, but honestly that was not what I was thinking, Lan. I hear the frustration that both of you are feeling, the sense that there is no good path forward. Is that a fair statement of where we are here?

HENRY: Yup.

LAN: I guess so.

In this tense interaction, Henry and Lan reenacted their quarrel, which itself rehearsed an experience that had occurred many times and which seemed inevitable to them. They were not so receptive to the therapist's suggestion that in looking to blame the other person, they were stuck in anger at each other from the past; they were overlooking a dynamic between them, which both had become deeply invested in maintaining. They struggled to be able to tolerate each other, with Henry being dismissive to Lan, and Lan constructing Henry as dangerous and retreating from engagement. Although the therapist recalled feeling powerless at that moment, this did not mean that he believed that the couple was inexorably moving toward divorce. The therapist's ability to mentalize was challenged, but he hung on to the idea that the immediate goal was to lower the temperature and to encourage both parties to mentalize. How could it be possible to make progress in curtailing such hostile interactions, with Henry's escalating affect and Lan's fear and need to shut down.

Epistemic mistrust had arisen and was presiding in Henry and Lan's relationship. The legacy of Henry's special status as the gifted son and Lan's history of being traumatized and being a survivor had come to a head. This had unfortunate implications for their daughters' epistemic trust, which seemed to exist when Lan was alone with her daughters but became strained when the whole family was together. The therapist did not feel optimistic about the fate of the couple, but he held on to the faith both that the couple loved and cared about their daughters and that they had vowed to be guided by protecting their daughters' best interests. It was also clear that although they would readily go headlong into conflicts, there were aspects of their life where they were able to function collaboratively.

EMBRACING MENTALIZED AFFECTIVITY AND STAYING TOGETHER

Henry and Lan came to couples therapy on the brink of ending their marriage. This was a shared affect in which both opted for the worst outcome, out of anxiety that this would happen. Through the course of their work with the therapist, they made the decision to stay together. This happened gradually, as they opened to the process and proved to themselves that they could contain conflicts to be less damaging. Could Henry become more aware of his escalating affect and recognize its effect on Lan, and could Lan find a way to remain engaged in the possibility of communicating with each other? About a year into the work, after the session in which they and the therapist had the following interaction, Henry and Lan returned the next week and announced the decision to remain married and work on their issues—which was clearly a relief to both of them:

LAN: [*after Henry looked over to her to start off the session*] We have been making time in bed at night to talk about our daughters, how they are so different, how things come easily for Ji-a which are difficult for Sarah, and how this is especially difficult for an older sister. As you know, this has been an issue for a long, long time . . .

HENRY: Sarah has always struggled at school. This was not easy for me, um . . . it was not easy for Lan either, to accept or to deal

	with. Sarah does not feel proud of herself—terrible to see really.
LAN:	Yes, but I want to talk about a recent conversation between us, because we both agreed that we end up focusing so much on Sarah that Ji-a gets the short end of the stick.
HENRY:	Yeah, and that has been a cause of conflict between the girls. Sarah's problems take up a lot of attention. I don't know how we can balance things better.
THERAPIST:	That's a really good question, but before we focus on balancing attention to your daughters, I wanted to point out that I was hearing something different between you, not just that you agreed about the situation with your daughters, but that you were able to talk calmly, putting your heads together. This is not something to ignore or take for granted.
LAN:	Well, I did have to ask Henry to stop looking at his phone. But he listened, and I also felt that he listened to me in the conversation.
HENRY:	That's fair—Lan was being sensible, and we both were able to see things pretty much in the same way.
LAN:	[*smiling*] I am just going to overlook the word "sensible" in what Henry just said.

The therapist and the couple laughed together at this moment, which, up to this point, was not a frequent occurrence in sessions. It was evident that Henry and Lan had become less likely to jump down each other's throats and to appreciate that they were able to find their way to a shared perspective. The therapist noted progress in being empathic with each other, in perspective taking, turn taking, collaboration, and openness to change. They were trusting each other and managing moments of mistrust without further damage. There are two things to note here about this couple: (a) They had begun to be able to engage each other without an automatic conflict ensuing; and (b) they underestimated having similar core values and that they had been managing their lives together in some respects, despite the high conflict between them. The problems that brought them to therapy were not resolved—however, when conflict emerged, it no longer happened with a vengeance. What this interaction demonstrated was some movement between them, affirming that they both had a great deal at stake in keeping the family together.

Discussing mentalized affectivity in couples is an area that has not been explored—so our remarks will be tentative, and hopefully there will be research that follows. In conceptualizing mentalized affectivity in couples, it makes sense to begin with the respective mentalized affectivity of each person. Mentalized affectivity exists in individuals; however, there is a sense in which mentalized affectivity is affected by couple, family, and group dynamics. In the case of Henry and Lan, their respective mentalized affectivity was weakened through the dynamic that pervaded their relationship, where his narcissism was heightened, and her sense of victimhood was reinforced. Contemplating divorce was an expression, no doubt, of the frustration of feeling that the relationship was making each of them less healthy as individuals.

Henry was articulate and able to identify emotions well. His relation to emotions seemed strategic, which could be quite effective at work—especially in the intense atmosphere of a hospital emergency room—but did go over so well at home. He was facile at labeling various emotions, and he had access to a wide range of them. Yet, Henry was much better at identifying his own emotions than those of others, and his obtuseness in responding to Lan's emotions was readily apparent. Henry's capacity to process emotions was impacted by his self-focused bias, as it led him to dispense with feedback from others too easily. In his relationship with his daughters, for example, he could motivate them and be encouraging, primarily with activities that he had introduced or was excited about. A consequence was that they ended up seeking out their mother when they were considering trying a new activity or if they were unsure about doing it, as she would help facilitate their thinking, rather than inhibit it. Henry was also able to express emotions. His strategic approach led him to be selective about how he expressed himself, and with Lan, when aroused, he would express himself vehemently, in a way that dominated her but also caused resentment. Henry needed to tone down his expression, diverting its hyperbolic form, if he wanted Lan to be open to hearing him. This was not exactly a matter of exercising cognition over affect, as Henry often had used his cognitive abilities to fuel his strong feelings. It helped Henry to be invested in change, when the therapist told him that he would be heard better if his emotions could be communicated in a form that was attuned to the other's response.

Lan's relation to emotions was tricky to read. As a first impression, she was cordial and appropriate, putting others at ease. Yet, there was much more going on under the surface, and there was something unintegrated between her high social level of functioning and her traumatic family history. Lan could identify emotions, but she had a low tolerance for negative affect. The denial of her father's mental illness scarred her, leaving her vulnerable to dissociated states when under stress. The dynamic with Henry reinforced this tendency, and it sometimes resulted in her feeling paralyzed from her usual level of functioning. During conflicts, Henry's assertiveness could be aggressive; it frightened Lan and invoked her earlier life experience of being in danger because of her father's state of mind. The couple's youngest daughter was attuned to her parents' fighting, when she would closely monitor and protect her mother. Lan's processing of emotions could be tenuous in these circumstances, although she was curious and thoughtful in couples therapy. Lan was able to express herself in small-sized social realms and within the family. Her capacity to express emotions was hindered by Henry, where she would retreat and withdraw from interacting. In one way, Lan fit the bill of "stonewalling," a commonly used term in couples therapy, but the term suggests that the person is making an intentional choice, which was not the case here. Lan found it helpful to remind herself that when she automatically withdrew from conflict, she was capitulating rather than standing up for herself. She announced clearly and forcefully in a session that she wanted her emotions to be heard.

In the previous section, we saw an example that was a turning point in the couples therapy, where Henry and Lan did not feel so pessimistic about staying together. A year and a half into the treatment, we have an example of an interaction of theirs that highlights mentalized affectivity. It is especially notable that the patients take the lead in the session, as they can mentalize without guidance from the therapist. The context is about a visit to Lan's mother, in the Bay Area (her father had developed dementia and resided in a nursing home). In the past, these visits had produced intense conflicts between Henry and Lan, as Henry liked to plan activities, such as hiking and kayaking, that Lan's mother would be excluded from and that would leave Lan feeling conflicted and caught in the middle of different demands.

THERAPIST: So how did the trip go? [*In the prior session, they had talked about the visit and had tried to anticipate how it would go.*]

LAN: Not bad, not bad . . . What do you think, Henry?

HENRY: Yes, I would agree with that.

LAN: But it was not exactly all fun and games . . . but we dealt with it, actually listening to each other, rather than trying to get our way, and that made a difference.

THERAPIST: Can you give me some more details?

LAN: Well . . . Henry was being his most charming self when we
            arrived and when we spent time with my mom . . . but he did
            keep mentioning that he wanted to go to a baseball game, to
            take the girls to see the newish stadium that is inside the city
            of San Francisco. My immediate internal response was
            negative because the traffic would be impossible getting
            there, but I chose not to respond by shooting down the idea.

HENRY: And I was willing to give up the idea . . . I could tell that Lan
            was under stress, dealing with her mom, visiting her dad, not
            to mention that the girls always need their share of the
            attention . . . There are more culturally valuable activities
            than going to a baseball game . . . the girls might have
            enjoyed it, but then again, um, I realize, they might have
            been ready to leave after the second inning.

LAN: I thought, "Wow, he does notice, he does care."

HENRY: I always cared, but now I try to ask myself how you might feel
            and why you might feel that way. By the way, we went out to
            dinner and had the best tacos and burritos that we have ever
            had. It was delicious. Wasn't it amazing?

LAN: Ha—they were good. But Henry, here's a question: Do you
            feel that I do that with you—pay attention to how you are
            feeling and take that into account?

HENRY: You do, I mean, you always have.

THERAPIST: I am guessing that it feels much better to be with a partner
            who is aware of your needs . . . Not only did you skirt conflict
            here, you found your way to a better place.

HENRY: Are you referring to the goat birria tacos? [*All three laugh.*]

It was evident that this couple was in a different place from when they
came to therapy ready to end the marriage. Anticipating possible conflicts
was an idea that the couple and the therapist had discussed together many
times, but the proof is in the pudding—and when they faced a situation
where Henry proposed doing something without Lan's mother, Lan
restrained herself in her response, rather than directly discouraging the
idea. Lan also noticed that Henry was not simply pressing to implement an
idea that he was excited about; indeed, he was even able to recognize that
his daughters might not be fully engaged in seeing a ball game. Henry

demonstrated an awareness of Lan's mental state, which he had had trouble being able to do in the past. Henry had become aware that being thin-skinned and reactive contributed to escalating conflict in the relationship. It is worth observing, too, that the couple was playful together, and a fraught incident turned into an enjoyable dinner together as a family. Henry's joke at the end symbolized a shift in his self-expression and that the couple was under less strain. Although the therapist played a minor role, this was consistent with a mentalizing approach that seeks to promote patients' taking the lead as much as they can do so.

Let us be specific about how we try to help patients integrate cognition with emotions. As we have explicated, we ask questions that determine whether (a) patients identify emotions—and which emotions are predominant, (b) patients modulate emotions when aroused or under stress—and whether they understand how the past influences their experience of emotions in the present, and (c) patients express emotions in a way that is communicative. However, we also pay attention to whether patients are able to tolerate difficult emotions—that is, hold on to states as meaningful, without immediately seeking to discharge them. In addition, we take stock of how patients use cognition in relation to affect—does cognition allow the emotion to live and become illuminated, or does cognition serve to subdue and limit affect? This last point is particularly important, as integration connotes an alternative to exercising cognition over affect; it entails a blending of cognition and emotion, in which the emotions are experienced and (re)valued.

As the therapist, one might find oneself wondering whether the couple's daughters noticed the change in their interaction. Although one may not know the answer to that question, there was confirmation that both daughters seemed to be more involved and thriving in their own lives, a consequence of the crisis resolving at home and their parents sustaining a less tense and explosive home life. As a conclusion of the work, Lan entered individual therapy to help her deal with her history of trauma, and Henry also intended to try individual therapy to continue to work on being more receptive to others and perhaps less demanding of himself (and others). The couple continued to grapple with their differences, but their conflicts were less damaging. They had not resumed a sex life, but they still hoped to do so. They did make progress in being able to laugh together and restore a sense of intimacy between them. They also moved to be able to recognize their differences and to give up the notion that the other person was the cause of their problems. And they became better at sustaining mentalization, and this activated a space for them to negotiate their differences with less rancor compared to when they began couples therapy.

CONCLUDING SUMMARY

- Mentalizing is the means to improve the capacity for trust in social communication. This is highlighted by therapeutic work in the context of couples work.

- Family and couples work offer unique opportunities to witness and intervene with patients' mentalizing.

13 CONCLUDING REMARKS

Bringing It All Together Is Never Easy

When asked about what the most challenging aspect of working with children is, most psychotherapists agree with the answer: the parents! As illustrated in this book and synthesized in this final chapter, there are a few understandable reasons that may explain why psychotherapists answer that way, among which are the following:

- It is complicated to keep both the parents' and the children's agendas in mind in a balanced way.

- Working with parents tends to awaken the therapist's own relational history, emotions, and attachment style.

- Therapists run the risk of overidentifying with the child, which is something that can interfere with their capacity to put themselves in the parents' shoes and mentalize them—often leading to parents feeling judged, blamed, or misunderstood.

https://doi.org/10.1037/0000341-014
Working With Parents in Therapy: A Mentalization-Based Approach, by N. Malberg, E. Jurist, J. Bate, and M. Dangerfield

- Therapists are often targeted and placed in the position to manage challenging parental behaviors stemming from the parents' feelings of despair, pain, shame, rivalry, envy, and rage.

- Teleological demands from parents are often responded to, by systems such as schools, in nonmentalizing ways. This often complicates the therapist's goal, when working with parents, of creating and offering a different way of thinking about their difficulties, as it implies a higher level of emotional commitment and a movement away from fixing the child as the main motivation to seek help.

- Helplessness breeds nonmentalizing, inhibiting a parent's capacity for curiosity and creativity in relationships.

Not uncommonly, therapists in community settings are placed in challenging and chaotic situations, where time with each patient is limited due to high clinical need and low resources—for example, the physical setup involves sharing offices or changing settings every session without much anticipation, and there is a lack of support and supervision for clinicians. They find themselves struggling with intense feelings while dealing with the chaos of a demanding mental health system organized around demands for efficacy and expediency of services. Even clinicians operating within a private realm encounter the stress of parents' and teachers' pressures to provide solutions via concrete strategies while they attempt to create a clinical picture of the family system and the child as separate but interdependent of each other. All of these situations challenge a clinician's capacity to reflect in a mentalizing fashion. Sometimes, therapists need to focus on issues of protection and safety first when working with a family. In the same fashion, a clear framework from which to work provides the clinician safety and protection from feeling overwhelmed.

A developmental framework seeks to create bridges between two parallel processes: the developmental journey of the child and that of the parent(s). Throughout this book, we have provided ample research and clinical evidence of the impact of working from a mentalization-informed framework, one that balances the focus between process and content. This is particularly valuable when working in the context of the diverse contemporary family—and often in the face of high levels of stress, challenging our capacity to maintain a therapeutic mentalizing stance. The proposed framework seeks to provide organizing principles in the context of highly disorganizing experiences and systems.

Mentalization is a developmentally based capacity that emerges in the context of the intersubjective space characterized by explicit genuine curiosity manifested both verbally and nonverbally. Working with parents from a developmental perspective requires an awareness of their relational histories. However, we often find ourselves learning about their history as we become new protagonists with whom to revisit, retell, and rewrite that history. A developmental approach to our work with parents makes no assumptions as to the parents' personality functioning or capacities for attentional or affect regulation. Nor does it make assumptions about the parents' potential or existing capacity to mentalize self or other. Because of this, it is important for the mentalization-informed therapist to explore their own potential triggers in the context of parenting.

As we have learned throughout this book, mentalizing is characterized by the capacity to be humble, empathic, playful, self-observant, trustful, curious, aware of the impact of our behavior on others, capable of taking different perspectives, and tolerating of the not-knowing stance. For obvious reasons, mentalizing is not an easy task—and even less so when confronted by the demanding work of trying to help parents who might be overwhelmed or suffering because of the difficulties they encounter in their parenting roles as well as in different moments of their children's developmental process.

Asen and Fonagy (2021) reminded us of the three primary areas in which it is important to try to develop mentalizing capacities—three areas that all therapists should keep in mind when working with parents, trying to hold a balance between them as much as possible: (a) mentalizing about oneself, (b) mentalizing about the other, and (c) relational mentalizing about the parental relationship and the family system. These three areas can be described separately, but, as Asen and Fonagy described, they are constantly in interaction:

> The extent to which individuals will experience being able to mentalize the self will depend on how they are treated by others, which, in turn, will be crucially dependent on how well they are able to see others' perspectives. The processes that enhance mentalizing in the three primary areas are of course also massively overlapping. (p. 39)

The therapist's main task is to try to improve or develop a parent's mentalizing capacities. The mentalization-informed framework that we introduce in this book offers a structured yet flexible place from which to carry out this complex and challenging task. However, we must remind ourselves of the limitations we all have as therapists—no matter how good our therapeutic models may be. We would want to focus here on the limitations that have to do with the impact experienced by therapists in their daily work—emotional impact that interferes with the therapists' capacity to mentalize, moving them into prementalizing modes that can handicap the therapeutic process as well as contribute to wearing out the therapist, with the risk of getting burnt out.

MENTALIZING THE THERAPIST AND THE VALUE OF SUPERVISION

When learning a new way of working, we tend to focus on the patient. In a similar way, when working in a team, professionals tend to listen to their colleagues' accounts on patients from a problem-solving mode, listening with the idea of what should be understood about the patient, what could be said, or what could be done. When offering training to mental health professionals, we tend to ask the following question: Has anyone ever ended a team meeting feeling worse than when you started? The sincere response in the room is always everyone raising their hands. From our perspective, this indicates that teams are not always fulfilling what should be the main function of any team: offering support and containment to the emotional impact experienced by colleagues in their daily care work.

A mentalizing approach is a two-person model, so we must bring in the therapist before we finish the book. When thinking about "holding a balance" in the mentalizing stance, we must also remember that it is not only between the different dimensions observed in the patients we work with but also within the therapist as an active participant of the therapeutic relationship. Central to a two-person model is acknowledging that while the therapist is nonjudgmental and open, they will inevitably have their own feelings within the context of the therapy—because they are human. What should make therapists different during their work is the capacity to observe their own feelings in the moment instead of acting on them. And this is a skill that a mentalizing therapist helps their patients to do, as well. Parents tend to arouse strong feelings in therapists, perhaps for two reasons:

- We have all had parents, and working with parents arouses our own attachment histories.

- We have all been children and can often put ourselves in the shoes of children and are therefore at risk of being judgmental of parents.

Furthermore, who we are as individuals shapes the reactions that we have to our patients. And despite whether we ourselves are parents, similarities and differences will be brought to the surface. Therapists who are not parents themselves may feel intimidated and unsure of what they have to offer. Those who are parents to similar-age children may find themselves reflecting on their own choices and ways of responding and may be more empathic to certain situations, depending on their own personal experiences. Whether the therapist is a parent themselves or not, they may feel frustrated or angry at parents they work with, often out of a sense of urgency about how a child is being affected.

From a psychodynamic perspective, the impact of the wide range of communications from the patient toward the therapist has always been considered and worked through around the concept of countertransference. It has also valuably been described as ways of understanding levels of preverbal communication, which the therapist can acknowledge through the emotions they may be experiencing during the sessions. From a mentalizing-informed perspective, we think it is important for the therapist to try to maintain, as much as possible, this self-observing stance. In other words, what the therapist's *resilient capacity* implies is the ability to recover their mentalization as soon as possible in the inevitable and rather frequent moments in which they will lose this capacity—especially if they are available enough to receive the impact of parents' communications, both verbally and nonverbally. To "be available" means to tolerate a *stance of safe uncertainty,* to be able to tolerate a not-knowing stance, to be aware of how our own personal history and current personal situation may interfere in the understanding or assessment of the parents we are working with.

This is clearly a difficult and demanding task, but to try to highlight a core aspect of the mentalizing stance, we must remind therapists of the importance of their humble approach and profound respect toward human suffering—that of not only the people they are working with but also themselves. Therapists should not feel ashamed of falling into prementalizing modes when working with parents. Instead, therapists should feel ashamed if they never feel anxious, afraid, confused, or angry with the parents they are working with—and would do themselves a great service to remain cognizant of the fact that they can guarantee their best care for their patients only if they first and continually take care of themselves.

Therapists are often left wondering about the impact of their interventions. From a mentalization-informed perspective, we can say that therapeutic intervention has been successful when we end the treatment process leaving parents (a) in a place where their curiosity toward themselves and others has improved and (b) with the awareness of how much—and what—they need from the other parent, or someone else, in order to be able to recover their capacity to mentalize when it is lost.

Mentalizing is relational: It is born in relationships, it develops in relationships, and we all need a relationship to be able to recover it when lost—either an internalized relational experience to turn to in case of necessity, or a trustful external relationship. As mentalization theory influences therapists, we know that modeling is a key aspect of our work with patients, so we must also be reminded of how important it is to model our own needs of support and help to deal with situations that overwhelm us in particular moments.

CONCLUDING SUMMARY

The following is an outline of the process of working with parents from a relational and developmental framework, one that integrates the key clinical theoretical and practice elements necessary for a mentalization-informed approach to working with parents:

- A detailed and accurate assessment and formulation of the parent's overall functioning, with the goal of creating a profile that includes the parent's
  - predominant prementalizing modes of functioning
  - attachment styles
  - temperament
  - relational history and presence of adverse childhood experiences
  - personality organization
  - strengths and vulnerabilities
  - ability to identify, process, and express emotions (mentalized affectivity)
- Outline a formulation that will guide us in determining where to start working, based on the parent's mentalizing profile:
  - working at establishing a balance in our work with parents, between a cognitive and affective level, with a special focus on parents' mentalized affectivity as a protective factor.
  - working on development of epistemic trust with parents (being aware of both verbal and nonverbal communications that elicit the motivation toward new social learning).
  - exploring the ghosts and angels in the nursery, as a way of helping parents create a coherent narrative of their own relational experiences, which includes both their strength and vulnerabilities.
  - helping parents understand the core issues and developmental issues of each developmental stage and supporting them in making links between their own histories and those of their children.

- working back and forth with parents, in the developmental line of mentalization, during each developmental stage, using the techniques that have been detailed in each chapter, following the building blocks of mentalizing:
  - attention regulation
  - affect regulation
  - explicit mentalization
- keeping in mind the value of working therapeutically with the goal of "holding the balance" in the four dimensions that facilitate the emergence of mentalization during our therapeutic interactions with parents.
- cultivating the integration of cognition and affect—that is, mentalized affectivity in parents' relationships to each other and to their children.

Working with parents, like being a parent, is a complex endeavor. One with ups and downs, filled with doubt, ambivalence and at times, hopeful and joyful moments. Working with parents is central and necessary in the context of child and adolescent psychotherapy as well as in our work in adult psychotherapy with those who are parents. Having a clear framework which holds the mind and guides the actions of the therapist, facilitates and encourages better therapeutic alliance, increased treatment adherence as well as the generalization of what has been learned in the context of a safe and predictable therapeutic relationship.

Appendix A

ASSESSMENT MEASURES FOR MENTALIZING REFLECTIVE FUNCTIONING

The following are clinical-research measures used in the process of working with parents. These measures can support the process of assessment and formulation, as well as the focus of the treatment plan. Some of the measures mentioned here require specialized training in order to be used as research tools; however, they can also provide valuable structure in the context of initial meetings with parents and during the process of clinical work with adults.

REFLECTIVE FUNCTIONING

Observational Measures

1. Parental Reflective Functioning

   Slade, A., Aber, J. L, Bresgi, I., Berger, B., & Kaplan, M. (2004). *The Parent Development Interview–Revised* [Unpublished protocol]. The City University of New York.

   Contact: Arietta Slade (https://pditraininginstitute.com)

2. Assessment of Reflective Parenting in Interaction

   Normandin, L., Leroux, A., Ensink, K., Terradas, M. M., & Fonagy, P. (2015). *Reflective Parenting Assessment coding manual* [Unpublished manual]. Laval University.

   Contact: Lina Normandin (Lina.Normandin@psy.ulaval.ca) and Karin Ensink (Karin.Ensink@psy.ulaval.ca)

3. Reflective Functioning Coding System

Fonagy, P., Target, M., Steele, H., & Steele, M. (1998). *Reflective-Functioning Manual Version 5 for application to Adult Attachment Interviews* [Unpublished manuscript]. University College London.

Contact person: Howard Steele (SteeleH@newschool.edu)

Self-Report Measures

1. Reflective Functioning Questionnaire (RFQ)

Fonagy, P., Luyten, P., Moulton-Perkins, A., Lee, Y. W., Warren, F., Howard, S., Ghinai, R., Fearon, P., & Lowyck, B. (2016). Development and validation of a self-report measure of mentalizing: The Reflective Functioning Questionnaire. *PLOS ONE, 11*(7), Article e0158678. https://doi.org/10.1371/journal.pone.0158678

Available at: https://www.ucl.ac.uk/psychoanalysis/research/reflective-functioning-questionnaire-rfq

2. Parental Reflective Functioning Questionnaire (PRFQ)

Luyten, P., Mayes, L. C., Nijssens, L., & Fonagy, P. (2017). The Parental Reflective Functioning Questionnaire: Development and preliminary validation. *PLOS ONE, 12*(5), Article e0176218. https://doi.org/10.1371/journal.pone.0176218

Available at: https://www.ucl.ac.uk/psychoanalysis/research/parental-reflective-functioning-questionnaire-prfq

Contact: Patrick Luyten (p.luyten@ucl.ac.uk)

3. Mentalized Affectivity Scale (MAS)

Greenberg, D. M., Kolasi, J., Hegsted, C. P., Berkowitz, Y., & Jurist, E. L. (2017). Mentalized affectivity: A new model and assessment of emotion regulation. *PLOS ONE, 12*(10), Article e0185264. https://doi.org/10.1371/journal.pone.0185264

Available at: https://www.mentalizedaffectivity.net/scale

Brief Mentalized Affectivity Scale (B-MAS) is included in this appendix.

Contact: Elliot Jurist (ejurist5@gmail.com)

ATTACHMENT

Observational Measures

1. Adult Attachment Interview

    George, C., Kaplan, N., & Main, M. (1984). *Adult Attachment Interview* [Unpublished manuscript]. University of California, Berkeley.

    Contact: Naomi Gribnau Baum (ngbReliability@gmail.com; https://www.attachment-training.com/training/)

2. Patient Attachment Coding System (PACS)

    Talia, A., Miller-Bottome, M., & Daniel, S. I. F. (2017). Assessing attachment in psychotherapy: Validation of the Patient Attachment Coding System (PACS). *Clinical Psychology & Psychotherapy, 24*(1), 149–161. https://doi.org/10.1002/cpp.1990

    Contact: Alessandro Talia (alessandrotaliapsy@gmail.com)

Self-Report Measures

1. Experiences in Close Relationships Scale (ECR)

    Fraley, R. C., Waller, N. G., & Brennan, K. A. (2000). An item response theory analysis of self-report measures of adult attachment. *Journal of Personality and Social Psychology, 78*(2), 350–365. https://doi.org/10.1037/0022-3514.78.2.350

    Available at:

    http://labs.psychology.illinois.edu/~rcfraley/measures/relstructures.htm

    https://fetzer.org/sites/default/files/images/stories/pdf/selfmeasures/Attachment-ExperienceinCloseRelationshipsRevised.pdf

ADVERSE CHILDHOOD EXPERIENCES

Self-Report Measures

1. 10-item Adverse Childhood Experiences questionnaire

    Available at: https://developingchild.harvard.edu/media-coverage/take-the-ace-quiz-and-learn-what-it-does-and-doesnt-mean/

2. Parent and Child Adverse Childhood Experiences questionnaires

Murphy, A., Steele, H., Steele, M., Allman, B., Kastner, T., & Dube, S. R. (2016). The clinical Adverse Childhood Experiences (ACEs) questionnaire: Implications for trauma-informed behavioral healthcare. In R. D. Briggs (Ed.), *Integrated early childhood behavioral health in primary care: A guide to implementation and evaluation* (pp. 7–16). Springer. https://doi.org/10.1007/978-3-319-31815-8_2

Contact: Anne Murphy (amurphy1@montefiore.org)

3. Pediatric ACEs and Related Life Events Screener (PEARLS)

Thakur, N., Hessler, D., Koita, K., Ye, M., Benson, M., Gilgoff, R., Bucci, M., Long, D., & Harris, N. B. (2020). Pediatrics adverse childhood experiences and related life events screener (PEARLS) and health in a safety-net practice. *Child Abuse & Neglect, 108,* Article 104685. https://doi.org/10.1016/j.chiabu.2020.104685

Available at: https://www.acesaware.org/wp-content/uploads/2019/12/PEARLS-Tool-Child-Parent-Caregiver-Report-De-Identified-English.pdf

B-MAS

(Brief-Mentalized Affectivity Scale)

Instructions: Here are a number of statements about emotions that may or may not apply to you. Please indicate the extent to which you agree or disagree with each statement using the scale below.

Disagree strongly	Disagree moderately	Disagree a little	Neither agree nor disagree	Agree a little	Agree moderately	Agree strongly
1	2	3	4	5	6	7

1. ____ I try to put effort into identifying my emotions.

2. ____ When I am filled with a negative emotion, I know how to handle it.

3. ____ People tell me I am good at expressing my emotions.

4. ____ I often look back at my life history to help inform my current emotional state and situation.

5. ____ It is hard for me to manage my emotions.

6. ____ If I feel something, I prefer not to discuss it with others.

7. ____ I try to understand the complexity of my emotions.

8. ____ I am good at controlling my emotions.

9. ____ If I feel something, I will convey it to others.

10. ____ I rarely think about the reasons behind why I am feeling a certain way.

11. ____ I am good at distinguishing between different emotions that I feel.

12. ____ I often keep my emotions inside.

Scoring: "R" denotes reverse-scored items. Identifying: 1, 4, 7, 10R; Processing: 2, 5R, 8, 11; Expressing: 3, 6R, 9, 12R.

Reference for 12-item measure: Greenberg, D. M., Rudenstine, S., Alaluf, R., & Jurist, E. L. (2021). Development and validation of the Brief-Mentalized Affectivity Scale: Evidence from cross-sectional online data and an urban community-based mental health clinic. *Journal of Clinical Psychology, 77*(11). https://doi.org/10.1002/jclp.23203

Reference for 60-item measure: Greenberg, D. M., Kolasi, J., Hegsted, C. P., Berkowitz, Y., & Jurist, E. L. (2017) Mentalized affectivity: A new model and assessment of emotion regulation. *PLOS ONE*, *12*(10), Article e0185264. https://doi.org/10.1371/journal.pone.0185264

The B-MAS is copyright 2021 by David M. Greenberg and Elliot L. Jurist. Reprinted with permission.

MENTALIZING-INFORMED WORK WITH PARENTS– ASSESSMENT AND FORMULATION WORKSHEET

Reason for referral

Age and developmental level of all children

Family/household structure (e.g., married, divorced, other family members in home)

Salient aspects of identity and current circumstances (e.g., gender, sexuality, cultural background, religion, family immigration history, housing)

General functioning	ACEs/AREs
Intelligence	Abuse – Physical
	Abuse – Emotional
Reality testing	Abuse – Sexual
	Neglect – Physical
Neurological or cognitive differences	Neglect – Emotional
	Domestic violence exposure
Psychiatric diagnoses	Caregiver or adult with mental illness
	Caregiver or adult who abused substances
Substance use	Incarcerated caregiver
	Divorced or separated caregivers
Personality functioning and specific traits	Other ACEs/AREs:
Other	Significant losses:
	Other traumatic experiences:

Epistemic trust
(e.g., ability to turn to others, ability to take in and use information, ability to trust self, appropriate vigilance)

Adult attachment–Representation of relationships
(e.g., valuing of relationships, normalizing/minimizing, idealizing, angry preoccupation, vague preoccupation, fear)

Internal representation of self:

Integration of dimensions of mentalizing

Self-Other

Internal-External

Cognitive-Affective

Implicit-Explicit

Representation of child

Parental RF—Self-focused

Parental RF—Child-focused

Mentalized affectivity:

Identifying—Processing—Expressing

Breakdowns in mentalizing
(when/what happens)

Recovery or repair?

Prementalizing modes:

Teleological mode

Psychic equivalence mode

Pretend mode

Developmental level of mentalizing—Current functioning

Attention
regulation

Affect
regulation

Explicit
mentalizing

Strengths and resources

Angels in the nursery

Treatment goals: **Method of assessment** (if applicable)

1. ➡

2. ➡

3. ➡

Structure of therapy (e.g., individual adult or child, dyadic, family, couples; frequency)

Additional referrals recommended

MENTALIZING-INFORMED WORK WITH PARENTS ADHERENCE SCALE

How to use the scale:

The Mentalizing-Informed Work With Parents Adherence Scale was developed as a tool for assessment and reflection. It can be used to consider adherence in direct work with parents, regardless of the age of the child. This scale can be completed by an independent rater, clinician, observer, or supervisor.

The terms "adherence," "fidelity," "competence," and so on have different, but related, meanings. For the purposes of this scale, the term "adherence" is used to describe not only the use of specific techniques but also the capacity to hold the core mentalizing stance and the quality of the way in which the model is delivered. While the Mentalizing-Informed Work With Parents Adherence Scale sets out core principles and techniques that are expected to be present in a session that takes a mentalizing approach, these may look different, at different points in time, for each parent–therapist relationship. This scale will serve as a guide to help clinicians focus on areas of strength and areas for growth, during supervision, training, and self-reflection. The goal is for clinicians to learn to apply the mentalization-based treatment for children (MBT-C) stance and techniques with fidelity in practice.

When used as an evaluation tool for research or demonstrating capacity to work "on model," the scale can check adherence to the model and serve to identify aspects of treatment associated with positive change in the child. When being used by therapists or supervisors as an aid to developing fidelity to a mentalizing approach, it is recommended that clinicians spend 5 to 10 minutes after each session with a parent reviewing this scale and assessing the presence and skill level the clinician was at in the session.

Consistent with a mentalizing stance, the focus of this scale is not on what the clinician did "right or wrong" but is, rather, a process of reflecting on the work with parents—in order to make the implicit explicit, in terms of what you did or did not do, and attend to and explore the thoughts, feelings, and intentions that (a) were underlying your behavior as a clinician and (b) may have been underlying the behavior of the parent(s) in the session.

In order to assess parents' mentalized affectivity, we ask them questions about identifying, processing, and expressing emotions. Identifying emotions is captured by labeling emotions when the parents speak and noticing which emotions they refer to (positive and negative) and whether they refer to a wide range of emotions. Processing emotions leans more heavily into whether one feels the need to revalue them not only in order to fit a situation but also in light of one's own history. Expressing emotions typically denotes how they are communicated (in a form that others can take in and respond to or not) but also concerns allowing one to feel emotions fully, regardless of whether they emerge outwardly. If parents seem to struggle with all of these three, then the job of the clinician is to inspire curiosity about emotions.

We are all prone to slip into nonmentalizing modes when working with parents, as well as children, especially when they are emotionally dysregulated and not mentalizing. Therefore, it may be useful to use the scale in supervision, as a function of the supervisory relationship is to restore and facilitate our own mentalization. By practicing restoring our mentalizing functions in the context of supervision, we become better able to restore our mentalization when we are in the room with children and to help them to develop or restore their mentalizing capacities.

Assessment of Skill Level

1	2	3	4	5
Poor	Less than adequate	Adequate	Good	Very good

Mentalizing Stance and Core Principles	Presence	Skill Level
Adaptation to parent's developmental level of mentalizing (attention regulation, affect regulation, explicit mentalizing)		
Nonjudgmental stance		
Use of ostensive cues		
Not-knowing, curious stance		
Playful stance		
Responsive to parent's epistemic trust		

Mentalizing Techniques	Presence	Skill Level

Attention Regulation Interventions

Use of marked mirroring

Work toward joint attention and togetherness

Assume responsibility for structure and holding

Notice and name what is happening in the here and now

Highlight and bring attention to positive moments of genuine curiosity

Bring awareness to bodily experiences/ sensations/signals

Stop and stand, while staying in contact

Affect Regulation Interventions

Awareness and curiosity about perceptions and feelings

Regulation of arousal—taking an active role in keeping the arousal at a helpful level (not so high that people lose their capacity to mentalize, but not so low that the session becomes affectively flat)

Identify triggers

Use empathic validation in face of mentalizing breakdowns

Use clarification and challenging appropriately (i.e., increase arousal, as with pretend mode)

Integrate emotion and cognition (cognitive-affective dimension)

Explicit Mentalizing Interventions

Make the implicit explicit (implicit–explicit dimension)

Mentalize internal experiences in the here and now

Link mental states to behavior (internal-external dimension)

Play with perspective (self-other dimension)

Mentalize the therapeutic relationship

Other characteristic explicit mentalizing interventions:

(continues)

Assessment of Skill Level (*Continued*)

Mentalizing Techniques	Presence	Skill Level
Mentalized Affectivity Interventions		
Curiosity about emotions		
Identifying emotions–labeling, distinguishing; what emotions (specifically and whether positive and negative) and how many different kinds/degrees		
Processing emotions–adjusting/modulating but also reflecting in light of past history		
Expressing emotions–outwardly (communicatively or not), inwardly		
Interrupting prementalizing and restoring mentalizing		
Teleological mode–voice conflict, make internal processes explicit		
Psychic equivalence mode–empathic validation to regulate affect		
Pretend mode–gentle challenge and confrontation with reality		

Criteria for the Assessment of Skill Level

Each item listed on this scale requires the rater to indicate if the stance or technique was **Present** and, if the stance or technique was present, assign a rating for **Skill Level**, which refers to the clinician's demonstration of

- expertise, competence, commitment, and willingness to take well-judged relational risks

- appropriate timing and pace of intervention

- adapting to the fluctuating mentalizing state of the parents

- responding to where the parents are at specific times

1	2	3	4	5
Poor	Less than adequate	Adequate	Good	Very good

1 Poor	The clinician handled this skill in an unacceptable manner.
2 Less than adequate	The clinician handled this skill poorly (e.g., demonstrating lack of expertise, poor timing, unclear language, lack of understanding), in a less than average manner.
3 Adequate	The clinician handled this in a manner of an average, "good enough" clinician.
4 Good	The clinician handled this in a skilled manner that was better than average.
5 Very good	The clinician handled this in an extremely skilled and thoughtful manner.

An intervention is any visual or audible behavior/utterance of the clinician (for audio recordings or observable for video recordings or live supervision). This may be a single statement or a series of statements developing an interaction between the parent and the clinician.

Though frequency, extensiveness, and appropriateness of interventions are not rated separately, these aspects of an intervention should be considered when assessing skillfulness. For example, a highly skillful mentalizing intervention may be done only once in a session, but with depth (extensiveness) and appropriately. In contrast, frequent mentalizing interventions done in depth and at wrong timing might be overwhelming to the child and, therefore, rated lower in skill.

Skill level is not the same as effectiveness of intervention. A clinician may make an intervention that has a high level of skill, but it may not have an immediately observable effect, for a number of reasons. When rating a session, it is most helpful to assume that the clinician is *adequate* until proven otherwise. The assessor should then be able to define why a clinician moves below or above this "good enough" level of skill.

References

Aber, J., Slade, A., Berger, B., Bresgi, I., & Kaplan, M. (1985). *The Parent Development Interview* [Unpublished protocol]. The City University of New York.

Adkins, T., & Fonagy, P. (2017). *Coding reflective functioning in parents using the Five Minute Speech Sample procedure: Version 2* [Unpublished manuscript]. School of Social Work, University of Texas at Austin.

Ainsworth, M. D. (1985). Patterns of attachment. *The Clinical Psychologist, 38*(2), 27–29.

Ainsworth, M. D. S., Blehar, M., Waters, E., & Wall, S. (1978). *Patterns of attachment: A psychological study of the strange situation.* Lawrence Erlbaum.

Aival-Naveh, E., Rothschild-Yakar, L., & Kurman, J. (2019). Keeping culture in mind: A systematic review and initial conceptualization of mentalizing from a cross-cultural perspective. *Clinical Psychology: Science and Practice, 26*(4), Article e12300. https://doi.org/10.1037/h0101757

Altman, N. (1994). A perspective on child psychoanalysis 1994: The recognition of relational theory and technique in child treatment. *Psychoanalytic Psychology, 11*(3), 383–395. https://doi.org/10.1037/h0079554

Arnett, J. J. (2000). Emerging adulthood: A theory of development from the late teens through the twenties. *American Psychologist, 55*(5), 469–480. https://doi.org/10.1037/0003-066X.55.5.469

Arnett, J. J. (2015). *Emerging adulthood: The winding road from the late teens through the twenties* (2nd ed.). Oxford University Press. https://doi.org/10.1093/acprof:oso/9780199929382.001.0001

Artigue, J., & Tizón, J. L. (2014). Una revisión sobre los factores de riesgo en la infancia para la esquizofrenia y los trastornos mentales graves del adulto [Review of risks factors in childhood for schizophrenia and severe mental disorders in adulthood]. *Atención Primaria, 46*(7), 336–356. https://doi.org/10.1016/j.aprim.2013.11.002

Asen, E., & Fonagy, P. (2021). *Mentalization-based treatment with families.* Guilford Press.

Bacallao, M. L., & Smokowski, P. R. (2007). The costs of getting ahead: Mexican family system changes after immigration. *Family Relations, 56*(1), 52–66. https://doi.org/10.1111/j.1741-3729.2007.00439.x

Badoni, M. (2002). Parents and their child—and the analyst in the middle: Working with a transgenerational mandate. *The International Journal of Psychoanalysis, 83*(5), 1111–1131. https://doi.org/10.1516/1B7R-R8TG-MY2R-JCW1

Bartsch, K., & Wellman, H. M. (1995). *Children talk about the mind.* Oxford University Press.

Bastaits, K., & Mortelmans, D. (2017). Parenting and family structure after divorce: Are they related? *Journal of Divorce & Remarriage, 58*(7), 542–558. https://doi.org/10.1080/10502556.2017.1345200

Bate, J., Bekar, O., & Blom, I. (2018). A mother, a baby, and two treatment approaches: Discussing a switch case from CBT and mentalization perspectives. *Journal of Infant, Child, and Adolescent Psychotherapy, 17*(4), 328–345. https://doi.org/10.1080/15289168.2018.1526159

Bate, J., & Malberg, N. (2020). Containing the anxieties of children, parents and families from a distance during the coronavirus pandemic. *Journal of Contemporary Psychotherapy, 50*(4), 285–294. https://doi.org/10.1007/s10879-020-09466-4

Bate, J., Nikitiades, A., Hoffman, S., Allman, B., Steele, M., & Murphy, A. (2016). Attachment-based group therapy for children and parents. In C. Haen & S. Aronson (Eds.), *Handbook of child and adolescent group therapy: A practitioner's reference.* Routledge.

Bate, J., Prout, T. A., Rousmaniere, T., & Vaz, A. (2022). *Deliberate practice in child and adolescent psychotherapy.* American Psychological Association. https://doi.org/10.1037/0000288-000

Bateman, A., & Fonagy, P. (2004). *Psychotherapy for borderline personality disorder: Mentalization-based treatment.* Oxford University Press. https://doi.org/10.1093/med:psych/9780198527664.001.0001

Bateman, A., & Fonagy, P. (2012). *Handbook of mentalizing in mental health practice.* American Psychiatric Publishing.

Bateman, A., & Fonagy, P. (2016). *Mentalization-based treatment for personality disorders: A practical guide.* Oxford University Press. https://doi.org/10.1093/med:psych/9780199680375.001.0001

Beebe, B. (2005). Mother–infant research informs mother–infant treatment. *The Psychoanalytic Study of the Child, 60*(1), 7–46. https://doi.org/10.1080/00797308.2005.11800745

Beebe, B. (2006). Co-constructing mother–infant distress in face-to-face interactions: Contributions of microanalysis. *Infant Observation, 9*(2), 151–164. https://doi.org/10.1080/13698030600810409

Beebe, B., Jaffe, J., Buck, K., Chen, H., Cohen, P., Blatt, S., Kaminer, T., Feldstein, S., & Andrews, H. (2007). Six-week postpartum maternal self-criticism and dependency and 4-month mother–infant self- and interactive contingencies. *Developmental Psychology, 43*(6), 1360–1376. https://doi.org/10.1037/0012-1649.43.6.1360

Beebe, B., Jaffe, J., Buck, K., Chen, H., Cohen, P., Feldstein, S., & Andrews, H. (2008). Six-week postpartum maternal depressive symptoms and 4-month mother–infant self- and interactive contingency. *Infant Mental Health Journal, 29*(5), 442–471. https://doi.org/10.1002/imhj.20191

Beebe, B., Jaffe, J., Markese, S., Buck, K., Chen, H., Cohen, P., Bahrick, L., Andrews, H., & Feldstein, S. (2010). The origins of 12-month attachment: A microanalysis of 4-month mother–infant interaction. *Attachment & Human Development, 12*(1–2), 3–141. https://doi.org/10.1080/14616730903338985

Benbassat, N., & Priel, B. (2012). Parenting and adolescent adjustment: The role of parental reflective function. *Journal of Adolescence, 35*(1), 163–174. https://doi.org/10.1016/j.adolescence.2011.03.004

Benbassat, N., & Shulman, S. (2016). The significance of parental reflective function in the adjustment of young adults. *Journal of Child and Family Studies, 25*(9), 2843–2852. https://doi.org/10.1007/s10826-016-0450-5

Berthelot, N., Ensink, K., Bernazzani, O., Normandin, L., Luyten, P., & Fonagy, P. (2015). Intergenerational transmission of attachment in abused and neglected mothers: The role of trauma-specific reflective functioning. *Infant Mental Health Journal, 36*(2), 200–212. https://doi.org/10.1002/imhj.21499

Bick, J., Dozier, M., Bernard, K., Grasso, D., & Simons, R. (2013). Foster mother–infant bonding: Associations between foster mothers' oxytocin production, electrophysiological brain activity, feelings of commitment, and caregiving quality. *Child Development, 84*(3), 826–840. https://doi.org/10.1111/cdev.12008

Blos, P., Jr. (1985). Intergenerational separation-individuation: Treating the mother–infant pair. *The Psychoanalytic Study of the Child, 40*, 41–56.

Bonovitz, C. (2018). All but dissertation (ABD), All but parricide (ABP): Young adulthood as a developmental period and the crisis of separation. *Psychoanalytic Psychology, 35*(1), 142–148. https://doi.org/10.1037/pap0000128

Borelli, J. L., Stern, J. A., Marvin, M. J., Smiley, P. A., Pettit, C., & Samudio, M. (2021). Reflective functioning and empathy among mothers of school-aged children: Charting the space between. *Emotion, 21*(4), 783–800. https://doi.org/10.1037/emo0000747

Borelli, J. L., St John, H. K., Cho, E., & Suchman, N. E. (2016). Reflective functioning in parents of school-aged children. *American Journal of Orthopsychiatry, 86*(1), 24–36. https://doi.org/10.1037/ort0000141

Borelli, J. L., West, J. L., Decoste, C., & Suchman, N. E. (2012). Emotionally avoidant language in the parenting interviews of substance-dependent mothers: Associations with reflective functioning, recent substance abuse, and parenting behavior. *Infant Mental Health Journal, 33*(5), 506–519. https://doi.org/10.1002/imhj.21340

Bornstein, M. H. (2012). Cultural approaches to parenting. *Parenting: Science and Practice, 12*(2–3), 212–221. https://doi.org/10.1080/15295192.2012.683359

Bornstein, M. H., Britto, P. R., Nonoyama-Tarumi, Y., Ota, Y., Petrovic, O., & Putnick, D. L. (2012). Child development in developing countries: Introduction and methods. *Child Development, 83*(1), 16–31. https://doi.org/10.1111/j.1467-8624.2011.01671.x

Bowlby, J. (1969). *Attachment and loss: Vol. 1. Attachment.* Basic Books.

Bowlby, J. (1973). *Attachment and loss: Vol. 2. Separation.* Basic Books.

Bowlby, J. (1980). *Attachment and loss: Vol. 3. Loss.* Basic Books.

Bowlby, J. (1982). *Attachment and loss: Vol. 1. Attachment* (2nd ed.). Basic Books.

Bowlby, J. (1986). *The nature of the child's tie to his mother.* New York University Press.

Bowlby, J., & Ainsworth, M. D. S. (1951). *Maternal care and mental health* (Vol. 2). World Health Organization.

Brassell, A. A., Rosenberg, E., Parent, J., Rough, J. N., Fondacaro, K., & Seehuus, M. (2016). Parent's psychological flexibility: Associations with parenting and child psychosocial well-being. *Journal of Contextual Behavioral Science, 5*(2), 111–120. https://doi.org/10.1016/j.jcbs.2016.03.001

Brazelton, T. B. (1992). *Touchpoints: The essential reference: Your child's emotional and behavioral development.* Addison-Wesley.

Burcher, P., Cheyney, M. J., Li, K. N., Hushmendy, S., & Kiley, K. C. (2016). Cesarean birth regret and dissatisfaction: A qualitative approach. *Birth, 43*(4), 346–352. https://doi.org/10.1111/birt.12240

Callister, L. C. (2004). Making meaning: Women's birth narratives. *Journal of Obstetric, Gynecologic, & Neonatal Nursing, 33*(4), 508–518. https://doi.org/10.1177/0884217504266898

Cavanagh, M. R., Read, J., & New, B. (2004). Sexual abuse inquiry and response: A New Zealand training programme. *New Zealand Journal of Psychology, 33*(3), 137–144.

Center on the Developing Child. (n.d.). *Neglect.* https://developingchild.harvard.edu/science/deep-dives/neglect/

Chazan, S. (1995). The simultaneous treatment of parent and child. Basic Books.

Colarusso, C. (1992). *Child and adult development: A psychoanalytic introduction for clinicians.* Springer. https://doi.org/10.1007/978-1-4757-9673-5

Conger, R. D., Belsky, J., & Capaldi, D. M. (2009). The intergenerational transmission of parenting: Closing comments for the special section. *Developmental Psychology, 45*(5), 1276–1283. https://doi.org/10.1037/a0016911

Corriveau, K. H., Harris, P. L., Meins, E., Fernyhough, C., Arnott, B., Elliott, L., Liddle, B., Hearn, A., Vittorini, L., & de Rosnay, M. (2009). Young children's trust in their mother's claims: Longitudinal links with attachment security in infancy.

Child Development, 80(3), 750–761. https://doi.org/10.1111/j.1467-8624. 2009.01295.x

Csibra, G., & Gergely, G. (2009). Natural pedagogy. *Trends in Cognitive Sciences, 13*(4), 148–153. https://doi.org/10.1016/j.tics.2009.01.005

Dangerfield, M. (2012). Negligencia y violencia sobre el adolescente: Abordaje desde un Hospital de Día [Neglect and violence on adolescents: Approach from a day hospital]. *Temas de Psicoanálisis, 4*(2), 1–10.

Dangerfield, M. (2016). "Sense un lloc a la teva ment, sense un lloc al món." Aspectes tècnics del treball amb adolescents desatesos ["Without a place in your mind, without a place in the world." Technical aspects of work with neglected adolescents]. *Revista Catalana de Psicoanàlisi, 33*(2), 99–129.

Dangerfield, M. (2017). Aportaciones del tratamiento basado en la mentalización (MBT-A) para adolescentes que han sufrido adversidades en la infancia [Contributions of treatment based on mentalization (MBT-A) for adolescents who have suffered adversities in childhood]. *Cuadernos de Psiquiatría y Psicoterapia del Niño y del Adolescente, 63*, 29–47.

Dangerfield, M. (2020). *Estudio de las consecuencias psicopatológicas de las adversidades relacionales en la infancia y de la transmisión del trauma transgeneracional* [Study of the psychopathological consequences of relational adversities in childhood and the transmission of transgenerational trauma; Unpublished doctoral dissertation]. Universidad Ramón Llull.

Dangerfield, M. (2021a). El Proyecto ECID. Un modelo de intervención comunitario para adolescentes de alto riesgo desvinculados de la red asistencial [The ECID Project. A community intervention model for non-help-seeking high risk adolescents]. *Aperturas Psicoanalíticas* (68). https://aperturas.org/articulo.php?articulo=0001167

Dangerfield, M. (2021b). Working with at-risk mental states in adolescence. In T. Rossouw, M. Wiwe, & I. Vrouva (Eds.), *Mentalization-based treatment for adolescents: A practical treatment guide* (pp. 151–165). Routledge. https://doi.org/10.4324/9780429323928-10-14

Davis, D. E., DeBlaere, C., Owen, J., Hook, J. N., Rivera, D. P., Choe, E., Van Tongeren, D. R., Worthington, E. L., & Placeres, V. (2018). The multicultural orientation framework: A narrative review. *Psychotherapy, 55*(1), 89–100. https://doi.org/10.1037/pst0000160

de Haan, M. (2011). The reconstruction of parenting after migration: A perspective from cultural translation. *Human Development, 54*(6), 376–399. https://doi.org/10.1159/000334119

Delgado-Gaitan, C. (1994). Socializing young children in Mexican-American families: An intergenerational perspective. *Cross-cultural roots of minority child development* (pp. 55–86). Lawrence Erlbaum Associates.

Doss, B. D., & Rhoades, G. K. (2017). The transition to parenthood: Impact on couples' romantic relationships. *Current Opinion in Psychology, 13*, 25–28. https://doi.org/10.1016/j.copsyc.2016.04.003

Dreby, J. (2007). Children and power in Mexican transnational families. *Journal of Marriage and Family, 69*(4), 1050–1064. https://doi.org/10.1111/j.1741-3737.2007.00430.x

Duflos, M., Giraudeau, C., & Ferrand, C. (2020). What is emotional closeness between grandparents and their adolescent grandchildren? A systematic review. *Journal of Family Studies, 28*(2), 1–23. https://doi.org/10.1080/13229400.2020.1752771

Dunn, J., & Brown, J. R. (2001). Emotion, pragmatics and social understanding in the preschool years. In D. Bakhurst & S. G. Shanker (Eds.), *Jerome Bruner: Language, culture, self* (pp. 88–103). SAGE. https://doi.org/10.4135/9781446217634.n6

Duschinsky, R., & Foster, S. (2021). *Mentalising and epistemic trust: The work of Peter Fonagy and colleagues at the Anna Freud Centre.* Oxford University Press. https://doi.org/10.1093/med-psych/9780198871187.001.0001

Eells, T. D. (Ed.). (2011). *Handbook of psychotherapy case formulation.* Guilford Press.

Egeland, B., & Farber, E. A. (1984). Infant–mother attachment: Factors related to its development and changes over time. *Child Development, 55*(3), 753–771. https://doi.org/10.2307/1130127

Egyed, K., Király, I., & Gergely, G. (2013). Communicating shared knowledge in infancy. *Psychological Science, 24*(7), 1348–1353. https://doi.org/10.1177/0956797612471952

Ehrensaft, D. (2005). *Mommies, daddies, donors, surrogates: Answering tough questions and building strong families.* Guilford Press.

Ensink, K., Berthelot, N., Bernazzani, O., Normandin, L., & Fonagy, P. (2014). Another step closer to measuring the ghosts in the nursery: Preliminary validation of the Trauma Reflective Functioning Scale. *Frontiers in Psychology, 5*, 1–12. https://doi.org/10.3389/fpsyg.2014.01471

Ensink, K., & Mayes, L. C. (2010). The development of mentalisation in children from a theory of mind perspective. *Psychoanalytic Inquiry, 30*(4), 301–337. https://doi.org/10.1080/07351690903206504

Ensink, K., Normandin, L., Plamondon, A., Berthelot, N., & Fonagy, P. (2016). Intergenerational pathways from reflective functioning to infant attachment through parenting. *Canadian Journal of Behavioural Science, 48*(1), 9–18. https://doi.org/10.1037/cbs0000030

Erikson, E. H. (1994). *Identity and the life cycle.* W. W. Norton & Company.

Faircloth, C. (2014). Intensive parenting and the expansion of parenting. In E. Lee, J. Bristow, C. Faircloth, & J. Macvarish (Eds.), *Parenting culture studies* (pp. 25–50). Palgrave Macmillan. https://doi.org/10.1057/9781137304612_2

Fearon, R. M. P., Van IJzendoorn, M. H., Fonagy, P., Bakermans-Kranenburg, M. J., Schuengel, C., & Bokhorst, C. L. (2006). In search of shared and nonshared environmental factors in security of attachment: A behavior-genetic study of the association between sensitivity and attachment security. *Developmental Psychology, 42*(6), 1026–1040. https://doi.org/10.1037/0012-1649.42.6.1026

Fearon, R. P., Bakermans-Kranenburg, M. J., Van IJzendoorn, M. H., Lapsley, A. M., & Roisman, G. I. (2010). The significance of insecure attachment and disorganization in the development of children's externalizing behavior: A meta-analytic study. *Child Development, 81*(2), 435–456. https://doi.org/10.1111/j.1467-8624.2009.01405.x

Feduchi, L. (2016, April 14–16). *Evolución del encuentro terapéutico con el adolescente* [Evolution of the therapeutic encounter with the adolescent; Conference presentation]. *SEPYPNA XXVIII Congreso Nacional. La técnica en psicoterapia en sus diversas aplicaciones.* Burlada, Navarra, Spain.

Felitti, V. J., Anda, R. F., Nordenberg, D., Williamson, D. F., Spitz, A. M., Edwards, V., Koss, M. P., & Marks, J. S. (1998). Relationship of childhood abuse and household dysfunction to many of the leading causes of death in adults: The Adverse Childhood Experiences (ACE) Study. *American Journal of Preventive Medicine, 14*(4), 245–258. https://doi.org/10.1016/S0749-3797(98)00017-8

Fenichel, O. (1946). Endopsychic structure considered in terms of object-relationships: W.R.D. Fairbairn. *Int. J. Psa., XXV, 1944, pp. 70–93. The Psychoanalytic Quarterly, 15,* 541–543.

Fishbane, M. (2013). *Loving with the brain in mind: Neurobiology and couple therapy.* W. W. Norton & Company.

Fonagy, P. (2000). Attachment and borderline personality disorder. *Journal of the American Psychoanalytic Association, 48*(4), 1129–1146. https://doi.org/10.1177/00030651000480040701

Fonagy, P. (2006). The mentalization-focused approach to social development. In J. G. Allen & P. Fonagy (Eds.), *The handbook of mentalization-based treatment* (pp. 53–99). John Wiley & Sons.

Fonagy, P., & Allison, E. (2011). What is mentalization? The concept and its foundations in developmental research and social-cognitive neuroscience. In N. Midgley & I. Vrouva (Eds.), *Minding the child: Mentalization-based interventions with children, young people and their families* (pp. 11–34). Routledge. https://doi.org/10.4324/9780203123003

Fonagy, P., & Allison, E. (2014). The role of mentalizing and epistemic trust in the therapeutic relationship. *Psychotherapy, 51*(3), 372–380. https://doi.org/10.1037/a0036505

Fonagy, P., & Bateman, A. (2008). The development of borderline personality disorder—A mentalizing model. *Journal of Personality Disorders, 22*(1), 4–21. https://doi.org/10.1521/pedi.2008.22.1.4

Fonagy, P., Campbell, C., Constantinou, M., Higgitt, A., Allison, E., & Luyten, P. (2021). Culture and psychopathology: An attempt at reconsidering the role of social learning. *Development and Psychopathology,* 1–16. https://doi.org/10.1017/S0954579421000092

Fonagy, P., Gergely, G., Jurist, E. L., & Target, M. (2002). *Affect regulation, mentalization, and the development of the self.* Other Press.

Fonagy, P., Gergely, G., & Target, M. (2008). Psychoanalytic constructs and attachment theory and research. In J. Cassidy & P. R. Shaver (Eds.), *Handbook of attachment: Theory, research, and clinical applications* (pp. 783–810). Guilford Press.

Fonagy, P., & Luyten, P. (2009). A developmental, mentalization-based approach to the understanding and treatment of borderline personality disorder. *Development and Psychopathology, 21*(4), 1355–1381. https://doi.org/10.1017/S0954579409990198

Fonagy, P., Luyten, P., & Allison, E. (2015). Epistemic petrification and the restoration of epistemic trust: A new conceptualization of borderline personality disorder and its psychosocial treatment. *Journal of Personality Disorders, 29*(5), 575–609. https://doi.org/10.1521/pedi.2015.29.5.575

Fonagy, P., Luyten, P., Allison, E., & Campbell, C. (2017a). What we have changed our minds about: Part 1. Borderline personality disorder as a limitation of resilience. *Borderline Personality Disorder and Emotion Dysregulation, 4*(1), Article 11. https://doi.org/10.1186/s40479-017-0061-9

Fonagy, P., Luyten, P., Allison, E., & Campbell, C. (2017b). What we have changed our minds about: Part 2. Borderline personality disorder, epistemic trust and the developmental significance of social communication. *Borderline Personality Disorder and Emotion Dysregulation, 4*(1), Article 9. https://doi.org/10.1186/s40479-017-0062-8

Fonagy, P., Luyten, P., Campbell, C., & Allison, L. (2014, December). *Epistemic trust, psychopathology and the great psychotherapy debate.* http://www.societyforpsychotherapy.org/epistemic-trust-psychopathology-and-the-great-psychotherapy-debate

Fonagy, P., Luyten, P., Moulton-Perkins, A., Lee, Y.-W., Warren, F., Howard, S., Ghinai, R., Fearon, P., & Lowyck, B. (2016). Development and validation of a self-report measure of mentalizing: The Reflective Functioning Questionnaire. *PLOS ONE, 11*(7), Article e0158678. https://doi.org/10.1371/journal.pone.0158678

Fonagy, P., Steele, H., & Steele, M. (1991). Maternal representations of attachment during pregnancy predict the organization of infant–mother attachment at one year of age. *Child Development, 62*(5), 891–905. https://doi.org/10.2307/1131141

Fonagy, P., Steele, M., Steele, H., Moran, G. S., & Higgitt, A. C. (1991). The capacity for understanding mental states: The reflective self in parent and child and its significance for security of attachment. *Infant Mental Health Journal, 12*(3), 201–218. https://doi.org/10.1002/1097-0355(199123)12:3<201::AID-IMHJ2280120307>3.0.CO;2-7

Fonagy, P., & Target, M. (1996). Playing with reality: I. Theory of mind and the normal development of psychic reality. *The International Journal of Psycho-analysis, 77*(2), 217–233.

Fonagy, P., & Target, M. (1997). Attachment and reflective function: Their role in self-organization. *Development and Psychopathology, 9*(4), 679–700. https://doi.org/10.1017/S0954579497001399

Fonagy, P., Target, M., Steele, H., & Steele, M. (1998). *Reflective-Functioning Manual Version 5 for application to Adult Attachment Interviews* [Unpublished manuscript]. University College London.

Fonagy, P., Twemlow, S. W., Vernberg, E., Sacco, F. C., & Little, T. D. (2005). Creating a peaceful school learning environment: The impact of an antibullying program on educational attainment in elementary schools. *Medical Science Monitor, 11*(7), CR317–CR325.

Fox, R. A., Platz, D. L., & Bentley, K. S. (1995). Maternal factors related to parenting practices, developmental expectations, and perceptions of child behavior problems. *The Journal of Genetic Psychology, 156*(4), 431–441. https://doi.org/10.1080/00221325.1995.9914835

Fraenkel, P. (2019). Love in action: An integrative approach to last chance couple therapy. *Family Process, 58*(3), 569–594. https://doi.org/10.1111/famp.12474

Fraiberg, S., Adelson, E., & Shapiro, V. (1975). Ghosts in the nursery: A psychoanalytic approach to the problems of impaired infant–mother relationships. *Journal of the American Academy of Child Psychiatry, 14*(3), 387–421. https://doi.org/10.1016/S0002-7138(09)61442-4

Fraley, R. C., Waller, N. G., & Brennan, K. A. (2000). An item response theory analysis of self-report measures of adult attachment. *Journal of Personality and Social Psychology, 78*(2), 350–365. https://doi.org/10.1037/0022-3514.78.2.350

Freud, A. (1965). *Normality and pathology in childhood: Assessments of development.* Hogarth Press.

Fuller-Thomson, E., & Minkler, M. (2000). African American grandparents raising grandchildren: A national profile of demographic and health characteristics. *Health & Social Work, 25*(2), 109–118. https://doi.org/10.1093/hsw/25.2.109

George, C., Kaplan, N., & Main, M. (1984). *Adult Attachment Interview* [Unpublished manuscript]. University of California, Berkeley.

George, C., Kaplan, N., & Main, M. (1996). *Adult Attachment Interview* (3rd ed.) [Unpublished manuscript]. University of California, Berkeley.

Gergely, G. (2018). The social construction of the subjective self: The role of affect-mirroring, markedness, and ostensive communication in self-development. In L. Mayes, P. Fonagy, & M. Target (Eds.), *Developmental science and psychoanalysis: Integration and innovation* (pp. 45–88). Routledge.

Gergely, G., & Csibra, G. (2005). The social construction of the cultural mind: Imitative learning as a mechanism of human pedagogy. *Interaction Studies: Social Behaviour and Communication in Biological and Artificial Systems, 6*(3), 463–481. https://doi.org/10.1075/is.6.3.10ger

Gergely, G., Egyed, K., & Király, I. (2007). On pedagogy. *Developmental Science, 10*(1), 139–146. https://doi.org/10.1111/j.1467-7687.2007.00576.x

Gergely, G., & Jacob, P. (2012). Chapter Three—Reasoning about instrumental and communicative agency in human infancy. *Advances in Child Development and Behavior, 43*, 59–94. https://doi.org/10.1016/B978-0-12-397919-3.00003-4

Gladwell, M. (2013). *David and Goliath: Underdogs, misfits, and the art of battling giants*. Little, Brown and Company.

Gladwell, M. (2019). *Talking to strangers: What we should know about the people we don't know*. Little, Brown and Company.

Goldberg, B. (2011). Parental reflective functioning, emotion regulation, and stress tolerance: A preliminary investigation. *Yale Medicine Thesis Digital Library*, 1554. http://elischolar.library.yale.edu/ymtdl/1554

Gottman, J. M., & Gottman, J. S. (2015). *10 Principles for doing effective couples therapy*. W. W. Norton and Company.

Granqvist, P., Sroufe, L. A., Dozier, M., Hesse, E., Steele, M., van IJzendoorn, M., Solomon, J., Schuengel, C., Fearon, P., Bakermans-Kranenburg, M., Steele, H., Cassidy, J., Carlson, E., Madigan, S., Jacobvitz, D., Foster, S., Behrens, K., Rifkin-Graboi, A., Gribneau, N., . . . Duschinsky, R. (2017). Disorganized attachment in infancy: A review of the phenomenon and its implications for clinicians and policy-makers. *Attachment & Human Development, 19*(6), 534–558. https://doi.org/10.1080/14616734.2017.1354040

Grasso, D. J., Moser, J. S., Dozier, M., & Simons, R. (2009). ERP correlates of attention allocation in mothers processing faces of their children. *Biological Psychology, 81*(2), 95–102. https://doi.org/10.1016/j.biopsycho.2009.03.001

Gratz, K. L., & Roemer, L. (2004). Multidimensional assessment of emotion regulation and dysregulation: Development, factor structure, and initial validation of the Difficulties in Emotion Regulation Scale. *Journal of Psychopathology and Behavioral Assessment, 26*(1), 41–54. https://doi.org/10.1023/B:JOBA.0000007455.08539.94

Greenberg, D. M., Kolasi, J., Hegsted, C. P., Berkowitz, Y., & Jurist, E. L. (2017). Mentalized affectivity: A new model and assessment of emotion regulation. *PLOS ONE, 12*(10), Article e0185264. https://doi.org/10.1371/journal.pone.0185264

Greenberg, D. M., Rudenstine, S., Alaluf, R., & Jurist, E. L. (2021). Development and validation of the Brief-Mentalized Affectivity Scale: Evidence from cross-sectional online data and an urban community-based mental health clinic. *Journal of Clinical Psychology, 77*(11). https://doi.org/10.1002/jclp.23203

Grice, H. P. (1975). *Studies in the way of words*. Harvard University Press.

Grossmann, K. E., Grossman, K., & Waters, E. (2005). *Attachment from infancy into adulthood: The major longitudinal studies*. Guilford Press.

Han, M., Goyal, D., Lee, J., Cho, H., & Kim, A. (2020). Korean immigrant women's postpartum experiences in the United States. *MCN: The American Journal of Maternal/Child Nursing, 45*(1), 42–48. https://doi.org/10.1097/NMC. 0000000000000585

Hertzmann, L., Target, M., Hewison, D., Casey, P., Fearon, P., & Lassri, D. (2016). Mentalization-based therapy for parents in entrenched conflict: A random allocation feasibility study. *Psychotherapy, 53*(4), 388–401. https://doi.org/ 10.1037/pst0000092

Hoffman, M. B. (1984). The parents' experience with the child's therapist. In R. S. Cohen, B. J. Cohler, & S. H. Weissman (Eds.), *Parenthood: A psychodynamic perspective* (pp. 164–172). Guilford Press.

Holmes, J., & Slade, A. (2017). *Attachment in therapeutic practice*. SAGE.

Hrdy, S. B. (2009). *Mothers and others: The evolutionary origins of mutual understanding*. Harvard University Press.

Hughes, C., Devine, R. T., Foley, S., Ribner, A. D., Mesman, J., & Blair, C. (2020). Couples becoming parents: Trajectories for psychological distress and buffering effects of social support. *Journal of Affective Disorders, 265*, 372–380. https:// doi.org/10.1016/j.jad.2020.01.133

Jacobs, T. J., & Chused, J. F. (1987). Psychoanalysis of the young adult: Theory and technique [Panel report]. *Journal of the American Psychoanalytic Association, 35*(1), 175–187. https://doi.org/10.1177/0003065187 03500109

Johnson, S. (2011). *Hold me tight: Your guide to the most successful approach to building loving relationships*. Hachette UK.

Jurist, E. (2018). *Minding emotions: Cultivating mentalization in psychotherapy*. Guilford Press.

Jurist, E., & Sosa, M. P. (2019). Commentary on mentalization and culture. *Clinical Psychology: Science and Practice, 26*(4). Advance online publication. https:// doi.org/10.1111/cpsp.12302

Jurist, E. L. (2005). Mentalized affectivity. *Psychoanalytic Psychology, 22*(3), 426–444. https://doi.org/10.1037/0736-9735.22.3.426

Jurist, E. L. (2008). Minds and yours: New directions for mentalization theory. In E. L. Jurist, A. Slade, & S. Bergner (Eds.), *Mind to mind: Infant research, neuroscience, and Psychoanalysis* (pp. 88–114). Other Press.

Jurist, E. L., & Meehan, K. B. (2009). Attachment, mentalization, and reflective functioning. In J. H. Obegi & E. Berant (Eds.), *Attachment theory and research in clinical work with adults* (pp. 71–93). Guilford Press.

Jurist, E. L. (2010). Mentalizing minds. *Psychoanalytic Inquiry, 30*(4), 289–300. https://doi.org/10.1080/07351690903206496

Katznelson, H. (2014). Reflective functioning: A review. *Clinical Psychology Review, 34*(2), 107–117. https://doi.org/10.1016/j.cpr.2013.12.003

Kessler, R. C., McLaughlin, K. A., Green, J. G., Gruber, M. J., Sampson, N. A., Zaslavsky, A. M., Aguilar-Gaxiola, S., Alhamzawi, A. O., Alonso, J., Angermeyer, M., Benjet, C., Bromet, E., Chatterji, S., de Girolamo, G., Demyttenaere, K., Fayyad, J., Florescu, S., Gal, G., Gureje, O., . . . Williams, D. R. (2010). Childhood adversities and adult psychopathology in the WHO World Mental Health Surveys. *The British Journal of Psychiatry, 197*(5), 378–385. https://doi.org/10.1192/bjp.bp.110.080499

Kivity, Y., Levy, K. N., Kelly, K. M., & Clarkin, J. F. (2021). In-session reflective functioning in psychotherapies for borderline personality disorder: The emotion regulatory role of reflective functioning. *Journal of Consulting and Clinical Psychology, 89*(9), 751–761. https://doi.org/10.1037/ccp0000674

Knox, J. (2016). Epistemic mistrust: A crucial aspect of mentalization in people with a history of abuse? *British Journal of Psychotherapy, 32*(2), 226–236. https://doi.org/10.1111/bjp.12212

Kohlberg, L. (1981). *The philosophy of moral development: Moral stages and the idea of justice* (Vol. 1). Harper & Row.

Kovács, Á. M., Téglás, E., & Endress, A. D. (2010). The social sense: Susceptibility to others' beliefs in human infants and adults. *Science, 330*(6012), 1830–1834. https://doi.org/10.1126/science.1190792

Krishnakumar, A., & Buehler, C. (2000). Interparental conflict and parenting behaviors: A meta-analytic review. *Family Relations, 49*(1), 25–44. https://doi.org/10.1111/j.1741-3729.2000.00025.x

Kwon, K.-A., Jeon, H.-J., Lewsader, J. T., & Elicker, J. (2012). Mothers' and fathers' parenting quality and toddlers' interactive behaviours in dyadic and triadic family contexts. *Infant and Child Development, 21*(4), 356–373. https://doi.org/10.1002/icd.1746

Lebow, J., & Rekart, K. N. (2007). Integrative family therapy for high-conflict divorce with disputes over child custody and visitation. *Family Process, 46*(1), 79–91. https://doi.org/10.1111/j.1545-5300.2006.00193.x

Lewis-Fernández, R., Aggarwal, N. K., Lam, P. C., Galfalvy, H., Weiss, M. G., Kirmayer, L. J., Paralikar, V., Deshpande, S. N., Díaz, E., Nicasio, A. V., Boiler, M., Alarcón, R. D., Rohlof, H., Groen, S., van Dijk, R. C. J., Jadhav, S., Sarmukaddam, S., Ndetei, D., Scalco, M. Z., . . . Vega-Dienstmaier, J. M. (2017). Feasibility, acceptability and clinical utility of the Cultural Formulation Interview: Mixed-methods results from the *DSM-5* international field trial. *The British Journal of Psychiatry, 210*(4), 290–297. https://doi.org/10.1192/bjp.bp.116.193862

Leyton, F., Olhaberry, M., Alvarado, R., Rojas, G., Dueñas, L. A., Downing, G., & Steele, H. (2019). Video feedback intervention to enhance parental reflective functioning in primary caregivers of inpatient psychiatric children: Protocol for a randomized feasibility trial. *Trials, 20*, Article 268. https://doi.org/10.1186/s13063-019-3310-y

Lieberman, A. F., Padrón, E., Van Horn, P., & Harris, W. W. (2005). Angels in the nursery: The intergenerational transmission of benevolent parental influences. *Infant Mental Health Journal*, *26*(6), 504–520. https://doi.org/10.1002/imhj.20071

Lieberman, A. F., & Van Horn, P. (2005). Don't hit my mommy!: A manual for child–parent psychotherapy with young witnesses of family violence. Zero to Three.

Lieberman, A. F., & Van Horn, P. (2008). *Psychotherapy with infants and young children: Repairing the effects of stress and trauma on early attachment*. Guilford Press.

Liu, D., Wellman, H. M., Tardif, T., & Sabbagh, M. A. (2008). Theory of mind development in Chinese children: A meta-analysis of false-belief understanding across cultures and languages. *Developmental Psychology*, *44*(2), 523–531. https://doi.org/10.1037/0012-1649.44.2.523

Luyten, P., Campbell, C., Allison, E., & Fonagy, P. (2020). The mentalizing approach to psychopathology: State of the art and future directions. *Annual Review of Clinical Psychology*, *16*(1), 297–325. https://doi.org/10.1146/annurev-clinpsy-071919-015355

Luyten, P., & Fonagy, P. (2015). The neurobiology of mentalizing. *Personality Disorders*, *6*(4), 366–379. https://doi.org/10.1037/per0000117

Luyten, P., Fonagy, P., Lowyck, B., & Vermote, R. (2012). Assessment of mentalization. In A. W. Bateman & P. Fonagy (Eds.), *Handbook of mentalizing in mental health practice* (pp. 43–65). American Psychiatric Publishing.

Luyten, P., Mayes, L. C., Nijssens, L., & Fonagy, P. (2017). The Parental Reflective Functioning Questionnaire: Development and preliminary validation. *PLOS ONE*, *12*(5), Article e0176218. https://doi.org/10.1371/journal.pone.0176218

Lyons-Ruth, K., Bruschweiler-Stern, N., Harrison, A. M., Morgan, A. C., Nahum, J. P., Sander, L., Stern, D. N., & Tronick, E. Z. (1998). Implicit relational knowing: Its role in development and psychoanalytic treatment. *Infant Mental Health Journal*, *19*(3), 282–289. https://doi.org/10.1002/(SICI)1097-0355(199823)19:3<282::AID-IMHJ3>3.0.CO;2-O

Mahler, M. S., Pine, F., & Bergman, A. (1975). *The psychological birth of the human infant: Symbiosis and individuation*. Routledge. https://doi.org/10.4324/9780429482915

Main, M. (1996). Introduction to the special section on attachment and psychopathology: 2. Overview of the field of attachment. *Journal of Consulting and Clinical Psychology*, *64*(2), 237–243. https://doi.org/10.1037/0022-006X.64.2.237

Malberg, N. T. (2015). Activating mentalization in parents: An integrative framework. *Journal of Infant, Child, and Adolescent Psychotherapy*, *14*(3), 232–245. https://doi.org/10.1080/15289168.2015.1068002

Malberg, N. T. (2019). From reaction to reflection: Mentalizing in early childhood education. In M. Charles & J. Bellinson (Eds.), *The importance of play in early childhood education: Psychoanalytic, attachment, and developmental perspectives* (pp. 49–62). Routledge. https://doi.org/10.4324/9781315180090-5

Malberg, N. T. (2020). The baby in the cave. In K. K. Novick, J. Novick, D. Barrett, & T. Barrett (Eds.), *Parent work casebook*. IP Books.

Malberg, N. T., & Midgley, N. (2017). A mentalization-based approach to working with adolescents in groups. In C. Haen & S. Aronson (Eds.), *Handbook of child and adolescent group therapy: A practitioner's reference* (pp. 213–224). Routledge.

Malda-Castillo, J., Browne, C., & Perez-Algorta, G. (2019). Mentalization-based treatment and its evidence-base status: A systematic literature review. *Psychology and Psychotherapy: Theory, Research and Practice, 92*(4), 465–498. https://doi.org/10.1111/papt.12195

Marty, P. (1991). *Mentalization et psychosomatique* [Mentalization and psychosomatics]. Collection Les Empêcheurs de Penser en Rond.

Marvin, R., Cooper, G., Hoffman, K., & Powell, B. (2002). The Circle of Security project: Attachment-based intervention with caregiver–pre-school child dyads. *Attachment & Human Development, 4*(1), 107–124. https://doi.org/10.1080/14616730252982491

Masterpasqua, F. (2016). Mindfulness mentalizing humanism: A transtheoretical convergence. *Journal of Psychotherapy Integration, 26*(1), 5–10. https://doi.org/10.1037/a0039635

Meins, E., Fernyhough, C., Wainwright, R., Clark-Carter, D., Das Gupta, M., Fradley, E., & Tuckey, M. (2003). Pathways to understanding mind: Construct validity and predictive validity of maternal mind-mindedness. *Child Development, 74*(4), 1194–1211. https://doi.org/10.1111/1467-8624.00601

Meins, E., Fernyhough, C., Wainwright, R., Das Gupta, M., Fradley, E., & Tuckey, M. (2002). Maternal mind-mindedness and attachment security as predictors of theory of mind understanding. *Child Development, 73*(6), 1715–1726. https://doi.org/10.1111/1467-8624.00501

Meng, A. (2012). Informal caregiving and the retirement decision. *German Economic Review, 13*(3), 307–330. https://doi.org/10.1111/j.1468-0475.2011.00559.x

Merrick, M. T., Ford, D. C., Ports, K. A., Guinn, A. S., Chen, J., Klevens, J., Metzler, M., Jones, C. M., Simon, T. R., Daniel, V. M., Ottley, P., & Mercy, J. A. (2019). *Vital signs:* Estimated proportion of adult health problems attributable to adverse childhood experiences and implications for prevention—25 states, 2015–2017. *Morbidity and Mortality Weekly Report (MMWR), 68*(44), 999–1005. https://doi.org/10.15585/mmwr.mm6844e1

Midgley, N., Ensink, K., Lindqvist, K., Malberg, N., & Muller, N. (2017). *Mentalization-based treatment for children: A time-limited approach.* American Psychological Association. https://doi.org/10.1037/0000028-000

Miller, J. M. (2017). Young or emerging adulthood: A psychoanalytic view. *The Psychoanalytic Study of the Child*, *70*(1), 8–21. https://doi.org/10.1080/ 00797308.2017.1280286

Monaci, M. G., Gratier, M., Trevarthen, C., Grandjean, D., Kuhn, P., & Filippa, M. (2021). Parental perception of vocal contact with preterm infants: Communicative musicality in the neonatal intensive care unit. *Children*, *8*(6), Article 513. https://doi.org/10.3390/children8060513

Muller, N., & Midgley, N. (2020). The clinical challenge of mentalization-based therapy with children who are in "pretend mode." *Journal of Infant, Child, and Adolescent Psychotherapy*, *19*(1), 16–24. https://doi.org/10.1080/ 15289168.2019.1701865

Mundy, L. (2007). *Everything conceivable: How assisted reproduction is changing men, women, and the world.* Knopf.

Murphy, A., Steele, H., Bate, J., Nikitiades, A., Allman, B., Bonuck, K., Meissner, P., & Steele, M. (2015). Group attachment-based intervention: Trauma-informed care for families with adverse childhood experiences. *Family & Community Health*, *38*(3), 268–279. https://doi.org/10.1097/ FCH.0000000000000074

Murphy, A., Steele, H., Steele, M., Allman, B., Kastner, T., & Dube, S. R. (2016). The clinical Adverse Childhood Experiences (ACEs) questionnaire: Implications for trauma-informed behavioral healthcare. In R. D. Briggs (Ed.), *Integrated early childhood behavioral health in primary care* (pp. 7–16). Springer. https:// doi.org/10.1007/978-3-319-31815-8_2

Murphy, A., Steele, M., Dube, S. R., Bate, J., Bonuck, K., Meissner, P., Goldman, H., & Steele, H. (2014). Adverse Childhood Experiences (ACEs) questionnaire and Adult Attachment Interview (AAI): Implications for parent child relationships. *Child Abuse & Neglect*, *38*(2), 224–233. https://doi.org/10.1016/j.chiabu. 2013.09.004

National Scientific Council on the Developing Child. (2014). *Excessive stress disrupts the architecture of the developing brain: Working paper No. 3* (Updated ed.). https://developingchild.harvard.edu/resources/wp3/

Nauck, B., & Lotter, V. (2015). Parenting styles and perceived instrumentality of schooling in native, Turkish, and Vietnamese families in Germany. *Zeitschrift für Erziehungswissenschaft*, *18*, 845–869. https://doi.org/10.1007/s11618-015- 0630-x

Nelson, L. J., Padilla-Walker, L. M., Carroll, J. S., Madsen, S. D., Barry, C. M., & Badger, S. (2007). "If you want me to treat you like an adult, start acting like one!" Comparing the criteria that emerging adults and their parents have for adulthood. *Journal of Family Psychology*, *21*(4), 665–674. https://doi.org/ 10.1037/0893-3200.21.4.665

Normandin, L., Leroux, A., Ensink, K., Terradas, M. M., & Fonagy, P. (2015). *Reflective Parenting Assessment coding manual* [Unpublished manual]. Laval University.

Novick, K. K., & Novick, J. (2005). *Working with parents makes therapy work.* Jason Aronson.

Novick, K. K., & Novick, J. (2013). A new model of techniques for concurrent psychodynamic work with parents of child and adolescent psychotherapy patients. *Child and Adolescent Psychiatric Clinics of North America, 22*(2), 331–349. https://doi.org/10.1016/j.chc.2012.12.005

Nyberg, V., & Hertzmann, L. (2014). Developing a mentalization-based treatment (MBT) for therapeutic intervention with couples (MBT-CT). *Couple and Family Psychoanalysis, 4*(2), 116–135. https://doi.org/10.33212/cfp.v4n2.2014.116

Nyberg, V., & Hertzmann, L. (2018). A partnership of two therapeutic models: The development of mentalization based treatment–couple therapy (MBT-CT) within a psychoanalytic framework. *Couple and Family Psychoanalysis, 8*(1), 23–37.

Onishi, K. H., & Baillargeon, R. (2005). Do 15-month-old infants understand false beliefs? *Science, 308*(5719), 255–258. https://doi.org/10.1126/science.1107621

Otto, H. (2008). *Culture-specific attachment strategies in the Cameroonian NSO: Cultural solutions to a universal developmental task* [Unpublished doctoral dissertation]. Universität Osnabrück.

Parreñas, R. S. (2005). *Children of global migration: Transnational families and gendered woes.* Stanford University Press. https://doi.org/10.1515/9781503624627

Perreira, K. M., Chapman, M. V., & Stein, G. L. (2006). Becoming an American parent: Overcoming challenges and finding strength in a new immigrant Latino community. *Journal of Family Issues, 27*(10), 1383–1414. https://doi.org/10.1177/0192513X06290041

Petrowski, K., Pokorny, D., Nowacki, K., & Buchheim, A. (2013). The therapist's attachment representation and the patient's attachment to the therapist. *Psychotherapy Research, 23*(1), 25–34. https://doi.org/10.1080/10503307.2012.717307

Premack, D., & Woodruff, G. (1978). Does the chimpanzee have a theory of mind? *Behavioral and Brain Sciences, 1*(4), 515–526. https://doi.org/10.1017/S0140525X00076512

Puia, D. (2018). First-time mothers' experiences of a planned cesarean birth. *The Journal of Perinatal Education, 27*(1), 50–60. https://doi.org/10.1891/1058-1243.27.1.50

Raphael-Leff, J. (2019). *The psychological process of child bearing.* Routledge.

Read, J., Harper, D., Tucker, I., & Kennedy, A. (2018). Do adult mental health services identify child abuse and neglect? A systematic review. *International Journal of Mental Health Nursing, 27*(1), 7–9. https://doi.org/10.1111/inm.12369

Rinaldi, T., Castelli, I., Greco, A., Greenberg, D. M., Jurist, E., Valle, A., & Marchetti, A. (2021). The Mentalized Affectivity Scale (MAS): Development and validation of the Italian version. *PLOS ONE, 16*(4), Article e0249272. https://doi.org/10.1371/journal.pone.0249272

Rosso, A. M., Viterbori, P., & Scopesi, A. M. (2015). Are maternal reflective functioning and attachment security associated with preadolescent mentalization? *Frontiers in Psychology, 6*, Article 1134. Advance online publication. https://doi.org/10.3389/fpsyg.2015.01134

Rossouw, T. I. (2012). Self-harm in young people: Is MBT the answer? In N. Midgley & I. Vrouva (Eds.), *Minding the child: Mentalization-based interventions with children, young people and their families* (pp. 131–144). Routledge.

Rothbaum, F., Rosen, K., Ujiie, T., & Uchida, N. (2002). Family systems theory, attachment theory, and culture. *Family Process, 41*(3), 328–350. https://doi.org/10.1111/j.1545-5300.2002.41305.x

Rowen, J., & Emery, R. (2014). Examining parental denigration behaviors of co-parents as reported by young adults and their association with parent–child closeness. *Couple and Family Psychology: Research and Practice, 3*(3), 165–177. https://doi.org/10.1037/cfp0000026

Rubino, G., Barker, C., Roth, T., & Fearon, P. (2000). Therapist empathy and depth of interpretation in response to potential alliance ruptures: The role of therapist and patient attachment styles. *Psychotherapy Research, 10*(4), 408–420. https://doi.org/10.1093/ptr/10.4.408

Scannapieco, M., & Jackson, S. (1996). Kinship care: The African American response to family preservation. *Social Work, 41*(2), 190–196. https://doi.org/10.1093/sw/41.2.190

Scharfman, M. (1990). From past to present: Major contributors from child and adolescent analysis. In S. Dowling (Ed.), *Child and adolescent analysis: Its significance for clinical work with adults* (pp. 3–20). International Universities Press.

Schlesinger, H. (2013). *Endings and beginnings: On terminating psychotherapy and psychoanalysis.* Routledge.

Schuengel, C., Bakermans-Kranenburg, M. J., & Van IJzendoorn, M. H. (1999). Frightening maternal behavior linking unresolved loss and disorganized infant attachment. *Journal of Consulting and Clinical Psychology, 67*(1), 54–63. https://doi.org/10.1037/0022-006X.67.1.54

Seymour, S. C. (1999). *Women, family, and child care in India: A world in transition.* Cambridge University Press.

Shaheen, S. (2014). How child's play impacts executive function–related behaviors. *Applied Neuropsychology: Child, 3*(3), 182–187. https://doi.org/10.1080/21622965.2013.839612

Sharp, C., Fonagy, P., & Goodyer, I. M. (2006). Imagining your child's mind: Psychosocial adjustment and mothers' ability to predict their children's attributional response styles. *British Journal of Developmental Psychology, 24*(1), 197–214. https://doi.org/10.1348/026151005X82569

Sisk, D. A. (2020). *Working with parents in psychodynamic child psychotherapy* [Unpublished doctoral dissertation]. Institute for Clinical Social Work.

Siskind, D. (1996). The child therapist and the child's parents: A precarious alliance viewed from a psychoanalytic perspective. In J. Edward & J. B. Sanville (Eds.), *Fostering healing and growth: A psychoanalytic social work approach* (pp. 293–311). Jason Aronson.

Siskind, D. (1997). *Working with parents: Establishing the essential alliance in child psychotherapy and consultation.* Jason Aronson.

Siskind, D. (1999). *A primer for child psychotherapists.* Jason Aronson.

Slade, A. (2005). Parental reflective functioning: An introduction. *Attachment & Human Development, 7*(3), 269–281. https://doi.org/10.1080/14616730500245906

Slade, A. (2008a). Mentalization as a frame for working with parents in child psychotherapy. In E. L. Jurist, A. Slade, & S. Bergner (Eds.), *Mind to mind: Infant research, neuroscience, and psychoanalysis* (pp. 307–334). Other Press.

Slade, A. (2008b). Working with parents in child psychotherapy: Engaging the reflective function. In F. N. Busch (Ed.), *Mentalization: Theoretical considerations, research findings, and clinical implications* (pp. 207–234). Analytic Press.

Slade, A. (2009). Mentalizing the unmentalizable: Parenting children on the spectrum. *Journal of Infant, Child, and Adolescent Psychotherapy, 8*(1), 7–21. https://doi.org/10.1080/15289160802683054

Slade, A. (2014). Imagining fear: Attachment, threat and psychic experience. *Psychoanalytic Dialogues, 24*(3), 253–266. https://doi.org/10.1080/10481885.2014.911608

Slade, A., Aber, J. L., Bresgi, I., Berger, B., & Kaplan, M. (2004). *The Parent Development Interview–Revised* [Unpublished protocol]. The City University of New York.

Sperber, D., Clément, F., Heintz, C., Mascaro, O., Mercier, H., Origgi, G., & Wilson, D. (2010). Epistemic vigilance. *Mind & Language, 25*(4), 359–393. https://doi.org/10.1111/j.1468-0017.2010.01394.x

Sperber, D., & Wilson, D. (1986). *Relevance: Communication and cognition.* Blackwell.

Sroufe, L. A. (1988). The role of infant–caregiver attachment in development. In J. Belsky & T. Nezworski (Eds.), *Clinical implications of attachment* (pp. 18–38). Lawrence Erlbaum Associates.

Stanhiser, J., & Steiner, A. Z. (2018). Psychosocial aspects of fertility and assisted reproductive technology. *Obstetrics and Gynecology Clinics of North America, 45*(3), 563–574. https://doi.org/10.1016/j.ogc.2018.04.006

Steele, H., Steele, M., & Croft, C. (2008). Early attachment predicts emotion recognition at 6 and 11 years old. *Attachment & Human Development, 10*(4), 379–393. https://doi.org/10.1080/14616730802461409

Steele, H., Steele, M., & Fonagy, P. (1996). Associations among attachment classifications of mothers, fathers, and their infants. *Child Development, 67*(2), 541–555. https://doi.org/10.2307/1131831

Steele, M., Bate, J., Nikitiades, A., & Buhl-Nielsen, B. (2015). Attachment in adolescence and borderline personality disorder. *Journal of Infant, Child, and Adolescent Psychotherapy, 14*(1), 16–32. https://doi.org/10.1080/15289168.2015.1004882

Steele, M., Steele, H., Bate, J., Knafo, H., Kinsey, M., Bonuck, K., Meissner, P., & Murphy, A. (2014). Looking from the outside in: The use of video in attachment-based interventions. *Attachment & Human Development, 16*(4), 402–415. https://doi.org/10.1080/14616734.2014.912491

Steele, M., Steele, H., & Johansson, M. (2002). Maternal predictors of children's social cognition: An attachment perspective. *Journal of Child Psychology and Psychiatry, and Allied Disciplines, 43*(7), 861–872. https://doi.org/10.1111/1469-7610.00096

Stern, D. (1985). *The interpersonal world of the infant: A view from psychoanalysis and developmental psychology.* Basic Books.

Stern, D. (1995). *The motherhood constellation: A unified view of parent–infant psychotherapy.* Basic Books.

Stob, V., Slade, A., Brotnow, L., Adnopoz, J., & Woolston, J. (2019). The Family Cycle: An activity to enhance parents' mentalization in children's mental health treatment. *Journal of Infant, Child, and Adolescent Psychotherapy, 18*(2), 103–119. https://doi.org/10.1080/15289168.2019.1591887

Suárez-Orozco, C., & Suárez-Orozco, M. M. (2001). *Children of migration.* Harvard University Press.

Talia, A., Miller-Bottome, M., & Daniel, S. I. F. (2017). Assessing attachment in psychotherapy: Validation of the Patient Attachment Coding System (PACS). *Clinical Psychology & Psychotherapy, 24*(1), 149–161. https://doi.org/10.1002/cpp.1990

Talia, A., Miller-Bottome, M., Wyner, R., Lilliengren, P., & Bate, J. (2019). Patients' Adult Attachment Interview classification and their experience of the therapeutic relationship: Are they associated? *Research in Psychotherapy, 22*(2). Advance online publication. https://doi.org/10.4081/ripppo.2019.361

Talia, A., Muzi, L., Lingiardi, V., & Taubner, S. (2020). How to be a secure base: Therapists' attachment representations and their link to attunement in psychotherapy. *Attachment & Human Development, 22*(2), 189–206. https://doi.org/10.1080/14616734.2018.1534247

Target, M., Hertzmann, L., Midgley, N., Casey, P., & Lassri, D. (2017). Parents' experience of child contact within entrenched conflict families following separation and divorce: A qualitative study. *Psychoanalytic Psychotherapy, 31*(2), 218–246. https://doi.org/10.1080/02668734.2016.1268197

Teicher, M. H., Samson, J. A., Anderson, C. M., & Ohashi, K. (2016). The effects of childhood maltreatment on brain structure, function and connectivity. *Nature Reviews Neuroscience, 17*(10), 652–666. https://doi.org/10.1038/nrn.2016.111

Thakur, N., Hessler, D., Koita, K., Ye, M., Benson, M., Gilgoff, R., Bucci, M., Long, D., & Harris, N. B. (2020). Pediatrics adverse childhood experiences and related life events screener (PEARLS) and health in a safety-net practice. *Child Abuse & Neglect, 108*, Article 104685. https://doi.org/10.1016/j.chiabu.2020.104685

Tizón, J. (2019). *Apuntes para una psicopatología basada en la relación: Vol. III. relaciones emocionalizadas, intrusivas, actuadoras y "operativas"* [Notes for a relationship-based psychopathology: Vol. III. Emotionalized, intrusive, acting and "operative" relationships]. Herder.

Trnavsky, P. (1998). Strange situation behaviors in Chinese infants. *Child Study Journal, 28*(1), 69–88.

Tronick, E. Z. (1989). Emotions and emotional communication in infants. *American Psychologist, 44*(2), 112–119. https://doi.org/10.1037/0003-066X.44.2.112

Tsiantis, J. (2000). *Work with parents: Psychoanalytic psychotherapy with children and adolescents.* Karnac Books.

van IJzendoorn, M. H., & Kroonenberg, P. M. (1988). Cross-cultural patterns of attachment: A meta-analysis of the strange situation. *Child Development, 59*(1), 147–156. https://doi.org/10.2307/1130396

van IJzendoorn, M. H., Schuengel, C., & Bakermans-Kranenburg, M. J. (1999). Disorganized attachment in early childhood: Meta-analysis of precursors, concomitants, and sequelae. *Development and Psychopathology, 11*(2), 225–250. https://doi.org/10.1017/S0954579499002035

Varese, F., Smeets, F., Drukker, M., Lieverse, R., Lataster, T., Viechtbauer, W., Read, J., van Os, J., & Bentall, R. P. (2012). Childhood adversities increase the risk of psychosis: A meta-analysis of patient-control, prospective- and cross-sectional cohort studies. *Schizophrenia Bulletin, 38*(4), 661–671. https://doi.org/10.1093/schbul/sbs050

Vedam, S., Stoll, K., Taiwo, T. K., Rubashkin, N., Cheyney, M., Strauss, N., McLemore, M., Cadena, M., Nethery, E., Rushton, E., Schummers, L., Declercq, E., & the GVtM-US Steering Council. (2019). The Giving Voice to Mothers study: Inequity and mistreatment during pregnancy and childbirth in the United States. *Reproductive Health, 16*(1), Article 77. https://doi.org/10.1186/s12978-019-0729-2

Von Below, C. (2017). *When psychotherapy does not help . . . and when it does: Lessons from young adults' experiences of psychoanalytic psychotherapy* [Unpublished doctoral dissertation]. Department of Psychology, Stockholm University.

von Mohr, M., Mayes, L. C., & Rutherford, H. J. V. (2017). The transition to motherhood: Psychoanalysis and neuroscience perspectives. *The Psychoanalytic Study of the Child, 70*(1), 154–173. https://doi.org/10.1080/00797308.2016.1277905

Wang, Z. (2015). Theory of mind and children's understanding of teaching and learning during early childhood. *Cogent Education, 2*(1), Article 1011973. https://doi.org/10.1080/2331186X.2015.1011973

Wass, S. V. (2021). The origins of effortful control: How early development within arousal/regulatory systems influences attentional and affective control. *Developmental Review, 61,* Article 100978. https://doi.org/10.1016/j.dr. 2021.100978

Waugh, L. J. (2011). Beliefs associated with Mexican immigrant families' practice of *la cuarentena* during postpartum recovery. *Journal of Obstetric, Gynecologic, & Neonatal Nursing, 40*(6), 732–741. https://doi.org/10.1111/j.1552-6909.2011.01298.x

Weisner, T. S. (2014). The socialization of trust: Plural caregiving and diverse pathways in human development across cultures. In H. Otto & H. Keller (Eds.), *Different faces of attachment: Cultural variations on a universal human need* (pp. 263–277). Cambridge University Press.

Wellman, H. M. (1992). *The child's theory of mind.* The MIT Press.

Wellman, H. M., Fang, F., Liu, D., Zhu, L., & Liu, G. (2006). Scaling of theory-of-mind understandings in Chinese children. *Psychological Science, 17*(12), 1075–1081. https://doi.org/10.1111/j.1467-9280.2006.01830.x

Winnicott, D. W. (1960). The theory of the parent–infant relationship. *The International Journal of Psycho-Analysis, 41,* 585–595.

Winnicott, D. W. (1965). *The maturational process and the facilitating environment.* Hogarth Press.

Yerkes, R. M., & Dodson, J. D. (1908). The relation of strength of stimulus to rapidity of habit-formation. *Journal of Comparative Neurology and Psychology, 18*(5), 459–482. https://doi.org/10.1002/cne.920180503

Zahran, S. (2011). Type of parental socialization across cultures: A psychoanalysis review. *Psychology, 2*(5), 526–534. https://doi.org/10.4236/psych.2011.25082

Index

About the Authors

Norka Malberg, PsyD, is originally from San Juan, Puerto Rico. Dr. Malberg is an adult and child psychoanalyst who trained at the Anna Freud National Centre for Children and Families in London and The Western New England Psychoanalytic Society in New Haven, Connecticut. She obtained her clinical doctorate at University College London for her work with chronically ill adolescents in mentalization-based groups. She currently lives and practices in Barcelona, Spain, where she is in private practice and consults to multiple community mental health organizations. She is on the faculty of the Instituto Universitario de Salud Mental Vidal y Barraquer at Ramón Llull University in Barcelona and on the clinical faculty of the Yale Child Study Center and the psychology department at Rutgers University. Dr. Malberg is a mentalization-based trainer and supervisor for work with children, adolescents, and families. Her current research and clinical work focuses on the development of modifications of mentalization-informed interventions working in the context of trauma and autism, the impact of emigration on parental reflective functioning, and the development of mentalization-based group interventions for adolescents in community mental health settings. She is one of the coeditors of the *Psychodynamic Diagnostic Manual* (second edition) and a guest master clinician for the American Psychological Association video series.

Elliot Jurist, PhD, PhD, is a professor of psychology and philosophy at the Graduate Center and The City College of New York, City University of New York (CCNY, CUNY). From 2004 to 2013, he served as the director of the clinical psychology doctoral program at CUNY. From 2008 to the present, he has been the editor of *Psychoanalytic Psychology*, the journal of Division 39 (Society for Psychoanalysis and Psychoanalytic Psychology) of the American Psychological Association. He is also the editor of a book series, Psychoanalysis and

Psychological Science, from Guilford Press and author of a book in the series, *Minding Emotions: Cultivating Mentalization in Psychotherapy* (which has been translated into Chinese, Italian, and Spanish and was named Best Theoretical Book in 2009 by the American Board and Academy of Psychoanalysis). Dr. Jurist is the author of *Beyond Hegel and Nietzsche: Philosophy, Culture, and Agency* (MIT Press, 2000) and a coauthor, with Peter Fonagy, György Gergely, and Mary Target, of *Affect Regulation, Mentalization, and the Development of the Self* (Other Press, 2002); the latter has been translated into five languages and won two book prizes. He is also the coeditor of *Mind to Mind: Infant Research, Neuroscience, and Psychoanalysis* (Other Press, 2008). His research interests concern mentalization and the role of emotions and affect regulation in psychotherapy. His research lab has published a self-report measure, the Mentalized Affectivity Scale, which has been translated into 12 languages. In 2014, he received the Scholarship Award from Division 39 of the American Psychological Association. He is currently writing a book titled *When Therapy Met Memoir,* which is about references to therapy in contemporary memoirs. Dr. Jurist writes a Substack newsletter titled *Mental(izing) Health* (https://elliot4cc.substack.com/).

Jordan Bate, PhD, is an assistant professor at Ferkauf Graduate School of Psychology, Yeshiva University, in the School-Clinical Child Psychology Program, where she runs the Attachment and Psychotherapy Process lab and coleads the psychodynamic practicum in child therapy at the Max and Celia Parnes Family Psychological and Psychoeducational Services Clinic. Her research examines psychotherapy process and therapist effects through the lens of attachment theory and mentalization, with a specific focus on empirically studying training of therapists to improve interpersonal and relational skills. She is a coauthor of the book *Deliberate Practice in Child and Adolescent Psychotherapy* with Tracy Prout, Tony Rousmaniere, and Alexandre Vaz, which is part of the American Psychological Association's Essentials of Deliberate Practice book series. She is also a voluntary supervisor at Northwell Health, Lenox Hill Hospital, in the perinatal mental health service. She is the current president of Section II (Childhood and Adolescence) of the Society for Psychoanalysis and Psychoanalytic Psychology (Division 39) of the American Psychological Association. Dr. Bate has a PhD in clinical psychology from The New School for Social Research, where she worked under the mentorship of Miriam and Howard Steele and Jeremy Safran, and a BA in history and political science from Williams College. She maintains a private practice in New York City, where she works with children of all ages, parents, families, and individual adults.

Mark Dangerfield, PhD, is a clinical psychologist, psychotherapist (member of the European Federation for Psychoanalytic Psychotherapy and EuroPsy), and psychoanalyst (member of the Spanish Psychoanalytical Society and the International Psychoanalytical Association). He is the director of the Vidal y Barraquer University Institute of Mental Health, Ramón Llull University (Barcelona), and is lead Adaptive Mentalization-Based Integrative Treatment (AMBIT) trainer and Mentalization-Based Treatment for Adolescents (MBT-A) trainer and supervisor at the Anna Freud National Centre for Children and Families in London. Dr. Dangerfield has worked for over 25 years in pediatric hospitals and mental health services in Barcelona, Spain. He is also director of the Equipo Clínic de Intervención a Domicilio project at the Fundación Vidal y Barraquer, a pioneering project in Spain, where community-outreach mental health teams work with non–help-seeking adolescents and their families, based on the AMBIT model of the Anna Freud National Centre for Children and Families. He has directed research projects on the prevalence of adverse childhood experiences and their psychopathological consequences in adolescence, as well as on the risk of associated suicide attempts. He has also led a research study on the transgenerational transmission of relational trauma, reformulating the term "ACEs" as "adverse relational experiences" (AREs) in order to emphasize the relational dimension of these experiences. Dr. Dangerfield is a member of the Research Group on Mentalization and Evaluation of Psychological Interventions of the Vidal y Barraquer University Institute of Mental Health, Ramón Llull University (Barcelona).